# CIA Rogues and the Killing of the Kennedys

# CIA Rogues and the Killing of the Kennedys

## HOW AND WHY US AGENTS CONSPIRED TO ASSASSINATE JFK AND RFK

## Patrick Nolan
### Foreword by Dr. Henry C. Lee

Skyhorse Publishing

Skyhorse Publishing books may be purchased in bulk at special discounts for sales promotion, corporate gifts, fund-raising, or educational purposes. Special editions can also be created to specifications. For details, contact the Special Sales Department, Skyhorse Publishing, 307 West 36th Street, 11th Floor, New York, NY 10018 or info@skyhorsepublishing.com.

Skyhorse® and Skyhorse Publishing® are registered trademarks of Skyhorse Publishing, Inc.®, a Delaware corporation.

Visit our website at www.skyhorsepublishing.com.

10 9 8 7 6 5 4 3 2

Library of Congress Cataloging-in-Publication Data

Nolan, Patrick (Patrick Thomas)
  CIA rogues and the killing of the Kennedys : how and why US agents conspired to kill JFK and RFK / Patrick Nolan.
    pages cm
  Includes bibliographical references and index.
  ISBN 978-1-62636-255-0 (alk. paper)
  1. Kennedy, John F. (John Fitzgerald), 1917-1963–Assassination. 2. Kennedy, Robert F., 1925-1968–Assassination. 3. United States. Central Intelligence Agency–Corrupt practices. 4. United States. Central Intelligence Agency–History–20th century. 5. Conspiracies–United States–History–20th century. I. Title.
  E842.9.N64 2013
  973.922092'2–dc23
                          2013024614
ISBN: 978-1-62636-255-0

Printed in the United States of America.

# ACKNOWLEDGMENTS

I ESPECIALLY WANT to thank noted forensic scientist Dr. Henry C. Lee of Connecticut, without whom this work would not have been accomplished, and Arthur M. Schlesinger Jr., who encouraged me to keep writing. I wish to recognize investigators William W. Turner and Prof. Philip H. Melanson for their advice and assistance. My thanks also to Judge Robert J. Joling and Profs. Robert M. Hendrick and Maura Flannery. Archivists Judy Farrar, Misty Fitch, Rosemary Grossman, Nancy Zimmelman, Jessica Herrick, Mark Davies, Michael Levenstein, Rex Bradford, and the Mary Ferrell Foundation were especially helpful. I thank attorney Larry Teeter for his help, as well as attorney Gregory St. John. Others whom I greatly appreciate are my agent Grace Freedson, Bill Wolfsthal, Wesley Jacques, Emily Houlihan, and Lauren Burnstein at Skyhorse Publishing, and Peter Kilduff, Taivo Raig, and Tony Calabrese. And last, but not least, Theresa L. Nolan, John W. Nolan, Aideen F. Nolan, Patrick and Leanne Nolan, Mary and Andrew Fracchia, Joseph Nolan, and Bella Pangur Ban.

# DEDICATION

*To Aideen*

# TABLE OF CONTENTS

# FOREWORD

by
*Dr. Henry C. Lee*

F ROM A FORENSIC science point of view, there is much to be learned from the 1960s' assassinations of President John F. Kennedy and New York senator Robert F. Kennedy. In both cases, these men were killed at the peak of their popularity. While many have ascribed these murders to lone assassins, forensic evidence reveals inconsistencies, unanswered questions, and the likelihood of unaccounted-for gunmen.

The job of a responsible forensic scientist or criminalist is to reconstruct, if possible, how a particular crime took place. This determination is based on the available physical evidence. It is not the role of the forensic expert to speculate regarding the identity of those who may have been behind a crime or the planning of it. The professional forensic scientist leaves this part of the equation to the detectives and the justice system. We can only collect, analyze, and present the best evidence. It is up to others to draw conclusions from the body of evidence.

For more than forty years, I have investigated thousands of cases, both in my home base, Connecticut, and around the world. Through my work at the Connecticut State Police Forensic Science Laboratory and at the University of New Haven's Henry C. Lee Institute of Forensic Science, I have been fortunate to have had the opportunity to assist many people to find justice for their loved ones.

The Kennedy cases have intrigued forensic scientists throughout the decades since these assassinations befell America in the 1960s. The assassination of President Kennedy on November 22, 1963 in Dallas, Texas, is examined in my book *Famous Crimes Revisited*, coauthored with Dr. Jerry Labriola. My analysis of the evidence and studies conducted by other respected forensic scientists reveal that the bullet evidence, the ballistics, and the autopsy findings point away from the official Warren Commission version. More recently, I participated in the 2008 national symposium at the Cyril H. Wecht Institute of Forensic Science and Law at Duquesne University in Pittsburgh, Pennsylvania. At the conference, new bullet evidence was presented. The results of neutron activation (exact composition in parts per billion) of fragments recovered from the JFK assassination showed "no match"—that is, the batches of shells were different. This is an indication of a high probability that more than one weapon was fired.

In the assassination of Sen. Robert Kennedy, major inconsistencies also exist in the physical evidence recovered at the scene. The shooting took place as the senator walked through a crowded hotel kitchen pantry following his presidential primary election victory speech at Los Angeles's Ambassador Hotel on June 5, 1968. Kennedy was shot at point-blank range in the back of the head. However, the alleged gunman was firing from the front at a distance of several feet.

In the summer of 2002, one of the foremost experts on the case, Judge Robert Joling, donated his entire RFK assassination collection to the University of New Haven's Henry C. Lee Institute of Forensic Science archives. From Judge Joling's documents and photographs, it is clear that the ballistics and autopsy evidence in the case conflict with the official version of events. While dozens of eyewitnesses saw twenty-four-year-old Palestinian immigrant Sirhan Sirhan fire a .22 caliber handgun at Senator Kennedy, the physical evidence reveals a different story.

But such evidence alone cannot tell us why a crime occurred or how a plot developed.

In this latest work on these cases, author Patrick Nolan presents the culmination of more than a decade of research, much of which he has shared with me over the years. His thesis is backed up with compelling evidence and thorough documentation. He has taken what some considered to be open-and-shut cases and, through diligent analysis of facts and the evidence, has found some new answers to the questions surrounding the violent attempts to subvert the national will in the 1960s.

Mr. Nolan's early background in news writing and college teaching and his perseverance and devotion to this subject have given him the tools to make sound judgments in these controversial cases.

# Foreword

The goal of forensic science professionals is to find the truth. This is also Mr. Nolan's goal. At the end of the day, it is up to the reader to draw his or her own conclusions based on the best evidence. At the same time, I firmly believe—and I often remind myself and others—"The truth will always surface . . . someday."

*Dr. Henry C. Lee*
*New Haven, 2013*

**Dr. Henry C. Lee's** television series, *Trace Evidence: The Case Files of Dr. Henry Lee*, premiered on Court TV in June 2004. Dr. Lee is the former director of the Connecticut State Police Forensic Science Laboratory and currently Distinguished Professor of Forensic Science at the University of New Haven. He has assisted forty-six countries and investigated more than six thousand major crime cases worldwide.

# PREFACE

I N 1969, MAN landed on the moon. In 1977, Elvis died. In 2001, the United
States was attacked by terrorists; the 9-11 assaults did not, in any way, shape,
or form, involve the CIA. In contrast to these facts, there are conspiracy theorists
who mistakenly believe that the moon landing was faked, that Elvis lives, and
that 9-11 was an inside job. At the same time, there are those who lump together
all conspiracy theories and brand them as false. But in fact, as serious students
of history know, major conspiracies have indeed occurred in our nation's past.
In the cases of the John and Robert Kennedy assassinations, numerous hidden
facts related to these murders, uncovered over the years and pieced together
here, overwhelmingly debunk the official "lone-gun" scenarios.

Most Americans today realize that the CIA is saving their lives every day; the
Agency's intelligence-gathering networks, drone attacks, and other clandestine actions are critical to the war on terrorism. It wasn't always this way. This
book, *CIA Rogues and the Killing of the Kennedys: How and Why US Agents Conspired
to Assassinate JFK and RFK,* is the story of the CIA's darkest days—the 1960s.

Journalists typically answer five key questions when writing their reports:
who, what, when, where, and why. In this book, we will also examine in
depth the question of "how." How were the Kennedy brothers' assassinations
planned, executed, and covered up? The evidence shows conclusively that
both plots were based on a cunning variation of an appalling CIA operation
known originally as MKULTRA with a crucial twist incorporated: the program
utilized an unwitting fall guy in conjunction with hidden sharpshooters (not
to be confused with a "Manchurian Candidate"). It is this finding that forms
the framework for understanding the true story of the assassinations of the
Kennedys.

You may be familiar with the mantra, "if conspiracy theories were true,
someone would have talked by now and everyone would know the truth.

5

You can't keep a secret that long in this town." Washington, DC, may not be known for keeping secrets. But at the same time, we must remember that assassins also kill witnesses or are themselves eliminated by their backers; dead men tell no tales. Secondly, some secrets are bigger than others and take more time to surface. You'll recall that it was not until 2005 when we read the revelation that "Deep Throat" of Watergate fame was a quiet, unassuming, high-level bureaucrat named W. Mark Felt, the assistant director of the FBI. Mr. Felt had remained anonymous to the public at large for more than thirty-two years!

Another legend in the nation's capital depicts Watergate as the greatest political scandal in modern US history. Yet the break-in and its related sundry political crimes pale in comparison to the '60s assassinations. If one takes the time to dig beyond the falsehoods of crazed lone gunmen and magic bullets, it becomes evident that the facts surrounding the murders of President John F. Kennedy and his brother New York senator Robert F. Kennedy reveal a much greater scandal, one that begs to be explored in depth.

The goal of this book is to show, through forensic science and other resources, the identity of the primary individuals ultimately responsible for these horrific assassinations. A thorough examination and analysis of those who had ample motive, means, and opportunity concludes that only one small group stands alone: the CIA's Richard Helms and James Angleton and their rogue band of conspirators and mob allies. Their story is told in the chapters ahead.

This revisionist view of history will startle some historians, particularly those who recall the murder of Bobby Kennedy.

New York senator Robert Kennedy was shot at the Ambassador Hotel in Los Angeles moments after giving a rousing victory speech, having just won the California Democratic presidential primary. Minutes after midnight on June 5, 1968, as he walked behind the speaking platform and through a crowded kitchen pantry, he was shot in the back of the head and in the upper back at point-blank range. Sirhan Bishara Sirhan, a twenty-four-year-old Palestinian immigrant, was apprehended, gun in hand.

While Sirhan had indeed been firing, top forensic scientists concur that the evidence shows he could not have been the killer. There are three key reasons for this: bullets later test fired from his gun could not be conclusively matched to the victim's bullets. Kennedy was shot in the back, yet Sirhan was positioned in front of him. The fatal shots were fired from an inch away based on the powder burn evidence, yet Sirhan's gun was several feet away.

In addition, the alleged murder weapon held eight bullets, yet evidence of at least ten bullets was found. Witnesses have testified they saw two other gunmen standing next to Kennedy as he fell. Sirhan has no memory of the murder, even while under hypnosis. He also claims to have no memory of writing his forty-eight-page so-called diary, evidence the state produced to show premeditation. The psychiatrist who last examined Sirhan reported that he was not deranged in any way.

On April 23, 1969, Sirhan was sentenced to death in the gas chamber for assassinating Sen. Robert F. Kennedy. The sentence was reduced to life imprisonment in 1972 after California abolished the death penalty. At this writing, Sirhan is still imprisoned in a California jail. Since 1992, he had been at Corcoran State Prison, an hour north of Bakersfield. In November 2009, he was moved to Pleasant Valley State Prison in Coalinga, California,[1] some eighty miles east of Big Sur and two hundred miles northwest of Pasadena.

Robert Kennedy, forty-two, would most likely have been the next president of the United States. When he was shot, he was in the final stages of an electrifying presidential campaign. An anti-Vietnam War candidate, Senator Kennedy was projected to win the Democratic nomination over his main rival, also a peace candidate, Minnesota senator Eugene McCarthy. With a victory at the convention in Chicago, Kennedy's chances were excellent to have gone on and defeated Republican candidate Richard M. Nixon in the general election in November 1968. An examination of the facts, based on the best evidence, indicates that the elimination of Robert Kennedy from the race was a well-planned, cunning plot.

Four and a half years earlier, in November 1963, President John F. Kennedy had signed an order to begin the process of gradually withdrawing US troops from Vietnam. Several days later on November 22, 1963, while riding in a motorcade through the streets of Dallas, Texas, President Kennedy was assassinated. The Vietnam withdrawal order was immediately rescinded by the newly sworn-in President Johnson.

On the day President Kennedy was killed, CIA director John McCone drove over to Robert Kennedy's house in McLean, Virginia. According to author Richard Mahoney in his book, *Sons & Brothers: The Days of Jack and Bobby Kennedy*, Kennedy aide Walter Sheridan has revealed that when McCone arrived they went outside to the lawn, where Bobby asked him if the CIA had killed his brother. Shortly after, Bobby called a Washington location at which the CIA maintained a unit of anti-Castro Cuban operatives. These CIA handlers, an element within the Agency over which Richard Helms had overall authority, had been carrying out raids on Cuba and attempting to assassinate Fidel Castro. The unit was enraged over the Kennedy administration's decision to end hostilities toward Castro. Bobby spoke with a writer there, Haynes Johnson, who was chronicling the April 1961 Bay of Pigs invasion. Speaking of his brother's assassination, Bobby told him, "One of your guys did it," meaning the Cubans' CIA handlers.[2]

Bobby publicly went along with the Warren Commission investigation of the assassination, but did so to avoid media controversy while quietly planning his own route to the White House, a vantage point from which he could then try to bring both his enemies and the enemies of peace and democracy to justice.

President Kennedy was killed at age forty-six as he was about to run for a second term in 1964, which he surely would have won. His plans to make peace with the Soviet Union and Castro's Cuba, eloquently expressed in his June 1963 speech at American University, were anathema to many in the establishment, particularly at the top of the CIA. Kennedy's actions sealed his fate.

The alleged assassin, Lee Harvey Oswald, was a twenty-four-year-old ex-Marine living in Dallas, who was married with two infant children in 1963. He was arrested within hours of the assassination at a movie theater following the murder of a police officer and was charged with killing the president. Oswald was accused of firing a bolt-action rifle from a window on the sixth floor of the Texas School Book Depository building in Dealey Plaza in Dallas. As the car carrying the president, his wife Jacqueline, and Gov. John Connally and his wife passed by on Elm Street, shots rang out, hitting Kennedy in the head and back and also wounding Governor Connally. Fifty-one eyewitnesses later stated the shots came from the grassy knoll in front of the president, not only from the Book Depository building behind the motorcade. No one witnessed the alleged assassin in the window. Oswald was in fact observed minutes before and after the shooting sitting in the Book Depository lunchroom. Later investigations have shown that eyewitness reports, film evidence, Parkland Hospital doctors' testimony, and forensic evidence on the angle and direction of the bullets all indicate that the JFK assassination was carried out by three gunmen who fired four shots.

Oswald was gunned down two days after the assassination while being taken through the basement of the Dallas Police Station en route to the county courthouse. In the full glare of network TV cameras, local mobster

Jack Ruby silenced the government's prime suspect, thus eliminating the need for a trial.

As a Marine, Oswald had studied the Russian language and become fluent. He was assigned to a key US spy base in Japan. After nearly three years in the service, he was discharged, traveled to the Soviet Union, and married there. His ease of entry and exit, his access to financial resources, and other indicators have shown that his "defection" involved covert intelligence operations ongoing during this era. Oswald's closest associates were all CIA assets: George de Mohrenschildt a well-financed Dallas immigrant who assisted Oswald upon his return to the Dallas area from the Soviet Union; Captain Alexi Davison of Atlanta, a US embassy doctor whom he met with repeatedly in the USSR; and David Ferrie, a pilot who worked for CIA sponsored anti-Castro Cuban exile groups. When Oswald started his sole-member Fair Play for Cuba Committee chapter, his office was in the same building as David Ferrie's. But despite these intelligence connections, Lee Harvey Oswald had another side of himself that definitely was not in sync with the CIA's upper echelon: his admiration for President John F. Kennedy, according to Oswald's friends in Dallas.

Conventional wisdom holds that the alleged assassins, Sirhan Sirhan and Lee Harvey Oswald, were "nobodies" who wanted to be "somebodies." This classic line, used by many in the media and in government circles, implies that conspiracy theorists are people who refuse to accept that a man so "small" (i.e., Sirhan, Oswald) could kill a man so "big" (RFK, JFK). Those who think that revisionists think this way cannot accept the fact that a small cabal of intelligent—yet demented—men within their own government could be so ruthless and inhuman that they would embrace such diabolical plots.

Instead, these conventional "official line" writers believe that each assassination was carried out by a lone gunman. "Organized evil," or the concept of a conspiracy, is just too much for some to contemplate. At the same time, there are other writers who believe that there is such a thing as organized evil in society, such as the Mafia. But they refuse to accept the fact that rogue members of the CIA, the "good guys," could have acted with such malevolence. Indeed, for many historians, the assassinations are enigmas wrapped in emotions (to paraphrase Winston Churchill).

And then there are those conspiracy critics, many in positions of power in the media, in publishing, and in academia, who adamantly believe that advocating conspiracy theories is criminal because it will undermine the public's belief in government. On the contrary, as students of history can affirm, seeking the truth in public records promotes openness, and, in turn, strengthens our government.

And, of course, there are those in these same camps who know the truth—that CIA rogues and mobsters killed JFK and RFK—but publicly they deny such convictions, saying to themselves, "We don't want our enemies to know that sometimes we are as bad as they are."

Other powerful nationally known writers have stated that discussing conspiracies increases paranoia in the country. *The New York Times'* Anthony Lewis wrote simplistically in 1975 that the search for a conspiracy "obscures our necessary understanding, all of us, that in this life there is often tragedy without reason."[3]

The most common misconception of establishment pundits is the idea that the assassinations were carried out by an individual seeking fame, that is, "by a crazy person who wanted to make a name for himself." If this were so, then why is it that one of the alleged assassins protested the charges against him, and the other insisted he could not recall what had happened? Lee Harvey Oswald admonished his brother Robert, "Don't believe the so-called evidence against me."[4] And Sirhan B. Sirhan has spent the majority of his life behind bars while his attorneys have sought to have their client exonerated as a programmed pawn.

These two 1960s assassinations at issue involved similar methods, hidden gunmen, and innocent fall guys. The motive in each case was the continuation of the war against Communism in Vietnam and Cuba and the suppression of civil rights protest marches at home by eliminating key leaders who stood in the way. Only Richard Helms and James Angleton, the CIA's chiefs of counterintelligence, possessed the means of planning and executing this type of operation without drawing suspicion, albeit in part by relying on their closest officers: David Atlee Phillips, the head of CIA Latin American Affairs; E. Howard Hunt, sabotage expert; and other confidants. Helms and Angleton had two overriding motives: accumulating power and self-preservation. But there were other motives. They maintained a zealous desire to vanquish Communism in all its forms both abroad and at home. This was the Red Scare generation; several years younger than "Red-baiting" Republican senator Joseph McCarthy of Wisconsin, they and their contemporaries produced the Black List as they hunted alleged Communists in the military, in government, and in Hollywood. It was the McCarthyism of the 1950s that culminated in the assassinations of the 1960s. JFK and RFK chose to travel a different path. They confronted the rabid anti-Communism of their day. On issues of war and peace and civil rights, they listened to a different drummer, and because of this, they were cut down in their prime.

The CIA's Richard Helms also was motivated by factors within his psychological makeup. Through intelligence and charm, he maintained the illusion of normality. If we look beneath the surface (as we shall see when we examine his personality in detail ahead), we find an apparent pathological liar, one who acted like a man without a conscience who would do whatever he needed to survive and to get ahead. In fact, he exhibited the classic signs of a serious mental disorder—not insanity, but that of a closet sociopath.

Critics of conspiracy theories like to postulate that people in general cannot accept the irrational. Yet, the assassinations were not irrational by any means. Again, it is very difficult for shallow people to live with the hard, cold fact that individuals within their own government conspired to assassinate their leaders.

No one likes to believe that he or she has been lied to, or worse, that one has believed the lies. There are those whose egos cannot accept the fact that they were duped while others, less astute than they, were not fooled. Consequently, many of these "official line" believers naively look away. They would rather believe the popular delusion that these assassinations were utterly senseless and tragic and have no explanation than to have to face the brutal facts. Others say to themselves, *If I were wrong about the assassination conspiracy, was I also wrong about other important aspects of my life?* They resolve this anxiety by dismissing opposing points of view out of hand. The "lone nut" theories were promulgated to cover up the true accounts of two incredible losses. Upon closer inspection, history has had to be rewritten.

This work involves the use of the mosaic theory of intelligence gathering in which pieces of information are combined with other pieces to produce a composite. By connecting the dots, information that has been hidden from the general public for decades can emerge with force, clarity, and meaning.

Some key connections and conclusions herein have never before been published. They represent new knowledge stemming from an analysis of the available forensic evidence and an assessment of the work of several intrepid historians whose books are cited throughout. By following up their persistent investigative efforts and carefully fitting together the many pieces of the puzzle, we have arrived at a better understanding of modern American history.

Richard Helms and James Angleton took with them to the grave many of the secrets of the '60s assassinations. Helms died of bone cancer at home in Washington, DC, on October 22, 2002. He was eighty-nine. Angleton died of lung cancer, also in Washington, DC, on May 11, 1987, at age sixty-nine. Since then, enough evidence and related historical facts have been uncovered over the years to enable us to decipher both Helms's and Angleton's roles in relation to these murders during their thirty years of covert activities.

# 1

# *Richard Helms, The Strategist*

RICHARD HELMS WALKED briskly from a hearing room in Washington, DC, on April 28, 1975. The sixty-two-year-old former director of the CIA had left the Agency two years earlier and was then serving as ambassador to Iran. As he stepped into the hallway, he came face-to-face with CBS newsman Daniel Schorr. Suddenly Helms exploded, "You sonofabitch! You killer! You cocksucker! 'Killer Schorr'—that's what they ought to call you."[5]

For the normally reserved bureaucrat, publicly unleashing such a bizarre verbal assault seemed out of character. The hearing from which he had exited had consisted of four hours of questioning before the Rockefeller Commission regarding CIA attempts to assassinate foreign leaders. Schorr had been broadcasting news stories about the CIA–Mafia assassination conspiracies and was seeking a response from the director himself.

Clearly, newsman Schorr's presence alone had touched a nerve in the no-nonsense ex-director. Unaccustomed to such public scrutiny, Helms's cool demeanor had cracked under the pressure. Although he proved to be a master at keeping secrets, his outburst revealed an angry, violent side to his character. Another telling public reaction from Richard Helms that adds insight into his character was delivered during a lecture for students at Johns Hopkins University in the fall of 1972. Helms was asked if the CIA had tried to interfere in the election of Chilean president Salvador Allende in 1970. He responded to the student, "Why should you care? Your side won."[6] The elected Marxist leader was eventually overthrown and died in a CIA-assisted coup in 1973.

Another nonanswer from Helms—and again, one that showed his arrogance when involved in discussions related to the assassinations—transpired during the House Select Committee on Assassinations hearings in 1978. According to the *Washington Post's* George Lardner, during a break in the testimony, Helms got into a conversation with several reporters, one of whom asked Helms if he knew anything about a connection between Lee Harvey Oswald and the CIA or the KGB. Helms replied, "I don't remember." And then he added, "Your questions are almost as dumb as the Committee's."[7]

Helms's belligerent language and his practice of defending himself by going on the offensive were tools he used to protect himself and his secrets, for he was a man with much to hide. *The Man Who Kept the Secrets,* the title of author Thomas Powers's biography of Richard Helms, is a fitting description of his subject. Beneath Helms's outward appearance of restraint (the Daniel Schorr outburst being a major exception), the career spymaster was the embodiment of ambition. Tall, lean, and an avid tennis player, Helms also was intellectually gifted. His autobiography, *A Look Over My Shoulder: A Life In The Central Intelligence Agency,* leaves the impression that he spent much of his time putting out fires; the fact that most were of his own making is left untold.

By the same token, Helms writes that key CIA actions were always carried out with presidential approval.[8] Yet, in truth, Helms routinely kept a succession of presidents in the dark (detailed ahead).

Helms's unauthorized use of the Mafia in various operations was typical, particularly his attempts to eliminate Cuba's Fidel Castro. As Deputy Director of Plans, Helms hid this information from President Kennedy and his CIA director John McCone. Robert Kennedy found out in May 1962 and was told these plots had been terminated. In reality, Helms's field coordinator for the Castro assassination plots, William Harvey, continued to use the Mafia into 1963.[9] When questioned about these CIA-mob assassination conspiracies in the 1975 Senate investigation, Helms replied, "I'm really surprised I did not discuss it with him (Director McCone) at the time."[10] According to Helms's assistant, George McManus, the main reason Helms did not tell his boss about mob involvement in assassination conspiracies was because McCone would have considered it "morally reprehensible."[11]

Helms was born Richard McGarrah Helms on March 30, 1913, in St. Davids, Pennsylvania, outside of Philadelphia. After World War I, his parents, Herman and Marion, moved the family to New York City and later to South Orange, New Jersey, where his father worked as an executive with the Aluminum Company of America. Young Richard attended Carteret Academy. In

1929, when Richard was sixteen, his family—including Richard, his older sister Elizabeth, and younger brothers Pearsall and Gates—departed for Europe. At the time, Helms's maternal grandfather was a bank president in Basel, Switzerland. Helms was enrolled in Le Rosey, a private preparatory school on Lake Geneva. This is the same school the Shah of Iran, Mohammad Reza Pahlavi, attended.[12] Although the Shah was six years younger than Helms, the fellow alumni became very close in their later lives, and particularly when Helms was appointed ambassador to Iran by President Richard Nixon in March 1973.

Helms completed his schooling in Europe at age eighteen in 1931 and returned to the United States after his acceptance at Williams College in western Massachusetts. He graduated second in his class in 1935 and decided to go into the field of journalism. In part because of his foreign language skills, he was able to hook up with the United Press in London and soon after was sent to Berlin. In 1936, he was with a small group of reporters who interviewed Adolf Hitler in Nuremberg. The newsmen had been invited to a luncheon with the Führer during a weeklong Nazi Party Congress meeting. Helms notes in his autobiography that this was two years before the terror of the Nazi's plans became clear with the outbreak of anti-Semitic violence known as Kristallnacht on November 9, 1938.[13] On that night, more than two hundred synagogues were set aflame, ninety-one people were killed, and twenty thousand were arrested and taken to concentration camps. The following year in September 1939, Germany attacked Poland, starting World War II.

Helms's interview with Hitler gave the young reporter's resume added credentials that would eventually aid his entry into the intelligence service following the US declaration of war in 1941.

When twenty-four-year-old Helms left Germany in 1937, he decided he wanted to become a newspaper publisher and realized that the best route to this goal would be to learn the business side of the industry. He joined the *Indianapolis Times* and soon moved up to the position of advertising manager. In September 1939, Helms married Julia Bretzman Shields, a local divorcée who had two children from a previous marriage, James and Judith. After the Japanese attack at Pearl Harbor on December 7, 1941, Helms joined the Navy and moved his family to his parents' home in South Orange, New Jersey. Helms and his wife Julia had one child, a son named Dennis.[14]

During his war service in the US Navy, Lieutenant Helms was initially assigned to track enemy submarines off the coast of New York. Soon after, he was transferred to the Office of Strategic Services (OSS), the precursor of the Central Intelligence Agency, under the command of General William J.

Donavan. Helms trained at an OSS farm in Maryland and was sent to Washington, DC. Later in the war, Helms worked in intelligence offices in London and Paris. He and his fellow officers were the beneficiaries of the most successful espionage operation of World War II in Europe—the breaking of the German code by allied cryptologists—an operation code-named ULTRA.

For a short time, Helms worked closely with Allen Dulles, a World War I spymaster who would eventually become CIA director (1953–1961). Helms and Dulles, who was then Chief of Mission in Berne, Switzerland, met at General Dwight Eisenhower's headquarters when Germany surrendered on May 8, 1945.[15]

It was Helms's fluency in the German language that helped him earn the position of station chief in post-World War II Berlin. There, his spy career focused on Russian KGB activities in Germany and Eastern Europe, tracking down former Nazi spies, and appropriating intelligence from them that the Axis powers had collected regarding the Soviet Union. Helms remained with the OSS after his discharge from the Navy in 1946 as the Cold War began in earnest.

When the CIA was formed in 1947 with the passage of the National Security Act, Helms stayed on under the new umbrella agency. James Angleton, another master spy who had spent World War II working with the OSS in Italy, also stayed. Together, Angleton and Helms would form a twenty-five-year partnership in covert operations.[16] The enigmatic Angleton was a very thin man, four years younger than Helms, and was known as an intellectual. He had graduated from Yale before the war and attended Harvard Law School for a year. His father, Lt. Col. James H. Angleton, had worked for a US firm in Italy and, with the outbreak of war, the elder Angleton also wound up working in intelligence under General Donovan. By 1946, his son Jim went on to become the OSS station chief in Rome.[17]

Meanwhile, his friend Richard Helms was also on a fast track. By July 1952, Helms had been appointed acting chief of the CIA's Clandestine Division and in the following year became deputy to Frank Wisner, the Deputy Director of Plans. In this position, Helms was in charge of all covert action operations.[18]

With the appointment of Allen Dulles as Director of Central Intelligence in 1953, Helms began to lay the groundwork for a program that became known as operation MKULTRA. The "ULTRA" is no doubt a nod to the great contribution of the operation that broke the Nazi code in World War II. As for the initials "MK," the words "mind control" come to mind, though the origin of this code name has never been found.

The Agency's behavior control program was built upon research experiments carried out during the Korean War (1950–1953). At that time, North Korea had developed so-called "brainwashing" techniques for use in obtaining "confessions" from American prisoners of war. In the face of the Communist challenge, the US military sought to prepare its soldiers for survival in the event they were captured by the enemy. Research on hypnosis was conducted to attempt to protect America's intelligence services from such tactics being used against them. Indeed, CIA Director Allen Dulles did not take Soviet and Chinese Communist threats lightly; he intended for his behavioral research specialists to break new ground in the quest for mind control knowledge.

Helms in the directorate of plans (covert operations) and Angleton in counterintelligence guided this new mission. Together they formed the "perfect storm." Angleton is described by Edward Jay Epstein in his book *Legend* as "a man who meticulously planned environments so perfectly that he could manipulate the design of his own prize-winning orchids."[19] Indeed, Helms and Angleton's goal was much more than just defensive techniques and truth serums; they were intent on finding out if a human could be programmed to carry out "executive action" operations, which in CIA terminology meant assassination.[20]

The behavior control program was initiated under the auspices of the CIA's Office of Security. In addition to researching information based on North Korean field work, the CIA dug deeper, researching experiments found in captured Nazi documents. At the close of World War II, top German spy Commander Reinhard Gehlen escaped the approaching Russians and fled to the Americans, bringing with him a treasure trove of Nazi and Russian intelligence files.[21] Richard Helms worked closely with the Gehlen network of former German spies to penetrate Soviet intelligence and uncover Communist activities in West Germany. It was not until June 2006 that the National Archives in Washington released twenty-seven thousand pages of declassified post-World War II documents revealing the extent of the CIA's collaboration with ex-Nazis. For example, memos from the 1950s show that the CIA hid knowledge of the whereabouts of notorious Nazi war criminal Adolf Eichmann who had escaped to Argentina. The reports indicate that the CIA feared that his capture would expose their use of former Nazis, and that he would reveal the CIA's efforts to undermine Communist influence in West Germany.[22] Eichmann was captured by Israeli intelligence in 1960, tried, and executed.

Helms's intelligence gathering in Germany focused on Soviet activities, but at the same time, he explored in earnest the newly discovered ex-Nazi files, in particular those studies and reports that contained data on what the German scientists had learned about the subject of human programming. Helms and Angleton would use this information to plan their future in the world of espionage.

The captured Nazi research documents showed that the most gruesome Nazi experiments conducted at death camps were the so-called "aviation series" in which prisoners were used to test various survival factors for the military. For example, at Dachau, inmates were immersed in cold water to determine how long a downed pilot would last in frigid seas. Other inmates died in pressure chambers designed to simulate high-altitude environments. Less horrific experiments carried out by Nazi scientists were conducted in order to find ways in which to control prisoners and make them reveal secret information. This psychopharmacological research involved the combined use of mescaline and hypnosis.[23] It was the results of these experiments that most interested Richard Helms and American intelligence.

Under Helms's guidance, behavioral medicine scientists from across the US were recruited to investigate a curious mix of concepts: creating amnesia, understanding bioelectrics, and attempting to harness parapsychology. Soon, this newly contracted legion of psychiatrists began to test mind-altering drugs in conjunction with hypnosis.

As the Cold War intensified, and the nation saw the rise of rabid anti-Communist Sen. Joseph McCarthy, a sense of paranoia emerged regarding the Soviet Union and Communist efforts in the field of mind control. The so-called "mind control gap" would provide a strong impetus for greater CIA funding. However, in later years, it was publicly revealed that in reality the Soviets' work in this area had been much exaggerated.

The Agency's MK experiments started out in 1950 as project BLUEBIRD. Day-to-day tasks were run by the CIA's Sheffield Edwards, who several years later would become a key player in Helms's CIA–Mafia operations involving Cuba. The leadership of BLUEBIRD changed hands soon after when Morse Allen, a rigid anti-Communist from Naval Intelligence, was brought in to run the program. After consulting with various psychiatrists, Allen introduced the use of electro-shock treatments to the mind control repertoire. Gradually, the agency learned to use combinations of various methods to achieve amnesia in its subjects.[24]

The CIA's mind control research program was renamed ARTICHOKE in 1952.[25] Such code words are typically meaningless except to the originator. In this case, it is interesting to note that a vegetable is also the term for what could happen if an experiment went awry and the subject's memory was lost permanently. Most of the subjects tested did not know the nature of the tests being given to them. This was considered an important requirement by the experimenters in order to produce dependable results.

Hypnosis and drugs were central elements of the programs that encompassed CIA mind control and behavior modification research of this era. Much of the records of this work have been destroyed, but it is estimated that the CIA may have used thousands of subjects in its behavior modification experiments.[26] The subjects chosen by the CIA included prisoners, foreigners, prostitutes, mental patients, and drug addicts.[27] These individuals were picked because, due to their social and economic circumstances, they typically would have little recourse if they discovered the true nature of their predicament. They were also the types of subjects who would not be prone to question if they had been unwittingly drugged, because drugs were a normal part of their culture anyway.[28]

For several years, the CIA had tested the use of hypnosis in interrogations and on unwitting subjects under Operation ARTICHOKE.

At the time of this writing, several US congressmen and veterans' groups are sponsoring a bill that will provide medical care for American military personnel who unknowingly took part in military research between 1954 and 1973. Paralleling the CIA's experiments, it is estimated that thousands of US soldiers were exposed to dangerous chemicals, biological weapons experiments, and radioactive agent tests sponsored by the Pentagon in operations worldwide.

Unwitting subjects in CIA mind control research were typically administered a knockout drug to compel them into the program. After a subject was temporarily "appropriated," the individual would be taken to a secure place for the conditioning to be conducted. Experiments were carried out in such places as prisons, safe houses, and hospitals or other clinic-type settings. Besides studying individual responses, the research also involved the testing of various drugs, hypnosis, and the administering of electroshock treatments.[29] One of the researchers' objectives was to determine the best equation for achieving temporary control over a subject without his knowing it, and at the same time obliterating any memory of the experience.

Today's so-called date rape drug, commonly known as "roofies" or Rohypnol, is a successor of the drugs used during the CIA's mind control testing era. Drug Enforcement Administration publications describe Rohypnol as a benzodiazepine. It is a round, white pill slightly smaller than asprin. Colorless, odorless, and tasteless, when it is added to a drink, it has approximately ten times the potency of Valium. It causes loss of memory. Today, the most common drug used in sexual assaults, next to alcohol, is Gamma Hydroxy-Butyrate (GHB), also known as Liquid E, Liquid X, or Woman's Viagra.

More so than mescaline and marijuana, the most studied drug in the CIA's history was LSD, the hallucinogenic known in the lab as lysergic acid diethylamide. Ironic as it may seem, the LSD craze of the '60s originated with the CIA's mind control experiments.[30] Dr. Albert Hofmann discovered LSD in Basel, Switzerland, in 1943 while he was a researcher for Sandoz Pharmaceuticals, now part of Novartis. He had been searching for a blood circulation stimulant when he accidentally ingested a fungus found on wheat that he was testing. Describing the feeling, he recalled, "I had the idea I was out of my body. . . . I did not know how it would finish."[31] The drug arrived in America six years later, when researchers in Boston seeking a cure for schizophrenia set to work testing it. The CIA started to consider uses for LSD in 1951 and in the following year began funding research at Boston Psychopathic.[32] Eli Lilly & Company of Indianapolis was contracted to make batches of the new drug, and soon experiments were being conducted at several major US universities including Harvard, Baylor, the University of Minnesota, and the University of Maryland.[33]

The most well-known instance of LSD testing by the CIA involved the tragic case of an agent named Dr. Frank Olson, a biochemist in the Special Operations Division. At a CIA meeting in a lodge in western Maryland on November 19, 1953, Olson and others were unwittingly served LSD mixed in Cointreau by Sid Gottlieb, head of the CIA's Technical Services Staff Chemical Division. Olson reportedly became psychotic. A week later, after being taken to a CIA-approved doctor in New York, Olson either jumped or fell from a tenth-floor window at the Statler Hotel.[34] His wife Alice and his three children were kept in the dark regarding the events surrounding his death for twenty-two years. Then, in 1975, the LSD trip was revealed following the Rockefeller Commission investigation of the CIA. A lawsuit was avoided when the Olson family accepted a cash payout of $750,000 from the federal government.[35] However, once again, the case has resurfaced.

Frank Olson's sons Eric and Nils Olson of Frederick, Maryland, recently sued the federal government, claiming that, in fact, the CIA had killed their father. According to a November 28, 2012 story by Associated Press reporter Frederic J. Frommer, the sons, who were nine and five years old at the time, are seeking unspecified compensation and previously withheld documents. The sons say they have evidence that their father was pushed from the New York

City hotel window. They believe he was killed because he had begun to have serious concerns over the Agency's MKULTRA practices.

In another recent case, six veterans filed suits on January 7, 2009 in San Francisco stating that they had volunteered for military experiments to test mind control techniques using LSD and that they were not adequately told of the nature of the tests. The veterans are suing the CIA, the Department of Defense, and other agencies. They allege more than 7,800 servicemen were involved in the experiments, which were conducted in the 1950s and 1960s at the Edgewood Arsenal outside Baltimore, Maryland.[36]

Bars were ideal places for the agency to initiate contact with unwitting subjects for induction into research experiments utilizing drugs and hypnosis. In strip clubs in particular, one would easily find a fringe element of subjects who, it could be safely assumed, would keep the operation out of mainstream cognizance. Many of these individuals had negligible credibility and few resources. If something were to go awry, such subjects had little recourse. In addition, a bar situation made it easy for someone to slip a "mickey" into the drink of an unsuspecting patron. Of course, in topless bars, dancers provided an abundance of distractions for operatives to carry out their devious tasks.

Soon, mind control testing routinely involving the use of drugs—with LSD being administered to unwitting subjects—was being carried out on US college campuses.[37] These top secret studies were initiated by Richard Helms with approval of CIA Director Allen Dulles. They worked closely with James Angleton, head of the counterintelligence group, and scientist Sid Gottlieb, who directed the operational experiments.[38] World-famous neurologist Dr. Harold Wolff of Cornell University Medical Center in New York was hired during this period to study both chemical and nonchemical mind-altering techniques. He became an expert in the study of brainwashing and understanding the effects of sensory deprivation. As a cover for its work, Dr. Wolff established a study group, the Human Ecology Society, which was actually a funding mechanism for CIA behavioral research.[39] During the 1950s, the Society received more than three hundred thousand dollars in CIA funds.[40] Dr. Wolff's society kept CIA money flowing into research at Cornell and later Rutgers and concealed the Agency's activities from public view.

The Agency's Directorate of Science and Technology, Office of Research and Development, and the Technical Services Staff gradually built on its successes in its studies of LSD and ways of controlling human behavior, and, in turn, the Agency broadened its mandate. Agency researchers began to work towards finding a drug that would simulate a heart attack and drugs that would create amnesia in subjects. They also sought the ultimate objective: to find out if a human could be programmed to carry out "executive action" operations, which, in CIA terminology, meant assassination.[41]

On April 13, 1953, Richard Helms's proposal for a new mind control program called MKULTRA was approved by Allen Dulles. For reasons of security, Helms's program was "exempted . . . from normal CIA financial controls."[42] MKULTRA initially commenced operations by secretly funding LSD research at universities across the country: Columbia University in New York, University of Illinois Medical School, the University of Oklahoma, and the University of Rochester, among others. The grants were supplied by the CIA through nonprofit foundations.[43]

In the following year, 1954, the ARTICHOKE program, noted above, was turned over to the MKULTRA team headed by Sid Gottlieb, a Bronx PhD in Chemistry, and hypnosis case officer John Gittinger, an Oklahoma psychologist.[44] The MK program was more extensive and complex than ARTICHOKE, and it included additional research facilities at various universities that had been enlisted as well.

The three goals of MKULTRA originally were: "to induce hypnosis very rapidly in unwitting subjects, to create durable amnesia, and to implant durable and operationally useful posthypnotic suggestions."[45] Essentially, a subject would be made to do something and not remember it. James Angleton's counterintelligence staff, known for conducting the most secretive operations, took on the task of field experimentation. His researchers found that with some subjects, they were able to develop very successful techniques for both rapid induction into a trance state and creating amnesia.[46]

At this point, Helms's MK group proposed the operational use of a hypnoprogrammed assassin. A 1954 CIA memorandum released under the Freedom of Information Act reveals that the ultimate intent of the MK behavior control program was to create unwitting assassins. The heavily redacted (blackened out) memo contains a disturbing and prophetic line that indicates that this method of eliminating an enemy could be useful against "a prominent politician or, if necessary, an American official."[47]

If a programmed assassin or a hypno-programmed patsy could be created, US intelligence wanted to be the first to do it. However, after several years of testing, it was becoming clear to those in charge of the Agency's behavior modification program that *total* control over a subject would produce a vegetable,[48] and at the same time, *limited* control would produce an individual with some unpredictability.[49] Neither would be acceptable risks, given the tasks required by the head of the CIA's Clandestine Services, Richard Helms.[50]

The goal of the program—to create a programmed assassin who could neutralize an enemy target on command without disclosing his or her agency affiliation (a "Manchurian Candidate")—produced *unreliable* results. Either the subject was too drugged to function or aware enough to be unpredictable. However, the research proved to be most successful in creating a patsy, a fall guy who could be framed for a murder while actually being innocent. The assassination would be carried out by hitmen hidden on the sidelines while the patsy would appear to have committed the crime, thus protecting the identity of the actual assassins. The technique of producing such a patsy involved the use of drugs and hypnotism, hence the term "hypno-programmed fall guy." The success of the program hinged on creating temporary amnesia in the mind of the patsy in order to both ensure the secrecy of the true nature of the operation and enable the agency to guarantee plausible denial.

Again, when the Agency realized that the goal of drugging and hypnotizing a subject for the purpose of having him perform an assassination and not recall it later was too chancy, it sought easier, more effective ways to kill someone without being detected. One modified version involved the use of a patsy. Forensic case evidence has found that in this approach, the drugged and hypnotized (programmed) subject would *not* fire the lethal shots. Instead, the murder would be carried out by hit men concealed at the scene. The programmed subject—the innocent fall guy or patsy—would be apprehended. The patsy could be holding a weapon or even firing unwittingly (shooting blanks, of course, which would prevent the hidden gunmen from being hit.) The actual hidden assassins could easily escape while the patsy received the blame. Through its research, the CIA learned that a fall guy, who would appear to have committed a particular deed and would have no memory of it, could be created in three months' time.[51]

A patsy is an individual who does not commit a crime but is blamed for it. To ensure a successful operation, the actual assassins hidden on the sidelines would be expert marksmen. The crucial test for programming a patsy would be the successful creation of amnesia with the certainty that it would hold up during subsequent police interrogation. The subject's memory of the posthypnotic suggestion—for example, to be at a certain location at a specific time—the programmed act itself, and the identity of the hypnotist, all had to be irretrievable.

The term used to describe a hypno-programmed fall guy is an unwitting "patsy." The common name for a programmed assassin is a "Manchurian Candidate." Obviously, the difference between the two is significant. The term "Manchurian Candidate" originated with the publication of author Richard Condon's 1959 bestselling novel by that name. The movie followed in 1962, directed by John Frankenheimer and starring Frank Sinatra, Laurence Harvey, Janet Leigh, and Angela Lansbury. In *The Manchurian Candidate*, Soviet and Chinese Communists brainwash an American POW in Manchuria. The soldier is programmed through the use of hypnosis and sent to assassinate the president of the United States. His cue was the phrase, "Why don't you pass the time by playing a little solitaire?" An accompanying cue, seeing the queen of diamonds, activated the hypno-programming. He then killed without remembering what he had done.[52] Because of this movie, the moniker "Manchurian Candidate" gave many conspiracy theories the reputation of being Hollywood fantasies.

However, it is no fantasy that between 1960 and 1963, the CIA's operational hypnosis experiments for counterintelligence were not only conducted, but achieved the goals sought. Helms's group mastered the technique of quickly inducing hypnosis in unwitting subjects that had been developed by the Technical Services Staff working with MKULTRA. At the same time, work accelerated on efforts to create lasting amnesia and to successfully give workable posthypnotic suggestions.[53] Such suggestions included inducing subjects to perform unwitting acts that ranged from following simple prompts from a handler on cue to firing a pistol. New York psychiatrist and hypnosis expert Dr. Herbert Spiegel, when asked about his feelings concerning the efficacy of programming a subject, said that he believes such conditioning is "definitely attainable."[54] In addition, forensic scientists familiar with the history of hypnosis have confirmed that a person's reluctance to commit a crime can be overridden if the person is conditioned to believe the act being committed has a high moral purpose.[55]

The methods involved in creating an unwitting fall guy were a well-guarded CIA secret. Initially, most of the experiments were conducted in Montreal, Canada. Under the tutelage of Richard Helms, the CIA financed some of its most intense and prolonged behavior modification treatment programs out of the country.[56] Helms believed that by removing this type of research to hospitals outside US borders, another layer of secrecy was added to these activities.

Finding subjects on which to experiment was a relatively easy matter. In those days, patients who were clinically depressed or suffering from other psychological maladies did not have the luxury of modern medications. Absent the designer drugs of today, their best hope for relief or a cure was thought to be temporary institutionalization. In the 1950s, individuals with moderate to severe psychological diagnoses who could financially afford hospital care would typically be committed by loved ones to an institution for a brief stay. It was expected that they would eventually come out mentally healthy and able to cope with the world once again. It is now known that throughout the 1950s and the 1960s, some of these patients were unwittingly subjected to CIA-funded experimentation involving new drugs such as LSD. Patients also were accorded the latest "benefits" of sensory deprivation.[57] In addition, records of CIA-funded programs in Montreal indicate that many patients were administered advanced forms of electric shock treatment in connection with behavior modification and amnesia induction research.[58]

One such Agency-funded program in Montreal was directed by Dr. D. Ewen Cameron.[59] One of Cameron's purported goals was to find a cure for schizophrenia, and according to the records of his work, he would go to almost any lengths to achieve his objective. His method involved "de-patterning" his patients, which meant erasing the person's mind of past behaviors, at least temporarily. He would use drugs, long periods of sleep, and electric shock to effect this change in the patient. The amnesia aspect of the program was of vital interest to the CIA and its main purpose in funding this work.[60] Cameron started using sensory deprivation in 1957, along with drugs and electric shocks. He eventually reached a point where he actually proposed performing terminal experiments on subjects.[61] He died in 1967 at age sixty-six, having never found any cures. The damage he caused to patients' minds was in many cases found to be permanent.[62]

Other scientists who had learned from Cameron picked up where he had left off. In fact, CIA-financed programs of this type—rapid induction into hypnosis and creating amnesia—continued throughout Richard Helms's tenure.[63]

By 1960, Helms was chief of operations under Deputy Director of Plans Richard Bissell. Bissell was a high-tech visionary who had developed the U-2 spy plane program in 1954 and satellite photo reconnaissance in 1961, giving the CIA high-resolution pictures of Soviet and Chinese military sites on a regular basis.[64] While Bissell pursued these remarkable achievements, he built his own staff, and, for the most part, left Helms to his own devices.[65]

It was during this time that a four-year-long feud between Helms and Bissell ensued.[66] The brilliant and creative Bissell had been appointed in 1958 by CIA director Allen Dulles to the DDP post, a job Helms had been vying for. Helms would later state that he was "surprised and disappointed"[67] at this turn of events, considered it a vote of no confidence, and called Bissell a "peculiar choice."[68] Helms reportedly felt demeaned and became abrasive.[69] Soon, his resentment caused his relationship with Bissell to deteriorate into hostility.[70] In his isolation, Helms quietly but aggressively pressed ahead, hunting for results in his and Angleton's top secret MK programs, among other covert activities.

One of those covert operations on the front burner was a plot to oust Cuba's popular dictator Fidel Castro, who had come to power in 1959. Within weeks of President John F. Kennedy's inauguration, a CIA-trained army of twelve hundred exiled anti-Castro paramilitary forces attempted to retake the island of Cuba. In the ensuing debacle at the Bay of Pigs on April 17, 1961, the invaders were overwhelmed and soundly defeated by Castro loyalists. President Kennedy had found out about the CIA's plan to invade Cuba shortly after coming into office in January 1961. Relying on the judgment of the elite in the US intelligence community, he had allowed the ill-conceived plan to move forward. Afterwards, the intelligence planners in charge of the invasion blamed Kennedy for not providing more support, particularly from the air. However, as General Maxwell Taylor has pointed out, even a US air strike would not have affected the outcome, mainly because Cuban antiaircraft batteries were so strong.[71] In addition, Kennedy knew an aerial attack clearly would have created even more political problems both at home and abroad. The president felt that he had been grossly misled. As he struggled to negotiate freedom for the prisoners of war, he vowed to break the CIA "into a thousand pieces and scatter (it) to the winds."[72]

In 1962, following the resignation of CIA Director Dulles and Richard Bissell at the behest of President Kennedy, Helms moved up to the position of Deputy Director of Plans under Director John McCone.[73]

By mid-1963, a majority of Americans supported President Kennedy. He had established the Peace Corps, initiated the Nuclear Test Ban Treaty, and extended an olive branch to the Soviet Union. It is interesting to note, regarding the mission of the Peace Corps, that according to its first director, Sargent Shriver, who was married to Kennedy's sister Eunice, during this time Richard Helms submitted a request recommending that CIA agents be placed in the Peace Corps. Kennedy immediately ordered Helms to keep the CIA away. The president knew Helms's plan could cause the Peace Corps to lose all of its credibility.[74]

In a speech at American University in Washington, DC, in June 1963, Kennedy delivered one of his most memorable lines, one that marked a significant departure in Cold War politics. The president promised to "make the world safe for diversity." Behind the scenes, Kennedy had agreed *not* to invade Cuba and also had begun to plan a military withdrawal from South Vietnam.[75] Indeed, President Kennedy was viewed by most Americans as a peacemaker. Yet, to the extreme right wing, Kennedy was seen as having capitulated to the Communists. His groundbreaking political moves had violated primary tenets of Cold War ideology. To many within the CIA, Communism was a monolithic threat, and its ethos was world domination. The Right felt America's place in the world demanded that the administration actively seek to overthrow leftist regimes where feasible. While hardly extreme by today's political standards, many in government and in the military-industrial complex advocated exporting democracy by military means. Some held an even more distorted worldview. These extremists had become convinced that America's future would not be secure until President Kennedy was removed from the White House.

Meanwhile, at the CIA, Helms's MK drugs and hypnosis research continued unrestrained, largely without the knowledge of Director McCone and the administration. As noted above, one of the most common covers for the CIA's hypnosis testing was the pretense of giving medical treatment.[76] Finally, in 1963, political pressure led to the suspension of some of the CIA's unwitting drug testing. Besides hospitals outside the United States, at this point safe houses within US borders operated by the CIA were being routinely used as locations for the Agency's unwitting testing of drugs. Such tests involved surreptitiously administering a drug to a subject without his or her knowledge. When CIA director John McCone had obtained sufficient information about this widespread practice, he ordered it suspended. In addition, the Agency's Inspector General John Earman wrote that such manipulation of unwitting subjects was "distasteful and unethical."[77] McCone recommended that the safe houses be closed, and two years later, two key sites were shut down, one in New York and one in San Francisco.

Richard Helms, meanwhile, fought vigorously to save the programs. The longtime clandestine services veteran believed that unwitting testing of subjects was crucial to his division's work, despite the reservations of others in government. Helms wrote to his superior, "We have no answer to the moral issue."[78] He and other zealots at the Technical Services Staff saw their research as far more important than the fate of their subjects. Helms insisted that "in the field of covertly administered chemicals" it was incumbent upon the United States to keep up with the Russians.[79] This line evidently was a ruse to gain funding and support from the highest level of the Agency, since it is now believed that the United States was far ahead of the Soviets in this area.

Richard Helms—the Agency's most powerful promoter of behavioral research and mind control programs—made sure that any changes to his units would only be cosmetic. As you will see, Helms's MK programs played key roles in the assassinations of President John F. Kennedy in Dallas, Texas, on November 22, 1963, and Sen. Robert F. Kennedy in Los Angles, California, on June 5, 1968.

Six months after the assassination of President Kennedy, in June 1964, Helms changed the name of the MKULTRA program to MKSEARCH.[80] This was actually much more fitting, given that its key task at that point was searching for and finding appropriate subjects, individuals who could be conditioned to become suitable unwitting fall guys.

MKSEARCH focused mainly on testing psychochemicals on individuals. The operation's head scientist, Sid Gottlieb, had by this point made substantial headway in his investigations of "knockout drugs, stress-producing chemicals, and mind-altering substances."[81]

Another team under the direction of Dr. Stephen Aldrich worked out of a several hundred-acre farm in Massachusetts.[82] During the late 1950s and early 1960s, Helms's staff had found top scientists and then financed their work with CIA funds channeled through various foundations, university hospitals, and correctional institutions.

With the ascension of Lyndon B. Johnson to the presidency following the assassination of President Kennedy and Johnson's victory in the 1964 presidential elections, Helms solidified his position in the Agency. He focused on guiding the CIA's role in the rapidly expanding war in Southeast Asia and at the same time advancing its top secret mind control and behavior modification programs. On June 30, 1966, President Johnson appointed Richard Helms Director of the CIA, succeeding Vice Admiral William F. Raborn Jr., who had served from April 1965 through June 1966.[83]

By 1967, many new chemicals and drugs were becoming available to the Agency, courtesy of the CIA's contacts within the pharmaceutical industry. When these drugs could no longer be tested on subjects in safe houses, other venues were opened up. For example, one testing site was a prison, the California Medical Facility at Vacaville. Between 1967 and 1968, the CIA paid a psychiatrist there more than ten thousand dollars to experiment on hundreds of inmates.[84]

At the same time the MK programs were expanding, so, too, was the CIA's war in Southeast Asia. Most Americans did not know at this point that President Kennedy, just days before he was assassinated, had drawn up departure plans for Vietnam. After he was assassinated, the Pentagon canceled the plans and in late 1963 began to increase military aid to South Vietnam.[85]

The year 1967 saw American troop strength in Vietnam climb to nearly a half-million. While Johnson continued to bomb North Vietnam, the number of US troops killed in the war was escalating daily. In 1966 and 1967, more than fifteen thousand Americans died in Southeast Asia.[86] Finally, the heir apparent to the presidency, Robert Kennedy, broke with President Johnson in a speech on the Senate floor over the war in Vietnam. It was March 2, 1967. He saw the war for what it was and spoke of this to his fellow senators: "It is we who live in abundance and send our young men out to die. It is our chemicals that scorch the children and our bombs that level the villages. We are all participants."[87]

In this powerful anti-war speech, Kennedy stated that we all were responsible for the war, focusing on the victims. He implied that the United States should take the high road and that peace and negotiations should be paramount. Without stating it, his remarks were meant to finally announce that the war, which originally had the support of his brother and himself, had been a mistake. The noble cause of defending democracy had turned into a civil war in which the United States was in support of a corrupt regime. Pride and saving face had taken over America's consciousness. At that point, a majority of the country believed we should never back down, that victory was necessary at virtually any cost. Those who voiced an opposing view were considered traitors, especially by many in the military and the intelligence community. To some of them, Bobby Kennedy had no doubt become a marked man.

Meanwhile, Senator Kennedy saw the war's grave impact on people at home. Civil unrest was growing dramatically. During the summer of 1967, the worst race riots in the history of the country broke out in several major cities; there were fires in Cincinnati while Black Panthers with rifles paraded in Sacramento.[88] Then in July, Newark and Detroit exploded as rioters burned buildings, looted stores, and shot at the police. From July 12 to 17, twenty-six people were killed in Newark. In Detroit a week later, rioting broke out with a fury that left forty-three people dead. Michigan Governor George Romney called up the National Guard, and President Johnson sent in tanks to restore order to the city. New York, too, saw violence in Spanish Harlem. Police were stationed on virtually every street corner in the *barrio*.[89]

In a letter to President Johnson, civil rights leader Martin Luther King Jr. wrote from Atlanta, "The chaos and destruction which now spreads through our cities is a blind revolt against the revolting conditions which you so courageously set out to remedy as you entered office in 1964. The conditions have not changed." Dr. King went on to term the violence in Detroit as "the externalization of the Negro's inner torment and rage."[90]

While President Johnson was vilified by both civil rights activists and anti-war protesters, Republican Richard Nixon—whom John F. Kennedy had defeated in 1960—quietly waited for the 1968 presidential election year to arrive. The intelligence community and the military also played a key role in the dynamics of this period.

Richard Helms's domestic spying program—dubbed Operation CHAOS, run by James Angleton—was set up in an attempt to curb race riots and anti-war demonstrations by discrediting the protesters. Tactics included mail opening, black-bag jobs (home and office break-ins), telephone wire taps, and surveillance.[91] As part of this assault on civil liberties, in 1967, according to law professor Christopher H. Pyle at Mount Holyoke College in South Hadley, Massachusetts, the army was recruited because of its vast manpower to assist in the task of collecting information on hundreds of thousands of innocent Americans. Pyle had firsthand knowledge; as an army intelligence captain at that time, he was one of those who exposed this flagrant abuse of power.[92] According to Pyle, he and some fifteen hundred soldiers dressed in plainclothes illegally infiltrated college groups and black organizations. Their orders were to cause enough mischief to disrupt dissident activities and thereby prevent future protests. Pyle would work later on in the 1970s for Sen. Sam J. Ervin's subcommittee on Constitutional Rights and for Sen. Frank Church, who uncovered further illegal surveillance being carried out by the CIA and the FBI.

Towards the end of 1967, the war in Vietnam continued to escalate, and the CIA moved into high gear in virtually every way, both at home and abroad. President Lyndon Johnson's war of attrition was not going well, yet he refused to change course, despite the carnage in Vietnam. According to Arthur Schlesinger Jr., Henry Kissinger said that at cabinet meetings President Johnson would plead with Secretary of Defense Robert McNamara, "Tell me how I can hit them in the nuts."[93]

Johnson's ratings in the polls continued to slip and by the end of 1967, McNamara was dismissed as secretary of defense.[94] He eventually became head of the World Bank. Meanwhile, President Johnson clung to his faith in American power and might, envisioning victory, and blindly followed the CIA's lead.

The Agency that year had begun a program of destroying Communist Vietcong ammunition depots. Known as Operation PHOENIX, the plan called for infiltrating Vietnamese villages and hamlets that served as ammo dumps for the guerrillas. According to Vietnam's foreign minister Nguyen Co Thach,

Operation PHOENIX "wiped out many of our bases," and forced many of the Communist forces to flee to Cambodia.[95] The operation was extremely destructive. Disaffected CIA operatives, many of whom had disbanded following the Bay of Pigs fiasco in Cuba, found their services and contract roles were again in demand.

At home, the CIA also built up its forces by recruiting and illegally training municipal police to be able to work on various projects on an as-needed basis.[96] A key job was that of gathering intelligence, as noted above, to neutralize the activities of race rioters and anti-war protesters. Two high-level police officers at the Los Angeles Police Department who were on contract were Manny Pena and Hank Hernandez. Both would play critical roles in the official investigation into the assassination of Robert Kennedy.[97] Indeed, their efforts would ensure that the official story would be simply a case of a "lone gunman." As we shall see, witnesses who saw other gunmen were either ignored, or, in one way or another, convinced that their versions were not correct.[98]

This widespread use of intelligence personnel for domestic operations allowed Helms's MK units to effectively accomplish their mission in several important ways: namely, to find suitable subjects, condition the subjects to carry out posthypnotic suggestions, and produce amnesia to ensure plausible denial. It was at the end of 1967 that twenty-four-year-old Palestinian immigrant Sirhan Sirhan would disappear from his home in Pasadena, California. He would return three months later with amnesia regarding the time gap. MKSEARCH was a key element in the assassination conspiracy that felled Sen. Robert F. Kennedy four months later on June 5, 1968 at the Ambassador Hotel in Los Angeles (and Martin Luther King Jr. before that, on April 4, 1968 at the Lorraine Motel in Memphis, Tennessee.)

In addition to these shocking murders, the Vietnam War continued unabated in 1968, and Richard M. Nixon was elected president in November, keeping Richard Helms on board as Director of the CIA. Also in that year, Helms divorced his wife of twenty-nine years, Julia Bretzman Shields, and married Cynthia Ratcliff McKelvie.

During Nixon's first term from 1968 through 1972, Richard Helms's attention was focused on assassination cover-up operations. Scores of witnesses in the JFK case were found dead, many from unexplained heart attacks, suicides, car accidents, and violent murders. A number of witnesses involved in the RFK assassination were also shot at. Then, as the next presidential election campaign moved into high gear, a popular Southern candidate, former Alabama governor George Wallace, was shot on May 15, 1972 in Laurel, Maryland. The candidate survived, but his legs were paralyzed, and he lived the rest of his life in a wheelchair. Wallace had been a major threat to Nixon's ambitions for a second term because of his strong support in the South from both conservative Democrats and Republicans. His withdrawal from the race handed the '72 election to Nixon, who would badly defeat the peace candidate, Democratic senator George McGovern of South Dakota. The assailant who had attacked Governor Wallace, Arthur H. Bremer (another "crazed lone gunman"?), was convicted and is currently serving a life sentence.

One month after the attempted assassination of George Wallace, the Watergate office complex, headquarters for the Democratic National Committee in Washington, DC, was broken into. On June 17, 1972, five burglars were discovered and taken into custody. Two were former CIA and one was a current Agency employee. Ostensibly, their mission had been to bug the offices in order to provide valuable campaign intelligence for the Nixon camp. But more importantly, the telephonic eavesdropping would provide Helms and Angleton with the most critical information they needed to know: namely, whether or not the Democrats had broken the "MKULTRA code," that is, if the opposition had discovered who was behind the assassinations.

As the Watergate story gained traction in the media, President Nixon knew that the news reports could cripple his campaign. With the election only six months away, he turned to his CIA director Richard Helms for help, but Helms, who disavowed any knowledge of the break-in, refused. Nixon then asked his top aide, H. R. Haldeman, to meet with Helms. The two met with presidential assistant John Ehrlichman on June 23, 1972 in Ehrlichman's office. Once again, Helms was asked who was behind the break-in, and the CIA director insisted that he was not connected in any way. Then Haldeman relayed a message from President Nixon: "The president asked me to tell you this entire affair may be connected to the Bay of Pigs, and if it opens up, the Bay of Pigs may be blown . . ." [99]

According to Haldeman, Helms suddenly became uncontrollable, shouting at those in the room, "The Bay of Pigs had nothing to do with this. I have no concern about the Bay of Pigs." A stunned Haldeman replied, "I'm just following my instructions, Dick. This is what the President told me to relay to you." Helms then calmed down. [100]

The key to understanding Helms's violent outburst is knowing that the "Bay of Pigs" refers to the Kennedy assassination. This is the code word used throughout the Nixon Watergate tapes. Clearly, President Nixon suspected that Helms was linked to the assassinations.

As noted above, despite Watergate, in November 1972 Nixon won a second term as president, defeating McGovern in a landslide victory. CIA Director Helms, on the other hand, fearing the worst, abruptly shut down the Agency mind control programs that he had so assiduously fostered.[101] Together with Sid Gottlieb, chief MK scientist, Richard Helms deliberately destroyed the MKULTRA files in January 1973. However, the two men overlooked the program's financial records. Several boxes of these documents were discovered four years later and made available to the Senate.[102]

Within days of the destruction of the main MK files by Helms and Gottlieb, on February 2, 1973, President Nixon relieved Helms of his post at the Agency and Sid Gottlieb retired from federal service. In return for giving up the directorship of the CIA, Helms was appointed by Nixon to the ambassadorship of Iran, a location which Helms had requested.[103] At that time, Iran was under the reign of the Shah Mohammad Reza Pahlavi, a strong US ally who had been installed by the CIA in 1953. The Shah held onto power with Helms's help through the use of CIA-trained secret police known as the SAVAK.

It was not until August 3, 1977 that the MKULTRA financial records became known to the general public for the first time when the US Senate Select Committee on Intelligence issued its joint hearing report. But despite the hearings, the public still did not know what the files meant. This is because many of those connected with these clandestine programs who appeared at the Senate Hearings routinely deceived both Congress and the press.[104] For example, one agent who had supervised one of the Agency drug-testing safe houses renounced any direct knowledge of such places.[105] Another witness who denied testing various drugs on humans had, in fact, been the person who wrote the proposal to carry out the very same testing.[106] And one foundation head, who had operated a CIA front, claimed his budget was 25 to 30 percent Agency-funded, while the true figure, according to the government's own documents, was more than 90 percent.[107]

Richard Helms's long government career came to an end when Jimmy Carter defeated President Gerald Ford and took the oath of office in January 1977. After Helms's replacement arrived in Iran, the sixty-four-year-old ex-spy chief set up shop in Washington working as a business consultant specializing in international investments. He named his firm Safeer, an Iranian word meaning "ambassador." Helms's retirement from the government would prove to be personally more tumultuous than any of his days at Langley.

In the same year he departed his post in Iran, Helms was indicted for perjury for having lied to the Senate Foreign Relations Committee during his

February 1973 ambassadorship confirmation hearings. The senators were inquiring about American intervention in Chile, specifically a 1970 CIA operation in which Helms had directed covert activities designed to prevent the election of Socialist President Salvador Allende in that copper-rich country.[108] The Agency was successful three years later when a CIA-assisted military coup overthrew the Chilean government and installed a military dictatorship led by Gen. Augusto Pinochet. The US-backed regime tortured and killed more than three thousand people during its sixteen-year reign.[109] In Helms's testimony before the Senate, he had kept secret the fact that the CIA had funneled millions of dollars to Allende's opponents. In the end, Helms knew there was no way out. He pleaded guilty. The judge fined him two thousand dollars and handed him a suspended two-year sentence.[110] Helms was allowed to keep his government pension.

The truth regarding Helms's brutally efficient career in covert operations first began to surface when President Gerald Ford came into office. Ford had ascended to the presidency when Richard Nixon resigned in disgrace in August 1974. It was during a routine media interview five months later in January 1975 that President Ford innocently mentioned to *The New York Times'* managing editor, A. M. Rosenthal, that the CIA had been involved in foreign assassinations.[111] Earlier, Ford's CIA Director, William Colby (September 4, 1973 to January 30, 1976) had ordered all CIA personnel to divulge any wrongdoing they were aware of within the CIA's past.[112] The so-called "Family Jewels," a 693-page report initially kept confidential, contained evidence of CIA assassination plots in Africa and the Caribbean. Eventual disclosure of this information, while infuriating Richard Helms,[113] led directly to the Rockefeller Commission investigation of 1975, which looked into a multitude of assorted illegal Agency domestic activities. This was followed in 1976 by the Senate Select Committee to Study Governmental Operations with Respect to Intelligence Activities, chaired by Sen. Frank Church, an Idaho Democrat. Known as the Church Committee, this body disclosed the Mafia–CIA connection. And finally, the House Select Committee on Assassinations set about reexamining the John F. Kennedy and Martin Luther King Jr. shootings in 1976 through 1978.

Despite all of these investigations and hearings, little has been written about the thread that runs through most of the Helms era, namely, the activities associated with operations such as MKULTRA. Helms's ultimate goal for these programs was for the CIA to be able to conduct assassinations without being implicated, to kill without being blamed. Indeed, a series of coups and assassinations of foreign and domestic leaders began in 1953 and would continue for the next twenty years. Although the CIA was cleared of direct involvement by the various congressional investigations, there was evidence of Agency funding backing these activities. All of the victims of these assassinations were leaders advocating policies inimical to the interests of the United States in terms of economics and military advantage during the Cold War. Congress and the media accepted the CIA's denials as plausible. Today, however, much of Richard Helms's testimony over the years regarding CIA fingerprints on the planning, execution, and cover-ups of numerous assassinations is known to have been false. In November of 2005, at a Bethesda, Maryland conference sponsored by the Assassination Archives and Research Center, G. Robert Blakey, the House Assassinations Committee Chief Counsel, commented regarding information that the CIA had provided his committee. Blakey stated, "I have no confidence in anything the Agency told me."[114]

Again, Helms was in a unique position from the early 1950s through the early 1970s to know about virtually every CIA covert operation going on. As liaison between Washington and the field, he had a "need-to-know." At the same time, there is no evidence that any of the presidents in office during this twenty-year time period ever ordered any assassinations. Indeed, coups in various countries were approved. However, the expectations were that a new, more favorable regime would be installed, and the deposed leader would be allowed to flee into exile or be deported, not killed. Richard Helms, on the other hand, routinely operated without the advice or consent of the president. Indeed, there are numerous instances in which Helms did not inform his superiors of the extent of his plans nor the nature of key operations, particularly in the case of the CIA–Mafia assassination plots. One reason for Helms's secrecy was the fact that he knew the Oval Office would consider such actions "completely out of bounds,"[115] as John McCone stated in reference to covert actions planned against Cuba in August 1962.

Nevertheless, during the Helms era between 1953 and 1973, there were nearly a dozen CIA-backed foreign coups or coup attempts. Most of these regime changes involved assassinations. Coups took place in Iran in 1953, Guatemala in 1954, Indonesia (attempted) in 1958, Congo in 1961, Cuba (attempted) in 1961, Dominican Republic in 1961, Iraq in 1963, South Vietnam in 1963, revolutionary Che Guevara was killed in Bolivia in 1967, and finally, Chile in 1973. In the United States, political leaders were shot in 1963—President Kennedy; 1965—Malcolm X; 1968—Rev. Martin Luther King Jr. and Sen. Robert Kennedy; and in 1972—Governor George Wallace (attempted assassination).

Political assassination as a tool of foreign policy was outlawed in the United States in February 1976 under Executive Order 11905. In his autobiography, Richard Helms wrote that he disagreed with this ban on assassination in the event the United States was in a state of war. He considered assassination to be an effective method to defeat an enemy.[116] Obviously, Helms felt that the Cold War was in fact warfare taking place under the radar.

During his years in the CIA, Helms became an expert at recruiting and training foreigners to conduct covert action operations. As he moved up the ladder—Helms was primarily with the Directorate of Plans (also known as Clandestine Services)—he was able to draw on a variety of specialists from a wide array of nations. His foreign contract operatives ranged from anti-Castro Cubans to pro-Shah Iranians. Helms's foreign connections could be counted on to carry out clandestine missions of all types, including assassinations.

Helms's preference for using foreigners in sensitive operations is alluded to in his biography by Thomas Powers. Powers writes that Helms considered it of the utmost importance to keep the CIA's hands clean: "If inherently noisy things had to be done, it was better to let someone else do them."[117]

For Helms, "noisy things" were to be approached with caution and discretion. His goal, as demonstrated in his plans for MKULTRA, was to be able to eliminate an individual without the Agency being blamed. This was Helms's primary reason for using foreigners as assassins rather than his own personnel. Protecting the Agency (and himself) from exposure was paramount. The issue of right or wrong was practically irrelevant to Helms, or as he himself once called this concern, "the soggy mass of morality."[118] Ethics and empathy were not part of Helms's vocabulary. Instead, his chief worry in terms of assassination was that the hitman would later talk, due to guilt, too much alcohol, mental instability, or job disaffection. Helms feared that such exposure could lead to retribution against the Agency and long-term political repercussions. In addition, he knew that being found out meant that he and his coconspirators could easily be fired, but on a wider scale, it meant almost certain reprisals against the United States. Despite the risks involved, Helms pressed ahead, confident that he could avoid unwanted blowback, first, by having foreigners do his dirty work, and secondly, by making good use of his top secret MK programs.

Another secret to Helms's success in these clandestine endeavors was his use of "compartmentalization." This concept simply means that information is strictly compartmented, that is, information is given to one officer, but perhaps not to another officer working at the next desk. By keeping sensitive information regarding top secret operations (for example, assassinations) limited to only those who needed to know, even at the highest levels of command, security could be achieved. This compartment technique enabled the CIA to deceive presidents, oversight committees, and the media for decades. As Helms writes in his memoir, "In the secret operations canon, it is axiomatic that the probability of leaks escalates exponentially each time a classified document is exposed to another person—be it an Agency employee, a member of Congress, a senior official, a typist, or a file clerk. Effective compartmentation is fundamental to all secret activity. . . . The potential for leaks—deliberate or accidental—is vast."[119]

Another effective strategy used by Helms to keep sensitive operations out of the public eye was to create cover stories within the Agency. These invented tales were told by covert operations officers to other officers who were working next to them in order to keep them from knowing about certain activities. Helms describes this tactic thusly: "Within the Agency offices, cover stories within cover stories had to be invented to explain the presence of the specialists and the various closed doors to their fellow officers."[120] In this way, by creating stories of fictitious operations, the actual programs such as MKULTRA were carried out with very few Agency staff even aware of their existence.

Some historians who have interviewed Agency personnel have recorded these stories that had erroneously been told as truth and they have believed many of them. One cover story blamed the Kennedys, both John and Robert, for the attempts to murder Fidel Castro and the assassination of South Vietnamese despot Ngo Dinh Diem. Yet there is no evidence of such plotting. The facts actually point to Richard Helms and his close confidant, CIA officer William Harvey, as the lead planners. Harvey admitted to the Church Committee in the mid-1970s that both he and Helms intentionally kept their anti-Castro–Mafia alliance secret from then CIA Director John McCone.[121] Helms, Harvey, and Angleton all believed extraordinary means were justified during the Cold War. For them, this period of tension between East and West was more than just ideological warfare; it was an international struggle to defeat the Soviet Union and Communist China, to crush Marxism both abroad and at home using whatever means were at their disposal.

These men also had their reputations to uphold—their notoriety had been born in Berlin at the very start of the Cold War. William Harvey, for example, had led the digging of a secret underground tunnel into the Soviet sector, resulting in an intelligence coup. When President Kennedy once asked who in the CIA most resembled Ian Fleming's agent 007, the Agency sent Harvey to meet with him. The sight of the overweight, balding, and heavy-drinking

Harvey prompted Kennedy to inquire as to whether he had "as much luck with women as James Bond."[122] Harvey apparently took himself much more seriously. His sobriquet for the Kennedys, in private, was "fags."[123]

Helms's chief of counterintelligence, James Angleton, has been described as a "spooky figure." His gaunt face, shrouded office, and eccentric ways added to his mystique.[124] Angleton's contribution to the CIA's covert efforts was to design secret operations that would foil Soviet intelligence—KGB—espionage activities in critical locations. But beyond containing the "Soviet menace," Angleton's role was to fully support Helms's goals both abroad and at home. Helms abundantly praised Angleton and considered him the "dominant counterintelligence figure in the non-Communist world." Helms once stated, "Jim had the ability to raise an operational discussion not only to a higher level but to another dimension."[125] The MK (mind control) programs certainly fit this description of "another dimension." In MKULTRA and other operations, Helms spearheaded programs that would ensure that culpability for an assassination would be placed on others outside the CIA. The most sophisticated method, as we have seen, involved using expert marksmen who would shoot from the sidelines while unwitting fall guys—drugged and hypnotized programmed patsies—would be arrested for the crime. Incredibly, some historians have written, "Oswald may have been a patsy, but why did he do it?" Yet a "patsy" by definition is someone who did not do it.

The Helms-Angleton programs not only raised assassination operations to another dimension, but these new operational techniques were available for other uses as well, including stymying assassination investigations. A wide variety of similar tactics were employed to effectively neutralize witnesses in order to cover up assassinations. As we shall see, numerous witnesses to the various political assassinations died mysterious, untimely deaths. Writers also were targeted, as well as jurists and others whose lives somehow intersected with an assassination. Some examples include the sudden death of columnist Dorothy Kilgallen of New York, who had interviewed Oswald's assassin Jack Ruby; she was not a drug user, yet she died of a drug overdose. And a US attorney who many thought would reopen the Robert Kennedy case, Robert L. Meyer, was found dead of a heart attack in an Orange County courthouse parking lot. He had no history of heart problems.[126] (Tragic deaths in the Martin Luther King Jr. case include William Sartor, a *Time* magazine stringer who was investigating the assassination; he also died from an overdose although he did not use drugs. And Memphis judge Preston Battle was found dead from a heart attack one morning while at his desk. He had been considering a motion to reopen the case of James Earl Ray in the King assassination.)

CIA-connected mobsters Sam Giancana and John Rosselli were both killed before they could be brought in to testify at the Senate Assassination hearings. Both had considered themselves immune from prosecution because of their work for the CIA. In 1975, Chicago's Giancana was shot seven times while preparing a meal in his kitchen, and in July of the following year, Rosselli was found dismembered and stuffed in a drum floating off the Miami coast.[127] Numerous ordinary people who were witnesses to the assassinations and who knew too much also died early deaths, as we shall see ahead.

# 2

# *The Sociopathy Test*

A CRITICAL ELEMENT for success in Richard Helms's chosen profession of espionage and covert operations was deception. But for spymaster Helms, there were no limits to its use, particularly when addressing congressional committees and the media. Indeed, it was a key character trait of his. As we shall see, his extreme use of falsehoods actually may have crossed the line into the realm of the pathological. In the following pages, some of Helms's major public prevarications are examined.

One way in which Helms was able to keep his activities secret, according to his autobiography, was to invent cover stories.[128] These myths were told to certain CIA officers to keep them from knowing about programs other officers were involved with. Granted, this was an excellent method to hide various operations and to maintain security. But eventually, the Agency's culture under Helms became imbued with lies.

A prime example of this is Helms's use of organized crime. In his autobiography, Helms claims he had little regard for the mob and calls them "thugs."[129] Yet in reality, his division of the CIA maintained very close relationships with various mobsters, even after having been warned by Bobby Kennedy about such involvements. In fact, in June 1963, six months prior to President Kennedy's assassination, according to Senate Intelligence Committee records, Helms's lieutenant, Bill Harvey, was still meeting with John Rosselli, the Mafia's chief assassination coordinator.[130]

Helms "was a master of telling different people different stories to suit his purposes,"[131] states John Marks in his book, *The Search for the Manchurian Candidate*.

Marks provides as one example the time Helms was telling the Warren Commission that the Soviets were incapable of effectively forcing someone to perform an action through drugging, and at the same time, Helms was writing to his boss, DCI John McCone, insisting that he was disturbed over the Soviets' "aggressiveness" in the use of chemicals being administered covertly. Helms was, at the time, pushing for McCone to continue his division's drug experiments on unwitting subjects.[132]

In another chapter in his autobiography, Helms blamed Moscow for fabricating documents and planting stories in European newspapers to show that the CIA was involved in the assassination of President Kennedy.[133] Based on the facts, the Soviets did not have to fabricate them.

Helms devoted his resources to protecting his cover domestically as well. In 1967, when New Orleans district attorney James Garrison began his investigation into the assassination of President Kennedy, then CIA Director Richard Helms was so upset he sent in agents to attempt to sabotage the case.[134] In addition, according to the House Committee investigating the assassination, Helms planted CIA agents on Garrison's staff.[135] Garrison had had New Orleans millionaire businessman Clay Shaw arrested on March 1, 1967 on charges that he was a central figure in the plot to kill the president. (Lee Harvey Oswald had lived in New Orleans several months prior to the assassination and was connected with several Agency contacts there.) Clay Shaw had founded the International Trade Mart and had served as an informant for the CIA's Domestic Contact Division from 1948 to 1956.[136] According to Helms, after 1956, Shaw ended his Agency involvements because he had "lost interest."[137] The truth is quite the opposite. Shaw's interest in CIA activities in New Orleans had greatly increased by the early 1960s, a time when the CIA and anti-Castro Cubans had begun to establish a key paramilitary camp north of the city. Not surprisingly, with Helms's aid, Shaw was acquitted in early 1969. He died of cancer in 1974.[138]

On the subject of President Kennedy, Richard Helms's memoir abounds with distortions. For example, in discussing Kennedy's Vietnam policies, Helms wrote that if Kennedy had lived, he would not have withdrawn US troops from South Vietnam early in the conflict, based on the president's actions toward Cuba.[139] Yet, as seen above, this is precisely what Kennedy did do. On November 20, 1963 at the Honolulu conference, Kennedy announced the withdrawal of one thousand troops. As for Kennedy's policies toward Cuba, he, in fact, displayed unusual restraint there as well when he withheld the follow-up aerial attack at the Bay of Pigs.

Another significant deception involving the Kennedy assassination, this one emanating from Helms's Mafia liaison, John Rosselli, occurred in early 1967. Rosselli told a Washington lawyer, Edmund Morgan, that Castro had planned the Kennedy murder to get back at the Kennedys for the early coup attempts. Morgan passed this ruse along to Washington columnist Drew Pearson, who published the story on March 3, 1967.[140] Clearly, the false leak was an attempt by Helms's CIA to cover its tracks yet again.

Probably the most substantial act of deception by Helms was his response to the Warren Commission following President Kennedy's assassination. Indeed, investigators have since discovered that much of the evidence Helms gave the Commission was fabricated documentation.[141] For example, the entire trip Oswald was alleged to have taken to the Cuban embassy in Mexico City in the weeks prior to November 22, 1963 has been found to have been staged by Helms's subordinate David Phillips. The operation was designed to link Oswald to Cuban and Soviet Communists. Helms gave this "red herring" information to the Warren Commission to create the appearance that Oswald intended to work with the KGB. But none of the evidence checks out. The Agency's film, eyewitnesses, photos, and voice tapes all fail to identify the actual Oswald in Mexico.[142]

In another falsehood, Helms told the House Select Committee on Assassinations on August 1, 1978 that Oswald was not a CIA agent and had had no contact with the CIA.[143] The truth is that one of Helms's most trusted associates, David Phillips, also known as Maurice Bishop, met with Oswald two months before the Kennedy assassination. Despite Helms's assertions, anti-Castro Cuban leader Antonio Veciana disclosed on March 2, 1976 that CIA agent Phillips met with Oswald in Dallas in September 1963.[144] After the Senate Intelligence Committee studied Oswald's relationships and activities in the Marines, the Soviet Union, New Orleans, and Dallas, Sen. Richard Schweiker of Pennsylvania stated, "Oswald had intelligence connections . . . the fingerprints of intelligence" were all over him.[145]

Following President Kennedy's death, Richard Helms, who, we have noted, was a former newspaperman, set out to enlist the media in his effort to protect himself and the Agency from accusations, suspicion, and criticism related to the assassination. Helms's cover-up plan included a memo that he wrote to prepare agents for discussions with politicians and newspaper editors advising them how to react to conspiracy theories. The memo contained four points agents should make. One: "no significant new evidence has emerged which the (Warren) commission did not consider." This was obviously false. New witnesses, not heard by the Commission, were continually being interviewed and their stories published. Two: "critics usually overvalue particular items and ignore others." Clearly, it was the government investigators who were avoiding pieces of evidence that did not fit the official version. Indeed, this was a common practice of the Warren Commission. Three: "conspiracy on the large scale often suggested would be impossible to conceal in the United States." In fact, the conspiracy involved very few, very secretive men, and even then it could not be kept concealed; bits and pieces of the plot were uncovered from the very start. And four: "Oswald would not have been any sensible person's choice for a coconspirator. He was a loner, mixed-up, of questionable reliability, and an unknown quantity to any professional intelligence service." The truth is, Oswald was quite stable, as we shall see. He was well-liked in school and in the Marines. He was a loyal and responsible son, brother, and husband (his wife Marina has stated that he was "a good husband"—not an abusive spouse as some have reported). He was a caring father of two infant children, worked hard, and paid his bills. But the primary reason that Richard Helms's division chose Oswald to be on their payroll was because he could easily be manipulated into becoming an unwitting fall guy and framed for the murder of a president.[146] So, in essence, Helms's four points for reporters, editors, and columnists in fact amounted to a covert operation of total deception carried out to cover up the truth behind the Kennedy assassination.

Helms's world of deception is clearly revealed in his autobiography, as we have seen above. Another example of his avoiding responsibility for controversial covert actions is his recollection of Operation PHOENIX during the Vietnam War. The operation included infiltration of the Viet Cong in the villages. Some sixty thousand Communists were reported to have been eliminated because of this program.[147] Helms states in his book that this was a South Vietnamese-run program, not CIA.[148] Yet multiple intelligence experts have documented the fact that PHOENIX was established in 1967 by the CIA under Richard Helms and managed by then CIA officer William Colby.[149] Helms also may have denied the CIA's role in PHOENIX to slight Colby, who became Helms's nemesis when, as director (1973–1976), Colby sought to gather information regarding the Agency's bankrupt practices.

Helms also denies in his book any and all CIA assassinations. To back this up, he references Senator Church's investigation that stated the final report showed the CIA never assassinated anyone.[150] The report was based on the fact that at the time the Agency was not forthcoming with relevant documents for the committee. Not long after, the evidence began to mount that showed the CIA had at least facilitated and had paid others to carry out assassinations, rendering Helms's version fiction.

Helms's most repeated line in his book states that he only acted with presidential approval.[151] Once again, more deception. The truth is that Helms never told his superiors what was really going on if he could help it. For example, Helms states that his violations of the CIA charter in 1968 were ordered by President Lyndon Johnson. These violations included wiretapping, mail opening, break-ins, unwitting drugging and hypno-programming of individuals, and assassination operations. There is, in fact, no evidence that President Johnson was aware of these activities.

Another example of Helms's tendency to strain credibility in his written version of events is his story of being given an ambassadorship by President Nixon in 1973. At the time, Nixon was removing Helms as director of the CIA and offered him an embassy post, to which Helms replied that the job had "never crossed (his) mind."[152] John Ehrlichman suggests in his novel that the truth is Helms blackmailed Nixon.[153] Most likely, Nixon knew too much about Helms's past and was afraid this knowledge could end up implicating himself. Helms also states that he is "not sure why" he picked Iran for his ambassadorship.[154] He fails to acknowledge that he had had a long and close relationship with the Shah of Iran, Mohammad Reza Pahlavi. The two men had attended the same prep school in Switzerland and twenty years earlier in 1953, Helms had helped place the Shah in power. In addition, Helms's choice of Iran also would have given him a respite from the limelight as Watergate began to dominate the headlines.

As noted earlier, Helms lied during his confirmation hearings for the embassy position on February 7, 1973. He told the Senate Foreign Relations Committee that the CIA and the United States had no involvement in the Chilean coup.[155] The truth eventually surfaced despite the fact that Helms, when questioned by several Congressional committees, sounded like an "amnesia victim."[156] In 1977, Helms was indicted for perjury on eight counts and pleaded guilty. As noted earlier, he received a two-year suspended sentence and was fined two thousand dollars.[157] During his plea-bargain proceedings, Helms defended his lies by telling the judge, "I had found myself in a position of conflict. I had sworn my oath to protect certain secrets. I didn't want to lie. I didn't want to mislead the Senate. I was simply trying to find my way through a difficult situation in which I found myself."[158]

Richard Helms was obviously "truth-challenged." In fact, some would label him a pathological liar. This characteristic of consistently lying is known to be a key symptom of the sociopathic personality when found in combination with a number of other symptoms exhibited by such individuals. Sociopathy is a serious mental disorder; however, it is not insanity. The cluster of symptoms that make up this mental disorder will be examined in the following pages. Although it is too late to psychoanalyze Richard Helms, it is possible to study his known behavioral characteristics. By comparing Helms's profile to profiles of psychiatrically certified sociopaths, we then can clearly demonstrate whether his behavior falls into the sociopathic range. One widely used method that forensic psychiatrists utilize to facilitate such comparisons involves the Psychopathy Checklist devised by Robert D. Hare, PhD.[159] The terms "psychopathy" and "sociopathy" are interchangeable; they only differ in the sense that the former is used by those who view the disorder as genetic, and the latter is used by those who feel the cause is based on factors within the social environment. Ahead, we will explore the historical figure of Richard Helms from this psychoanalytical perspective. Our information is drawn from Helms's autobiography, his definitive biography, congressional testimony, and his media responses. The results, based on the facts developed herein, reveal a correlation between Helms and evidence of sociopathy.

Sociopaths are *not* like most individuals who have mental disorders. While mentally unstable people are not in control of their emotions or have lost contact with reality, this is not the case with sociopaths. They function normally in these respects, but without any sense of empathy. They have no conscience.

Again, although sociopaths have a serious mental disorder, they do *not* exhibit symptoms of insanity. For example, there is no stress or disorientation. While at the office, Richard Helms was busy planning assassinations, but after work, he socialized with the Washington elite. One political scientist in the 1970s described Helms as "a tall, elegant man with a quiet voice and piercing eyes."[160] The widow of publisher Walter Ridder, Marie Ridder, considered Helms "a very sweet, well-meaning man" and the wife of historian Arthur Schlesinger Jr., Alexandra, once told a reporter, "He (Helms) was a friend of ours. We played tennis with him."[161]

Despite the fact that sociopaths are often pathological liars, they can be cordial, charming, or unusually intelligent. They try to keep their ruthlessness hidden. Richard Helms was a soft-spoken man who usually conducted himself as the most normal of bureaucrats (excluding his outburst with CBS's Daniel Schorr noted above and his other unusual comments to the media). Experts in forensic psychiatry say this is normal for a sociopath. Besides the appearance of normality, sociopaths also exhibit another common characteristic: following a sudden outburst triggered by their sensitive natures, they abruptly return to normal, completely composed as if nothing unusual had happened.[162] This is precisely the behavior exhibited by Helms when confronted by Daniel Schorr (recall that Helms called Schorr a "killer" and a "cocksucker" before settling down).

In the 1970s, some notorious sociopaths in the United States—who were more commonly referred to as psychopaths—were John Gacy, a contractor who killed thirty-two young men in Illinois and buried them under his house; Kenneth Bianchi, one of the Hillside Stranglers, responsible for twelve murders in the Los Angeles area; and Ted Bundy, who killed several dozen young women and was finally executed in Florida.[163] Obviously, most sociopaths do not murder people. However, it is important to note that the assassinations of the 1960s were the tip of the iceberg. In subsequent years, numerous witnesses were killed to keep the truth from getting out. These serial murders started with the first witness killed, Lee Harvey Oswald.

The twelve key symptoms that describe this syndrome of sociopathy, according to Dr. Hare, are divided into two categories: interpersonal characteristics and social deviance. "The former are: glibness, egocentricity, a lack of remorse, a lack of empathy, deceitfulness with tendency to be manipulative, and shallowness of emotions. The social deviance traits are: impulsiveness, poor behavior control, a need for excitement, lack of responsibility, early behavior problems, and adult antisocial behavior."[164] Dr. Hare cautions that his lists are simply tools; more in-depth analysis and obviously, medical training, would be required for a diagnosis. Nevertheless, a "thumbnail sketch" of the sociopath's profile when compared to a subject's known characteristics can be revealing.

Starting at the top of the checklist, Helms was typically glib. His answers to questioners were smooth, but typically without substance. He was a detached figure. In fact, his entire biography by Thomas Powers, cited above, contains a miniscule number of anecdotes from those who worked closely with him. Even CIA Director Allen Dulles described Helms by mustering only a simple line: "he was useful," adding that he "knew how to keep his mouth shut."[165] Helms's egocentricity was often observed, but of course, this was not unusual among Washington's power elite. He considered himself superior to others and strove for power and control. When his career was briefly blocked for a time, he became bitter and resentful. When he attained the top position in the Agency, he directed it as his personal fiefdom. A lack of remorse was pervasive in his writings and interviews. He exhibited no concern for those individuals who were eliminated through coups and assassinations that he had facilitated, nor did he show any interest in their families and friends. He rationalized his illegal activities and denied any personal responsibility. His lack of empathy becomes evident when we look at the lives of those who were unwittingly drugged and experimented on during his MKULTRA research. This was manipulation at its worst. Helms's persistent deceitfulness regarding his role in such illegal activities is well documented. And his personal reaction to the toll his directives inflicted on his many victims and targets fully demonstrates the shallowness of his emotions.

In the category of social deviance, Helms's actions mirror the Hare checklist quite well. For starters, they were impulsive. In fact, although Helms paints a picture of cautiousness in his autobiography, his covert operations were typically reactive and poorly thought out. In the realm of behavior control, as seen above, Helms reacted aggressively to the slightest provocation, lashing out with sudden verbal abuse. He played the role of conformist on the surface and actually became a very successful tennis player. But in his secret world of intelligence, he continually sought for ways for his division to kill without getting caught. The next symptomatic trait, the need for excitement, was realized daily as he moved his key staff swiftly toward the goal of achieving a workable MKULTRA program. Helms was living on the edge. At the same time, the tendency to exhibit a lack of responsibility was also apparent in this endeavor. Helms denied any responsibility for the foreign coups and assassinations of the 1950s and 1960s, let alone those in the United States. As for adult antisocial behavior, this characteristic too is epitomized in the mind control programs of the Helms era. Experimenting on people's minds without their knowledge and approval is the ultimate in antisocial behavior.

This last characteristic of the sociopath—antisocial behavior—is consistent with Helms's tendency to take advantage of the vulnerable and to exploit the weak without concern for right and wrong.[166] In the Agency under Helms, it was acceptable to be a hustler, finding subjects for the MK program, and to be a con man, manipulating subjects with drugs and hypnosis and then programming them to be unwitting fall guys. Indeed, some sociopaths' cons are very elaborate, according to Dr. Hare.[167] MKULTRA was just such a con. Rather than pity the vulnerable, persons who are sociopaths choose the vulnerable as their victims. Helms chose society's marginal people as his test subjects and as fall guys. As one sociopath in Dr. Hare's study stated while referring to such victims, "They're used to it. They don't whine to the police."[168]

Another common trait of sociopaths is their lack of allegiance.[169] As we have seen above, Helms was not loyal to any of his superiors and would operate independently without their advice or consent. He was out for himself and sought to achieve his own sense of satisfaction through power and domination. We also see this reflected in his home life. For example, Helms barely mentions his only child, Dennis, in his autobiography. This theme of indifference is typical among sociopaths. They also always blame others for their troubles. Large doses of finger pointing fill Helms's autobiography. This same characteristic is a subset of their need to deceive, which was noted earlier. Another common trait of sociopaths is their irresponsible use of their organizations' resources.[170] MKULTRA is a classic example of such a diversion of funds. When all of the research and operational costs are totaled and weighed against the ethics and the purpose of such a program, the irresponsibility is appalling.

An intelligent sociopath can be the most destructive, and Helms was at the top of his class. They are focused individuals who aim to achieve their goals. At the same time, they are opportunists who ignore the rules, forging ahead with no inner controls.[171] Again, they lack a conscience.

The motivations of sociopaths vary. However, common reasons for their crimes include retribution, satisfaction, and rage. All three motives certainly fit Helms's situation. In addition, according to forensic experts, sociopaths' murders are "businesslike" and without distress.[172] The assassinations and the killings of witnesses during the cover-up of the assassinations, when viewed as MKULTRA operations, indeed fit this mold. In looking back to when New York writer Dorothy Kilgallen was drugged and thereby eliminated and so many other witnesses turned up dead, the sociopath's mantra emerges: "nothing personal."

Helms used his education, social connections, and charm to gain the trust of others and to rise rapidly in the Agency. These characteristics, when combined with an obsession for power and the manipulation of others, are routinely manifested in the realm of sociopathy. In analyzing Helms, according to experts, another key determinant in sociopathic profiles that need to be taken into account is the fact that their "instincts are savage."[173]

Sociopaths seek positions of power over the lives of others. They are driven to obtain roles in which they will have this power. Helms created just such a role in MKULTRA and spent his entire career trying to perfect it through testing drugs on unwitting subjects, carrying out hypno-programming experiments, and plotting coups, assassinations, and cover-ups while manipulating others. But how does a sociopath maintain such a high position of power?

According to psychiatrists, "they keep up a consistent appearance of normality."[174] In Helms's case, he reached the top spot in the CIA and went on to be appointed ambassador to Iran. He did not end up in jail as most sociopaths do. This was because he was able to maintain the illusion of normality. Experts add, however, that the sociopath's "cloak of respectability is thin."[175] According to experts, "a cornered sociopath will adopt a posture of righteous indignation and anger in an attempt to scare off his accusers."[176] Again, we saw an example of this when Helms verbally attacked CBS's Daniel Schorr.

Unfortunately, according to forensic psychologists, in many cases, sociopaths' "tracks are hidden by normal people who have succumbed to their charm."[177] This is clearly the case with Helms, who was known to ingratiate himself with his seniors. White House officials, congressmen, and pundits protected Helms, having been unaware of his covert activities throughout his career.

Many people still believe that Helms was normal, despite the evidence to the contrary. From a psychological point of view, experts have found that sociopaths "use their titles as masks that others are loathe to look behind. . . . We believe in (them) because we assign to the individual the integrity of the role itself."[178] This was especially true during the Cold War era when leaders such as Helms claimed to be fighting the spread of Communism. Indeed, during the Helms era, many writers were surprisingly gullible. Nationally known newsmen, including scribes at *Time* magazine and the Washington-based Scripps Howard News Service, other major news outlets, wire services, newspapers, and broadcast networks were hoodwinked. Otherwise insightful and widely read conservative columnists echoed the official government line. Of course, many such writers also feared the humiliation of coming to grips with having been taken in.

Even as late as 1983, Richard Helms continued to be protected and even honored by high US government officials. He had received the Distinguished Intelligence Medal upon leaving the CIA in February 1973. In May 1983, he was awarded the William J. Donovan Medal. And in October 1983, President Ronald Reagan awarded Helms the highest award given for work in the field of intelligence, the National Security Medal.[179]

After being exposed as a liar following his sentencing, Helms told the media that he agreed with his attorney that he would wear his conviction like a "badge of honor."[180] This is typical of a sociopath's reaction. They have no sense of humiliation. They know the rules, but they do not feel they should be held accountable for their actions. They are legally sane, but they have a serious mental disorder. They have no conscience.

To summarize this chapter, the CIA's Richard Helms was the prime motivator and key intellect behind the Agency's mind control (MK) programs of the 1950s and 1960s. Helms's objective was to establish a method by which political assassination could be carried out by the CIA without the Agency being suspected. Through the MK experiments involving drugs and hypnosis, Helms developed a program in which an unwitting fall guy was produced who would be erroneously blamed for a murder while the actual hitmen were hidden on the sidelines.

Richard Helms facilitated, planned, and oversaw numerous assassinations, both foreign and domestic, during his CIA career. In addition, scores of important witnesses were silenced as part of Helms's cover-up of these assassinations. Helms and his key allies believed that by means of assassination they were ridding the world of leaders they considered inimical to their right wing, anti-Communist views.

Forensic psychology reveals evidence that Helms's personality was similar to the classic pattern of a sociopath. His role in fostering the CIA's MKULTRA programs, given the operations' purposes and results, offers us a window on these sociopathic characteristics. Some of these traits included his deceitfulness, manipulation, aggressiveness, dominance-seeking, lack of allegiance, lack of remorse, egocentricity, shallow emotions, detachment, indifference, and irresponsibility.

Some historians and authors, such as Gerald Posner (*Case Closed*), have erroneously concluded that Lee Harvey Oswald, the accused assassin of John F. Kennedy, was a sociopath. The alleged killer of Robert F. Kennedy, Sirhan B. Sirhan, has also been wrongly portrayed as one. But, in fact, these "loners" were mentally sound individuals, both unknowingly selected by the CIA's MKULTRA program, unwittingly conditioned to be pawns, and framed for murders for which they were not responsible.

How these young men, Oswald and Sirhan, became unwitting fall guys in two of the most extraordinary rogue Agency assassination operations in US history will be fully examined later in this book.

# 3

# *James Angleton, The Tactician*

P ROBABLY THE CLOSEST confidant and subordinate of Richard Helms's was the CIA's eccentric, longtime chief of counterintelligence, James Jesus Angleton, a Yale graduate who was four years younger than Helms.

Angleton was born on December 9, 1917 in Boise, Idaho, the son of James Hugh Angleton of Illinois and Carmen Mercedes Moreno of Nogales, Mexico. The parents had met when the elder Angleton was serving with the US military south of the border.[181] James Jesus was the oldest of four children, two boys and two girls.[182] Their father, Hugh, a vice president at National Cash Register, moved the family to Dayton, Ohio, in 1927. The family relocated to Milan, Italy, when James was fifteen, after his father took over the company operations in that city.[183] James attended high school at Malvern in England and entered Yale in New Haven, Connecticut, in 1937.[184] While his future boss, Richard Helms, had found his academic niche in journalism, Angleton's most avid interest in school was the world of poetry. He collaborated in founding a college poetry journal, *Furioso*, in which some of the leading poets of the day were published, including Ezra Pound and E. E. Cummings.[185]

Angleton graduated from Yale in 1941 and went on to Harvard Law.[186] He left school when World War II started and was drafted into the army in March 1943.[187] With help from a college professor and his father Hugh, who had become an Army intelligence officer, Angleton eventually was assigned to the Office of Strategic Services (OSS), the forerunner of the CIA. He was first stationed at the Italian desk in London. It was here that the young Corporal learned the craft of counterintelligence, which is essentially keeping secrets safe, tracking down enemy spies, and neutralizing double agents.[188] By the end of the war, James had been promoted to First Lieutenant and was named chief of the Rome office, a position for which he had been cleared to read messages decoded from ULTRA, the famous German code that the Allies had cracked early on in the war.[189]

Angleton's grades in school had not been outstanding,[190] yet he was considered by his teachers to be highly intelligent and mature.[191] His personality was seen as "quiet, (with) good manners." According to one Yale classmate, he was "a mysterious person . . . with mysterious contacts," (though it is uncertain what exactly this means).[192] Another source described the young Angleton as an insomniac who would play poker all night while at Yale. One roommate said "he never thought he was wrong."[193] It was during his college years that he reportedly became a fervent anti-Communist.[194] One other observed personality trait, one that would prove quite useful in his future endeavors, was the fact that he was seen as someone who had "infinite patience."[195]

Descriptions of Angleton's personality while in school were similar to those exhibited in the army. One colleague in basic training considered Angleton a "genius" and very "secretive."[196] A classmate in officer training described him as "extremely brilliant, but a little strange."[197] Later on, when stationed in Italy, some colleagues called him "the poet" because of his choice of reading material. They also called him "the cadaver" due to his thin, pale look. Some characterized him as "weird" and said he "lived in another world."[198] It was also said that he "dominated" and "intimidated" his subordinates.[199]

It was Angleton's unique ability to design unusual covert operations and to operate so secretly that established his place within the Agency and sustained his durable career. Israeli statesman, Teddy Kollek, once described Angleton this way: "Jim is by no means an ordinary person. He is an original thinker."[200] Angleton's boss during most of his CIA years, Richard Helms, termed Angleton "a strange, strange man."[201]

As we shall see ahead, Angleton held a paranoid view of the world. At the same time, he displayed classic symptoms of someone supremely confident in his capabilities and in his ability to survive, and also dangerous to anyone who threatened his uber-right wing worldview.

At age twenty-five in July 1943, after four months in the Army, Angleton married a college sweetheart, Vassar student Cicely Harriet d'Autremont, who came from a wealthy family with homes in Duluth, Minnesota,[202] and Tucson, Arizona.[203] Although she stayed married to James until his death, they separated three times "out of frustration," said Cicely.[204] She added her husband worked "very strange hours," and "you could never ask him any questions about his work." She said that when his work associates came to the house, the phones were unplugged and the curtains were drawn.[205]

The couple had three children, a son and two daughters. But, according to Cicely, "the kids saw little of their father."[206] Angleton was known among close colleagues for his drinking habits, which frequently consisted of double martini lunches and Bourbon after work.[207] Clearly, alcohol influenced Angleton's behavior and judgment. Cicely outlived her husband by twenty-four years; he died in May 1987, and she died at age eighty-nine on September 23, 2011 at home in Virginia.[208]

Angleton settled down with his young family in Arlington, Virginia, following World War II, an ideal location to live given his new job.[209] After having returned home from Europe on December 20, 1947, he had joined the newly created CIA.[210] His records describe him as tall and very thin, at six feet eleven inches and 150 lb.[211] He was gaunt, wore thick glasses,[212] and chain-smoked.[213] He also appeared "stooped," and his voice was extremely low.[214] One historian described him as "lean, unsmiling," and noted that Angleton had gained a "fearsome reputation" at the CIA in a few short years due to his work countering the spies of the new enemy, the Soviet empire.[215]

At this point in the postwar world, the Soviets were firming up their control of Eastern Europe and making inroads in intelligence in the West. Angleton's office led the operations to neutralize communist actions in Turkey, Greece, France, and Italy.[216] Angleton specialized in "psychological operations" which, in Italy in particular, meant fixing elections by paying off candidates in order to stop a left-wing takeover.[217] Angleton was fluent in Italian and French and could speak some German,[218] but his strongest suit was his skill at gaining information through stealth, i.e., bugging.[219] This endeared him to Allen Dulles (CIA Director from 1953 to 1961) and Richard Helms (CIA Director from 1966 to 1973)[220] and enabled his rapid climb to the top ranks of the CIA. He had developed friendships with both Dulles[221] and Helms[222] since his OSS days, and would report intelligence scoops to them directly—even information from Washington social parties[223]—ignoring the chain of command.[224]

In the eyes of the rest of the Agency, Angleton came to be seen as a remote and mysterious figure,[225] a "loner" who knew the details of all of the important clandestine operations ongoing.[226] He was labeled "a misguided genius" by one staffer,[227] and an "arrogant" individual who treated others with "disdain," according to one Defense Intelligence Agency officer.[228]

In 1949, Angleton was appointed head of the CIA Office of Special Operations,[229] and in 1951, in addition to his regular duties, he was given a key post, the Israeli Desk.[230] CIA Director Allen Dulles, who was appointed by President Dwight Eisenhower in 1953, named Angleton chief of counterintelligence in December 1954.[231] The importance of this position to the Agency should not be underestimated. As Angleton once stated, "If you control counterintelligence, you control the intelligence service."[232]

Both Dulles and Helms exerted little control over Angleton, allowing him to operate with an "unaudited funding source," which he used to build his secret empire.[233] All three men were strong believers in covert operations.[234] Helms was "gifted at guiding and controlling covert actions"[235] and Angleton was gifted at inventing them.

It was Angleton's ability to act without accountability and with the utmost secrecy that would be crucial to his carrying out the most significant operations of the 1960s, particularly his illegal domestic forays. During these years, according to many CIA staffers, Angleton "was seldom seen."[236] However, covert operations linked to his division provide some clues as to his whereabouts, as we shall see ahead.

Angleton's reported suspicions of a wide range of national leaders and policymakers give us a glimpse into his paranoid worldview. The personalities Angleton suspected of being Soviet spies or "moles" included British Prime Minister Harold Wilson,[237] Nixon's secretary of state Henry Kissinger,[238] and JFK aide and noted historian Arthur Schlesinger Jr. (Schlesinger had voiced his opposition to the CIA's Bay of Pigs operation plan that Kennedy had inherited from Eisenhower).[239] Angleton also reportedly believed President Kennedy himself was "a KGB mole"[240] because of JFK's secret diplomatic efforts to initiate peaceful coexistence with Russia, North Vietnam, and Cuba.

In the early 1960s, Angleton became even more paranoid when his wartime friend, a British spy named Kim Philby, turned out to be a KGB agent.[241] CIA psychologist Dr. John Gittinger has stated that this news from the Soviet Union of his close colleague's betrayal "shattered Angleton's life in terms of his ability to be objective about other people."[242]

A succession of CIA directors all knew Angleton as someone who consistently stuck to his "unbending Cold War views."[243] At one Washington party in the mid-1960s, Angleton and one of his subordinates reportedly shocked the Canadian counterintelligence chief Leslie James Bennett with their radical, right-wing ideology. During their conversation, they spoke of how they supported the infamous Sen. Joe McCarthy and his Communist witch hunt.[244]

Indeed, according to CIA psychologist Dr. Jerrold Post, from Angleton's point of view, there existed "a careful Soviet master plan to take over the world."[245] Dr. Post also has reported that Angleton tended toward a paranoid personality, adding that it may have helped him perform his job. However, he asserts that this condition, when combined with his drinking, adversely affected his powers of critical judgment.[246]

At the same time, Angleton was known for his great attention to detail. His covert operations reflected this attribute. This characteristic also emerged in his hobbies, which included making jewelry, fashioning lures for fly fishing, and growing orchids.[247] These pastimes neatly fit his need for a "cover" or a "legend." Such "everyman" activities helped conceal from relatives, friends, and neighbors the true nature of his business, which, of course, involved planning and participating in covert operations many times around the clock.

While Angleton was extremely secretive regarding his actual work activities, he did share with his wife at least one example of his surreptitious side. According to Cicely, one night in mid-1963, he climbed a wall and broke into the French Embassy in Washington. Once inside, he and others located the French intelligence service's code book and other documents and photographed them. The black-bag job was ostensibly carried out to uncover potential "moles" (KGB double agents) that may have penetrated this key US ally's ranks.[248] However, there is another equally important reason that Angleton was so desirous of decoding French intelligence communications. President Kennedy, using his own channels (avoiding the CIA), was secretly attempting to obtain President Charles de Gaulle's help in mediating a peace agreement with North Vietnam, a plan strongly opposed by right wingers at the CIA.

Angleton's "mole-hunting" became legendary within the Agency, but it now appears that the campaign to oust enemy double agents was itself a cover for other more nefarious activities, as we shall see. At the end of his career, in the mid-1970s, when Angleton was asked to publicly account for his activities, he clung to his story that he had been hunting KGB infiltrators. The Director of the CIA, William Colby, at that point investigated these claims. The result: "they found not one single shred of hard evidence" against mole-hunt suspects.[249]

Beside protecting Agency secrets from its enemies, as chief of counterintelligence, part of Angleton's mission was to penetrate the Soviet Union. Throughout the late 1950s and early 1960s, Angleton and Helms worked closely in running operations against the Soviets. Prior to spy satellites and at the beginning of the high-altitude, U-2 spy-plane missions, obtaining human intelligence on the ground was indispensable. One of the major intelligence projects of this era was Angleton's "fake defector program."[250]

When we examine the brief career of Lee Harvey Oswald (ahead), we can see that he was clearly a player in this counterintelligence program. Oswald "defected" at the end of 1959 to the Soviet Union. At that time, one of the main CIA contacts at the American Embassy in Moscow—for both Russian spies who were working for the United States and for fake American defectors—was a US Air Force officer named Dr. Alexi Davison.[251] It is known that the doctor was not only a top American spy, but at the same time a friendly contact of Lee Harvey Oswald during his stay in the Soviet Union.[252]

Defectors slipping into the United States from the Soviet Union were also handled by Angleton. One of the highest ranked was KGB officer Anatoliy Golitsyn, who defected in December 1961.[253] While much of his pronouncements proved to be unfounded, Angleton and Helms used Golitsyn's warnings of the Soviet threat to justify much of their actions in Africa, Southeast Asia, and South America.

Angleton was "imbued with a war psychology . . . [l]egality was not questioned . . . it was not an issue," the FBI's William Sullivan once said of CIA counterintelligence chief James J. Angleton.[254] One early example of Angleton's disregard for the law of the land was evidenced by his infamous mail-opening program known as operation HT/Lingual, designed by Angleton and approved by Helms in 1955.[255] The operation, which was carried out without the knowledge of the US Post Office, involved opening all mail incoming and outgoing between the Soviet Union and New York. Eventually, some four-teen thousand letters per year were being steamed open, the contents photographed, and the envelopes resealed. The film was developed by the CIA and the information obtained was analyzed at headquarters. Angleton reportedly commented that the effort was "worth the risk" and that if needed, he could always blame a fall guy,[256] a consistent theme of his. By 1971, leaks and complaints from constitutional rights groups began to reach Post Office Inspector Bill Cotter.[257] Finally, in 1973, CIA Director James Schlesinger (February–July 1973) and deputy William Colby ended the HT/Lingual mail openings,[258]over Angleton's objections.[259] By then, the list of illegalities in Angleton's repertoire also included home and office break-ins, phone eavesdropping, and the use of informants,[260] many of whom were embedded in various political groups, universities, and the media—all within US borders.

All of these covert techniques were needed for Angleton to accomplish his most sophisticated top secret program of all, MKULTRA, the use of hypnosis and drugs to create a fall guy. By 1960, units under Angleton had begun to accelerate "operational experiments" involving hypnosis. One agency memo emphasizing the importance of this research indicated that this program "could provide a potential breakthrough in clandestine technology."[261]

The breakthrough came with the achievement of the capability of ordering a subject—under the influence of drugs and posthypnotic suggestions—to perform an action and not recall it later. For example, a subject could be controlled to the point where he would pull out a weapon and fire without remembering later what had happened. However, since the subject's aim and reliability was far too unpredictable, this technique could not be used by itself. It would also include the use of clear-headed, well-hidden, backup sharpshooters who would carry out the actual shooting. The hypnotized, clueless "patsy" would end up being the fall guy who would be apprehended and charged with the crime, thus allowing the true assassins to escape.

Angleton's MK operational experiments consisted of three parts: "induce hypnosis rapidly on unwitting subjects; create durable amnesia; and implant hypnotic suggestions that were 'operationally useful.'"[262]

All of this research involved numerous unwitting subjects—many from the military, college campuses, and prisons to drinking establishments and places where those on the "fringes" of society would meet. To carry out these experiments and covert operations in secret, Angleton pursued his agenda by employing the panoply of illegal resources listed above in addition to unwitting drugging. As noted earlier, from the mid-1950s through the mid-1970s, hundreds of soldiers were tested with drugs at Edgewood Arsenal Laboratories in Maryland. (Many of these veterans nationwide have at this writing filed law suits against the federal government seeking medical compensation for having been used as guinea pigs.)[263]

Back at Langley, Angleton kept his office staff busy by having his employees spend their time studying old Soviet spy cases, according to CIA general counsel Lawrence Houston.[264] Angleton's chief of operations, Newton Scotty Miler, who was responsible for running the shop while the boss was away, "kept the wheels turning."[265] Given Helms and Angleton's finely tuned system of "compartmentalization" of information, the home office staff was no doubt totally unaware of some of the most significant and substantive covert operations (i.e., information known by the field operatives stayed with their handlers, and very little was put in writing.).

While Angleton and Helms were developing their MK plan, they were also in the process of implementing various other assassination techniques. A variety of methods would be used in their attempt to kill Cuban premier Fidel Castro in order to take over Cuba. (The CIA's involvement in assassination plots did not come to light until President Gerald Ford mentioned it in a *New York Times* interview in the mid-1970s.[266])

In 1961, when JFK arrived at the White House, the Cuban invasion plan was already set to go. President Kennedy approved it, based on unreliable CIA assurances, and allowed the Agency to sponsor (without direct US support) a force of anti-Castro Cubans in an amphibious landing attack scheduled for Cuba's southern shore at the Bay of Pigs in April 1961. The operation was a total disaster. Kennedy took full responsibility and eventually fired CIA Director Allen Dulles and others for the tragic miscalculations of the doomed Cuban takeover bid. Kennedy replaced Dulles with John McCone, a Republican defense contractor.[267] Meanwhile, Richard Helms and James Angleton managed to remove themselves from the aftermath of the debacle. The furtive pair stayed on the job and avoided repercussions while quietly strengthening their clandestine operational capabilities.

Helms and Angleton had at this time also secretly initiated a plan in which they had enlisted the support of the Mafia without presidential knowledge. The plan involved one of Helms's top lieutenants, William Harvey, who was given the responsibility of hiring mobster Johnny Rosselli to have Castro poisoned.[268] When Attorney General Robert Kennedy discovered the Agency's mob ties, he ordered the relationship to cease. His order was ignored.[269] Evidence of mob links later surfaced in both the JFK and RFK assassination cases, as we shall see ahead.

In 1962, after Soviet missiles were found on the island of Cuba, President Kennedy famously negotiated withdrawal of the weapons by the Russians. But in the midst of JFK's efforts to obtain a peaceful resolution, the CIA's William Harvey launched an undercover operation involving sending in teams to support a military strike inside Cuba. When Robert Kennedy learned of this, he had Harvey removed from covert ops. Helms reassigned Harvey to a new post as station chief in Rome.[270]

By 1963, both William Harvey and Johnny Rosselli loathed Bobby Kennedy.[271] CIA counterintelligence chief James Angleton's worldview also was diametrically opposed to John and Robert Kennedy's leadership. Angleton did not believe that diplomacy with the Soviet Union would win the Cold War.[272] Rather, he was convinced that his Agency covert operations alone could save democracy across the globe.[273]

While many voters believed President Kennedy, too, was a "Cold Warrior," over time he had grown into the office of the presidency and had matured in his perspective on international relations. His evolved Cold War strategy included quietly expanding negotiations with the Russians, the Cubans, and the North Vietnamese. In Kennedy's American University speech of June 1963, we can see how his view of reality stands in stark contrast to James Angleton's paranoia.

"So, let us not be blind to our differences—but let us also direct attention to our common interests and to the means by which those differences can be resolved. And if we cannot end now our differences, at least we can help make the world safe for diversity. For, in the final analysis, our most basic common link is that we all inhabit this small planet. We all breathe the same air. We all cherish our children's future. And we are all mortal."[274]

On the day of President Kennedy's assassination, Angleton's whereabouts have been officially reported as his having been at a meeting with French officials regarding a suspected KGB mole in the French intelligence service.[275] Again, much of Angleton's double agent "mole hunt" pronouncements have rung hollow for many observers over the years. This is primarily because, as CIA Director William Colby once stated, the CIA never caught a spy on Angleton's watch.[276] It is much more likely that the mole hunt stories were a cover for his actual primary activities.

In hindsight, rather than hunting moles, as one of the planners of MKULTRA, he was guiding the search for unwitting fall guys, overseeing their conditioning, and devising their missions. In conjunction with such operations, it was also necessary to direct the hunt for anyone who may have had knowledge of his programs, and particularly any information relating to President Kennedy's assassination—knowledge that differed from, or contradicted, the official version. A similar, massive cover-up was carried out several years later in the wake of Sen. Robert Kennedy's assassination. To conceal the true facts concerning these plots, it was necessary to keep a tight lid on numerous individuals including eyewitnesses, investigative reporters, law enforcement officials, courageous politicians, and a host of others, all seeking the truth. The number of those who were "neutralized" for their knowledge over the years is statistically shocking. Author Peter Janney, in his book *Mary's Mosaic* on the death of JFK's friend Mary Pinchot Meyer, cites writer Jim Marrs's 1989 analysis of some one hundred individuals who knew some aspect of President Kennedy's murder conspiracy and who died within twenty years of the assassination. "More than thirty people on this list had been killed in violent gun-related circumstances."[277] Why?

One month after the JFK assassination, counterintelligence chief James Angleton sought and was given by Richard Helms the job of liaison to the

Warren Commission investigating the president's death. Angleton continued to manage JFK assassination matters for the CIA until the end of his career.[278] It is now known that much of the information he gave to the Warren Commission, and to Congressional hearings later on, was false. He protected the Agency at every turn.

When Angleton was asked by one Congressional committee investigator to describe the nature of counterintelligence, he responded: "to construct a 'Wilderness of Mirrors' in which the opponent would be forever lost and confused."[279] If there were an assassination cover-up manual, what approach could be more fitting than this?

A prime example of Angleton's strategy following the president's murder in Dallas is revealed in the case of Yuri Nosenko. The Warren Commission had just begun its investigation when a Russian KGB agent named Yuri Nosenko, thirty-seven, defected to the United States in February 1964 and claimed that he had firsthand knowledge of Lee Harvey Oswald's stay in the USSR. Nosenko, the son of a high-level Soviet bureaucrat, had been serving in the USSR's SCD (KGB internal security), similar to the FBI.[280] In fact, he had been a deputy in the division that monitored foreigners in the country.[281] In that position, Nosenko reported that he had reviewed information concerning Oswald upon Oswald's arrival in Moscow in October 1959 and also examined follow-up files after the JFK assassination. Nosenko stated that he was certain that the KGB had no involvement with Oswald nor any connection with the murder of President Kennedy.[282] While Helms and Angleton had accepted Nosenko's request to defect, after he arrived in Washington they claimed they did not believe his Oswald story.[283] Clearly, Angleton wanted Oswald to be seen as a possible Soviet agent and Nosenko to be viewed as having been sent by the KGB to deny Soviet involvement in the assassination. Consequently, Helms and Angleton in March 1964 had Nosenko locked up illegally[284] and had the Warren Commission keep Nosenko's testimony secret. The Warren Report was issued on September 28, 1964;[285] it contained no reference to the Soviet defector's assertions.

Nosenko was imprisoned for nearly five years and for much of that time he endured the mental torture of solitary confinement—no human contact, little food, little sleep, no medical care, no books, and no TV.[286] He was kept for more than two years in a windowless cell at Camp Peary, Virginia, and for the rest of the time in safe houses in the Washington, DC, area.[287] All the while, the Agency tried to break him through interrogations, to get him to "cooperate," [288] i.e., to get him to sign statements declaring that he was a "mole." He refused. Angleton and Helms could build no evidence against him.[289] By June of 1966, Helms had become CIA director.

Finally, in March 1969, nine months after Robert Kennedy's assassination, Helms allowed Nosenko to be released. His decision followed a Security Office report by the CIA's Bruce Solie in 1968 stating that Nosenko was a "bona fide" defector, and that some of his leads were excellent.[290] Another CIA report by John Hart in December 1976 also showed that Nosenko was indeed who he said he was.[291] Other legitimate Soviet defectors confirmed that Nosenko was not a fake defector,[292] and in September 1978, then CIA Director Stansfield Turner said that Nosenko's statements, and in particular his statement regarding Oswald, had been made in good faith.[293]

Angleton obviously knew Nosenko was not a KGB double agent, yet he termed the clearing of Nosenko "a whitewash"[294] and during the CIA hearings in the late 1970s, he even denied that he was responsible for imprisoning and nearly killing Nosenko. Yet, as Director Turner pointed out, Angleton was at Camp Peary and only Angleton could have approved these actions.[295]

Most likely, Angleton wanted to hold Nosenko as a fake in the event the JFK plot unraveled because he could then say Oswald was a KGB pawn and that Nosenko was sent to cover up Oswald's mission. As one British intelligence expert has been quoted as saying, "Angleton was more than capable of manufacturing evidence where none existed."[296]

The response of CIA Director William Colby in 1973 to the story of Angleton and Helms's jailing of Yuri Nosenko was clear: "that kind of intelligence service is a threat to its own people."[297] Upon his release, Nosenko received at least some redress. He was hired as an independent CIA consultant,[298] and in the fall of 1975 (after Angleton had been replaced by George Kalaris at counterintelligence), was brought back to Agency headquarters to speak about his life. He received a standing ovation.[299]

In the same year that Nosenko had defected to the United States, another intriguing case involving James Angleton occurred—one that was even more sinister. On October 12, 1964, Mary Pinchot Meyer, forty-three, ex-wife of Cord Meyer, a CIA colleague of James Angleton, was found murdered near her home in the Georgetown neighborhood of Washington. The case was never solved.[300] Mary was a beautiful woman, the daughter of a wealthy attorney, a Vassar graduate, journalist, and later in her life, an artist. Her sister, Tony, was married at the time to Ben Bradlee of the *Washington Post.* And, although only a very few knew at the time, Mary had had an ongoing affair with President Kennedy.[301]

The day after her murder, Bradlee and his wife went to her home to search for her diary, which they had learned about from another of Mary's close friends. To their surprise, they found family friend James Angleton inside. He, too, was searching for the diary. (Angleton's wife Cicely was also a friend of Mary's.) After the diary was eventually discovered in Mary's backyard ~~dio. To~~ gave it to Angleton to have it destroyed. The diary reportedly did relationship with the president, but he was not named in it. ~e, he and his wife later found out that Angleton had not _ uiary, and Tony asked for it back. She then burned it herself.[302]

At least two sources have stated that Angleton had to have been aware of Mary's affair with the president. Joe Shimon, a Justice Department and CIA operative,[303] and artist Kenneth Noland, another former lover of Mary's,[304] have stated that Angleton had had Mary's phone bugged. This was typical of Angleton's style—he would have wanted to know what the president was telling this woman, particularly since both she and Kennedy had serious reservations regarding the activities of the CIA.

Some historians feel that the release of the Warren Commission Report in September 1964 may well have been seen by Mary Pinchot Meyer as a massive cover-up of the assassination, and that this may have been a catalyst for her possibly planning to go public with her views of the president's murder. Mary had called another friend following the president's death, LSD guru Timothy Leary, to share her suspicions, her grief, and her fear. She told him, "They couldn't control him anymore. He was changing too fast. They've covered everything up. I gotta come see you. I'm afraid. Be careful."[305]

In the spring of 1965, six months after Mary's murder, Joe Shimon, who was also a CIA-mob liaison, reportedly confided to his daughter, Toni, what he knew about her death. After her many questions, Toni, then a college student and very close to her father, finally heard him say, "She (Mary Meyer) was eliminated because she knew too much."[306]

An intensive cover-up of assassination conspiracy information—related to both Kennedy brothers' deaths—took place during the years 1964 through 1970. Not so coincidentally, this is the same time period in which Angleton carried out his famous mole hunt,[307] an intensive search for KGB double agents who might have penetrated the CIA ranks. The mole hunt actions were directed domestically, toward Agency staff and others, in order to determine if any operatives were working for the enemy. For Richard Helms and James Angleton, did the enemy also include anyone working to uncover the truth in the Kennedy assassination cases? Angleton's boss, Richard Helms, fully supported the mole hunt, allowing Angleton to run his operations and investigations without close supervision. Interestingly, over its six-year existence, the mole hunt turned up not one penetration of the CIA.[308] However, numerous individuals who knew too much about the assassinations turned up dead.[309]

In the midst of this "purge," during these same years, grassroots opposition to the government began to emerge on college campuses and in urban churches as thousands took to the streets to condemn the war in Vietnam and also to voice their support for civil rights. Protests, ranging from nonviolent demonstrations to riots, exploded across the land.

In the face of this challenge, Richard Helms, who had been sworn in as Director of Central Intelligence on June 20, 1966, handed James Angleton a special, and illegal, assignment: to infiltrate the liberal Catholic publication *Ramparts,* a national magazine emanating from Berkeley that had been running anti-Vietnam War articles.[310] Angleton called the *Ramparts* articles "a Soviet plot," yet his covert investigation of the magazine's staff, editors, and writers ended with no foreign financial links being found.[311]

The *Ramparts* operation was but one small example of a nationwide program managed by James Angleton, a plan dubbed Operation CHAOS. Officially launched in 1967, the operation was ostensibly intended to determine if foreign governments were behind the antiwar protests and the civil rights movement. Under Operation CHAOS, Angleton monitored peace activists, radicals, and black leaders, infiltrating and penetrating their organizations.[312] The unit Helms and Angleton set up to carry out this domestic spying operation was called the Special Operations Group (SOG). In addition to investigating activists, their work also included "monitoring and harassing" numerous newspapers.[313]

In all, some six hundred names of Americans were on CIA watchlists.[314] The lists also included members of Congress. The SOG obtained information on these individuals through a variety of means: the use of informants, phone bugging—wiretaps and illegal entries—and home and office break-ins.[315] The methods used against protestors were also the essential tools needed for Angleton's MKULTRA operation, i.e., finding subjects, drugging them, conditioning them, and framing them.

Following Richard Helms's resignation (Helms was appointed ambassador to Iran by President Nixon) and the appointment of James Schlesinger as the new director of the CIA in early 1973, Schlesinger ordered Angleton to end Operation CHAOS.[316]

It is unknown whether the Watergate break-in in June 1972, carried out by a team mostly made up of CIA operatives, was in fact an Operation CHAOS mission. The goal of the failed burglary was to plant listening devices in the Democratic National Headquarters offices. But it is unclear who ordered the break-in or why. If indeed the order came from James Angleton, the purpose of the bugging may well have been to find out if the Democrats had obtained any information concerning who killed the Kennedys and if the leads were pointing in Angleton's direction.

The media's discovery of the CIA's Operation CHAOS and its spying on anti-war protestors began with a leak at the Justice Department. *The New York Times'* Seymour Hersh interviewed DCI Schlesinger's successor William Colby, who confirmed the leaks were indeed factual.[317] (Schlesinger had been appointed secretary of defense by President Nixon and William Colby had moved up to director of Central Intelligence on July 1, 1973.) On December 22, 1974, the *Times* published its story on Operation CHAOS along with the breaking news on HT/Lingual, the CIA mail-opening operation.[318] James Angleton, the chief architect and overseer of both operations, was interviewed two days later by CBS news correspondent Daniel Schorr. Angleton denied everything.[319] That day, December 24, 1974, DCI Colby fired James Angleton.[320]

In addition to Angleton's role in the CIA's years of illegal operations, Colby criticized Angleton's division for being "secretive and self-contained" and stated that he found "a total lack of cooperation."[321] Colby questioned Angleton's career, saying, "No one knew what he had done. I didn't."[322] It is known that the majority of Angleton and Helms's MKULTRA records were destroyed by Helms days before Helms departed the CIA.

Angleton stayed on at the agency for nine months following his forced resignation to "clear out his files." Hence, his actual retirement date was in September 1975.[323] During that year, then President Gerald Ford asked Vice President Nelson Rockefeller to investigate the stories by Seymour Hersh, and as a result, the select committee headed by Idaho senator Frank Church was established, as well as a House select committee.[324] During the hearings, Angleton reportedly met with the CIA liaison to Congress, Walter Elder. Forever believing the best defense is a strong offense, Angleton delivered his standard ploy: he cautioned Elder of a Soviet plot and advised him that the Church committee was "serving as the unwitting instrument of the KGB."[325] Thus, he maintained his "cover" until the end.

As if to publicly deny the relevations and accusations against the Agency, in 1975, the CIA awarded Angleton its highest medal for distinguished service.[326]

For the next twelve years, Angleton operated in retirement nearly as secretively as he had while working.

On May 11, 1987, Angleton died of lung cancer in Washington, DC, at the age of sixty-nine. He is buried in Boise, Idaho.[327]

This glimpse into the life and times of Richard Helms's right-hand man, longtime CIA chief of counterintelligence James Angleton, serves as a backdrop to our understanding of the lives of Lee Harvey Oswald and Sirhan B. Sirhan, detailed ahead.

Angleton was the genius behind the MKULTRA, unwitting, fall-guy plan, devising with Richard Helms the operational strategy and implementing it through sympathetic Agency and mob allies. Angleton also used his powerful arm of the Agency to carry out sustained and far-reaching covert actions designed to cover up the conspiracy through disinformation campaigns, domestic spying, break-ins, intimidation, and ultimately, the untimely deaths of numerous witnesses. Indeed, James Angleton was Richard Helms's secret weapon dedicated to the mission of making the 1960s assassination plots work.

# 4

# *Assassinations Past*

---

T O FULLY GRASP the MKULTRA assassination plans of Helms and Angleton, one must first examine the strategy and tactics of the Agency-backed foreign assassinations of the 1950s and early 1960s.

CIA operations involving assassination began in earnest in Iran in August of 1953 with the ouster of Socialist leader Mohammad Mossadegh. While Richard Helms was not yet operating at the highest levels of the Agency, by 1953, he was in charge of all covert operations, which was a critical role both tactically and strategically. For the next two decades, from 1953 to 1973, Helms not only knew what was going on in terms of foreign coups d'etat, he was intimately involved in the planning, execution, and cover-ups of many of them. James Angleton, as counterintelligence chief, was equally engaged. Although not all of the coups of this era involved assassination, many of them did, and in some cases, the deposed leader escaped or was executed later on.

## Iran

Iran's location on the Persian Gulf between Iraq and Afghanistan makes it a strategically valuable piece of real estate. In the Iranian coup of 1953, Helms was working on covert action operations under the Deputy Director of Plans, Frank Wisner. To implement their coup, seasoned professional and the head of the Agency's Middle East Department Kermit Roosevelt was brought in. He had earlier assisted the Shah, Mohammad Reza Pahlavi, thirty-four, in fleeing with his wife to Rome when rioting had broken out in the streets of Teheran.

Premier Mohammad Mossadegh, with popular support, took over the reins of power in Iran following the Shah's departure. Mossadegh wasted no time in expropriating the oil wells formerly owned by the Anglo-Persian Oil Company. He also immediately began to lay plans for using oil profits to modernize his country while leaning toward the Soviet Union to gain support for his efforts.

The CIA covert action operatives moved quickly. Key Iranian military officers were bribed to kidnap Mossadegh supporters and eliminate them. Large protests against the government were organized, and soon Mossedegh found himself in jail. The Shah returned to Teheran and was met by crowds of well-wishers supplemented by Agency-paid greeters. Meanwhile, back in Washington, CIA Director Allen Dulles (1953–1961) was applauded within the Agency for the efficacy of the operation. Ousted premier Mossadegh was released from jail three years later.[328]

It was during this time that the CIA also significantly increased its covert action staffing levels. By this point, several thousand Agency personnel were training in paramilitary activities at Camp Peary, known as "The Farm," located near Williamsburg, Virginia. Army officers were recruited and trained in guerilla warfare, and thousands of mercenaries were hired around the globe to fight for the CIA.[329]

## Guatemala

In 1954, the CIA turned its sights on Guatemala and the democratically elected government of Jacobo Arbenz. This small Central American country, situated below the Yucatan peninsula on the Pacific between Mexico and Honduras, is known for its abundance of bananas. Its president, Jacobo Arbenz, came to power in 1950 after serving as defense minister under President Juan Arevalo. Like his predecessor, Arbenz sought land reform and gained much popular support, including the allegiance of Guatemala's socialists. By 1954, Arbenz had legalized the country's small Communist Party and had taken over four hundred thousand acres of banana plantations owned by the United Fruit Company of the United States.[330] In Washington, the administration dropped any plans for a diplomatic solution and initiated plans for a CIA-backed coup. According to Richard Helms, at that point, "an ambitious covert action operation" was necessary to overthrow the government of Jacobo Arbenz.[331]

Helms has downplayed his role in this coup, yet at this time he was meeting with CIA Director Allen Dulles three times a week. The key planner in the Guatemalan plot was the CIA's Tracy Barnes, an attorney, working with Frank Wisner and Richard Bissell. Two other operatives, who were close associates of Helms's, were also involved: E. Howard Hunt and David A. Phillips.[332] At the time, Phillips was a propaganda expert working in Honduras. He would later play a major role with Richard Helms in coup attempts in Cuba and Chile.

The coup was based more on psychological warfare than military prowess. At the start, the CIA created a ruse, a disinformation campaign stating that Soviet arms were being delivered by ship to Arbenz.[333] US Navy ships were loaned to the agency for the operation in order to play the role of surface interception. Meanwhile, a Guatemalan officer in exile, Col. Carlos Castillo Armas, who had been trained in the United States, readied his CIA-backed army in Honduras for an attack on Guatemala.

Clandestine stations broadcasting fake battles hit the airwaves on May 1, 1954. The radio reports spread propaganda that Arbenz's forces were coming under fire from rebel forces. In Washington, Secretary of State John Foster Dulles condemned the Guatemalan government while the continual broadcasts and leaflet drops created panic in Guatemala City. Finally on June 18, 1954, Colonel Armas and his small army crossed from Honduras into Guatemala as several CIA-piloted rebel planes ran bombing runs. After a week and a half, President Arbenz's own confused army refused to support him. Arbenz resigned on June 27, 1954.[334]

Six years later, in 1960, a thirty-six-year civil war would break out in Guatemala. Some two hundred thousand lives were lost by the time it ended in 1996. Many were executed by the government death squads or were killed by the antigovernment guerrillas.[335]

## Indonesia

By 1958, less than four years after the CIA's removal of Mossadegh in Iran and Arbenz in Guatemala, the CIA turned in earnest towards Southeast Asia. Their target this time was the heavily populated multi-island nation of Indonesia led by a strong nationalist and maverick, President Sukarno. Indonesia lies below Malaysia, southwest of the Philippines, and encompasses the islands of Sumatra, Java, Borneo, and the Celebes. Sukarno was taking advantage of the Cold War to play off the Soviet-US rivalry and win huge amounts of aid from both sides. He was known for enriching himself and for his ambitious public works projects. However, at one point, a particular project on an island of his located north of Sumatra fell under US intelligence scrutiny. Sukarno was reportedly building an airfield that the CIA feared could someday become a refueling stop for Soviet military aircraft.

Once again, the CIA chose a dissident Indonesian army officer to be the point person for a coup. With Agency funding, the insurgents were trained and equipped on Sumatra. In February 1958, this rebel army declared the island of Sumatra independent. Sukarno wasted no time in attacking from the land, sea, and air. The insurgents could not stop the government forces and had little choice but to flee to the Celebes where they were rescued by US Navy ships.[336] During the fighting, Allen L. Pope, an American pilot who was flying for a CIA-owned company, was shot down on May 18, 1958. He ended up serving four years in jail.[337]

The failed coup was an embarrassing moment for the CIA. Richard Helms would later write off the debacle as simply a matter of too few CIA personnel being involved and rebels being poorly trained to fight.[338] At the time, however, the State Department issued denials to all reports that the CIA was involved in the insurrection. *The New York Times*, accepting these falsehoods, backed up the CIA and the Eisenhower White House, writing, "The United States is not ready . . . to step in to help overthrow a constituted government."[339] Meanwhile, Helms, who was the second in charge of Clandestine Services in 1958, knew that the administration's spokespersons were delivering disinformation. No doubt this gave him a certain comfort level.

## Congo

Two years later, in 1960, world attention turned to a central African colony known as the Belgian Congo, a land rich in copper and uranium, which is a building block for nuclear power. On June 30, 1960, in the capital city of Leopoldville (today Kinshasa), Belgium declared the Congo's fourteen million citizens independent. Some forty political factions vied for power with the elections going to the largest party, the Congolese National Movement led by thirty-five-year-old Patrice Lumumba, who became Prime Minister. The second largest vote-getter, Joseph Kasavubu, was named president. Lumumba had been a forceful and effective speaker during the Congo's struggle for freedom from Belgian rule. A graduate of missionary schools, he had risen from the ranks of a mail clerk to become a national hero. The Eisenhower administration, however, was wary of his designs on the Congo's mineral resources, which were controlled by Western investors.

Within weeks, civil unrest broke out across the country, fomented by groups seeking power. Antiwhite attacks prompted Belgium to send in troops to protect the minority white population. At the same time, the army revolted against the remaining Belgian officers who had stayed on to assist in the transition. Lumumba called for the United Nations to restore order. He also asked Premier Nikita Khrushchev for military advisors.[340] By August 1960, Soviet trucks and equipment began to arrive by plane.

The United States and other Western countries were heavily invested in the mines of Congo's southern Katanga Province. Because of the new Soviet presence, Lumumba was seen as a serious threat to their interests. This prompted the Katanga Province head, provincial leader Moise Tshombe, to call on the CIA and Belgium for assistance in a break-away bid.[341]

At Langley, CIA Director Allen Dulles stated that he had received President Eisenhower's approval and wrote to the CIA office in the Congo that Lumumba's removal (from office) should be a "high priority of our covert action."[342] Helms signed off on the order, and his staff quickly initiated plans to finance a Congolese army officer, Col. Joseph Mobutu, if he would lead a coup to overthrow Lumumba. Tshombe and other provincial leaders also were paid handsomely by the CIA for their cooperation. Meanwhile, Congolese President Kasavubu split the new government, dismissed Prime Minister Lumumba, and threw his support to Colonel Mobutu.

Mobutu launched the coup on September 5, 1960 with his army taking over the administration of the country, ordering the Soviet military to leave, and shutting down the Parliament. With CIA assistance, Mobutu placed Lumumba under house arrest and jailed his leading supporters.

At the same time, back in Washington, Richard Helms began to formulate an assassination plan. His technical advisor and lead MKULTRA scientist, Dr. Sidney Gottlieb, prepared a kit for the neutralization of Patrice Lumumba and delivered it to Leopoldville. Gottlieb's choice was a lethal germ agent made from equine encephalitis sleeping sickness. It was inserted into toothpaste and was supposed to be administered by having the Prime Minister brush his teeth with the toxic mixture.[343] This plan failed.

On November 2, 1960, Richard Helms's executive action unit, headed by William Harvey, sent instructions to a CIA agent in Leopoldville to implement the removal of Lumumba. This back-up plan involved using CIA contract agents to abduct the deposed Prime Minister and then assassinate him.[344]

Lumumba was able to escape briefly from his captors in December 1960, fleeing to his stronghold in Stanleyville (Kisangani) in the north. He was captured and on January 17, 1961, flown to Elisabethville and taken to a safe house. There, he and two aides were shot in the head by CIA-paid Belgian mercenaries.[345]

The explanation given by the Mobutu government for Lumumba's death was that he had been killed by opposition forces while trying to escape custody.

Following the assassination, a CIA officer in the Congo reported driving around Lulumbashi, Congo, with Lumumba's body in the trunk of his car, not knowing exactly where to bring it. This is according to John Stockwell, who was the chief of the CIA station in Angola in 1975.[346]

News of the murder was not made public until February 13, 1961. President Kennedy, who had been in office less than one month, was notified by UN Ambassador Adlai Stevenson. The president had had no knowledge of the CIA's plans and was reportedly shocked and discouraged by the news. He had studied the Congo situation while in the Senate and had often spoken about it during his campaign. He was fully aware of Lumumba's standing in the community of developing nations. In fact, many Washington observers thought Kennedy would have tried to have had Lumumba released from home arrest had he already been installed in office at the time the coup occured.[347]

## Cuba

The plan to stage a coup in Cuba and to assassinate Cuban Premier Fidel Castro was initiated in 1960 during the Eisenhower administration. The island of Cuba, located only ninety miles from Key West, Florida, had been a popular resort and gambling mecca from the 1930s and into the 1950s. Mafia-owned casinos and US businesses thrived under the dictatorship of Fulgencio Batista. A popular revolution led by Castro, then thirty-two years old, his brother Raul, and the charismatic Ernesto "Che" Guevara, overthrew Batista on January 1, 1959.

Initially, the peasant revolution was seen as benign by the United States. Castro placed great emphasis on public education, universal health care, and land reform. At the same time, he soon began to close down the mob casinos in Havana and imprisoned mobsters, along with opposition leaders and students. He expropriated US businesses and confiscated the homes of the wealthy. Middle-and upper-class Cubans fled in droves to Florida where they started new lives. The Eisenhower White House, which had been cautiously watching the Cuban revolution unfold, decided to take action to remove Castro when he announced he would accept Soviet support for his regime. In May of 1960, the CIA began plotting to assassinate Castro. The plan called for this action to be quickly followed by a coup that would install the anti-Castro exiles in positions of power.

Richard Helms later denied being a part of the planned coup—code-named Zapata—yet senior CIA officials have reported that he did indeed play a key role in running the operation. These officials are amazed that Helms was able to keep his signature off documents related to the venture.[348] Allen Dulles, CIA director; Gen. Charles P. Cabell, USAF, deputy director; and Richard Bissell, clandestine services chief, all depended on the expertise of Helms and his associates, James Angleton, William Harvey, David Phillips, and E. Howard

Hunt, to execute the plethora of details. At first, the plan involved training a small group of Cubans in guerilla warfare at a CIA base in Panama. These new guerilla fighters would in turn work with CIA instructors to teach a larger group of Cuban exiles in Guatemala. It soon became clear, however, based on intelligence reports, that infiltration of Cuba would be nearly impossible. Dissidents who would collaborate with the infiltrators were nowhere to be found; they were either in Castro's jails or had fled the country. Hence, the plan was changed from infiltration to a CIA-backed exile invasion.[349] The landing site chosen for the attack was at the Bay of Pigs (*Bahia de Cochinos*), a remote area on the south coast of Cuba, some ninety miles southeast of Havana. It was felt that this location would offer better protection for the invaders.

The CIA program called for killing Castro immediately prior to the attack. The planned method of execution was to be poison pills. It is important to note that President Kennedy was never informed of this plot to kill Castro, nor of the CIA's ZR/RIFLE or Executive Action (assassination) program. However, Kennedy did know of and approved the plan for the invasion of the exile army.[350] As noted earlier, Kennedy also accepted full responsibility for the disastrous results.

Again, the planning of Castro's assassination began during the Eisenhower administration. Interestingly, two of Helms's colleagues (who would both become known as Watergate burglars eleven years later) played key roles in the CIA's planning of the Cuban coup attempt: E. Howard Hunt led the formation of the "Cuban Revolutionary Council," the exile coalition, and Bernard L. Barker helped arm the invasion force with CIA-funded weapons. In the fall of 1960, just prior to the Nixon-Kennedy election, Richard Helms's closest associates, James Angleton and William Harvey, recruited the Mafia to hit Castro.[351] Both Angleton and Harvey would never think of taking such actions without Helms's approval. The CIA liaison with the mob was former FBI agent Robert A. Meheu, who had previous experience in carrying out various assignments for the Agency. Meheu met with Johnny Rosselli of the Chicago mob at a Beverly Hills restaurant in September 1960 and offered his organization $150,000 to eliminate Castro. The offer was accepted by the families with the obvious expectation that by helping the CIA, pressure on the mob from the Feds would be substantially removed.[352] Moreover, the plot would be expected to result in a regime change in Cuba and the return of the Havana casinos to Mafia ownership.

The CIA's Technical Services Staff and its toxins expert Dr. Sidney Gottlieb produced poison pills (botulinum toxin) and had them delivered to Rosselli in Miami in March of 1961. They were to be flown in to Cuba and handed off to a mistress of Castro's or a dissident who was close to him and then slipped into his drink.[353]

This was not the first time US intelligence had enlisted Mafia support. During the 1940s and 1950s, they cooperated when fighting Communists in Sicily and in other parts of the globe. The CIA's choice of Rosselli to handle the assignment was based on his long history of assassination. He had been involved in some thirty hits during his career.[354] He started out working for Al Capone and later the Giancana crime family. At the same time, he was seen as a sophisticated, well-read individual and was a colleague of Frank Sinatra. He had moved to Los Angeles in the 1920s and helped establish the Chicago mob in Las Vegas in the 1950s.[355] His efforts to help reestablish the Mafia in Havana, however, were doomed to failure.

Clearly, the pills destined for Castro's bedroom never made it. When the fifteen-hundred-man force of CIA-backed commandos arrived at the reefs of the Bay of Pigs on April 17, 1961, they were met by a force of two thousand Cuban soldiers. Upon word of the landing, Castro immediately sent in twenty thousand reinforcements. The anti-Castro Cuban Brigade was led ashore by two American CIA agents, despite an order by President Kennedy that no Americans be included in the attack.[356] Indeed, the Agency not only ignored the president, but it had also led him to believe that US intelligence had indicated that an uprising against Castro was probable. This was fantasy, the wishful thinking of many, including Washington insiders, Cuban exiles, and Miami Mafia chieftain Santos Trafficante, who had been mob boss of Havana before Castro took power. We now know in hindsight, according to CIA documents released in 2005, that the Agency plan was in reality not just too optimistic, but in fact a CIA trap or a ploy to force Kennedy to order a military air strike. Kennedy stood his ground and refused.[357]

After two days of fierce fighting, the exiles surrendered. Their invasion force, known as Brigade 2506, had lost 114 men. Another 1,189 were captured, and the rest escaped. Over the next year and a half, Robert Kennedy steadfastly negotiated the release of the prisoners for fifty-three million dollars in food and medical supplies. The Bay of Pigs veterans were freed on December 23, 1962 and arrived in Florida on Christmas Eve.[358]

President Kennedy did not believe the United States should be in the business of murder.[359] He was well aware that foreign assassination missions, whether they succeeded or failed, could ruin his political reputation and America's respect in the world. Bobby Kennedy, his brother and main advisor, fully supported his wishes. At the same time, Bobby also believed strongly in the Cuban exiles' fight to free their country from a Communist dictatorship. Hence, while President Kennedy resisted plans that called for assassination, he allowed his brother Robert to keep the pressure on Castro's forces and to assist the exiles.

Bobby participated in this effort through the Special Group Augmented, a committee made up of national security and intelligence staff that assisted in coordinating the planning of various types of sabotage against Cuba. CIA-funded, anti-Castro, Cuban exiles struck from a key base in south Florida code named JM-WAVE, and other bases hidden in the United States, as they carried out raids on Cuban and Russian shipping.

During this time, the CIA's David Phillips (also known as Maurice Bishop), who had been an agent in pre-Fidel Havana, joined with an Agency contractor and Cuban exile Antonio Veciana and a Spanish Castro opponent Eloy Gutierrez Menoyo to form Alpha 66. This violent, paramilitary group's commandos led the most serious raids conducted against Cuba.[360]

Meanwhile, Richard Helms and his CIA associates continued plotting to kill Castro without presidential knowledge. The Church Committee found eight separate plots against Castro.[361] Secret reports on these unsuccessful CIA attempts on Castro's life—released during Senate hearings in the mid-1970s—reveal a bizarre collection of episodes that bring into question the mental balance of Richard Helms and his close subordinates. As noted earlier, Helms and William Harvey admitted they never told CIA Director McCone about their plots against Castro's life nor about their collaboration with the Mafia.[362] During the early 1960s, Helms's executive action team proposed numerous ways of murdering the Cuban Premier. These methods included poison pills (botulinum toxin) to be mixed in a drink (as noted above); a poison pen (to be used as a knife by a disaffected aide, a Major Rolando Cubela, code-named AM/LASH); a poisonous wetsuit (with TB in the breathing apparatus) to be given to Castro as a gift; poison cigars (dipped in botulinum toxin); an exploding cigar that would blow off his head; and an exploding seashell (Castro enjoyed skin-diving).[363] Both of the latter were too obviously American. After all this, a rifle and a pistol, both with silencers, were given to an anti-Castro exile leader to deliver to a Cuban dissident.[364] However, the only method known to have been actually attempted was the poison pills. Several tries were made to use them, none successfully.

In February 1962, Richard Helms took over chief responsibility for operations against Cuba from Richard Bissell, who had retired. The thrust of the plan, code named MONGOOSE, was to destabilize the Castro regime. Helms placed Gen. Edward G. Lansdale, USAF, in charge of managing the details. Lansdale's qualifications included putting down a guerilla uprising in the Philippines.[365] Lansdale was assisted by William Harvey.

Until mid-1962, as noted above, the Helms group in the CIA had kept knowledge of its assassination program secret from the Kennedys. However, on May 7, this clandestine program was revealed. The CIA's attorney, Lawrence Houston, met with Attorney General Robert Kennedy to ask him not to press mob leader Sam Giancana in a matter dealing with a Justice Department wiretap. Houston reasoned that in so doing, CIA secrets could be disclosed. Houston then told Kennedy that the CIA had hired the mob to assassinate Castro, and added that the program had been closed down (Houston was unaware that it was ongoing). Bobby believed that the plots were in the past and sternly replied, "I trust that if you ever try to do business with organized crime again, with gangsters, you will let the Attorney General know."[366]

In September of 1962, Helms replaced Harvey with New York attorney Desmond FitzGerald as the point person for Cuban actions. Over these several months, Harvey and Robert Kennedy had come to loathe each other. It was not only a personality conflict; the two men represented opposing viewpoints with regard to both policy and philosophy.[367]

The Cuban missile crisis of October 1962 brought the planet to the brink of thermonuclear war, and the aftermath of the crisis led to a totally different relationship with Cuba. President Kennedy had reached a peaceful agreement with the Soviets—the removal of their missiles from Cuban soil in return for the removal of US missiles from Turkey—and had brokered a deal that guaranteed a hands-off policy towards Cuba. In addition, in Washington, the Special Group Augmented was terminated, Operation MONGOOSE was ended, and anti-Castro Cuban bases in the United States were shut down, including a key base at Lake Pontchartrain in the New Orleans area. This turn of events embittered many in the exile movement and their CIA supporters.

The US agreement for the USSR to withdraw its missiles from Cuba had been contingent upon US nonaggression against Cuba. However, at this time, Castro was supporting military actions of his own outside Cuba in other Latin American countries. To counteract this, Robert Kennedy continued to back Bridgade leaders Dr. Manuel Artime, Roberto San Roman, and Enrique Ruiz-Williams and Alpha 66 raids on Russian freighters.[368]

Nevertheless, President Kennedy refused to allow the Helms faction within the CIA to conduct covert missions involving assassination. According to a

*New York Times* reporter, Tad Szulc, who interviewed Kennedy during this period, the president said that "he and his brother felt that the United States for moral reasons should never be in a situation of having recourse to assassination." John Kennedy later told an aide, Richard Goodwin, "If we get into that kind of thing, we'll all be targets."[369]

President Kennedy sought to avoid another Soviet-US crisis and warned the exiles concerning their actions. Simultaneously, the president offered Castro renewed relations if his military halted its interference in other Caribbean nations. Castro received word of Kennedy's initiative through a French journalist, Jean Daniel, who delivered the president's message to Havana.[370] By September 1963, the Cuban leader was convinced that his economy would have a better chance of improving if it were in the US orbit rather than as a Soviet satellite, and he sought a normalization of relations with Washington. Robert Kennedy was also on board, in support of his brother.[371] Just prior to John Kennedy's assassination, Castro was quoted as saying, "He (Kennedy) still has the possibility of being, in the eye of history, the greatest president of the United States . . . he has come to understand many things over the past few months. . . . You can tell him that I'm willing to declare (conservative Republican senator Barry) Goldwater my friend if that will guarantee Kennedy's reelection!"[372]

President Kennedy was assassinated days later. As we shall see, the Helms executive action team would use the plot to kill Castro as its cover to kill the president.

Years later, Robert Kennedy's wife Ethel traveled to Havana to visit Fidel Castro. At their meeting, she told him that her husband Bobby and his brother President John Kennedy had nothing to do with the attempts to kill him. Castro, who had numerous spies in the United States, replied, "I know."[373]

The myth that Robert Kennedy was behind the Castro assassination plots all started with Richard Helms. It was actually Helms who planned the operation assigning Bill Harvey as point person. Harvey, whom CIA veteran John Whitten later termed "a very dangerous man," brought in the mafia's Johnny Rosselli. All of this was done without the Kennedys' knowledge.[374] Years later, such CIA abuses came under government scrutiny in the 1975 Church Committee inquiries. Helms, who was then US ambassador to Iran, met with Henry Kissinger, then secretary of state, and lied to him, saying Robert Kennedy had "personally managed the assassination of Castro." Kissinger relayed this false information to President Gerald Ford and eventually to the media.[375]

## Dominican Republic

The attempts on Castro's life and the plot that killed Lumumba were authorized in the Eisenhower administration along with a third regime change—the overthrow of the Dominican Republic's long-time dictator, General Rafael Trujillo (1891–1961). Trujillo was seen as a tyrant who had ruled the sugar-rich country with an iron fist since 1930. Based in the capital of Santo Domingo, he and his family controlled every aspect of the country's business, politics, military, and courts to the dismay of United States corporate interests. The Dominican Republic consists of a mixed Spanish and African population and encompasses the eastern two-thirds of the large Caribbean island of Hispaniola; the western third of the island is French-speaking Haiti. It is strategically located between Cuba and Puerto Rico.

By 1960, the CIA began working with a small group of dissidents on the island in planning the assassination of the Dominican leader. Weapons were requested through the US ambassador in May and then approved by Richard Helms and delivered to Trujillo's opponents in January 1961.[376] The CIA's allies on the island reportedly received three pistols and three carbines. This hardware served to show American support because obviously, the dissidents, who included generals, already owned an abundant supply of guns. The key service provided by Helms's covert operators was the expertise in planning, logistics, and tactical support needed to successfully carry out the killing without repercussions from the dictator's family and other loyal Trujillo followers. When President Kennedy found out about the assassination plan in early May 1961, he told the American ambassador Henry Dearborn that the United States would not be involved in murder plots. Kennedy also wanted to ensure that any coup attempt would be planned in such a way that it would bring about a better government for the Dominican Republic.[377]

At the end of the month, on May 30, 1961, Trujillo's car was ambushed and the seventy-year-old leader was shot to death. Helms's associates, E. Howard Hunt and newly contracted Johnny Rosselli, were involved in the arrangements, although CIA participation was kept under deep cover.[378] In fact, when word reached the White House that Trujillo had been killed, the administration had no information whatsoever from the CIA regarding the Dominican rebels. The operation had been conducted in total secrecy, a characteristically Helmsian modus operandi. Later on, when President Kennedy was meeting with Sen. George Smathers of Florida, a friend of the president's, Kennedy mentioned that he was worried about the fact that the CIA was operating behind his back. The president added that "he believed the CIA had arranged to have . . . Trujillo bumped off."[379]

Civil war broke out in the capital of the Dominican Republic four years later, which prompted President Lyndon Johnson to send the Marines to Santo Domingo in April 1965 in order to protect US corporate interests. The following month, a cease-fire was established.

## Iraq

The next sovereign country destined to invoke CIA covert action was Iraq. Strategically located on the Persian Gulf in Southwest Asia, Iraq's rich oil fields were then controlled by foreign companies. Once again, corporate interests and the Eisenhower administration sought to maintain the status quo in the country by dealing swiftly with any perceived threats to American interests. As noted, the CIA had played a key role in neighboring Iran, located on Iraq's eastern border, in 1953. Iraq is bordered by Saudi Arabia and Kuwait in the south, Jordan and Syria in the west, and Turkey in the north. The Soviet Union was not much farther to the north. The 1950s saw Arab nationalism on the rise, particularly in Algeria, while at the same time Soviet influence was growing in Egypt and elsewhere. US doctrine at the time equated such threats with chaos, which, it was feared, would in turn lead to Communism.

In July 1958, Iraq erupted into turmoil with a bloody coup staged by Iraqi Army General Abdul Karim Kassem. Under Kassem, Baghdad renewed its ties to the Soviet Union and allowed the Communist Party to operate freely. In Washington, these actions were considered potentially harmful to Iraq's economic value, and in 1960, the CIA began to initiate plans for the removal of General Kassem.[380]

Richard Helms, then deputy director of operations, called the plot to assassinate Iraq's new leader "highly desirable." One method promoted by Helms was a poisoned handkerchief created by the CIA's technical services unit. The lethal nose cloth was delivered to Baghdad at the same time a group of opposition generals were leading a revolt. The rebels, members of the Baath Party, took Kassem into custody, and on February 8, 1963 he was executed by firing squad.[381] Iraq's new leader, Abdul Salam Arif, restored relations with the West. He was killed in a helicopter accident three years later and was succeeded by his brother, General Abdul Rahman Arif. Iraqi regimes rose and fell during the subsequent years of war with Israel. One Baathist member at the time of Kassem's ouster in 1963, a twenty-five-year-old named Saddam Hussein (1937–2006), would become dictator of Iraq in 1979.

## Vietnam

Helms's covert operators turned their focus from Iraq to Southeast Asia later in 1963 as they finalized their plans for the overthrow of the president of South Vietnam, Ngo Dinh Diem (1901–1963).

Vietnam is located on the South China Sea, with the Gulf of Tonkin on the northeastern coast. The country is bordered by China on the north and by Laos and Cambodia in the west. Formerly known as Indo-China, the region was colonized by France in the 1860s. Japan occupied the colony during World War II, and after Vietnam's liberation, the Vietnamese fought a war of independence from France. In a decisive battle at Bien Dien Phu in May of 1954, the Communist Vietminh forces under Ho Chi Minh defeated the French after two months of fighting. France withdrew, and in July 1954, based on the decisions of the Geneva Accords, the country was divided at the seventeenth parallel into two separate nations, North and South Vietnam. Ho Chi Minh ruled the North from the capital of Hanoi. The South was ruled from Saigon by Emperor Bao Dai until 1956 when Ngo Dinh Diem, a French-educated Catholic, was elected president of South Vietnam.[382] Diem was an autocrat with a very narrow constituency. He faced strong opposition from the native Buddhist population. At the same time, his administration was intent on eliminating a growing North Vietnamese-supported Communist guerrilla movement known as the National Liberation Front, or the Vietcong. Diem's younger brother, Ngo Dinh Nhu, the head of the South Vietnamese security police, played a major role in quelling Communist and Buddhist dissent.

The Saigon government was viewed in Washington as an ally in the struggle to block Soviet expansion into Southeast Asia. And since Diem represented the forces of anti-Communism, President Eisenhower initiated a program of sending US military advisors to assist the South Vietnamese troops. In all, he sent in 685 advisors.[383] The CIA also was deeply involved in the country and the Diem government.[384]

In January 1961, when President Kennedy entered office, he continued Ike's support for South Vietnam. Although the Pentagon requested thirty-six hundred troops, Kennedy initially sent in only five hundred more. Kennedy had been in Vietnam a decade earlier and had visited the French forces there. Based on his observations at that time, he told his brother Robert the United States should avoid any such involvement. After his election in 1960, Kennedy had lunch with General Douglas MacArthur, who had led US forces in the Pacific during World War II. The general warned Kennedy that it would be foolish to fight with ground forces on the Asian Mainland and that he should pursue diplomacy instead.[385] Kennedy agreed. The CIA clearly disagreed, and remained committed to defeating Communism in Vietnam.

Helms's CIA liaison with the South Vietnamese army was Lt. Col. Lucien Conein, who also was a colleague of E. Howard Hunt. Conein was born in Paris and raised in Kansas City. He retained his French citizenship, and when World War II broke out, joined the OSS. He fought alongside the French against the Japanese in Indo-China.[386] Following the Geneva Conference of 1954, Conein gradually built up a program in South Vietnam in which sabotage teams of anti-Communists would spy on the North, spread disinformation, and assassinate key officials. Conein's CIA's assassins were South Vietnamese volunteers trained at Danang or at US bases in the Pacific. They were flown into North Vietnam via Air America.[387]

Interestingly, at the same time in neighboring Laos, a Communist insurgency was ongoing in which the CIA also was heavily involved. It was President Kennedy's view that Laos should remain neutral in the cold war between the Communists and the West. To implement his plan, Kennedy sent Ambassador Averell Harriman to Laos to try to craft an agreement between the warring factions. When Harriman returned to Washington, Kennedy found out Agency operatives in Laos were sabotaging his plans.[388]

The CIA was working behind Kennedy's back in Vietnam as well. Quietly, Lucien Conein had been meeting with South Vietnamese generals to discuss overthrowing President Ngo Dinh Diem and replacing him with one of their own, a Vietnamese military leader. The CIA covert operations division, led by Richard Helms, believed that Diem was incapable of unifying the various groups in South Vietnam—the Catholics, the Buddhists, the students, and the peasants—to the extent required to meet the challenge presented by the North.[389] This branch of the Agency decided to install a president in South Vietnam who would be more aggressive in crushing the Communist insurgency.[390]

Kennedy felt that a coup would be risky both politically and militarily.[391] Helms's division knew this, yet they pressed ahead anyway, planning the details of the coup while at the same time claiming it was being initiated and propelled by the opposition generals within Diem's military.

From President Kennedy's point of view, a nonmilitary solution was the only sensible route out of Vietnam, and Diem was probably the only leader who could facilitate this plan. Kennedy's planned objective was to negotiate with the Soviets to create a neutral, stable region in Southeast Asia. The US presence in South Vietnam totaled twelve thousand troops by mid-1962.

Finally, in July, Kennedy asked his Defense chief Robert McNamara to begin preparing a withdrawal plan for American forces to be replaced by South Vietnamese troops by the end of 1965.[392] The gradual withdrawal order was actually signed by Kennedy and announced on November 20, 1963. It was two days before his assassination. In a National Security Action Memoranda, announced at the Honolulu Conference, Kennedy ordered the withdrawal of one thousand US troops. Four days after his assassination, on November 26, 1963, the order was reversed by President Johnson, who immediately began to escalate US activity against North Vietnam.[393] (South Vietnam fell to the North Vietnamese Communists in April 1975 and has remained Communist to the present day without any loss to American security. When Kennedy died, the US death toll in Vietnam stood at seventy-three. By the time the US had withdrawn a decade later, the total was fifty-eight thousand US soldiers dead.)

Kennedy had consistently believed the war was South Vietnam's, not America's. However, in 1962, Kennedy publicly supported the war in order to keep up morale in Vietnam and also to win in the upcoming 1964 presidential election. To do otherwise would have been political disaster and would have resulted in a Republican victory at the polls in November, which, in turn, would have meant a much greater loss of life in Vietnam.[394] By the end of 1962, the number of American troops killed in Vietnam was twenty.

Along with the war, unrest in Saigon reached a critical stage by June of 1963. That month a Buddhist monk, Quang Duc, sixty-six, immolated himself on a busy downtown street. In subsequent weeks others followed, killing themselves by fire in protest of dissident arrests by Diem's oppressive government. Kennedy urged the Diem administration to reform its policies and to accommodate the Buddhists, students, and other dissidents, to no avail.[395]

That summer, the CIA's Lucien Conein was secretly meeting with the South Vietnamese generals who would carry out the CIA's planned coup d'etat.[396] Soon after, Saigon regional commander Gen. Ton That Dinh, a key person, was also recruited.[397] Conein worked out the details and promised the generals that US support would follow the overthrow. The plan was not emanating from the White House, but from Helms's covert action group. It was a CIA operation to be unleashed on the Saigon administration because of Diem and Nhu's resistance to CIA oversight and the brothers' nationalist leanings. Diem was reportedly working toward a secret agreement with the National Liberation Front that would have created a coalition government with the Communists.[398] At the same time, Diem's brother and chief political advisor Nhu was making contact with North Vietnamese Prime Minister Pham Van Dong.[399] This was a betrayal in the eyes of the CIA; the Agency wanted a Communist defeat.

President Kennedy received word of the planned coup in August 1963. Harriman at the State Department and US Ambassador to South Vietnam, John Lodge, who had been Nixon's running mate in the 1960 election, were both in favor of overthrowing Diem. While the CIA's covert operations group moved forward in Saigon, at home, CIA Director McCone opposed the coup along with Defense Secretary McNamara, General Maxwell Taylor,[400] and General Paul Harkins. In communications with Robert Kennedy, Gen. Harkins stated his opposition to disrupting the Saigon administration and also warned Kennedy not to trust the CIA covert operations team in Vietnam.[401]

President Kennedy knew that any US involvement in a coup d'etat would send the wrong message to our allies. He repeatedly sought information from the CIA through Ambassador Lodge to determine the makeup of the proposed government. When he obtained little of any substance, he considered relieving Lodge of his duties.[402] Again, Kennedy was seeking less involvement in South Vietnam's affairs, not further entanglements. In his efforts to seek a peaceful solution, in October 1963 Kennedy told US ambassador to France James Gavin that he intended to reach out to General Charles de Gaulle for diplomatic assistance. Kennedy said he believed that "we will be able to get something done together" to find a way to bring peace to Vietnam.[403]

That same month, Kennedy sent a message to Ambassador Lodge regarding the possible coup: "no initiative should now be taken to give any covert encouragement to a coup." However, he added that Lodge should "build contacts with possible alternative leadership as and when it appears." Kennedy ordered Americans in Vietnam not to play a part in any coup attempt, but he did agree not to thwart a coup.[404]

Meanwhile, the clandestine CIA operations force in Saigon, led by Lucien Conein, was busy working behind the scenes without Kennedy's full knowledge. On November 1, 1963, the coup attempt was launched. That evening, opposition generals began shelling the Presidential Guard Barracks in Saigon. A surprised Diem was asked by the generals via a phone call to resign and was promised safe passage out of the country. He rejected their offer and fled with his brother Nhu to a villa in Cholon outside the capital shortly before his palace was shelled. The next day, while hiding in the French church of St. Francis Xavier, Diem negotiated the terms of his abdication by phone with General Duong Van Minh, known as "Big Minh." Minh had worked with CIA operatives in Diem's Interior Ministry. Unbeknownst to Diem, Minh gave the order for a captain to kill both Diem and Nhu after their arrest. Gen. Mai Huu Xuan, of Nhu's secret police, led a convoy of jeeps and an armored personnel carrier to pick up the fugitive brothers in Cholon. On the return trip to Saigon, the vehicle carrying Diem and Nhu stopped. Two officers in the convoy approached them and opened fire, killing them both. The bodies were delivered to General Minh's headquarters.[405]

News of the murders shocked President Kennedy. He is reported to have been in a meeting with General Taylor and others and upon hearing the report, jumped from his desk and rushed from the room.[406] Three weeks later, Kennedy, too, was assassinated.

In analyzing the coup d'etat in South Vietnam, it is clear that Kennedy had failed to fathom the violence that would result during the transfer of power. He had assumed Diem would have been ousted and allowed political asylum in a neighboring country. Ambassador Lodge notified Kennedy within days of the murders that "the coup would not have happened as it did without our [CIA] preparation." Yet a few months later, while speaking with *The New York Times*, Lodge denied any US involvement.[407]

A second coup, approved by the CIA, took place on January 28, 1964, just three months after Diem's demise. General Minh was replaced by General Khanh. The war worsened for the United States, as the Vietcong continued to take control of strategic hamlets.

A postscript to the Diem coup, and his assassination, points to the lengths to which the Helms era covert operations activities extended. Eight years later, in 1971, when Richard Nixon was president, Helms's protégé E. Howard Hunt, with Helms's assistance, had joined the Nixon administration as a consultant, specializing in setting up disinformation schemes in the "Dirty Tricks" department. In one covert disinformation operation, Lucien Conein was asked by Hunt to create a fake telegram that would make it appear that President Kennedy had ordered Diem's murder.[408] Hunt was planning to pass the document on to *Life* magazine in order to discredit the Kennedys, Ted Kennedy in particular. The ploy failed when *Life* reporter William Lambert questioned the authenticity of Conein's handiwork.[409]

E. Howard Hunt was finally arrested at the Watergate complex in 1972 for his role in the break-in at the Democratic National Committee's Headquarters. He served thirty-three months in prison. When he was released, approaching age sixty, his career in covert operations and propaganda was finished. Hunt had served in the navy in World War II and had joined the CIA in 1949 at age thirty-one. A Brown University graduate from Hamburg, New York, Hunt had started out his career as a novelist and published throughout his life; his talent in the CIA was writing disinformation. Hunt would die from pneumonia in Miami on January 23, 2007 at age eighty-eight.

A retired US ambassador, Samuel Hart, who knew E. Howard Hunt in the 1950s in Uruguay, characterized him as "totally self-absorbed, totally amoral, and a danger to himself and anybody around him."[410] Hunt clearly found his niche with colleagues like Angleton and Helms.

With the successful facilitation of numerous coups and assassinations abroad in the 1950s and early 1960s, the CIA's covert operations heads next turned to planning such operations at home.

# 5

# Lee Harvey Oswald, an Unwitting Patsy

ON THE THIRTIETH anniversary of President Kennedy's assassination, *Newsweek* magazine published a list of conspiracy theories. They ranged from the absurd idea that the killing was an accidental shooting by a secret service agent to a murder plot involving one of several groups including the Soviet KGB (State Security Committee), Cuba's Castro, anti-Castro Cubans, the Mafia, and the Central Intelligence Agency. In the latter scenario, a CIA Black Ops conspiracy, *Newsweek* noted that the Agency had had experience in the realm of assassinations. This theory viewed Lee Harvey Oswald as a CIA recruit and offered motives for the crime, namely, the Agency's angst over Kennedy's peace overtures to Soviet and Cuban Communists, and the president's firing of three top-level CIA officials. The *Newsweek* article then listed two "hitches" to this particular conspiracy theory. First, it purported that Oswald's framing would have taken "great logistical legerdemain." And, second, that it would have been a problem for the CIA to silence the actual assassins in order to shield the Agency from suspicion.[411]

The fact is, these two points hardly qualify as hitches. The CIA had been planning "logistical legerdemain" in its MKULTRA programs for more than a decade, thus bringing to the task in-depth knowledge, skill, and the requisite resources. Turning Oswald into a programmed fall guy may have been a very sophisticated operation, but it was one at which the CIA was uniquely adept. So, the framing of Oswald was less tricky than *Newsweek* could then fathom. Oswald was simply set up to be an innocent patsy; he was manipulated to

89

appear to have been an assassin. The actual assassins were hired guns, well-hidden sharpshooters, who quickly escaped following the shooting.

As for eliminating the true assassins, this would *not* have been a problem given the Agency's line of business at the time. When it came to silencing those who knew too much, CIA-Mafia-connected hired guns were readily available. We know that scores of witnesses died early deaths.[412] Indeed, the actual assassins were no doubt eliminated soon after the assassination in order to ensure their silence forever. The hitmen who killed them would not have known who they were nor why they were being bumped off, only that they (the hitmen) were being paid very well to do it.

In the previous chapter, we described Richard Helms's top secret CIA MKULTRA programs of the 1950s and 1960s. We discussed their development and their use in creating a cover for "executive action operations," i.e., assassinations. In this chapter, we will explore the assassination of President John F. Kennedy from this perspective. Specifically, we will look at how the alleged assassin, twenty-four-year-old Lee Harvey Oswald, was shepherded into the intelligence community as a young Marine, sent to Russia, and brought back home two and a half years later. We will see how he was employed in Agency undercover assignments in New Orleans and Dallas, unwittingly positioned to be a fall guy, framed for the murder of President Kennedy, and then murdered while in custody.

Oswald was accused of assassinating Kennedy by firing a bolt-action, Italian-made, Mannlicher-Carcano rifle at the president's motorcade from a sniper's nest on the sixth floor of the Texas School Book Depository on Elm Street in Dallas, Texas. On November 22, 1963, the sun came out in the late morning, and by midday the skies were clear and the air warm. A throng of well-wishers lined the city streets to greet the president and the First Lady. The crowds thinned out as the motorcade route approached Dealey Plaza, which led to the freeway. Kennedy and his wife Jacqueline sat in the back seat of the open limousine, behind Texas governor John Connally and his wife Nellie. Vice President Lyndon Johnson and his wife Lady Bird were in another limo farther back in the motorcade. On Houston Street, the president's vehicle slowed and turned sharply to the left onto Elm. Mrs. Connally smiled, turned to the president and said, "Mr. President, you can't say Dallas doesn't love you." He answered, "No, you certainly can't."[413] It was 12:30 p.m. As they passed the Texas School Book Depository, approaching the picket fence at the grassy knoll, shots rang out. Kennedy was hit in the back and in the head. He slumped onto his wife's lap. Governor Connally was hit in the back and critically wounded. Fifty-two percent of the witnesses would later testify that the shots came from the grassy knoll, 39 percent stated they came from the Book Depository, and some said both directions.[414] President Kennedy was pronounced dead at 1 p.m.

Within the hour, Dallas policeman J. D. Tippit was shot and killed next to his patrol car in the general neighborhood in which Book Depository employee Lee Harvey Oswald lived. Minutes later, at the nearby Texas Theater, Oswald was arrested after a struggle. On November 24, 1963, two days after the Kennedy assassination, Oswald was being led through the Dallas Police Station basement on his way to the county jail when he was shot in the stomach and killed. The gunman, local mobster and strip club owner Jack Ruby, died of cancer while in jail three years later.

With the alleged presidential assassin having been silenced, President Lyndon Johnson ordered an investigation and a report on the facts of the case, the so-called Warren Commission Report. As we now know, some witnesses were not truthful, some changed their stories, and some key witnesses were not included. Clearly, the goal of the Commission was to officially stop the rumors that were swirling around the case.[415] Even President Johnson suspected Cuba or the CIA had played a role in the assassination. Yet he felt that the best course of action, to avoid war and to calm the citizenry, was to close the case with the simple conclusion that Lee Harvey Oswald was the lone assassin.[416]

In the years since President Kennedy's death, mischaracterizations and deliberate deceptions regarding Oswald have been widely disseminated by the media.[417] Some of these falsehoods are the result of disinformation campaigns directed early on by the intelligence community. Its subtle use of the media succeeded in making it extremely difficult to ascertain the true story behind the plot to kill the president. However, when we analyze the facts of Oswald's short life from the perspective thus far established, i.e., Richard Helms's MKULTRA operations, a much clearer and more credible picture of the alleged assassin begins to emerge.

When one adds up the inordinate number of seemingly human errors in the investigation of the circumstances surrounding the assassination, taken together with all of the inconsistencies, the facts point solidly to Oswald's having been framed. More specifically, the evidence points in the direction of individuals at a high level within the CIA—Richard Helms, along with his closest cohort James Angleton, and several others. Indeed, authors who insist that Oswald was a lone nut are either naive or exploiting the official viewpoint for personal gain. In either case, their arguments help to continue the cover-up.

There are those who say that a conspiracy on a large scale would be impossible to conceal in the United States. They are right. It was impossible to conceal, even on a small scale.

In the chronological analysis ahead, we will describe how Richard Helms and James Angleton's MKULTRA operation was the underpinning of the JFK (and RFK) assassination plot, and through an understanding of this hypno-programming operation, we can explain many of the mysteries in the case. Again, the purpose of the programming was *not* to create an assassin, but to create a fall guy by planting highly incriminating information about an innocent person, while expert marksmen carried out the actual shooting. Oswald was framed.

Common symptoms of hypno-programming, as we shall see ahead, include mood swings and irritability; Oswald experienced both of these symptoms.[418] Another sign is unaccounted for time gaps among those who were unwittingly involved in the CIA's mind control research programs. There are a number of periods during which Oswald was missing for two or more weeks. One, for example, was in October 1962, a few months after having arrived with his family in Dallas.[419] These periods would have allowed time for him to have undergone conditioning phases, obviously unwittingly. He would have no memory of these times. The time gaps and resulting memory lapses also help to explain some of his intermittent marital troubles, i.e., "Where were you . . . why didn't you tell me?" Another sign of hypno-programming is Oswald's "diary," found with his belongings after the assassination. House Committee experts stated that it was written in his handwriting, yet without his articulation. They also maintained it was written in one or two days, yet it covers two years of his life.[420] The simplest explanation, and most logical, is that it is not a diary—it is a journal his handlers produced to create Lee's cover. And yet another sign of the hypno-programming of Oswald comes from a story told by a friend of his. On the day of the assassination, according to this friend, Lee brought a package containing curtain rods to work at the Texas School Book Depository, a package the Warren Commission would later surmise must have been the disassembled rifle being secreted into the building. Yet witnesses' descriptions of the package's dimensions clearly rule out such a weapon.[421] Oswald later said that he had no memory of this package.[422] Such is the nature of MKULTRA hypno-programming.

Lee Harvey Oswald was born on October 18, 1939 in New Orleans. His mother, Marguerite Claverie Oswald, was a nurse, and his father, Robert Oswald, was an insurance man. Lee's father died in August 1939, two months before Lee was born. Marguerite had two other children: Robert, who was born in 1934, and John Pic, born in 1931, a son from her first husband from whom she was divorced. During World War II, three-year-old Lee was placed in an orphanage with his two brothers until the war ended in 1945. Marguerite married again and took the boys back, but the marriage only lasted until 1948. The family moved to the Fort Worth, Texas, area, and within a few years, the older boys had joined the military—John enlisted in the Coast Guard and Robert in the Marines. In 1952, when Lee was thirteen, he and his mother moved to New York City, where John Pic was stationed. There they rented an apartment in the Bronx and stayed for two years.[423]

Oswald is commonly considered to have been a loner and an eccentric; this is hardly the case. At age fourteen, in 1953, Lee Harvey Oswald was elected president of his eighth grade class at P.S. 44 in the Bronx, New York.[424] Such elections are typically popularity contests. It was here that Lee also became an avid reader and at the same time an enthusiastic subway rider, exploring the big city, many times when he should have been in class.

Lee and his mother left New York in 1954 and returned to their roots in New Orleans where they briefly lived with Marguerite's sister, Lillian Murret, before finding their own apartment. The following year, as Lee was turning sixteen, he joined the Civil Air Patrol, a scouting-type organization.[425] It was there that he became acquainted with one of the group's leaders, a pilot named David Ferrie. According to an aide to Richard Helms, Ferrie was a pilot who worked for the CIA.[426] Indeed, Oswald's ties to the intelligence community actually extended back to his teenage years in New Orleans.

Ferrie was extremely unusual in many ways, including his appearance. Due to a hairless condition, known as alopecia areata, he would paint on his eyebrows and glue on a wig. He was known for his fanatical, right-wing political views and his connections to New Orleans mob boss Carlos Marcello. He had close ties to anti-Castro Cubans and Guy Banister, former FBI bureau chief in Chicago, with whom he shared an office at 544 Camp Street in New Orleans.[427] Like Ferrie, Banister was another rabid anti-Communist who had established CIA-backed, anti-Castro, Cuban groups in New Orleans and was believed to have been a gun runner for their cause. In this respect, he was akin to E. Howard Hunt who also was responsible for training anti-Castro paramilitary forces in the Miami area.[428]

Interestingly, one of David Ferrie's hobbies was that of master hypnotist, a talent that dovetails neatly into the MKULTRA hypno-programming activities of the agency.[429] He was also a homosexual pedophile and was fired from

Eastern Airlines for his illicit activities. Jim Garrison, the famed New Orleans District Attorney, once described Ferrie as twisted but at the same time, "genuinely brilliant."[430]

On February 22, 1967, shortly before he was to appear at Garrison's JFK assassination conspiracy trial, Ferrie was found dead in his home at age forty-nine. The cause of death was listed as a cerebral hemorrhage.[431] His life and Oswald's were intertwined, starting with their meeting at CAP in 1955 when Lee was sixteen, and again several months before the Kennedy assassination when Lee was twenty-three. Ferrie and Lee were also witnessed together in various locations outside New Orleans, as we shall see ahead.

After Oswald was arrested following the Kennedy assassination on November 22, 1963, a library card was reportedly found in his wallet; the card was David Ferrie's.[432] What's more, when Jack Ruby, Oswald's murderer, was arrested, it was discovered that Ferrie's name was listed in Ruby's address book.[433] Clearly, the intertwining of these three lives was not coincidental.

Lee and his mother left New Orleans and moved to Fort Worth, Texas, in July of 1956. One week after turning seventeen, on October 24, 1956, Lee followed in his brother's footsteps and joined the US Marine Corps.[434] He wanted a life of excitement, travel; one where he might even learn something and get paid doing it. Medical records from Oswald's military enlistment file show that his personality was far different than that which many historians have ascribed to him since the assassination. Rather than "irrational" and "unstable," as many writers have characterized him, his Marine medical records state Lee "consistently showed no signs of emotional problems or mental abnormalities."[435]

Friends of Oswald's in the service also had positive things to say about their comrade. One Marine in his unit, Zack Stout, said he felt that Lee, whose nickname was "Ozzie," could hold an intelligent conversation, read "deep stuff like *Mein Kampf*. . . or *The Decline and Fall of the Roman Empire*," and was "absolutely truthful, the kind of guy I'd trust completely."[436] Another Marine acquaintance, James R. Persons, said of Oswald, "He was easy to get along with. He was quiet . . . not one of those animal-like guys."[437]

A quiet intellectual. Indeed, he was not the typical Marine. But it was these gifts that led Oswald to a very unique career path and his ill-fated destiny. At Marine basic training in San Diego, Oswald was a poor shot and failed to achieve "Expert Marksman."[438] He scored the minimum qualification for marksman, which was to hit a 191 on a scale of 190–250 in target shooting. This is considered "a low marksmanship rating" by the Marine Corps.[439] His talents clearly lay elsewhere, and soon he would find himself in the oftentimes paranoid world of military intelligence.

The official story of Oswald's service time has led many historians to believe that after his graduation from basic training, the Marines sent him to bases in Florida and Mississippi for several months to train to become a radar specialist, after which they assigned him to Atsugi, Japan.[440]

However, based on statements from Oswald's fellow Marines in Japan, we know that Lee spoke fluent Russian. In fact, he spoke it so often he was given an additional nickname, "Oswaldskovich."[441] Russian is a very difficult language to learn, and without schooling, an improbable task. The official story asks us to believe that Oswald learned it in his spare time. Yet there is no evidence that this occurred. A close friend of Oswald's remarked years later that the Russian community in Dallas was "amazed by Lee's almost perfect command of the language . . . to know Russian as he did was remarkable—to appreciate serious literature—was something out of the ordinary."[442]

This puzzle persisted until the mid-1970s when information was released under the Freedom of Information Act that shed new light on Oswald's actual Marine training. According to Professor Philip Melanson (*Spy Saga*), a belatedly released transcript from an executive session of the Warren Commission, contained a telling line by J. Lee Rankin, chief counsel. Rankin is quoted as informing the members what the Commission had done to "find out what he [Oswald] studied at the Monterey School of the army in the way of languages."[443] Oswald had been sent to the military's premier language school, the Defense Language Institute (DLI), in Monterey, California, to study the Russian language.[444] This elite, interservice language school teaches a multitude of key "target" languages, preparing select troops from all branches of the military for work with the National Security Agency. The school's intensive nine-month courses consist of six hours per day of classes, plus homework. The job of military language graduates is typically in cryptological services (codebreaking) and interception of enemy messages, whether from tanks, ships, submarines, missile bases, or aircraft. Linguists are typically assigned to do intercept translation work, although some are used for interrogation duties.

Oswald's graduation from basic training in San Diego in January 1957 would place him at DLI in Monterey through September of 1957. This squares with the timeline for Oswald's arrival at Atsugi Air Base, Japan. At that time, Atsugi was the largest CIA base in Asia and home of the CIA's brand new supersecret spy plane, the U-2.[445] The U-2 had been developed by the CIA's deputy director Richard Bissell and was first launched in 1956. The aircraft could fly at an altitude of ninety thousand feet. Armed with the most advanced photo capabilities, it captured images of the vast majority of Soviet military installations.[446] The U-2 fleet was replaced by satellites in the mid 1960s.

Again, given Oswald's actual job in intelligence, it was not unusual that he would be listed as a radar control operator. Quite often, military intelligence specialists' duty assignments were fabricated as a cover.[447] Oswald's job title of Radar Specialist was used to maintain the secrecy of his language-related job, which was classified as top secret.

During Oswald's time in Japan, he was deployed with his unit to monitor minor crises in other parts of East Asia. These TDYs (temporary duty assignments) brought him to the Philippines during a regional threat in Indonesia in January 1958, and another flare-up sent him to Taiwan in September 1958.[448] However, most of his tour of duty was spent supporting the U-2 spy plane missions out of Atsugi, some twenty-five miles south of Tokyo. At the same time, another intelligence mission of a more intimate nature emerged in Oswald's life. He began to hang out at the bars in Tokyo where he met young Japanese women who were known to be providing information to the KGB. Lee's job was to give them disinformation regarding the U-2 spy plane program.[449] Apparently, he was paid well for his additional duties. According to Edward Jay Epstein (*Legend*), a night with a hostess at the elite Queen Bee club could cost more than a month's salary for a Marine of his rank (eighty-five dollars).[450] Yet Lee was never lacking money despite his extravagant lifestyle at the capital city's high-priced clubs.

Another indication of Oswald's spy work is revealed in his medical records. He was examined in September 1958 for the venereal disease gonorrhea and was treated on base. Instead of being disciplined for violating the Marine code of conduct, his records state that he contracted the disease "in the line of duty."[451]

Oswald was living on the edge in many ways, both on base and off base. And during his time at Atsugi, he reportedly had two run-ins with the military justice system. In April 1958, MPs (military police) arrested Lee for owning a derringer he had purchased in Japan; private weapons were not allowed. He no doubt felt that it was a good idea to carry protection in case his nightlife turned ugly. The gun was discovered when he accidentally dropped it in the barracks and it fired, grazing his arm.[452] Apparently, Oswald was not handy with weapons of any kind.

The second incident occurred in August of 1958 at the Enlisted Club on base. At one point during the night, Lee poured a drink over a sergeant's head. MPs took him away, and he ended up spending two weeks in the brig.[453] Eighteen-year-old Oswald obviously had not yet learned to hold his liquor.

Oswald's tour of duty at Atsugi, Japan, ended three months later, and in November 1958 he returned by ship to California. His new assignment was at El Toro Air Station located between Los Angeles and San Diego.[454] Knowing the true nature of Lee's work in the service, we have a clearer perspective of what happened next. During his nine months at El Toro, Oswald is believed to have been preparing for his next assignment and was also being "prepared," i.e., conditioned for it. He would often speak Russian to colleagues and subscribed to a Russian periodical. Certainly his superiors knew his true role.[455] Years later, his roommate at El Toro Air Station, James Botelho, who had since become a judge in California, was asked about Oswald's political leanings and his work after leaving the Marines. Judge Botelho stated, "Oswald was not a Communist or a Marxist. . . . Oswald was on an assignment in Russia for American intelligence."[456]

While Richard Helms's MKULTRA program was secretly busy—experimenting with unwitting soldiers, prisoners, and others—there was another intrepid intelligence program of theirs also ongoing at that time. It involved fake "defections." Through this program, which was run by counterintelligence chief James Angleton,[457] the CIA used individuals in the US military to penetrate the Soviet Union.[458]

In September 1959, Oswald received a "family hardship" discharge allowing him to separate from the Marines three months early. Beneath the façade of the official story, the facts tell a different tale. His discharge was a cover designed to disguise his new orders. In fact, there was no "hardship" in Lee's family for which he needed to go home. His mother had hurt her foot and fallen a year earlier, but had recovered very well.[459] The hardship discharge was a simple ruse to usher Lee into a program being run by Richard Helms and James Angleton in which military personnel were being sent behind the Iron Curtain. Under the guise of being defectors, US troops were being sent to Soviet Bloc countries to work undercover for US intelligence. In that same time period, between 1958 and 1960, there were seven Americans who defected to the Soviet Union. It is known that six of them returned home. However, it is unclear from State Department records exactly how many were spies, and how many, if any, were authentic defectors.[460]

Lee departed from El Toro Air Station in September 1959 and first went home to Fort Worth to see his mother. He explained to her that he planned to work in the import-export business. He also told his family that he intended to enroll in a college in Europe, ostensibly at the recently established Albert Schweitzer College in Churwalden, Switzerland.[461] The CIA had a substantial monetary investment in this college, perhaps due to its strategic location in a neutral country. Lee's college plan was a useful cover story, as well as a possible fallback position if the goal of secreting Lee into the Soviet Union was foiled.

Rather than having to wait weeks for his passport, Lee's arrived in mere days. His discharge paperwork also was concluded with unusual efficiency. Nine days after his separation from the Marines, on September 20, 1959, passport in hand, Lee departed from the port of New Orleans on a freighter bound for France.[462]

From LeHarve, he went to England to catch a flight to Finland. Researchers have discovered that Lee's itinerary at this point in his journey was very unusual: there were no commercial flights to Helsinki, Finland, matching his arrival there on October 11, 1959.[463] Of course, in his line of business, that would not present a problem that couldn't be easily solved. The CIA often used contract pilots flying private aircraft; remember David Ferrie.

Lee arrived by train in Moscow on October 16, 1959, two days before his twentieth birthday, and booked a room at the Metropole Hotel. He had received a six-day visa to visit the Soviet Union from the Soviet Consulate in Helsinki.[464]

After agent Oswald's arrival in Moscow, his actions indicate that he was not only a part of the CIA's "defector" program, but also an unwitting subject in the Agency's MKULTRA hypno-programming operation, as we shall see ahead. It should be noted here that Richard Helms, CIA Deputy Director of Plans, testifying before the Warren Commission five years later, falsely denied any Agency dealings with Oswald. Helms disavowed that "either in records or in the mind of any individuals that there was any contact had, or even contemplated with him." The fact is Lee's name appears in a 1963 CIA memo in which Helms refers to Agency "interviews with Lee Harvey Oswald" in 1960.[465] There are no other details in the memo. Another indication of Oswald's CIA affiliation is the fact that the young ex-Marine had a "201 file."[466] A 201 is a CIA personnel term that applies to individuals who are either CIA or have a contract with the Agency.

Despite his meager earnings in the Marines, with CIA backing, Oswald had no difficulty financing his travel expenses and accommodations en route to the Soviet Union and back to the United States. Lee had earned a total of $3,452 during his three years in the Marines.[467] Yet, according to the Warren Commission's accounting, Lee still had some $1,500 available for his travel expenses.[468] Clearly, his trip to Europe was funded by his secret employer, not from his own pocket. Since Lee had no known bank accounts, he obviously had a covert source of income that he used to finance his worldwide travels and later to support his young family. Oswald's finances show that he maintained a steady source of income. Indeed, it is telling that his "defection" to the Soviet Union at the height of the Cold War also had no ill effect on his eventual return or the ease with which he obtained government funding in June 1962 upon the conclusion of his Russian assignment.[469]

Lee arrived in Moscow on October 16, 1959 and spent two weeks at his hotel, no doubt preparing for his defection or being prepared by someone else. The prep work involved memorizing his lines for declaring his intentions and writing a letter to document his objective. On October 31, 1959, he entered the US embassy and declared that he was a Marxist and was renouncing his US citizenship. The US officials on duty were Richard E. Synder, the embassy's second secretary, a ten-year CIA career man who had served in Tokyo, and John McVickar, vice consul at the embassy.[470] Of course, they were not the only individuals to hear the announcement. It was known that the US embassy in Moscow was being bugged by the Soviets, and theirs in Washington by the United States.[471] So Oswald's announced defection immediately gave notice to the KGB to begin its assessment procedures of candidate Oswald. Richard Snyder was astute in Agency procedures and may well have known Lee was on a US intelligence mission. At the same time, since Agency operations were compartmentalized—to avoid being compromised—Snyder may not have known the full details of Oswald's status.

Lee presented Snyder his defection letter stating he wished for his US citizenship to be revoked and that he was applying for citizenship in the Soviet Union. The legal language suggests that Lee himself did not write the statement, that it had been prepared for him by his US compatriots either in the embassy or undercover elsewhere in the city.

Lee followed up by launching into a monologue on "American imperialism" and stating that he had information from his Marine days that he had decided to give to the Soviets, implying that his secrets could possibly involve the U-2 flights from Atsugi. Snyder told Oswald to return after the weekend to complete the paperwork.[472]

In real life, the Agency would have made quick work of any former Marine offering secret intelligence to the enemy. Lee would have been under lock and key posthaste. That is, of course, unless Snyder or other US embassy employees were aware of Oswald's mission. In this case, they would have known Lee would be providing disinformation designed to mislead Soviet intelligence, just as he had done at the Queen Bee in Tokyo.

After Oswald had departed the embassy, Snyder called the United Press International bureau in Moscow to give them the news tip. Speaking with the UPI's Robert Korengold, Snyder told him where he could locate Oswald to get the story.[473] Normally, this would not be the kind of news the Agency would publicize. But this case was different. The Agency was creating the Oswald legend—Lee's anti-American cover—by tying the media into his fake defection. The next day, the story hit the wire services and made news in the United States, including Fort Worth, Texas.

One other peculiar element of Oswald's defection announcement was Lee's unusual presentation. Apparently, while speaking to Snyder and McVickar, Lee delivered a monologue, albeit in an articulate manner, praising Marxism and condemning American "oppression." As Snyder recalled, "You could tell he'd been rehearsing. . . ." And McVickar wrote in a memo that it seemed to him Lee "was following a pattern of behavior in which he had been tutored by person or persons unknown."[474] Indeed. Such a performance can be elicited quite easily when the individual is properly conditioned.

After the UPI picked up Lee's story, he was contacted by two reporters with whom he agreed to be interviewed: Aline Mosby of UPI, whose article appeared soon after in Fort Worth, Texas, and Priscilla Johnson of the North American Newspaper Alliance, who interviewed Lee two days later. Both wanted to know Lee's motives and how he felt about leaving America, to which he responded again by parroting Soviet philosophy and themes on capitalist exploitation and class struggle in America. The first interview lasted two hours and the second four hours.[475] Both newswomen reported that Lee seemed to be lecturing them uninterruptedly, as if he were programmed. Again, such behavior occurs when a subject receives the proper conditioning; this is routine in the world of MKULTRA. Interestingly, for Priscilla Johnson, Lee's "defection" may not have been news to her. This is because, in addition to her journalism career, Johnson was working at the time on contract for the CIA. In fact, one of her articles about Oswald, published after his death, was used in a disinformation campaign to advance the legend of Lee as an avowed Marxist.[476]

While Lee anxiously waited in his Moscow hotel room for word from the Soviets regarding his residency status, he wrote home to his mother and his brother Robert. Lee knew there was a good possibility that he could be ejected from the Soviet Union.

After two weeks in Moscow, Oswald was told by Soviet authorities to leave the country,[477] no doubt because of his suspected motives; he had told them of his military background, but they had no proof that his story was true, nor was there any evidence that he had turned to their side. After all, he had been serving with the Marines just weeks earlier at the most secret US spy base in Asia.

At this point in time, according to his diary—which is also suspect—in despair, he allegedly tried to commit suicide by cutting his left wrist. The story states that he was found by a hotel maid in his room and brought to a hospital for stitches and then to an asylum for a few days before being released. Oddly, there are no reports of Lee ever telling anyone about this attempt, not even his wife Marina (described ahead); a scar found on his left arm was listed on the autopsy report, but it was not a deep wound; and finally, there are no Soviet medical records that show that this hospital visit actually happened.[478]

For the next six weeks, from mid-November 1959 to the end of December 1959, there was no sign of Oswald.[479]

Lee knew that his letters were being intercepted by the KGB. He also knew that one way to gain a resident permit would be by gaining KGB approval. Obviously, one of the most effective ways to accomplish this was to criticize America by adding disparaging lines about the United States in the letters home.

Letters allegedly written by Lee in Moscow were intercepted in New York by James Angleton's counterintelligence unit. These letters never made it to their destination in Texas but were instead sent to CIA offices in Washington, DC.[480] In one such letter to his brother Robert, the topic was "why I and my fellow workers and Communists would like to see the capitalist government of the United State overthrown." The letter seems more sophisticated than twenty-year-old Lee was up to writing, without assistance from an Agency writer, unless it was done unwittingly through an MKULTRA session in his room. (And, again, he was writing to gain acceptance by the KGB, which was routinely intercepting and reading letters to the United States.) The letter reads, "workers must form unions against their employers in the United States . . . because the government supports an economic system which exploits all the workers, a system based upon credit which gives rise to the never-ending cycle of depression, inflation, unlimited speculation, and war . . . Look around you, and look at yourself. See the segregation, see the unemployment and what automation is. Remember how you were laid off at Convair?"[481]

An uncharacteristically violent paragraph follows: "I want you to understand what I say now, I do not say lightly, or unknowingly, since I've been in the military as you know, and I know what war is like. . . . In the event of war, I would kill any American who put a uniform on in defense of the American Government—Any American."[482] It is clearly not the style nor content of typical messages between two brothers, unless, in fact, it was written "unknowingly."

Suddenly, on January 4, 1960, Lee was called by Soviet authorities and informed that he would be allowed to stay in the Soviet Union. His anti-American diatribe had worked.

With the words "kill any American," indeed, the letter shows precisely what MKULTRA was designed to do. MKULTRA was a way of creating incriminating evidence that would make it appear that the subject would carry out an assassination for his political beliefs. CIA counterintelligence chief James Angleton and agency writer E. Howard Hunt specialized in these tasks. The violent emotions of this letter also implied that Lee would even kill his own brother. This totally contradicts the nature of his relationship with Robert. In addition, the fact that Robert did not receive the above letter—it came from James Angleton's office[483]—makes it even more suspect.

There were a number of such letters written—most likely prepared during Lee's missing time gap from mid-November through December 1959. Given his circumstances, he no doubt had no knowledge of writing them. In essence, the letters served two purposes: first, to deceive the KGB into believing that Lee was an authentic defector, not a spy, and secondly, to pave the way for Lee's future by painting him as a bona fide Communist suitable for framing for a possible assassination at home.

Soviet authorities issued Oswald a resident permit, not Soviet citizenship, and gave him a job in a radio and television factory in Minsk, the capital of Byelorussia, some five hundred miles southwest of Moscow. He arrived there on January 7, 1960.[484]

Little is known about Oswald's activities in the Soviet Union, and most of our knowledge comes from a diary found with Oswald's belongings in Dallas after the assassination. It would seem to be an important document since the Warren Commission relied on it for information during its investigation, and Richard Helms even used it to support his contention that Lee Harvey Oswald was a typical defector.[485] Yet, the fact is that Helms may well have known a lot more about the diary than anyone else. Indeed, Lee may not have even known of its existence. It is not known when, where, or why the diary was written. It covers the period of Lee's life in Minsk from January 1960 through March 1961, about half of his two-and-a-half-year stay in the Soviet Union.[486] House Committee experts have analyzed the handwriting and stated they believe Lee wrote it, yet it is not written in his articulate, fluid style. However, they also state that it was written in one or two sittings.[487] In addition, based on its factual errors, analysts have determined that it was written at least a year after the dates given. Clearly, this is not a true diary, but one that was faked by someone.

Diaries are a common MKULTRA device. This is because they can provide tangible evidence with a clear motive and with a definite link to a particular individual. The methodology involves drugging and hypnotizing a subject and then commanding the person to write the words they hear, either taped or dictated. Upon completion, the subject has no memory of the writing or the content. The Oswald diary was written in only a day or two because Oswald was merely taking dictation while in an MKULTRA trance, writing a story as told by his CIA handler, a story that would create his "legend," or the appearance of a true defector. Again, he undoubtedly had no memory of writing it. So, while the diary does not furnish an accurate timeline of events in Lee's life in the Soviet Union, it does reveal a clue to his having been manipulated by his Agency handlers.

The diary's fictitious nature is evidenced by the numerous facts regarding events portrayed in the diary that have since been contradicted in witness interviews.

For example, the diary states that Lee's Russian wife Marina (more on their marriage ahead) was hospitalized for five days in September 1961 due to nervous exhaustion. The reason given for her ailment was her fear of being denied permission to leave the country with her husband. However, the facts indicate a totally different story. First of all, Marina denied this occurred, and there are no known hospital records to this effect. In addition, Marina must have been in her government's good graces at this time because the next month, in October 1961, she took a vacation, traveling several hundred miles southeast of Minsk to visit with her uncle Yuri Mikhailov in Kharkov.[488]

Another example of the diary's specious nature is the account of May 1, 1960, which places Lee at a party with friends in Minsk. This is the day that U-2 pilot Francis Gary Powers was shot down and captured by the Soviets. Yet, a couple of years later after Lee returned home, he told friends in Dallas that he had been in Moscow that day at a May Day celebration.[489] (The Soviet Union exchanged Powers for Rudolf Abel, a Soviet spy held in the United States, on February 10, 1962.)

The diary also contradicts itself. One entry has Lee stating that he went to the "theatre, movies, or opera almost every day. I'm living big and am very satisfied."[490] By contrast, another page has Lee complaining, "The money I get has nowhere to be spent. No nightclubs or bowling alleys. No places of recreation except the trade union dances. I have had enough."[491]

Anomalies, or more properly, fabrications, abound in Oswald's life. As with any intelligence operation, outsiders are faced with a hall of mirrors. Another odd example: in conversations in Texas after returning home, Lee told friends about his living quarters in Minsk, complaining how he had to live in a small room with a shared kitchen and bathroom facilities.[492] Yet, in the official view of his life, based on photos found with his belongings, Lee lived in a large apartment with a river view and two balconies, a phonograph, and the latest wardrobe.[493]

Nevertheless, based on interviews and other documents, it appears the following is true: in Minsk in the spring of 1961, Lee met an attractive young woman at a dance and fell in love. Her name was Marina Prusakova, nineteen, a pharmacy assistant at the local hospital. She had grown up in Leningrad, and after her mother died, she had moved to Minsk where she lived with her aunt and uncle. The uncle was Col. Ilya Vasilyevich Prusakov, an officer in the MVD (similar to our FBI), which no doubt made Lee's life more interesting.[494] Lee and Marina married just six weeks later in May 1961.[495] And in the following February, their first child, June, was born.[496]

By 1962, Lee was planning his return home with his new wife and child. The US embassy was efficient and cooperative in handling their passport and visa issues. But the Soviets were less so, allowing the process to drag on for several months.

At the US embassy, one of Lee's contacts was a top CIA asset named Dr. Alexi Davison, a US Air Force captain. He befriended the Oswalds and was particularly helpful to Marina, making sure that she received a proper physical examination. Before they left Russia, Dr. Davison asked them to be sure to look up his mother who lived in Atlanta, Georgia. There is evidence that Lee and Marina's flight stopped in Atlanta en route home to Dallas, but it is not known if they in fact connected.[497]

What is known is that the CIA's Dr. Davison had a vital additional duty at the embassy as a top CIA officer. Several months after the Oswalds had departed, the Soviets released evidence that Dr. Davison was part of the most important CIA spy ring ever uncovered in the USSR. While Dr. Davison made it back safely to his home in Atlanta, his Russian contact, Col. Oleg Penkovsky, was tried by the Soviets and executed. It was Penkovsky's information regarding Soviet missiles that played a key role in helping the United States succeed in defusing the Cuban missile crisis.[498]

The CIA contacts in Lee's life and his travels are legion. Richard Synder at the US embassy expedited Marina's visa application and the State Department made sure she was exempted from immigration quotas. The reasoning: "it was in the interest of the United States."[499] The fact that she was a niece of a Soviet secret police officer and married to a man who had shown the ultimate in disloyalty to his country by offering to disclose top secret military intelligence apparently was unimportant. A true defector may well have faced prosecution for treason or a serious investigation into what information may have been divulged. But in Lee's case, a simple apology was sufficient.

Oswald maintained his cover and prepared to move on to a new assignment, this time in the United States. Under James Angleton and Richard Helms, the CIA had no qualms about conducting domestic operations.[500] And many of these were carried out without the Kennedy administration's knowledge, particularly with regard to anti-Castro Cuban activities in New Orleans and other cities.

In Moscow, as Lee and family were readying to depart, the embassy's Richard Snyder provided Lee with a government loan for $435 to help with travel expenses.[501] On June 1, 1962, the Oswalds took a train to Holland and spent several days in Amsterdam in a rented house. It appears that the layover served as Oswald's Agency debriefing location. The couple, with child, departed from Rotterdam by ship and arrived in Hoboken, New Jersey, on June 13, 1962.[502] Once again, Lee received help from CIA-connected personnel. A man named Spas Raikin, a member of a Travelers Aid society, met the Oswalds at the dock and drove them to a New York City hotel. Raikin had been an officer in the anti-Communist organization called American Friends of Anti-Bolshevik Nations.[503]

Lee's brother Robert also wired two hundred dollars to Lee to help him out with the flight home. The family flew out of New York bound for Fort Worth on June 14, 1962.

The ease of their exit from the Soviet Union and their return to the United States at the height of the Cold War more than hints at Lee's CIA involvement. What's more, Oswald and family had arrived home with financial assistance from a US intelligence front organization.[504] And, finally, most telling is the fact that Lee was not prosecuted for having threatened to disclose knowledge he possessed of US, U-2 intelligence, information that he had acquired in the service.[505] Interestingly, Lee's mother Marguerite is known to have spoken about her twenty-two-year-old son's line of work while he was abroad in 1961, letting out that he was on an undercover intelligence assignment in Russia.[506]

The Oswalds were happily reunited in June 1962 when Lee, Marina, and baby June arrived in Dallas and were met by Lee's brother Robert and wife Vada. They initially stayed at Robert's house in Fort Worth and at Marguerite's for a few weeks until they found their own apartment.[507] At the same time, Lee picked up a job working in a shop, Leslie Welding Company, a louver door factory in Fort Worth.[508]

Lee was inordinately dependent on others because of the fact that he did not have a driver's license and had never learned how to drive a car.[509] So, for Lee, finding a job, securing an apartment, and even grocery shopping were tasks that needed to be carefully arranged. His was not the life of a "loner." Indeed, he was fortunate to have had the security of knowing he had a support network behind him.

The CIA's domestic operations at that time were highly secretive.[510] But, as in the Agency's foreign work, the mission was the same: to *monitor*, that is, to attend meetings of individuals who posed a threat to the national interest; to *infiltrate*, or feign support for the group; and finally, to *penetrate*, which means to lead or direct the group.[511] Ostensibly, the objective of the domestic spying, much of which was illegal, was to unearth connections between groups in the United States and funding sources in Moscow or elsewhere in the Communist world. But this was merely pretense. Helms and company knew that the 1947 CIA Charter prohibited domestic spying without Congressional authorization; this turf belonged to the FBI.[512] Helms also knew that his MKULTRA programs—in which numerous individuals in the United States were drugged, hypnotized, conditioned, and continually monitored—were totally out of bounds. As a result, Helms sought to make CIA activities at home appear linked to foreign operations. The CIA's overall domestic spying project, which would formally become known as Operation CHAOS in 1967, carried out mail openings and the monitoring of antiwar student groups such as SDS (Student for a Democratic Society).[513] Some of the CIA's suspected domestic targets in the early 1960s included the ACLU (American Civil Liberties Union), CORE (Congress of Racial Equality), and FPCC (Fair Play for Cuba Committee).[514] In Lee's case, it appears that he did not know until the end of his short life that his assignments were also designed to make him appear to be working for the enemy, not just posing as one.

The CIA's Domestic Contact Service section head in Dallas at that time was J. Walton Moore. Another individual, believed to have been a longtime CIA asset and friend of Moore's, was a Russian immigrant named George de Mohrenschildt, fifty-one. The two, along with de Mohrenschildt's wife Jeanne, would dine together every couple of weeks at George and Jeanne's Dallas home. Moore also knew Lee Harvey Oswald and asked George to link up with the young newcomer.[515] George took his job seriously. According to his attorney, Patrick Russell, the relationship between Oswald and de Mohrenschildt was "deeper than friendship," and he once stated, "I personally have always felt that George was a CIA agent."[516]

Despite their twenty-eight-year age difference, Oswald and George de Mohrenschildt shared the bond of intelligence work. In the 1950s, George had traveled for months inside Yugoslavia while working as a petroleum engineer for a CIA subsidiary, American CoOperation Administration. This organization was a predecessor of another CIA front, the Agency for International Development.[517] De Mohrenschildt was quite successful in obtaining important intelligence for the CIA. In fact, his usefulness was acknowledged by Richard Helms in a memo he wrote at the time.[518] Upon returning from his mission to Eastern Europe, George was debriefed in Dallas by agent Moore.[519]

Sen. Richard S. Schweiker of Pennsylvania once stated, while serving on the Church Committee in 1975, the "fingerprints of intelligence" were all over Oswald's background.[520] Indeed, the same can be said of George de Mohrenschildt.

De Mohrenschildt was born in Russia in 1911, the son of nobility. He fled at a young age to Poland during the Bolshevik revolution. During World War II, he was a spy—some sources claim he worked for the Allies, and some say he was with the Nazis.[521] As noted earlier, Richard Helms and other OSS officers had recruited Nazi spies after the war to counter the Soviet threat. At any rate, de Mohrenschildt served as a spy in Mexico during World War II and worked in Latin America for US oil companies after the war had ended. In 1952, he settled in Dallas.[522] There he became a loyal Republican, a passionate anti-Communist, and a well-known member of the White Russian Community. He was known as a world traveler, yet had no discernible income and lived very comfortably.[523] Besides working in Yugoslavia, he spent months in Guatemala at the same time a CIA base there was preparing anti-Castro Cubans to launch the Bay of Pigs invasion.[524] Later, he worked in Haiti when the CIA was planning a coup in that country. He reportedly received two hundred thousand dollars in a Haitian bank account shortly after the Kennedy assassination.[525]

De Mohrenschildt's son-in-law, Gary Taylor, who was married for a time to George's daughter Alexandra, saw George's influence on Lee Harvey Oswald firsthand. Taylor once stated "whatever his [de Mohrenschildt's] suggestions were, Lee grabbed them and took them, whether it was what time to go to bed or where to stay."[526] As Oswald's closest friend in the fall of 1962, George de Mohrenschildt introduced Lee and Marina to several residents who were part of an elite social network connected to the Russian-speaking community in Dallas. George also arranged parties in the fall and winter of 1962 for them, although most of his guests appear to have been non-émigrés. For example, one of his parties included four geologists, all from Magnolia Laboratories, which was located in the Dallas-Fort Worth area: Volkman Schmidt, Everett Glover, Richard Pierce, and Norman Fredricksen. Norman was the son of the director of Radio Free Europe, a government propaganda service.[527] They all wanted to hear about Lee's discoveries in the USSR. Even today—given Russia's prodigious oil and gas reserves—geologists are intrigued by Russia. Other guests at George's parties included two individuals from the defense industry: attorney Max Clark, former head of security at Convair Aircraft Corporation (his wife Gali was a Russian immigrant),[528] and Michael Paine, a man known as a "creative genius" at Bell Helicopter.[529] Paine's wife, Ruth, was also introduced to the Oswalds and became close to Marina. When both wives were temporarily separated from their husbands, they would stay together at Ruth's home. Ruth, a matronly woman, was temporarily separated from Michael soon after the Oswalds' arrival, so she invited Marina Oswald to stay with her at times when Lee was away from home. Interestingly, Ruth's father, William Avery Hyde, had retired from AID, the same CIA-backed agency that Michael Paine's brother was working for and which George de Mohrenschildt had worked with.[530]

After three months working at the welding shop, Lee took up George de Mohrenschildt's suggestion to move to Dallas and a new job.[531] Not surprisingly, the new assignment involved photographic work connected to U-2 spy plane photos. The firm, Jaggars-Chiles-Stovall, an aerial photo maps and graphics company, held military contracts for specialized or classified intelligence printing work.[532] According to Jay Edward Epstein's *Legend*, Lee was missing again for one month at this time—his residence unknown.[533]

This same time frame was one of the most perilous in US history—the Cuban Missile Crisis. A U-2 reconnaissance flyover had picked up signs of Soviet nuclear missile sites being installed in Cristobal, Cuba on October 14, 1962. For thirteen days the world waited, fearing we had reached the brink of extinction. President Kennedy overruled his generals who wanted to bomb Cuba. He chose to implement a blockade and quarantine. He also began secret negotiations via cable messages with Soviet Premier Khrushchev. Finally, on October 28, 1962, the Russians gave up and sent word that they would dismantle their missiles and launchers and send them home.[534]

For anyone connected with the U-2 intelligence program, no doubt, during this crisis, all bets were off. Presidential advisors in the Oval Office and the War Room were viewing photographic enlargements of the U-2 evidence on a minute-by-minute basis around the clock. And, again, Lee was on the front lines at a firm that processed such photos. According to Jeanne de Mohrenschildt and her daughter Alexandra, George had assisted in placing Lee at Jaggars-Chiles-Stovall. Lee lived initially at the YMCA for a few days until he found an apartment.[535]

Rather than "missing," it is probably more accurate to say that Lee was not allowed to disclose where he was during this time period of a national emergency. As tensions rose, so did caution, particularly for those in intelligence.

After the crisis had passed, Lee found another apartment, this one on Elisabeth Street. He moved in on November 4, 1962, and Marina arrived two weeks after. Later that November, Lee, Marina, and their daughter June enjoyed Thanksgiving dinner at brother Robert's house in Fort Worth. It was a special occasion as Lee's half-brother brother John Pic and his family were there to join in the family reunion.[536]

It was during this time that Lee's finances were stabilizing. He paid back the two hundred dollar debt to his brother, the money he had borrowed for the flight to Dallas-Fort Worth from New York.[537] He also retired his State Department loan of $435, funds he had used to help finance his family's departure from the Soviet Union.[538]

Oswald worked steadily for six months at the Jaggars-Chiles-Stovall graphics company, from October 1962 to April 1963.[539] Interestingly, a fellow worker who trained him on the cameras and printing equipment was also an intelligence alum. His name was Dennis Ofstein, the same age as Lee, and he, too, was a Russian language specialist. He had served in the Army Security Agency, which is part of the National Security Agency. The two men became close and spoke in Russian with each other. When Lee told him he had worked in Minsk, Dennis said he just assumed it was for the US military.[540] Lee would discuss with him various types of Soviet military equipment and facilities, according to Dennis. This was an interest Lee also shared with his mentor George de Mohrenschildt.[541] While Lee maintained his cover as a leftist, he was also very close to de Mohrenschildt, whose beliefs were far to the right. Indeed, George was a dominant presence in his life and helped him out at important junctures in his life. In intelligence terms, George fit the profile of an Agency "handler."

Lee's role in the intelligence community while based at Jaggars-Chiles-Stovall consisted of working with classified aerial photos and translating signs and other Russian words from Cyrillic to English as needed. However, more intense and more public missions lay ahead for Lee. He would work in New Orleans in the summer of 1963 and back again in Dallas in the fall of 1963. As we shall see, his work appears to have been monitoring the anti-Castro and the pro-Castro camps in those cities, ostensibly to ferret out foreign spies. But it was this cover—Lee as a leftist—that also would be used to create a motive and in turn facilitate his being framed for President Kennedy's assassination.

Turning briefly to Lee's homelife, we can see that here, too, all is not as it seems. If we look at the record, Lee's wife Marina said her husband had been "a good family man" in her February 4, 1964 Warren Commission interview. It was in her September 1964 interviews that she changed her story.[542] No doubt she feared deportation if she did not, as we shall see ahead. As a result of her later stories, some authors have portrayed Oswald as an abusive spouse. Clearly, Lee was not a violent man; this evidence was no doubt manufactured to impugn Lee's character. According to accounts from his family and acquaintances, Lee was essentially unostentatious, a man who cared deeply for his wife and child, who had friends, and who paid his bills.

Again, this picture contrasts sharply with the official version of Oswald's life. There are many reasons for this. As noted earlier, Lee's letters and his "diary" were specifically designed to paint him as a potential assassin. In Agency MKULTRA experiments, such documents were produced in the subject's own handwriting through the use of drugs and hypnosis, a process called "automatic writing." The writings were accomplished by having the drugged and hypnotized subject respond to a stimulus, for example, being commanded to take dictation, to transcribe a tape, or simply to answer questions in writing, after which the subject would have no memory of the writings.

This conditioning or programming as described above also involved post-hypnotic suggestions whereby commands could be given to the subject that would be triggered at a later time—without the subject recalling the source of the command.

The symptoms that Lee exhibited prior to his arrival in Dallas, his rapid speech while lecturing as if by rote, and automatic writing—all signs of MKULTRA hypno-programming and manipulation—began to reoccur in the fall of 1962. Another indication of conditioning is a peculiar facial expression described as a half-grin, yet sullen look and glaring eyes.[543] Yet another is irritableness that was not there before.[544]

Edward Jay Epstein, in his book *Legend*, described episodes of Lee's exhibiting these symptoms at various dinner parties with Dallas's White Russian community. At one get-together, Lee gave a three-hour lecture on American policies regarding Cuba.[545] He referred to the United States as "imperialist," and reportedly appeared "obsessed" with the subject.[546] At another time, he sat in silence wearing the "half-smile and squinty eyes."[547] Not surprisingly, Marina wanted time away from him, and several times she did, in fact, accept a standing invitation from Ruth Paine to temporarily move in with her.[548]

Again, one side effect of conditioning, suggested by investigator Philip Melanson, is exhibiting irritability. In Lee's case, apparent conditioning had instilled in him a feeling of anger that his family and friends had noticed. It is not difficult to imagine being very annoyed at not knowing what was happening to oneself. Imagine not recalling recent events that had happened in one's life and the lives of others, having strange feelings and desires, and exhibiting new behaviors. While some pundits also have suggested that Oswald was deranged, there is no evidence of this. In fact, the military doctors who evaluated Lee in the Marines found him to be a normally functioning person.

During this time in Dallas, Lee had opened a post office box. In January 1963, he reportedly received a mail order pistol, a .38 caliber Smith & Wesson, for $29.95, from Seaport Traders of Los Angeles.[549] The weapon was ordered by A. J. Hidell. Not long after this, a rifle was ordered and received at the same post office box, also for A. J. Hidell.[550] However, it is not known if Lee actually placed these orders, nor if he picked them up.[551] If Lee had been planning to shoot someone, he certainly would not have bought a gun through mail order. He simply would have purchased one at a local gun shop to avoid a paper trail.

While Lee may have felt a pistol would be necessary for protection in the dangerous world of covert operations, the rifle purchase was hardly an item in which he would have had any interest. His handlers, on the other hand, had considerable need for Lee to be linked to these weapons, particularly if he were to be set up as a fall guy and framed for murder.

The named buyer of the weapons, A. J. Hidell, was thought by the Warren Commission to be Oswald's alias. A forged draft card with the name Alek James Hidell with a photo of Lee reportedly appeared in Lee's billfold after the assassination. However, Dallas police Sgt. Gerald Hill, who first emptied the wallet, made no mention of this card during an interview with radio newsmen that day.[552] The fake ID evidently was added afterwards to try to connect Lee to the weapons.

Lee had an acquaintance who had served in the Marines with him whose nickname was "Hidell," John Rene Heindel of New Orleans.[553] The name also appeared as A. J. Hidell, Chapter President, on a membership card for the Fair

Play For Cuba organization, which also was found on Lee.[554] As we shall see ahead, this organization, FPCC, had no members in Dallas nor New Orleans, the two cities Lee worked in; the membership card was simply a part of Lee's cover.[555]

The rifle allegedly used in the assassination was shipped on March 20, 1963 from Klein's Sporting Goods in Chicago to A. Hidell at post office box 2915 in Dallas. It was a single-shot, bolt-action, World War II Mannlicher-Carcano 6.5 mm. The cost was $21.45.[556] It should be noted that following the assassination, Dallas detectives found no fingerprints on the rifle. It then was sent by the FBI to Washington for analysis. Bureau experts also found no fingerprints on it, and it was returned to Dallas. Back in Dallas, a palm print allegedly was found under the barrel when the gun was in a disassembled state.[557] To many researchers, the only way a print could have been missed was if it were taken later from Oswald's body. (And this could have been accomplished through a simple black-bag job at the local morgue.)

At the same time that the rifle was allegedly purchased, in March of 1963, the Oswalds had moved to 214 West Neely Street in Dallas, to a second-floor apartment with a small terrace in back. It was here, according to the official version, that Lee was photographed while holding a rifle in one hand, a leftist newspaper in the other, and wearing a pistol on his belt. This photo and a similar one were allegedly found in Lee's belongings in Ruth Paine's garage following the assassination. Lee was shown one of the pictures in jail and he denied it was him. He stated that it was faked. The photo showed his face superimposed on a photo of someone else, he stated. He also added that he was familiar with photography (having worked at Jaggars-Chiles-Stovall).[558] When the photo was published on the cover of *Life* magazine on February 21, 1964, it made short work of Lee in the eyes of public opinion.[559]

Photo experts have since analyzed the prints and found clear evidence that the shots were faked. One of the experts was Major John Pickard of the Canadian Department of Defense and another was past president of the Evidence Photographers International Counsel, detective Malcolm Thompson, who was recommended by Kodak and Scotland Yard.[560]

Their analysis found, first, that the shadows on the face do not correspond to the shadows on the ground—the face shot was taken when the sun was high in the sky, and the body shot was taken when the sun was low in the sky. Secondly, the chin on the face does not resemble Lee's. It is square, while Lee's is more pointed. And third, the experts discovered a faint line that reveals the demarcation between the body shot and the pasted-on head.[561]

Another discrepancy in the photo was found in the comparison of the size of the Mannlicher-Carcano to the height of Oswald. Measuring the two, experts found a significant difference between the photo and the true measurements of Lee and of the rifle: either the man is five inches shorter than Lee, or the rifle is 2.4 inches longer than the Mannlicher-Carcano.[562]

Finally, the photos were obviously shot on a sunny day. Marina Oswald told the Warren Commission that she had taken the incriminating pictures on March 31, 1963. Yet according to US Weather Bureau reports for that day in Dallas, it was a cloudy, rainy day.[563]

Obviously, the Warren Commission's claim that Marina Oswald took the pictures is a fabrication. With respect to the camera used, similar problems developed.

First, it should be noted that police did discover photo equipment with Lee's belongings in Ruth Paine's garage. One item was a Minox,[564] a small West German camera that uses 9.2 mm film, about one-quarter the size of 35 mm film. The Minox has a close-focusing lens and is designed for copying documents. It is an espionage camera and yet another indication of Lee's actual profession.

As for the camera allegedly used in the backyard, Marina told investigators on February 6, 1964 that she could not remember what type of camera was used, American or Russian. On February 18, she stated that the camera was grey and boxlike. On February 25, she was shown a photo of an Imperial Reflex camera and she said that that was it. A small American-made camera was reportedly obtained by Lee's brother Robert from the Paine home two weeks after the assassination, despite the fact that Dallas police had thoroughly searched the house several times before that date and had not found it. Robert reportedly turned this camera over to the FBI on February 24, 1964. Researchers have noted the lack of credibility of this chain of evidence since on this particular issue, no witness interviews or testimony exist.[565]

The alleged photos of Lee with a rifle were found in the Paine garage by Dallas police. Interestingly, no other photos, such as snapshots of the Oswald family, were found anywhere. After a number of searches, the rifle photos suddenly appeared. It should be noted that the discovery by Dallas police occurred when Ruth Paine had left the house to go grocery shopping, leaving the house open for investigators.[566] She had allowed the authorities complete access to her house even when she went to the store, thus making the planting of photos and a camera a simple operation.

The handlers of Lee Harvey Oswald were obviously proficient in the dirty tricks department. They had covertly sent at least two operatives to Lee's back yard, including a photographer and an accomplice dressed in black, bringing with them a rifle, the newspaper, and a pistol. They took the shots and later in the lab pasted a portrait of Lee over the face, rephotographed it, and printed new copies. Later, after the assassination, the photos and the camera were planted with Lee's belongings in the garage at Ruth Paine's, the house in Irving where Marina was staying at that point in early December 1963. In the aftermath of the assassination, Marina knew that if her husband could be framed so convincingly, without anyone speaking up on his behalf, a similar fate could befall her and her daughters if she did not go along with the program. (Oswald's second child, Rachel, was born on October 20, 1963, a month before the assassination.) Indeed, Marina lied prodigiously to the FBI and to Warren Commission counsel simply because she was afraid that if she did not say what the investigators wanted her to say, she would be deported.[567]

Returning to where we left off, the previous spring on West Neely Street, Lee's work at Jaggars-Chiles-Stovall was winding down and his more public political activities were about to begin. In March of 1963, Lee was notified by his supervisor that his job at the photographic defense contractor lab would end on April 5, 1963. He had been working there for six months. When Lee's friend Dennis Ofstein heard the news, he asked Lee what he planned to do next. Lee answered cheerfully that he could be going back to Russia.[568] He was keeping in character. Lee's acting as if his goal was to be able to return to the Soviet Union, via Mexico and Cuba, was part of his cover, a theme in his legend. However, his immediate destination was New Orleans where he would get to meet with a number of anti-Castro Cuban leaders while at the same time posing as a pro-Castro activist.

Lee's departure from Jaggars-Chiles-Stovall in April 1963 was reportedly due to too many errors in his photographic work.[569] Earlier, Lee had left Leslie Welding in Fort Worth after three months. Lee and George de Mohrenschildt had spoken at the time about his having been fired, yet Lee's supervisor at Leslie Welding had reported that his work had been fine. In fact, the job at Leslie Welding had led to Lee's assignment at Jaggars-Chiles-Stovall.[570] But whether Lee quit or was fired from his multiple jobs, one thing is clear: Lee's handlers wanted to create a work history for Lee that gave the appearance of Lee as being an "unstable" character, one who could not hold onto a job. And in this effort, they were successful.

On April 10, 1963, during Lee's first week at home after leaving the photographics business, an incident occurred in Dallas that made it into *The New York Times*. A retired Army Major General, Edwin A. Walker, was shot at that night while sitting in his study at home. The gunman missed.[571] According to the police, the shot had come through a window in the back of the house. A witness who heard the shot, Walter Kirk Coleman, a neighborhood teenager, said he saw two men escape by car.[572] The police reported that they had investigated an incident outside the general's home two nights earlier when two men were spotted checking out the Walker house.[573] In addition, another neighbor, Ms. Ross Bouve, stated that she owned a dog that routinely barked at strangers, but on that night, the dog was silent. She said her dog was "very sick" the next two days and that she believed that someone must have drugged her dog.[574] The gunman and accomplice were never found. The evidence that detectives recovered from a wall in General Walker's house indicated that a 30.06 had been fired. (Which, by the way, is distinctly different from the 6.5 mm gauge of the alleged Oswald rifle.)

After the assassination of President Kennedy and Lee's subsequent murder, Marina Oswald stated in an FBI interview on December 3, 1963 that it was Lee who had fired the shot that narrowly missed General Walker,[575] despite the fact that there was no evidence linking Lee to the incident or to the rifle.[576] Ahead we will examine Marina's credibility, her palpable fear for her future, and the Warren Commission's take on her story. But first, it is interesting to note who General Walker was.

General Edwin Walker was not a favorite of President Kennedy's, and the feeling was mutual. Walker was a former infantry commander who regularly preached right-wing propaganda and John Birch Society views to his troops—in violation of federal law. In Walker's view of the world, Harvard University and even *Mad* magazine were agents of Communism.[577] The general considered Kennedy "weak" on Communism and unwilling to confront the Soviets militarily.

President Kennedy reacted to these assaults from the right by delivering speeches across the country attacking the paranoid right wing in the military. He stated that America's "basic good sense . . . has always prevailed," and he expressed confidence that Americans would ignore the war-mongers among us.[578] At the same time, his Secretary of Defense, Robert McNamara, warned Congress, "the military establishment is an instrument—not a shaper—of national policy."[579]

In September of 1962, retired General Walker showed up in Oxford, Mississippi, where James Merideth sought to become the first black student at the University of Mississippi. Walker, a die-hard segregationist, joined the battle lines opposing integration. In the ensuing riot, two men were killed and

166 wounded.[580] Outraged, Attorney General Robert Kennedy ordered Walker arrested, held in a psychiatric prison in Missouri, and charged with insurrection. His lawyers appealed to friends in Congress who had Walker released.[581] Seven months later, in April 1963, Walker was shot at in his Dallas home.

Less than one year after the shooting, Marina Oswald became the main witness to the Warren Commission who tried to involve Lee in the Walker murder attempt. In her story, she stated that Lee had said he was going to typing class that night, April 10, 1963, and that he came home late and told her what he had done. She said he told her he had buried the rifle near some railroad tracks. George de Mohrenschildt and his wife Jeanne visited Lee and Marina, at West Neely St. three days later, on Saturday night, April 13, 1963. During the Warren Commission hearings, Jeanne added to Marina's story when she said she had noticed a rifle in a closet at the Oswalds. This contradicted Marina, who had stated that Lee had dug up the rifle on Sunday night; it would have still been in the ground on Saturday. Marina then changed her story to say Lee brought the gun home late on Saturday. And then George added to the story, saying that they had arrived so late at the Oswalds on Saturday that they awakened Marina and Lee.[582] By this juncture, the credibility of both Marina and the de Mohrenschildts had reached the breaking point.

To add to the Walker story, Ruth Paine told authorities during the investigation that the Secret Service had found a note inserted in a book she had sent to Marina. The note was in Russian allegedly written by Lee to Marina. Marina claimed it pertained to instructions Lee left for her in case something happened to him. It listed mundane items he had taken care of, such as having paid the rent and the water and gas bills, the location of his personal papers file, and the location of the post office. There were also requests for her to contact the embassy if anything happened to him, to save press clippings "should there be anything about (him) in the newspapers," and finally, he provided her with the location of the jail, if he were "alive and taken prisoner." The note is undated and unsigned. Marina claimed it was left before the Walker incident.[583]

Two major problems with this note are, first, there is no question that there would have been press clippings if Lee were to have been arrested for a shooting. Secondly, the embassy would have quickly distanced itself from Marina for political reasons if she were in any way connected to the shooting of a public official.[584] Clearly, the note is not related to the Walker incident. Most likely it portends to Lee's very real concerns regarding his own future, given the nature of his undercover work, and the security of his family. In the event that his handlers turned on him and he disappeared or died trying to prevent a coup attempt, Lee wanted to ensure that his wife was prepared. In such a scenario, Lee wanted his wife to maintain his records until he returned, and if he did not come back, he sensed that Marina would find that the Soviet Embassy could be more helpful to her.

In analyzing Marina's General Walker story, it is important to note the fact that the Warren Commission also knew that Marina had at one point ridiculously stated that Lee had tried to assassinate Richard Nixon![585] Nixon was not even close to their area at the time.[586] As Norman Redlich, assistant to J. Lee Rankin, the Warren Commission's General Counsel, stated, "Marina Oswald has lied to the Secret Service, the FBI, and this (Warren) Commission on matters of vital concern. . . ."[587] Marina admitted as much, stating on February 4, 1962, during the investigation, "If I didn't want to answer, they told me that if I wanted to live in this country, I would have to help in this matter. . . ."[588] And Robert Oswald testified, "they were implying that if she did not cooperate . . . in so many words, that they would perhaps deport her from the United States and back to Russia."[589]

In evaluating Marina Oswald's fabrications regarding the photos, the camera, and the rifle, one is left with the strong impression that individuals from MKULTRA were no doubt at the ready to help her when it appeared that she had trouble remembering her story.

The bottom line is that Marina was coached.[590] And the Warren Commission's acceptance of Marina's story is evidence of the insidious nature of the framing of Lee Harvey Oswald. The Walker incident shows the depth of planning and the level of expertise of which Lee's handlers were capable. As noted, James Angleton and E. Howard Hunt were known to specialize in such operations. Whether a Walker enemy had tried to shoot him, or whether the shooting was staged, the event produced a major payoff down the road in establishing a bio for Lee as a political assassin in order to cover up the true conspiracy.

During the last three weeks of April 1963, after leaving Jaggars, Lee worked to establish his bona fides in various undercover intelligence tasks. Initially, these entailed contacting leftist organizations and obtaining their literature and distributing it on street corners. These routine operations were designed in order for Lee to start the process of making contacts and obtaining information from left-wing extremists, as well as their opponents on the radical right. At this time, one of the CIA's key goals was to link domestic leftist groups to the Soviet Union or Cuba to discredit them and to legitimize the CIA's spying at home. According to a FBI memo, the CIA had informed the Bureau that it was planning to "plant deceptive information that might embarrass the Committee (the Fair Play for Cuba Committee)."[591] For his part, Lee wrote to the American Communist Party newspaper, *The Worker*, and to the Socialist Workers' Party national headquarters. He informed them that he was available if they needed photographic work done "for the cause."[592] He also subscribed to *The Worker* and the *Militant* newspapers. In mid-April, Lee was reportedly seen one day handing out pro-Castro literature in Dallas at Main and Ervay Streets.[593] And on April 21, 1963, he wrote to the Fair Play for Cuba Committee (FPCC) office in New York City asking for pamphlets, applications, and membership cards.[594] In the letter, he wrote that while distributing literature he had worn a sign that read HANDS OFF CUBA, VIVA FIDEL![595]

As a side note, it is interesting that the FBI reported to the Warren Commission that it had seen these letters (having intercepted them) prior to the assassination. The Bureau said it gained access to them as part of its follow-up work with those who were "defectors." This being the case, it is odd that they did not detect the arrival of a rifle and a pistol at Box 2915, Lee's Dallas post office box. That is, unless, of course, the weapons never reached their destination (i.e., they were intercepted by Lee's handlers).[596]

It was through Lee's letter-writing and pamphleteering activities that Lee's handlers were able to reinforce the image of Lee as a Marxist and to start building his public reputation as being anti-American and a potential assassin. As for Lee's true affiliations, FBI investigators reported during the Warren Commission investigation that despite Lee's activities, he was not, in fact, a Communist Party member in Dallas nor in New Orleans. He never attended a Communist Party meeting and was unknown in Communist Party circles in both cities.[597] Furthermore, of Lee's associates, none were leftists; George de Mohrenschildt, David Ferrie, and Guy Banister were all right wingers.[598]

Ten days after the de Mohrenschildts had visited the Oswalds in April 1963, Lee and Marina left Dallas. The Oswalds and the de Mohrenschildts would not meet again. Marina and June, the baby, moved in with Ruth Paine in Irving on April 23, 1963. The next day, Lee gathered his belongings into his duffel bags and took a bus to New Orleans; their plan was for Marina to join him when he was settled in an apartment and into his new job. Meanwhile, this same week, the de Mohrenschildts also left Dallas. On May 1, 1963, the de Mohrenschildts departed for an extended stay in Haiti. George, the "petroleum engineer," reportedly had been contracted by the Haitian government's Francois "Papa Doc" Duvalier for work involving developing "various natural resources."[599]

According to information obtained by the House Assassinations Committee, George also took a trip to Washington, DC in May 1963, during which he met with CIA officials for reasons unknown. The Committee also discovered that following the assassination, de Mohrenschildt received between $200,000 and $250,000 in his Haitian bank account. No additional details are available.[600]

The close friendship of George and Lee became a subject of intense interest when the House Select Committee on Assassinations convened fourteen years later. As the Committee's investigation into President Kennedy's assassination progressed, George de Mohrenschildt was tracked down in South Florida by freelance writer Edward J. Epstein and separately by Committee investigator Gaeton Fonzi. Epstein met first with George in a Palm Beach hotel. Fonzi arranged an appointment with George's daughter Alexandra for his interview with him at home.[601] On March 29, 1977, several hours before they were to meet, George de Mohrenschildt was found dead in his bedroom. The cause of death was apparently due to a 20-gauge shotgun blast to the mouth. The coroner reported his death a suicide.[602] However, his widow Jeanne later told reporters that she believed that her husband was murdered. She said George worked in intelligence. She also stated that she believed that Oswald was in US intelligence as well. She called Lee "a very kind, very meek person," and she said that both she and George believed that Lee was innocent in the assassination of President Kennedy.[603]

Moving to New Orleans in late April 1963 was a homecoming of sorts for Lee Harvey Oswald. He was born in the Big Easy, and as noted earlier, had left to live in Texas and in New York and had come back with his mother in his teenage years. He had been a member of David Ferrie's Civil Air Patrol unit there and a year later had enlisted in the Marines. Lee's first call on his return to New Orleans on April 25, 1963 was to his aunt Lillian Murret and her husband Charles "Dutz" Murret, who invited him to stay at their house. They had helped out Lee and his mother when they lived in New Orleans during Lee's childhood. It was a colorful household given Dutz's line of work—he was a bookmaker for the Carlos Marcello mob family. At this point in time, Marcello was fighting a deportation order by Attorney General Robert Kennedy. The case was due to come in court in November 1963.[604]

Lee stayed with the Murrets for three weeks and spent time getting reacquainted with them and with a favorite cousin Marilyn Murret, a school teacher. Soon Lee found an apartment at 4907 Magazine Street in the center of the city. When he called Marina at Ruth Paine's house for them to arrange to come down, Marina told Ruth and baby June, "Papa loves us."[605] Ruth Paine drove Marina and the baby to be with Lee at the new apartment in early May 1963. Marina reportedly enjoyed the change of scenery and walks with Lee in the French Quarter.

Lee started his job on May 9, 1963, working as a machine repairman at a downtown coffee shop located not far from his apartment, the William B. Reily Company.[606] Reily was an avid right-winger and "financial supporter" of the Free Cuba Committee, which was part of a CIA-front organization, the anti-Castro Cuban Revolutionary Council (CRC). The CRC was connected to both Cuban exile and Mafia activities.[607] And just around the corner from Reily's, at 544 Camp Street, was the office of Lee's friend David Ferrie whose work involved flying commando raids over Cuba in support of CIA-backed anti-Castro Cuban organizations. Ferrie worked for Guy Banister. Banister, as noted above, was an ex-Naval intelligence officer and former Chicago FBI bureau chief. At this point, he was living in New Orleans and was allegedly supplying weapons for CIA-backed, anti-Castro, Cuban organizations. His cover was Guy Banister Associates, a detective agency. He was a John Bircher, a Minuteman, and the founder of the Anti-Communist League of the Caribbean. He was also an alcoholic and a man known to be violent. His secretary, Delphine Roberts, has reported that he regularly worked with anti-Castro Cuban militants and that he received CIA funding.[608]

According to a 1967 CIA memo, disclosed through the Freedom of Information Act, there were twenty-six CIA employees at this time in New Orleans running various operations, including a mail-intercept program.[609] One agency member was Clay Shaw, also known as Clay Bertrand, a local businessman who ran the International Trade Mart. Shaw had served with the army as a military intelligence officer during World War II and after the war joined the CIA's Domestic Operations Division.[610] According to the CIA's Victor Marchetti, Shaw, along with David Ferrie, E. Howard Hunt, and others had assisted in the CIA's planning of the Bay of Pigs invasion.[611] As noted earlier, it was Clay Shaw who in 1967 was charged by New Orleans District Attorney Jim Garrison with conspiracy to assassinate the president.[612] Richard Helms was so concerned over the matter that he requested CIA personnel in New Orleans to help Shaw.[613] At the end of the trial, which was made famous in Oliver Stone's film *JFK*, the jury decided it did not have enough evidence. Shaw was found innocent on March 1, 1969.[614]

One focus of the Agency's efforts in 1963 was to support the Cuban Revolutionary Council, noted above, a CIA front that received millions of dollars in funding. The CRC's mission was to recruit Cuban exiles for the planned war on Castro's Cuba. E. Howard Hunt, based primarily in Miami, oversaw key elements of this recruiting program.[615] And in New Orleans, the CRC's main office was located at 544 Camp Street, the same old three-story building that served as the office of Guy Banister. Banister's secretary and her daughter, who maintained a photo studio one floor above Banister's office, both stated that they had seen Lee Harvey Oswald visiting with Guy Banister.[616] Another guest of Banister's was none other than the top Mafia liaison to the CIA, Johnny Rosselli. According to Mrs. Roberts, Rosselli visited Banister several weeks before the assassination.[617]

Banister's relationship with David Ferrie apparently was very close. Ferrie assisted Banister's organization as a pilot and from time to time flew mob boss Carlos Marcello of New Orleans, who was a player in the CIA's attempts to kill Fidel Castro. Ferrie also instructed anti-Castro recruits at a camp outside New Orleans. On at least one occasion, Ferrie brought Lee with him to observe the ongoing guerilla training.[618] It was soon after this that the FBI raided the Lake Ponchartrain camp, in accordance with the Kennedy administration's wishes for the sabotage of Cuba to cease. The federal agents picked up a ton of TNT and materials for making napalm and apprehended eleven Cuban exiles and mob associates, all of whom, using their CIA connections, were released shortly after.[619].

Another CIA agent in New Orleans who knew Ferrie and Banister, and was aware of Lee's meeting with them was William Gaudet, a twenty-year veteran. Gaudet stated in a 1977 interview that although he knew Oswald, he did not know what he was working on. Concerning the Kennedy assassination, Gaudet stated that he felt Lee was innocent.[620]

Clearly, Lee Harvey Oswald's role in the world of Banister and Ferrie and CIA operations in New Orleans was simply a continuation of the undercover tasks he had been performing for six years—first in Japan with the Marines and later in the USSR as a "defector."

Thirteen years later, this topic of Lee's activities in New Orleans was raised by Colorado senator Gary Hart at a Senate Intelligence Committee hearing in 1976. Senator Hart asked, "Was (Oswald's) public identification with the left a cover for a connection with the anti-Castro right?"[621] While Helms and Angleton stonewalled such lines of inquiry, this was clearly the case. Oswald's assignment in New Orleans was ostensibly for him to pose as a leftist until the Agency could eventually place him as a mole inside Cuba. Working "behind enemy lines," he would be able to obtain and transmit valuable human intelligence data back to the United States. We also know, of course, Lee's leftist role-playing was simultaneously—and covertly—intended by his Agency handlers to ultimately frame him, when the time was right.

No doubt Lee was told by his handlers that he was the perfect candidate to go to Cuba—that he had all the right stuff—all he needed was for Cuban intelligence to notice him protesting against the United States on TV, and he would win their approval. Lee soon began implementing a series of media events or incidents that would draw the attention of local radio and TV news reporters. Again, Lee had already lived the life of a covert operator in Japan and in the USSR. But for this twenty-three-year-old spy, to be a mole in Cuba— the island nation ninety miles from US shores that was still a flashpoint in international relations—was a rare opportunity. To accomplish this objective, he would have to be accepted as a fervent believer in Castro's cause. And due to US restrictions, he would need a visa from a third country, such as Mexico, to be able to then travel to Cuba.

To establish his credentials, Lee wrote to the Fair Play For Cuba headquarters in the end of May 1963. He indicated that he intended to start a local chapter of the FPCC in New Orleans.[622] Lee also had one thousand pamphlets printed with the headline: "Hands Off Cuba!" He listed his office address on the inside back cover. It read "544 Camp Street, New Orleans, LA," which was Guy Banister's address.[623]

From May through August 1963, Lee stayed in New Orleans with his wife and daughter June. Marina was pregnant with her second child, due to arrive in October. According to Lee's cousin Marilyn Murret, "they were perfectly happy. He was very devoted to Marina. He seemed to love his child very much."[624]

Lee spent much of the summer reading. During this time, he borrowed thirty-four books from the New Orleans Public Library. As noted earlier, Lee apparently used David Ferrie's library card. Ferrie later disavowed any relationship with Oswald. Yet two witnesses in New Orleans reported that Ferrie was panic-stricken after the assassination and asked them about a library card belonging to Lee. In addition, when the Secret Service questioned Ferrie, they asked whether he had lent his card to Oswald.[625]

Not surprising, many of the books Lee borrowed that summer were James Bond spy novels. According to Warren Commission investigators, they included Ian Fleming's *From Russia With Love* and *Goldfinger*. Four of the books were on Communism in China and in Russia. Lee also took out *Profiles in Courage* by President Kennedy.[626] Indeed, Lee's aunt, Lillian Murret, and her daughter

Marilyn, both said that Lee "liked the president and admired his wife."[627] They were not alone. The Warren Commission would later note that Ruth Paine's husband, Michael, and members of the Russian-speaking community in Dallas, all testified that Lee had "favorable feelings" towards President Kennedy.[628]

Lee enjoyed his summer reading list and in fact, it was not until late August that he actually began to carry out his political action operations in earnest. There was one exception, however—June 16, 1963. On that day, Lee appeared on the wharf where the Navy's USS *Wasp* was anchored. He spent the afternoon handing out Fair Play for Cuba Committee recruiting pamphlets to the sailors.[629] Lee was the only member in his FPCC chapter, and his was the only chapter in the southeastern United States, except for Tampa, Florida.[630] At about this time, Lee also wrote a letter to *The Worker*, the American Communist Party's newspaper, located at 23 West 26th Street in New York City. Lee asked for their literature so that he could hand it out. He also enclosed membership cards from his own chapter for the Communist Party's leaders Gus Hall and B. Davis. Lee wrote:

> "As a longtime subscriber to *The Worker* I know I can ask a favor of you with full confidence of its fulfillment.
>
> "I have formed a "Fair Play for Cuba Committee" here in New Orleans, I think it is the best way to attract the broad mass of people to a popular struggle.
>
> "I ask that you give me as much literature as you judge possible since I think it would be very nice to have your literature among the "Fair Play" leaflets (like the one enclosed) and pamphlets in my office.
>
> "Also please be so kind as to convey the enclosed "honorary membership" cards to those fighters for peace Mr. Gus Hall and Mr. B. Davis."[631]

Obviously, the purpose of the letter was to create a paper trail connecting FPCC with Communists in the United States.[632]

One other significant step Lee took that month was to apply for a new passport. He filled out the paperwork on June 24, 1963. The passport was issued to him the next day, thanks to exceptional connections in the right places.[633]

Lee left his job at Reily Coffee on July 19, 1963—once again, fired for "poor work habits"—yet he left smiling, and implied to acquaintances that he had more important work ahead.[634] He had worked there for two months. Interestingly, the same day Lee had been hired at Reily Coffee another young friend of David Ferrie's also was hired, a man named Dante Marachini.[635]

After Lee left, Marachini and three other Reily employees also departed. They, however, went on to work at the same place—the local NASA (National Aeronautics and Space Administration) facility. The three were Alfred Claude, the man who had hired Lee; Emmett Barbee, Lee's boss; and John D. Branyon, Lee's coworker.[636] Obviously, the Reily firm was more than a coffee shop as evidenced by its alumni's later assignments in the aerospace defense industry. The fact that the infiltration of the shop occurred at the same time as Oswald's employment also bolsters the view that at that point the firm was a cover for a domestic spy operation.

The next assignment Lee Harvey Oswald took on after Reily's was a speaking engagement—his first since his news interviews in Moscow. The talk was scheduled at Spring Hill College in Mobile, Alabama, where Lee's cousin Eugene Murret was enrolled as a seminarian. Lee spoke to a class of Jesuit students concerning his stay in the USSR and his views on the philosophy of Marxism.[637]

During August 1963, Lee hit the jackpot in terms of media attention. In just about two weeks, the period from August 9 to August 21, Lee was on radio and TV and in the newspapers. He and his media-savvy handlers knew precisely how to generate stories that would pave the way for Lee's planned penetration of Cuba. It all started on Friday, August 9, 1963, when Lee began handing out Fair Play for Cuba leaflets on Canal Street and protesting US policies toward Cuba. At one point, the owner of a nearby men's clothing store, Carlos Bringuier, approached Oswald and an argument broke out. Bringuier was a member of the Miami-based anti-Castro group, the Cuban Student Directorate (or DRE, *Directorio Revolucionario Estudiantil*), and his primary interests involved training Cuban exiles for paramilitary raids on Cuba. A scuffle ensued. One policeman on the scene said the fight looked staged.[638] The fact is, Lee and Carlos knew each other. According to Carlos, he and Lee had discussed Cuba at length in his shop just a few days earlier and were in agreement. At any rate, both Lee and Carlos were arrested for breach of peace. Lee spent the night in jail.[639] While behind bars, Lee spoke with New Orleans Lt. Francis Martello and the FBI's John Quigley. Keeping in character, Lee exaggerated the size of his single-member FPCC chapter, stating it had thirty-five cardholders.[640]

In the morning, a friend of the Murrets bailed him out, and the following Monday, Lee went to court and paid a ten-dollar fine. Outside the courthouse, he was filmed by a local TV station, WDSU-TV. Lee's next media event was on August 16, 1963, at the International Trade Mart. Again, Lee was filmed by a TV crew as he handed out literature.[641] A local radio producer, William Kirk Stuckey found out about the protests and invited Lee on his show, *Latin Listening Post*, a venue for controversial figures. On August 17, 1963, Lee taped a half-hour interview in Stuckey's studio at WDSU. The station's news director, John Corporon, had it edited down to four-and-a-half minutes for the show. Soon after, Stuckey found out from the local FBI that Lee, an ex-Marine, had been a "defector" to Russia, making Lee's story all the more interesting. A second show was arranged in which Lee debated his adversary from the week before, Carlos Bringuier, along with another anti-Communist speaker, Edward Scannell Butler. While the two men "exposed" Lee's past on the air, Lee maintained his composure. He emphasized his belief in Marxism rather than Communism and steadfastly maintained his view that US relations with Cuba were wrong-headed.[642] Lee had done all he could do to pass the pro-Castro litmus test. The next step would be to obtain the documents in Mexico that would permit him to travel to Cuba.

But first, Lee's handlers had other plans in mind. In the end of August 1963, David Ferrie drove Lee some one hundred miles north of New Orleans to the small town of Clinton, Louisiana. One other passenger rode with them on this unusual excursion into the Louisiana countryside. It is believed to have been Guy Banister, based on witness descriptions, although some researchers have said the third member on the excursion was Clay Shaw. But this is unlikely given Shaw's position in the hierarchy of both the community and in the world of covert operations.

Whisking along in a black Cadillac, Ferrie drove his associates, Lee and Guy, to a voter registration drive in Clinton. According to testimony from the House Assassination Committee hearings in 1978, the three were identified after the fact by several witnesses including the town marshal and the registrar of voters. The voter drive was sponsored by the Congress of Racial Equality (CORE) and was organized to bring unregistered minorities into the electoral process. While Ferrie and Banister sat in the black Cadillac and watched, Lee waited in line for hours, only to be told when he reached the registration desk that he did not meet the residency requirement. Lee reportedly explained that he was in the area to seek employment as an electrician at a nearby hospital. Yet, since he had not lived in the town long enough, nor in fact, at all, he was informed that he would be unable to register at that time. He thereupon politely walked away.[643]

Some researchers have viewed this episode as merely part of that era's surveillance operations commonly carried out by the CIA. Many blacks, including Martin Luther King Jr. and Malcolm X, were closely monitored by the Agency at this time. Antiwar groups and civil rights organizations, such as CORE, also were targeted. Operatives routinely infiltrated them and reported back to their superiors a head count of how many had attended the activity and what future events they were planning.[644] But in the sleepy town of Clinton, Louisiana, voter registration was hardly an action that would have endangered the CIA. Ferrie, Banister, and Oswald were on a different sort of mission. Rather than testing the voter registration process, it is much more likely that Ferrie and Banister were testing a far more sophisticated process: Richard Helms's MKULTRA conditioning process. And their subject was Lee Harvey Oswald.

Again, David Ferrie is known to have been a master hypnotist.[645] He possessed an essential skill required in MKULTRA operations. The uses of hypno-programming are numerous and varied. They can range from simply confusing a subject to confusing investigators after the fact; erasing memories of recent actions to creating incriminating circumstances. Hypno-programming, or conditioning, can be used to embed a "moral imperative." Conventional wisdom holds that "under hypnosis you won't do anything you normally wouldn't do." However, as noted earlier, this commonly accepted rubric has an overriding axiom known as the moral imperative. According to this principle, for subjects under hypnosis, a need to take action in a way that is morally right (in their own minds) takes over, or becomes imperative. For example, if the average hypnotized subject believes that innocent, defenseless people are in some way threatened by imminent danger, he or she will want to take some action to try to protect them. Under this principle, a subject can be given information and commands but will respond in accordance with the subject's own morals, even taking actions that override inhibitions to achieve what the subject believes is right for him. By the same token, a hypnotist can trick a subject into doing something against his or her will by triggering the moral imperative. In such a case, the hypnotized subject is given erroneous information and commanded to carry out an action. The subject then obeys the command, believing that his or her action is morally right and therefore imperative.[646]

It is known that the effectiveness of hypnotism as a programming tool depends in large measure upon the individual being hypnotized. The subject must have passions that can be exploited. Lee was brought up with an affinity for the underdog. In political terms, he was philosophically a supporter of civil rights. It would have taken very little to motivate him beyond the usual MKULTRA conditioning technique. This involved an unwitting drug dose, perhaps in the form of a "mickey," along with a posthypnotic suggestion embedded in his subconscious mind.

As for the purpose of the testing, his handlers no doubt were requested by their superiors to verify that Lee's responses to programming cues would be predictable. It was essential to know that they could maintain control over Lee's behavior when required. For example, Lee was not an electrician, yet he applied and interviewed at a hospital for an electrician's job. There also was no reason whatsoever for him to have joined a voter registration drive in rural Louisiana. Yet he waited in line for hours. Lee fulfilled his handlers' expectations, unwittingly verifying his continued suitability for manipulation. Of course, even Lee's handlers may not have been privy to knowledge of Lee's eventual role, given the Agency's compartmentalization of tasks. The actions that their subject would take in November in Dallas and the way in which he would be framed for the assassination were top secret plans known only by a very few.

As the summer of 1963 drew to a close, Lee's direct handlers at this point, David Ferrie and Guy Banister, were busy preparing Lee for his departure from New Orleans and his return to the Dallas area. The two key CIA assets were relinquishing their responsibilities related to Oswald and turning over "care and control" to Richard Helms's close lieutenant, CIA chief of Cuban operations based in Mexico City, David Atlee Phillips.

Phillips, forty, was also known as Maurice Bishop.[647] He was a native of Fort Worth, Texas, and was fluent in Spanish. During his twenty-five years in secret operations, he had spent three years working for the CIA in Havana, from 1958 to 1961, posing undercover as "proprietor, David A. Phillips, Public Relations."[648] In 1963, he was supervising one of the CIA-backed, anti-Castro groups' most militant leaders, Antonio Veciana, founder of Alpha-66. On September 1, 1963, Phillips and Veciana met at the Southland Building in Dallas. According to Veciana, prior to their meeting, he (Veciana) had seen Phillips speaking with a man whom he later recognized as Lee Harvey Oswald.[649] Lee was described as "quiet, strangely preoccupied."[650] These symptoms are not typical of Lee. However, such a condition, a mild trancelike state, is quite common among those who have undergone MKULTRA hypno-programming. When subjects are properly conditioned, this state can be triggered by a specific sight, sound, or command embedded in a posthypnotic suggestion. Once in this state, the subject, in this case, Lee, would be functioning enough to follow a direction, but little else. Upon coming out of it, there would be no memory of having been under nor any recall of what had transpired.

Phillips's CIA specialty was psychological warfare operations, covert action, and propaganda. He was close to E. Howard Hunt and had worked with him in organizing the Bay of Pigs operation. Prior to this, posing as a PR consultant in Havana, [651] Phillips oversaw CIA agents at the same time the covert operations staff was beginning to recruit Mafia personnel to oust Fidel Castro.

Richard Helms eventually promoted Phillips to CIA Chief of the Western Hemisphere. At this point in 1963, Phillips's task was to link Lee Harvey Oswald to Fidel Castro so that the assassination could be blamed on Cuba.[652] Throughout his career, Phillips continually denied any connection with any alleged plotters in the JFK assassination. Then, just before he died in 1988, he called his brother James. According to David Phillips's nephew, Shawn, his father (James) was not on speaking terms with his brother, suspecting that David was involved in the assassination. James asked him again if he had been in Dallas the day President Kennedy was killed. David, on his deathbed, replied, "yes," whereupon Shawn's father hung up the phone.[653]

In September 1963, while Phillips and company were continuing to plan and carry out anti-Castro operations in the Caribbean, in defiance of the White House, President Kennedy was quietly pursuing peace with the Cuban leader. Kennedy's goal was to entice Fidel into joining the US side, cutting his ties to the Soviet Union. Kennedy had already ordered the FBI, the Coast Guard, and other departments of the federal government to stop the Cuban exiles' operations against Cuba.[654] To open up a channel of communication with the Castro government, President Kennedy chose William Attwood, his Special Advisor to the United Nations. From September through November of 1963, Attwood met secretly with Castro representatives at the UN to discuss JFK's initiative. The president's brother Robert, the Attorney General, was also reportedly in favor of the talks. The other key people in the loop were Ambassador Averell Harriman and Secretary of State McGeorge Bundy. Kennedy's plan for negotiations to normalize relations with Castro was expected to move to the next level in the end of November 1963. In fact, Kennedy had scheduled to meet with Attwood after his (Kennedy's) return to Washington following his trip to Dallas,[655] a meeting that would never take place.

The *Dallas Morning News* announced in its September 13, 1963 edition that the president's planned visit to Dallas was set for either November 21 or 22, 1963.[656] On cue, Lee's handlers began to put the final phase of their plans into action. While the president intended to normalize relations with Castro, David Phillips and the Helms and Angleton faction of the CIA were bent on overthrowing Castro. Eliminating Kennedy and blaming it on pro-Castro Cubans obviously would end CIA and mob issues with the president. But, equally important, by accusing Cuba of such a deed, the Agency (and its Mafia associates) would easily win America's approval for a second Bay of Pigs invasion.

On September 20, 1963, one week after the people of Dallas found out about President Kennedy's plan to visit their city in the end of November, Marina Oswald's friend Ruth Paine of Irving, Texas, drove to New Orleans. Ruth had offered to care for Marina, now eight months pregnant, and to bring her and her baby June back with her. In return, Marina had offered to help Ruth with her Russian language studies.[657] Lee and Marina agreed, and on September 23, 1963, Marina and June rode with Ruth to the Paine household in Irving, located between Dallas and Fort Worth. Lee would meet up with them at Ruth's home a week and a half later. However, at this point in time, Lee did not yet know where his actual covert work would be taking him next. According to Ruth's husband Michael, Lee had mentioned moving to Houston or possibly Philadelphia.[658]

Conveniently, when Marina moved in with Ruth Paine, she and her husband—who had two children of their own—were separated. Michael had his own apartment and at the same time continued to help Ruth maintain the house. He also had no problem with Ruth having live-in guests.[659] As we shall see, the Paines played an interesting role in Lee's life during the weeks ahead. Indeed, it appears that they took over where George de Mohrenschildt, David Ferrie, and Guy Banister had left off.

The week and a half between Marina's move into Ruth's house and the day Lee arrived, while only ten days, has been a much-disputed timespan. As we shall see, Lee's handlers fully utilized this ten-day period to their advantage. It was an opportune time to create additional false evidence with which to frame him.

On the evening of September 26, 1963, three days after Marina and baby June had unpacked their bags in Irving, Lee appeared several miles away in Dallas in the company of two Latin-looking men. The trio, led by a man named "Leopoldo," drove up to the Crestwood Apartments, a largely Cuban residence, and knocked on the apartment door of tenant Sylvia Odio. When Ms. Odio, twenty-six, a wealthy Cuban refugee, answered the door, Leopoldo introduced himself, his associate "Angelo," and Lee as "Leon Oswald," an American.[660]

Leopoldo did most of the talking, speaking in Spanish, which Lee did not understand.[661] Leopoldo explained that they had just come from New Orleans (where Lee had been living), and that they would be taking a trip soon (Lee reportedly was planning to travel to Mexico City).[662] Leopoldo said the three were members of an anti-Castro group that had been founded by Sylvia's father's friend, Manolo Ray. The organization was called JURE, *Junta Revolucionaria*. He told Sylvia that the purpose of their visit was to raise money to fund raids on Cuba.[663] Sylvia's father, Amador Odio, had owned a trucking company in Cuba until his arrest and imprisonment in Cuba for his anti-Castro activities two years earlier in October 1961. Amador and his wife Sarah had ten children of which Sylvia was the oldest. Sylvia had married and moved to Puerto Rico and had four children of her own. However, her husband left her, and in March 1963, she moved with her children to Dallas to live with her sister Annie, seventeen.[664]

Leopoldo's conversation with Sylvia lasted some twenty minutes, and based on some of his statements, it seemed that he knew Sylvia's father. At the end of his pitch, he asked Sylvia to write letters in English for them to send to area businessmen in order to raise funds for the cause. Sylvia made no promises, and was, in fact, suspicious of the three men.[665] It should be noted that her sister Annie also saw the three men at the door.[666]

Lee remained silent during the visit. He was also observed wearing "an odd-looking, half grin on his face."[667] As noted earlier, this peculiar facial expression just happens to be one of the unique identifiers of possible conditioning, i.e., a sign of MKULTRA hypno-programming. Physically, Lee was at Sylvia Odio's doorstep. But mentally, he may well have been simply following a posthypnotic command and had no recall later of the entire incident.

The next day, Leopoldo phoned Sylvia Odio and continued the mission of attempting to paint Lee as a potential assassin. He asked her what she thought of "Leon." During the conversation, he spoke as if he wanted her help in getting Lee into Cuba, presumably to eliminate Castro. Leopoldo said, "Our idea is to introduce him to the underground in Cuba . . . he is kind of nuts." Leopoldo mentioned that Lee was an ex-Marine and a marksman. He stated that Lee had said, "Kennedy should have been assassinated after the Bay of Pigs" by anti-Castro Cubans, and added that Kennedy "deserved" it.[668] Clearly, the phone call to Sylvia was meant to further implicate Lee Harvey Oswald in the assassination to come.[669]

In response to Leopoldo's questions, Sylvia said that she could not help them.[670] She was privately afraid of releasing any information about her father's friends, for fear it would place them, or her family, in jeopardy. Sylvia later wrote to her father regarding the three visitors. He replied that he did not know the men and told her to be careful.[671]

Following the assassination of President Kennedy, when Sylvia turned on the TV coverage and saw the alleged killer, she fainted.[672] A friend of Sylvia's who knew her story of the visit of the three men notified the FBI who took her testimony.[673] The Warren Commission would later state that Lee was not in Dallas in September 1963 at the time Ms. Odio and her sister claimed.[674]

The Commission claimed Lee had taken a bus to Mexico City on that date, September 26, 1963.[675] To explain the Odio visit, the Commission produced anti-Castro guerrilla Loran Eugene Hall and said he and two associates were the three Odio visitors, not Lee Harvey Oswald and associates. Hall later told the FBI that his (Hall's) story of visiting Odio was fiction.[676] Exactly who had advised Hall to create the story to protect the Commission was not resolved. Finally, in the House Assassinations Committee final report in 1979, the committee concluded it "was inclined to believe Sylvia Odio."[677]

While Lee was accompanying two anti-Castro Cubans on a visit to Sylvia Odio's apartment in Dallas, another covert operation to further malign Lee was being set in motion at the CIA station in Mexico City, home of Agency disinformation specialist David Phillips.[678] Phillips was the CIA's chief of Cuban operations and ran the bulk of the covert activities in the region. His close friend, E. Howard Hunt, who was also a protégé of Richard Helms, was known to visit him often at his home in Mexico City.[679] Phillips reported directly to the CIA station chief, Win Scott, one of Richard Helms's colleagues from the pre-CIA, OSS era. Scott retired six years after the JFK assassination and remained in Mexico. Not surprisingly, when Scott died in 1971, James Angleton flew to his home in Mexico City and cleaned out his safe.[680]

According to the Warren Commission, Lee Harvey Oswald reportedly spent six days in Mexico City, from September 27 to October 3, 1963.[681] But as we shall see, the eyewitness testimony later developed revealed that an imposter was playing the role of Oswald. The imposter had attempted to tie Lee to a Soviet Embassy liaison in Mexico City. The liaison was allegedly linked to a Soviet assassination unit.

The distance from New Orleans to Houston is approximately four hundred miles; Houston to Laredo, Texas, is another three hundred miles; and from there to Mexico City is about five hundred miles, for a grand total of twelve hundred miles. It's at least a full two-day road trip. The Warren Commission claimed Lee "probably" took a bus from New Orleans on Wednesday September 25, 1963 and headed to Houston. Yet no witnesses recalled seeing him on that trip.[682] According to the FBI, the next day, an American claiming to be Lee Harvey Oswald traveled by bus from Houston to Nuevo Laredo, Mexico, to Mexico City. En route, the man told passengers that he had been a Marine who had defected to the USSR, and was traveling to Cuba via Mexico.[683] Lee Harvey Oswald's nature was known to be quite reserved and low-key. Yet this man was outgoing and social. He introduced himself to two Australian women, a Dr. John McFarland and his wife, and an Englishman named Albert

Osborne, according to the FBI. Osborne claimed to be a missionary and world traveler, yet had no discernible source of finances and was using an alias, "John Bowen." The FBI reported that his answers to questions were "inconsistent and unreliable."[684] Consequently, the true identity of the man seated with him on the bus who claimed to be Oswald was difficult to discern.

One explanation for the extroverted behavior of the passenger who called himself Lee Oswald could be, once again, MKULTRA conditioning. However, it is more likely that Lee was being impersonated. His own whereabouts could well have been in an Agency safe house. As noted earlier, such places were routinely used by the Agency for conducting unwitting drug experimentation. At any rate, a Lee Harvey Oswald registered at the Hotel Comerico in Mexico City on Friday, September 27, 1963, according to the Warren Commission.

The Cuban and the Soviet embassies in Mexico City were situated one block apart. About noon that day, September 27, a man claiming to be Oswald walked into the Cuban Embassy. He was greeted at the reception desk by the assistant to the Cuban Consul, Silvia Duran, a young English-speaking Mexican woman.[685] The man said he was Lee Harvey Oswald and asked for a visa to Cuba in order to go to the Soviet Union, according to the Warren Commission. He explained that he was a member of the Fair Play for Cuba Committee and showed his membership card. Ms. Duran said that she would need the Soviet Embassy's approval to issue him a visa. The man left and returned later that day, saying he had spoken with Soviet officials and that they had granted him the necessary permission. Ms. Duran then made a call to the Soviet Embassy for verification and reported to the visitor that it would take three to four months for his paperwork to be finalized.[686] Both the Cuban and the Soviet consulates were bugged at this time, and audio tapes were being made by the CIA, William Colby, CIA director, stated in 1975.[687]

According to the FBI, the American who claimed to be Lee spoke with a contact at the Soviet Embassy named Valery Kostikov who was reportedly part of a KGB sabotage and assassination unit. The man also stated that he wished to help the Cuban revolution and he voiced his feelings against America.[688] This conversation was taped, according to the CIA, but Helms never released the recordings to the Warren Commission.[689]

When Ms. Duran told the American his visa application would take months, he became angry and began ranting, whereupon Ms. Duran's supervisor, Cuban Consul Eusebio Azcue, appeared and ordered the man to leave the premises.[690] After the assassination of JFK two months later, Azcue viewed news footage of Lee Harvey Oswald in custody and realized that he had confronted an imposter. He stated that the man he had met was about thirty-five years old and had blond hair. Oswald was twenty-four and had dark hair.

The fact that someone had posed as Lee Harvey Oswald at the Cuban Embassy two months before the assassination of President Kennedy is evidence of a frame-up. However, the evidence was not publicized immediately; it took years to emerge. In fact, in Silvia Duran's statements for the Warren Commission in 1963, she positively identified Lee as the visitor,[691] but when she was shown actual film footage of Lee some fourteen years later, she then confirmed that the man she had met in September 1963 at the embassy was not Lee Harvey Oswald.[692]

After the assassination, Silvia Duran was arrested by Mexican police at the behest of the CIA, interrogated, and held for several days. She initially went along with the Warren Commission story. In 1979, Irish investigator Anthony Summers interviewed Ms. Duran after the House Assassinations Committee had finished its work. He showed her film footage of Lee Harvey Oswald that had been shot in New Orleans years earlier. Ms. Duran stated, "The man in the film is not like the man I saw here in Mexico City."[693] She described the man as "short," her size, five feet three inches. Lee was six inches taller at five feet nine inches. And she said the man had lighter hair than Lee.[694] The man's identity remains unknown.

According to the Warren Commission version of events, Lee departed Mexico City on October 3, 1963 via bus to Dallas. But the evidence, the passenger manifest, is missing. Investigators, reportedly from the Mexican government, confiscated it and a copy of it, in the days following the assassination. The documents were never returned and their whereabouts are unknown.[695]

A week later, around October 10, 1963, David Phillips's disinformation unit at the CIA's Mexican City office in charge of Cuban matters sent a message concerning Lee to the FBI, the navy, and the state department. The communication stated that a man named Lee Oswald, a former defector, had contacted the Soviet Embassy in Mexico City asking if he had received any messages. It contained a physical description of an American male, thirty-five years old, six feet tall with a receding hairline. It was clearly not the real Lee Harvey Oswald.[696] But that was irrelevant. The Phillips report enabled the agency to later imply linkage between Lee, the JFK assassination suspect, Communist Cuba, and the Soviet Union.

On the day of the assassination, the CIA sent the FBI a photo of the man it had described as Lee Harvey Oswald visiting the Soviet Embassy in Mexico City. When it was determined that the older, heavyset individual in the picture was not Lee, Richard Helms claimed there must have been some kind of mix-up. The man remains unidentified.[697]

It should be noted that when Lee was in custody following the assassination, he was questioned by Secret Service agents Thomas Kelley and Forrest Sorrels, among others. Both of these individuals told Warren Commission investigators that they had no recollection of Lee mentioning traveling to Mexico or wanting to go to Cuba. And when asked by Dallas police if he had taken such a trip, Lee stated that he had never gone to Mexico City.[698]

Beyond the "innocent mix-up" of the photo of the man at the Soviet Embassy who was not Lee, there is also the issue of the voice recordings obtained from the bugs in the embassy. Agents in the Dallas FBI office reportedly listened to the audio surveillance tapes and reported that the voice was not Lee's. They informed the Secret Service on the day after the assassination, November 23, 1963.[699] FBI Director J. Edgar Hoover wrote to President Lyndon Johnson, "the Central Intelligence Agency advised that on October 1, 1963, an extremely sensitive source had reported that an individual identified himself as Lee Oswald, who contacted the Soviet Embassy in Mexico City inquiring as to any messages. Special agents of this Bureau, who have conversed with Oswald in Dallas, Texas, have observed photographs of the individual referred to above and have listened to a recording of his voice. These special agents are of the opinion that the above-referred-to individual was not Lee Harvey Oswald."[700]

When the Warren Commission asked CIA Deputy Director Richard Helms to resolve this discrepancy, and other questions about Lee's alleged visit to Mexico, Helms ducked the issue. He answered, "disclosure could compromise CIA sources and methods."[701]

David Phillips was questioned about these audio tapes in 1976. He claimed that the CIA had routinely recycled and destroyed them.[702] The House Assassination Committee also wanted to know why no photos were ever produced of Lee visiting the Soviet Embassy. Phillips replied that the CIA's surveillance cameras were down at the time.[703] The CIA reported in 1975 that their cameras at the Soviet Embassy were not operational on weekends and that at the Cuban consulate, the camera was broken. However, years later in 1989, writer Anthony Summers uncovered information from interviews with House investigators that two CIA employees had lied, and that indeed, the cameras had been working properly.[704] Furthermore, they were operational on weekends, and had backups as well. In addition, Agency informants inside the Cuban Embassy reported after the assassination that Lee had not been there; the irate visitor was someone else. As for the audio tapes, CIA staffers who transcribed them have since reported that the voice was speaking in broken Russian; Lee was quite fluent.[705]

None of these latest findings by Anthony Summers were reflected in the House Select Committee on Assassinations report in the late 1970s. The committee had hit a stone wall when seeking answers from the CIA. To resolve this impasse and to accomplish its task on time and on budget, the committee chose a policy of acceptance with respect to the Agency. This miscarriage of justice was vividly described by writer David Talbot in his worthy chronicle *Brothers*. He notes, for example, that CIA division chief David Phillips was grilled by the House Assassinations Committee in 1977. Phillips chain-smoked his way through pointed questions posed by the committee's chief deputy counsel Robert Tanenbaum, a New York prosecutor. When Tanenbaum produced the Hoover memo indicating that Oswald was being impersonated in Mexico City, Phillips simply rose from his chair and left the room.[706] Later on at another point during the course of the Committee's work, Phillips was interrogated by House investigator Dan Hardway, a Cornell Law student. This time, Phillips saw evidence mounting that showed US-backed, anti-Castro Cubans were connected to him. Nevertheless, in the end, the House Committee chose to limit its report and avoided naming CIA officials. The Committee concluded that President Kennedy "was probably assassinated as a result of a conspiracy" and simply stated that the conspiracy may have included anti-Castro Cubans and the mob.[707]

In October 1963, a month before the JFK assassination, according to the FBI, mobster Jack Ruby of Dallas met twice in Miami with the Mafia's chief anti-Castro-CIA liaison, Johnny Rosselli. As noted earlier, Rosselli had been recruited by the CIA's Bill Harvey for work in connection with James Angleton's operation ZR/RIFLE, the plots to kill Castro.[708] The substance of the October 1963 Ruby-Rosselli meetings is unknown.[709] However, it is apparent that eventually a plan was put in place for the mob to eliminate a number of key witnesses in the aftermath of the JFK assassination, starting with the murder of Lee Harvey Oswald who was shot by Jack Ruby on November 24, 1963 in the basement of the Dallas police station.

Returning to our story, on October 3, 1963, Lee registered at the local Dallas YMCA. Marina, pregnant with her second child, was living with Ruth Paine in nearby Irving, at 2515 West 5th Street.[710] Lee visited with them the next day, October 4, and stayed through October 6, 1963.[711] Lee stayed briefly at the YMCA and then at a rooming house on North Marsalis Street for a few days before moving in to an apartment at 1026 North Beckley Street in the Oak Cliff section of Dallas.[712] This small rooming house is situated on a wide boulevard on a rise west of the city skyline. According to Lee's landlord, at this point, Lee was using the name O. H. Lee. Marina later stated that Lee wished to remain incognito.[713] It is also very possible that he was trying to lose the two men with whom he had been seen at Syliva Odio's apartment. He may have realized that he was being manipulated and consequently tried to separate his family life from his work life, temporarily at least, while he attempted to discern the situation in which he found himself.

Interestingly, another tenant in the small house was a housepainter named John Carter who worked with a Hank Killam. Hank's wife was Wanda Joyce Killam, an employee of Jack Ruby's at the Carousel Club. It is not known if Hank knew of any connection between Lee and Jack Ruby. Hank was questioned continually after the JFK assassination, according to his brother Earl, and finally ended up escaping to Pensacola, Florida. Four months later, in March 1964, Hank was found dead, lying next to a broken plate glass window at a department store. His throat was slit. Oddly, the coroner ruled his death an accident.[714]

Just as George de Mohrenschildt had helped Lee find an apartment, Ruth Paine was instrumental in getting Lee the room at North Beckley Street. You will recall that Lee did not have a driver's license. Ruth Paine served as his driver. Lee registered at the North Beckley Street address on October 14, 1963.[715] The next day, Ruth made a few phone calls and found him a job at a building in which one of her neighbors worked—it was known as the Texas School Book Depository at 411 Elm Street in Dealey Plaza in Dallas. Ruth's neighbor, Linnie Mae Randle, reportedly told Ruth about a job her brother, nineteen-year-old Wesley Frazier, had at the Book Depository. Ruth called the supervisor, Roy Truly, and Lee was interviewed and hired. He started work the next day, October 15, 1963.[716] His job duties involved filling book orders for school book publishers. Although essentially Ruth Paine got Lee his job, its location in Dealey Plaza certainly implies that the choice was not without Lee's handlers' approval, if not their own covert action arrangements.

That weekend, an event of much greater importance in Lee's life occurred at Parkland Hospital. On October 20, 1963, Marina gave birth to their second child, Audrey Marina Rachel Oswald.[717] Lee eagerly hitched a ride out to Irving nearly every weekend to visit with his family. It has been reported that upon seeing Rachel for the first time, "Lee even wept a little."[718]

Lee's relationship with Ruth Paine and her husband Michael was not much different than the ties he shared with George de Mohrenschildt, David Ferrie, and others: he saw the Paines as being on the same "team" as he. As for his clandestine role, he no doubt assumed that he was not the only one in his extended "family" who was receiving assignments and dutifully carrying them out. As noted earlier, such work is highly compartmentalized; one does not know the reasons for a given task, nor the tasks of others with whom they live day in and day out. They are not allowed to discuss their work with each other, or with anyone for that matter. Such is the nature of the business. Looking at Lee's circumstances from this perspective, we can see that Lee fully trusted Ruth and felt confident with her caring for his wife and children. Also, we can more easily understand Ruth's actions during this period, serving as Lee's driver, helping him find a place to live, and making calls to place him in a job at the Texas School Book Depository.

In Lee's mind, no doubt the new job was another "cover" that would allow him to carry out his actual assignments, which at this point were focused on the American Civil Liberties Union (ALCU). It is clear that Lee's handlers wanted to establish a link between the Fair Play for Cuba Committee and the ACLU. Lee, playing the role of a leftist activist, would make that happen. On October 25, 1963, just a week and a half after starting his new job, Lee attended an ACLU meeting in Dallas. He went with Michael Paine and Paine's close friend and coworker at Bell Labs, Raymond Krystinik, and his wife.[719] According to the Warren Commission, Lee spoke at the meeting, voicing his concerns regarding the John Birch Society and its reported intolerance towards Jews and Catholics.[720] Lee also expounded on his views of Socialist philosophy, sparking an argument with Ray Krystinik, and then spent the evening defending himself in a heated debate.[721] Lee ended up joining the ACLU and later reportedly wrote a letter to the American Communist Party to discuss ways in which to make the ACLU more leftist. The source of the letter, dated November 1, 1963, appears to be Lee's handlers once again attempting to connect the ACLU with the Communist Party. It is evident that the letter is not Lee's writing style.[722]

> Could you advise me as to the general view we had on the American Civil Liberties Union? And to what degree, if any, I should attempt to heighten its progressive tendencies? This Dallas branch of the ACLU is firmly in the hands of "liberal" professional people (a minister and two law professors conducted the October 25th meeting). However, some of those present showed marked class-awareness and insight.[723]

You'll recall that Helms's lieutenants David Phillips and E. Howard Hunt both were known for their writing skills, particularly in the field of disinformation.

In this same timeframe, it appears that Lee was receiving money orders from an unknown source (read, his handlers) via Western Union, addressed to a payee at the YMCA. Warren Commission investigation witness C. A. Hamblen, a Western Union manager, stated that Lee had come in to pick up money orders on several occasions. Another Western Union employee, Aubrey Lewis, told a similar story. The Warren Commission found no existing records to this effect and finally concluded that the transactions were imaginary. Interestingly, the person whom the apparent witnesses had seen also had sent a telegram to the Secretary of the Navy in Washington, DC. It is known that Lee had written to the Secretary of the Navy regarding his honorable discharge from the Marine Corps; Lee had been given a family hardship discharge, but after his "defection" to the Soviet Union, this was changed to an unsatisfactory rating rather than honorable.[724] Apparently, Lee had considered this to be a simple bureaucratic error and had appealed to Washington for an upgrade. As for Lee's funding source, any Agency links to Lee Harvey Oswald were kept well hidden from the Warren Commission.

Returning to November 1, 1963, this date was a critical point in US international relations. As discussed earlier, South Vietnamese president Ngo Dinh Diem was assassinated in Saigon in a CIA-sponsored coup. The murder was carried out without President Kennedy's knowledge. Indeed, it was at this point that John Kennedy began to fully realize the power and the sinister nature of key individuals within the CIA.[725]

At the same time, in Irving, Texas, on this day, an FBI agent knocked on the front door of Ruth Paine's house and asked Marina if he could speak with Lee Harvey Oswald. Lee was out, but Marina listened and found that her visitor, FBI Special Agent James P. Hosty Jr., apparently was investigating Lee's pro-Castro activities.[726] He also sought information on Lee's residence, his job, and his family. Hosty left but returned four days later, on Tuesday, November 5, 1963. Both Lee and his brother Robert later made the claim that Hosty had harassed Marina. As for Marina, she stated later that the FBI visit had greatly bothered Lee, and that Lee had asked her to get Hosty's name, phone number, and car license plate number if he came around again.[727] Special Agent Hosty's background was quite inauspicious: he was known to have been a frequent bridge player with a man named Robert Surrey who was an assistant of Major General Edwin Walker. It was Surrey who on November 22, 1963 published the hand-outs that greeted President Kennedy in Dallas with the words, "JFK Wanted For Treason."[728]

On November 6, 1963, Lee visited the Dallas FBI field office intending to meet with agent Hosty. Hosty was out at the time, so Lee left a note for him (which we will discuss shortly).[729] Jumping ahead momentarily, on November

22, 1963, only two weeks later, when President Kennedy was assassinated in Dealey Plaza and Lee Harvey Oswald's name was released as a suspect, Hosty told Dallas Police Lt. Jack Revill, "We know this guy . . . (he's) a Communist." Lieutenant Revill relayed the information to Police Chief Jesse Curry who released it to the press. Hours later, the agent in charge of the FBI's Dallas office, Gordon Shanklin, asked Chief Curry to disavow this statement, claiming his source had been mistaken.[730] Chief Curry took back the statement.

Clearly, Gordon Shanklin must have realized that admitting that the FBI had had dealings with Lee Harvey Oswald prior to the assassination would have made it appear that the FBI did not watch the prime suspect closely enough and therefore failed to protect the president. Shanklin wished to shield the FBI from bad publicity. At the same time, Shanklin may have also feared the possibility of a conspiracy in the murder of the president and would have wanted to keep the FBI from being implicated in any way. He, therefore, moved quickly to eradicate any presumed linkage between Oswald and the FBI.

That afternoon following the assassination, when Lee was arrested and searched by the Dallas police before being interrogated, officers found in Lee's personal address book the name of agent Hosty. The book included Hosty's address, phone number, and license plate number.[731] Soon after, Hosty entered the room in which Lee was being interviewed. Lee abruptly lashed out in anger, accusing Hosty of having terrorized his wife by threatening to have her deported back to the Soviet Union.[732] Hosty quickly disappeared and refrained from any further sessions with Lee.

Two days later, on November 24, 1963, Lee was shot and killed by Jack Ruby. Hours later, Hosty destroyed the note that Lee had left at his office. Following the orders of his superiors, Hosty flushed the note down a toilet.[733] CIA disinformation expert David Phillips later published accounts of this incident and attempted to further impugn Lee's reputation. Phillips asserted that Lee's note to FBI Special Agent James Hosty had said that Lee planned to "blow up the FBI and the Dallas Police Department." Years later, Phillips finally admitted in testimony before a Congressional committee that his statements were untrue. The actual contents of Lee's note to Hosty read: "If you have anything you want to learn about me, come talk to me directly. If you don't cease bothering my wife, I will take appropriate action and report this to the proper authorities."[734]

Besides the obvious attempt by Helms's operatives to paint Lee as a malcontent, it appears Lee's handlers also may have used the FBI to harass Lee's family in order to create additional false evidence of Lee as an unstable hothead.

During the two-week period before the assassination of President Kennedy, numerous sightings of Lee were later reported by witnesses, besides his visits to Western Union, and to the Dallas FBI office. However, as previously discussed, we know that an Oswald stand-in was used at the Cuban Embassy in Mexico City. This clandestine legerdemain by Lee's handlers does not appear to have been limited to Mexico. For example, a man who claimed to be Lee Oswald made an appearance at a Lincoln-Mercury car dealership in Dallas on November 9, 1963. The man spoke with salesman Albert Guy Bogard stating, among other things, that he was coming into money. He took a test drive. Yet the real Lee Harvey Oswald did not know how to drive. In addition, Bogard told the Warren Commission that the man did not look like the Owald he later saw in the news.[735]

Another sighting that was reported later took place at an indoor rifle range on November 16, 1963, a Saturday. Witnesses Sterling Wood, thirteen, and his father, a dentist, Dr. Homer Wood, were shooting that day at the Sports Drome Rifle Range in Dallas. Both later claimed that the man firing next to them was Oswald. They said he was shooting an Italian carbine and was with another man who drove a recent model car. The other man did the driving. That particular Saturday, Lee did not go to Irving to see his family because Mrs. Paine was having a private party. The Warren Commission later dismissed the various sightings at this rifle range, saying all of the witnesses were mistaken for one reason or another. Again, of course, the commission did not wish to entertain the concept of Lee having a possible accomplice, thus opening the door to a conspiracy case. So while the Woods' testimony was dismissed, it is interesting to note that the Woods both correctly identified photos of Lee and, in fact, the details of their story do match up more than those of the other witnesses.[736] Perhaps the man they saw was a look-alike, or a planted double impersonating Lee. Another possibility, given the nature of the covert actions being directed against Lee at this point in time, is the existence of Helms's MKULTRA conditioning activities. As we shall see ahead, a similar occurrence took place in Sirhan Sirhan's life just days before the assassination of Sen. Robert F. Kennedy in 1968. Based on descriptions of Sirhan's behavior, his firing-range visit clearly was the result of a posthypnotic suggestion. Sirhan's unusually rapid speech, glassy eyes, and intense concentration were all classic signs of hypno-programming. As in the case with Lee, another unknown man accompanied Sirhan, driving him to and from the range. Indeed, the firing-range events in the lives of both Sirhan and Lee added the final touches to the overall plans designed to frame these two unwitting fall guys.

# 6

# November 22, 1963, the Assassination of President John F. Kennedy

I N WASHINGTON, DC, on November 19, 1963, just before President Kennedy was to leave for Dallas, Richard Helms walked into the Oval Office with a large canvas bag in hand. He told Kennedy that a cache of arms from Cuba had been picked up by the CIA on a Venezuelan beach. (One CIA official later stated that this so-called evidence—an attempt to show that Cuba was exporting revolution in the Caribbean—most likely had been fabricated by Helms to incriminate Fidel Castro.)[737] Helms then opened the bag and pulled out a submachine gun. Surprised that Helms had gotten through security, the President cracked, "it gives me a feeling of confidence."[738] Three days later, President Kennedy was dead.

With the 1964 presidential election on his mind, Kennedy had planned his trip to Texas in part to mend a political split in the Democratic Party in the Lone Star State. He wanted to bring together Texas's conservative Gov. John Connally and liberal Sen. Ralph Yarborough. Kennedy hoped that the presence of his vice president, Texas native Lyndon B. Johnson, would help them to settle their differences for the good of the party.[739] In the upcoming 1964 elections, Kennedy was confident that he would beat his Republican opponent Sen. Barry Goldwater of Arizona. He also was hopeful that his popularity would be reflected in Congress where he felt his legislation would have an excellent chance of passing. The president was also optimistic for peace with the USSR in South Vietnam, Berlin, and Cuba. In fact, he hoped to travel to Russia in his second term.[740]

On Thursday, November 21, 1963, the president and the First Lady left Washington, DC, by plane and arrived that afternoon in San Antonio, Texas, where they received a warm reception. They were also well received later in the day in Houston and that night, they stayed in Fort Worth at the Texas Hotel. Early the next morning, November 22, 1963, the president came across an advertisement while reading the *Dallas Morning News*. The ad read: "Welcome, Mr. Kennedy, to Dallas." It went on to criticize Kennedy's policies, stating that he had "scrapped the Monroe Doctrine in favor of the Spirit of Moscow," that his administration had gone "soft on Communists," and that he was ignoring the Constitution. Kennedy aide Arthur Schlesinger has reported that the president was momentarily upset; Kennedy asked, "How can people write such things?"[741]

Later in the morning, Kennedy loosened up. In a brief speech outside the hotel, the president told the audience, "Mrs. Kennedy is organizing herself. It takes longer, but, of course, she looks better than we do when she does it."[742]

President Kennedy next spoke at a Fort Worth Chamber of Commerce breakfast after which the entourage departed by plane from Fort Worth. A few minutes later, they landed at Love Field in Dallas. Crowds lining the streets cheered the first couple as they drove past on their way into the city.

Before Lee Harvey Oswald arrived at work at the Texas School Book Depository on Elm Street in Dallas, he would frequently start his day with breakfast at the Dobbs House. This restaurant became the subject of some speculation after the assassination due to reports that both Jack Ruby and Dallas police officer J. D. Tippit also patronized the place. At any rate, two waitresses, Mary Dowling and Dolores Harrison, reported that they had served Lee a number of times and later recognized him on TV after the assassination. The last time they saw him, on November 20 or November 21, 1963, they noticed something out of character or peculiar about him. Mary Dowling reported that he was "nasty" to her and had cursed at her about his breakfast. Dolores Harrison, who had prepared Lee's eggs "over light," said that he had complained that they were too hard, but he had eaten them anyway. Ms. Dowling noted that Officer Tippit was there at the time and that he had noticed Lee, but she felt that he did not know Lee.[743] Whether or not Tippit and Ruby were monitoring Lee, it is interesting to observe Lee's uncharacteristic outburst towards his waitress. As you may recall, such behavior—including intense irritability—is symptomatic of someone undergoing hypno-programming conditioning.

When Lee was not at work at the Texas School Book Depository during weekdays or with his family in Irving on weekends, on a number of weekday evenings he visited a Dallas strip club known as the Carousel that was owned by Jack Ruby.[744] The Warren Commission later claimed that there was no evidence that Lee knew Ruby.[745] Nevertheless, based on at least eight eyewitness accounts, it is evident that Lee was a patron of Ruby's nightclub. You will recall, as noted earlier, a fellow boarder at Lee's rooming house, Jack Carter, was friends with one of Ruby's employees at the Carousel, Wanda Killam.

The eight eyewitnesses who had seen Lee at the Carousel Club[746] include five strippers, a musician, a magician, and the emcee. The dancers were Karen Carlin (also known as Teresa Norton and Little Lynn),[747] Janet Conforto (a.k.a Jada),[748] Kay Helen Coleman Olsen (a.k.a Kathy Kay),[749] Bobbie Meserole (a.k.a Shari Angel),[750] and Beverly Oliver, who worked next door at the Colony Club.[751] The musician was drummer Bill Willis,[752] the magician was William Crowe Jr. (a.k.a Bill DeMar),[753] and the master of ceremonies was Walter Weston.[754]

Another connection to the Carousel Club involved Ruth Paine's husband Michael's good friends Mr. and Mrs. Raymond Krystinik. Several weeks before the assassination, on the night Krystinik was introduced to Lee at the ACLU meeting noted above, Raymond and his wife went out to Jack Ruby's Carousel Club.[755]

Interestingly, strip clubs appear in the lives of the two other alleged assassins of the 1960s documented herein: Sirhan Sirhan patronized clubs in Southern California, as did James Earl Ray in Canada. This seemingly coincidental behavior may appear unimportant on the face of it. But in fact, as we shall see ahead, these individuals were being similarly handled. Men's clubs offered safe, dimly lit places for handlers to carry out various control activities on their unwitting subjects. It is known that MKULTRA activities were typically initiated through the use of a "mickey" dropped into an unsuspecting subject's drink. After the unwitting subject slipped into a drugged condition, he or she could be easily secreted to other locations, where—through MKULTRA programming—various posthypnotic suggestions could be planted.

On Thursday, November 21, 1963, at the Texas School Book Depository, Lee took a late morning break from work and asked coworker, young Buell Wesley Frazier, if he would give him a ride that evening to Irving. Frazier was the same person from whom Lee had been hitching rides on weekends to see Marina and the children. Frazier asked him why he was going on a Thursday, and Lee explained that he wanted to pick up some curtain rods to bring to his apartment. That evening, Frazier drove Lee to Irving, and the next morning, November 22, 1963, Lee appeared at Frazier's house for the ride back to work. You'll recall that Frazier lived with his sister, Mrs. Linnie Mae Randle, near the Paine's house. As Lee opened the door to Frazier's car and stepped in, he placed a package wrapped in brown paper on the backseat. Both Frazier and his sister later claimed they saw it. And they were the only witnesses known to have seen it. In their descriptions later before Warren Commission counsel, they both said the package was about two feet long, which was much shorter than the sample bag counsel showed them. They were also asked to pinpoint precisely where in the back of Frazier's car the bag was placed. The distance between the points measured twenty-seven inches. But the bag found at the Texas School Book Depository was thirty-eight inches long and the disassembled rifle was 34.8 inches. Frazier also recalled that Lee carried it under his armpit, cupping the other end in his palm. It would have been impossible to carry it this way if it had been a rifle.[756] Finally, after arriving at work, no employees recalled seeing Lee carrying anything with him.[757]

Again, Frazier and his sister claimed to have seen the package, and based on their descriptions, it was too small to contain a disassembled Mannlicher-Carcano 6.5 mm rifle. Frazier stated that Lee told him he was bringing curtain rods to his North Beckley Street apartment. Interestingly, according to Dallas police, Lee later said that he had no knowledge of the curtain rods that Frazier told the police about.[758]

Looking at this matter from Lee's handlers' perspective, it was important for them to establish that Lee brought a weapon into the building if they were to convincingly show that Lee was the gunman. Their problem may have been solved simply and expeditiously by asking Lee to bring in curtain rods from Irving to the Texas School Book Depository on the morning of the planned assassination. Such an order, to bring home curtain rods, could have been viewed by Lee as a necessary item for his new apartment, either for his own privacy or to help out another resident or perhaps the landlady. At the same time, it is important to remember the modus operandi of those who were guiding this operation. Experts in the field of covert action at that time were able to induce an action from an unwitting subject (who had been conditioned) through the use of a posthypnotic suggestion. Again, Lee's handlers clearly were adept at Richard Helms's MKULTRA conditioning. As described earlier, a drug covertly administered, at a bar, for example, would render the subject powerless. Hypno-programming, a combination of hypnosis and drugs, enabled handlers to embed various triggers that later on could be used to induce a trancelike state in the subject. Such conditioning would allow Lee's controllers to issue simple commands that he would carry out and not recall later. As noted above, Lee stated that he could not recall at any time telling

Buell Wesley Frazier anything about curtain rods, according to Dallas police interrogators.[759] The curtain rods served Lee's handlers' goal of creating further incriminating evidence, fabricated in order to frame Lee for the assassination of President Kennedy.

The planners of the assassination knew that any investigation after the fact would view the curtain rod story as a simple cover for secreting the rifle—purportedly hidden in Mrs. Paine's garage—into the Texas School Book Depository. Yet there is no evidence of a gun in the garage, and as Marina Oswald later stated, as far as she knew, her husband never owned a rifle.[760]

It is known that one of Richard Helms's disinformation experts who ran Agency operations in Mexico City, David Atlee Phillips, was in Dallas at this time. Recall that he had been witnessed with Lee in the city in September 1963, and also that on his deathbed in July 1988, he stated in a phone conversation with his brother James that he was indeed in Dallas the day President Kennedy was assassinated.[761]

As for Lee Harvey Oswald, after he arrived at work with Buell Wesley Frazier on Friday morning, November 22, 1963, he went about his usual job duties in the Book Depository. The president's motorcade route through downtown Dallas had been published in two city newspapers three days before the assassination, on November 19, 1963. But the map did not indicate that the route would detour off Main Street and onto Elm Street. It simply showed the route as going through the triple underpass at the west end of Dealey Plaza and onto the Stemmons Freeway en route to a planned engagement at the Trade Mart.[762] In interviews with Texas School Book Depository employees later, it was found that the majority did not know until Friday morning that the president's motorcade would pass by their building. It is not known if Lee knew the president's route. However, it is known that on the morning of November 22, Lee was conversing with coworker James Jarman Jr. on the first floor when he noticed people gathering outside. He asked Jarman why, and Jarman replied that the president was coming. Lee asked from which direction, and Jarman told him that he had heard that it would probably be from Main Street to Houston Street and down Elm Street.[763]

The Texas School Book Depository is situated on Elm Street. The large, seven-story brick office and warehouse building marks the northeast corner of Dealey Plaza. The plaza slopes down from Houston Street to the Triple Underpass, which is a railroad bridge at the west end of the plaza. On the north side of the plaza, just west of the Book Depository, is a concrete art deco style pergola built in the 1930s and next to this (heading west) is a wooden stockade fence and several trees. The stockade fence is at the top of a rise known as the grassy knoll. Behind the fence is a parking lot and rail yards. In the rail yards, the Union Terminal's North Tower rises fourteen feet above the parking lot.

On November 22, 1963, the tower supervisor on duty, thirty-eight-year-old Lee Bowers Jr.,[764] noticed an out-of-state car drive into the parking lot and behind the stockade fence and slowly depart just before noon. Another arrived and left at 12:25 p.m. Between these two cars, a third car pulled in and departed at approximately 12:15 p.m. It was a black 1957 Ford with Texas plates and was being driven by a white man, probably between the ages of twenty-five and thirty-five. Interestingly, he appeared to be talking into a microphone. Bowers later told the Warren Commission that the driver was "holding something up to his mouth."[765]

Bowers also stated that he spotted two men at the fence at this point in time, both strangers to him; neither were railroad employees. One was a heavier, middle-aged man and the other was in his mid-twenties.[766]

At the same time, at the upper end of Dealey Plaza, another witness, Carolyn Walther, was standing on Houston Street before the motorcade arrived. She looked up at the Texas School Book Depository building and saw two men in the windows next to the southeast corner on the sixth floor. She later told the FBI that one of the men was wearing a white shirt and was carrying a rifle. The other man was dressed in a brown suit.[767]

Another observer in Dealey Plaza, Arnold Rowland, was standing with his wife on Houston Street between Elm Street and Main Street. While waiting for the president's arrival, he looked up and saw a man in a light shirt with a rifle standing back from a sixth floor window of the Depository.[768] He mentioned it to his wife,[769] and also noted the time on the Hertz clock above the building. It was 12:15 p.m.[770]

Another witness, Robert Hughes, was filming with an 8-mm movie camera at the corner of Main and Houston. When the motorcade approached from Main Street, he filmed the dark blue presidential Lincoln as it turned from Houston Street onto Elm Street at 12:30 p.m.[771] In the background, he captured the Texas School Book Depository. The film shows two men in a sixth floor window standing about ten feet apart.[772] Hughes stopped filming just moments before the shooting started.[773]

At Elm Street and Houston, alleged witness Howard Brennan looked up at the Texas School Book Depository as soon as he heard the sound of gunfire.[774] He claimed that he saw an assassin in a sixth floor window. Later, he was asked by the FBI to identify the suspect in a police lineup. He was unable to do so. And, again, during the Warren Commission's reconstruction of the shooting, he was unable to even see a figure in the window of the Depository. Yet, for the final report, Brennan suddenly changed his story and stated that the gunman was Lee Harvey Oswald.[775]

Meanwhile, as we look at Lee's movements during this timeframe, it is clear that Lee was in the Book Depository lunchroom both before and after the gunfire. A foreman at the Depository, William Shelley, walked to the first floor to have lunch at ten to twelve that day. Shelley later testified that he had met and talked with Lee at that time.[776] Another coworker of Lee's, Eddie Piper, a janitor, also told the Warren Commission counsel that he had spoken with Oswald on the first floor. This occurred at noon.[777]

Witness R. E. Carolyn Arnold, a secretary at the Texas School Book Depository, later told the FBI that she had walked to the front door steps to wait for the president's motorcade to drive by, and while on the way to the front door, she believed that she saw Lee on the first floor. This was at approximately 12:10 p.m.[778] In all, about ninety people worked at the Depository and a majority of those present that day went outside to catch a glimpse of the president and the First Lady.[779]

The key witness in Dealey Plaza was fifty-eight-year-old Abraham Zapruder,[780] a dress manufacturer, who was shooting a Bell and Howell 8-millimeter movie camera with a telephoto lens.[781] Shortly before the motorcade arrived, he decided to position himself on the grassy knoll overlooking Elm Street. He climbed up onto a four-foot high concrete pedestal next to the pergola. His assistant, Marilyn Sitzman, stood by him to steady him.[782] It was Zapruder's twenty-two seconds of film that would later be used to provide the baseline for determining the timing of the shots and the directions from which the shots were fired.

Dealey Plaza, pictured from above, is shaped like an arrowhead pointing to the west. The shaft is Main Street, the base of the arrowhead is Houston Street, the upper side is Elm Street, and the lower side is Commerce Street. The point of the arrow is the railroad bridge and triple underpass.

The route of the president's motorcade followed Main Street until it met Houston Street, and then it took a right onto Houston and a sharp left onto Elm Street. First came the motorcycle policemen. They were followed by the lead car, which was driven by Dallas Chief of Police Jesse Curry and included two Secret Service agents, Forrest Sorrels and Winston Lawson, and County Sheriff J. E. Decker. Next came the presidential limousine, a 1961 Lincoln convertible. President Kennedy sat on the right side of the rear seat, with Jacqueline Kennedy at his left. Texas governor John Connally sat in front of the president, with his wife Nellie on his left. Secret Service agent William Greer was in the driver's seat, and agent Roy Kellerman sat to his right. To the rear of the president's vehicle, four motorcycle policemen followed, two on each side. The follow-up car came next, a 1955 Cadillac convertible carrying eight Secret Service agents (including four on running boards on the sides) and two of the president's aides, David Powers and Kenneth O'Donnell. The vice president's car followed, a Lincoln convertible, with Vice President Lyndon Johnson in the right rear, Lady Bird Johnson next to him in the center, and Texas senator Ralph Yarborough on the left side. In the front seat was agent Rufus Youngblood on the right and Texas State Highway Patrol Officer Hurchel Jacks, who was driving. This car was followed by another of Secret Service agents and Dallas police. The rest of the motorcade included vehicles carrying Dallas mayor Earle Cabell and his wife Elizabeth, Texas congressmen, other local dignitaries, and the press. A final police car and several motorcycles completed the caravan.[783]

At 12:30 p.m., the motorcade reached Elm Street. As the president's car slowly passed by Texas School Book Depository, gunfire erupted in Dealey Plaza. It lasted six seconds. When it was over, President Kennedy was dead and Governor Connally was wounded.[784]

Jacqueline was seen climbing out onto the trunk to retrieve part of her husband's skull. Her bodyguard, Secret Service agent Clint Hill, immediately leaped from the running board of the follow-up car and pushed her back into the seat to protect her as the motorcade sped under the railroad trestle and onto Stemmons Freeway in the direction of Parkland Hospital.[785]

At the same time, at the front door of the Texas School Book Depository, motorcycle officer Marrion L. Baker jumped off of his bike and, with gun drawn, rushed into the building. He was assisted by Book Depository manager Roy Truly. The policeman first ran into the lunchroom where he found Lee sipping a soft drink. According to Truly, Officer Baker asked him, "Does this man work here?" Truly said, "Yes." Later on, Truly stated that Lee did not seem afraid nor excited. Lee was "not out of breath, (he was) calm and collected."[786]

Another witness, Mrs. Robert Reid, a clerical supervisor, stated that she had run back to her office moments after the gunfire and also noticed Lee. He was holding a Coke in his hand, she stated.[787]

Meanwhile, in Dealey Plaza, police searched for the source of the gunfire and discovered something which turned out to be very unusual. Patrolman J. M. Smith, who was posted near the front of the Book Depository, was told by witnesses that shots had come from the bushes at the grassy knoll. He hurried up the slope and into the parking lot behind the knoll with his gun drawn. As he approached a man there, the man flashed an ID and said he was Secret Service.[788] Yet the Warren Commission later confirmed that there were no Secret Service agents in the area—all of the Secret Service agents present for the president's visit had continued on to Parkland Hospital in the motorcade in accordance with Secret Service rules.[789]

Another law enforcement officer, Deputy Constable Seymour Weitzman, stated that he ran into the railroad yards adjacent to the Book Depository where, he claimed, "Secret Service . . . were also present;"[790] And Dallas police Sgt. D. V. Harkness testified that after the gunfire he ran to the rear of the Texas School Book Depository where he met up with some men who told him they were Secret Service agents.[791]

Again, the Secret Service has confirmed that none of its agents were in Dealey Plaza, on the grounds around the Texas School Book Depository, or at the railroad yard at the time of the assassination.[792] Oddly, the Warren Commission did not pursue the identities of the imposters nor their roles in the conspiracy.

As for Lee Bowers, the railroad tower man, he has stated that he was looking at the stockade fence when he heard at least three shots and saw "a flash of light or smoke."[793] It is quite possible that the two men he saw there threw the weapon into a car trunk and drove away.

The gunman in the Texas Book Depository would have had no problem exiting the building. It is known that the back of the Depository was not secured by police for up to twenty-five minutes after the assassination. So the actual gunman could easily have escaped via that route.[794]

Lee Harvey Oswald at this point obviously must have known what had happened. Although he may not have heard the shots or the screams of bystanders, he certainly would have heard the multitude of sirens as police converged on Dealey Plaza. Realizing what had happened, he apparently decided to go home immediately and then, given his role in covert intelligence, he no doubt hoped to meet up with his control agent. He would leave work and catch a ride back to his room, first taking a bus and then a cab. Lee also may have sensed who was behind this horrific killing and he may well have felt that a frame-up was in the making. His handlers, meanwhile, who had planned to incriminate him, knew that it was critical at this juncture to direct Lee's movements. Their use of posthypnotic suggestions could easily have been part of their plan to lead Lee to his ultimate fate. A simple command, such as "when you hear sirens, go to the Texas Theater to await instructions," is all that would have been necessary.

The Texas Theater was located at West Jefferson Boulevard, about a mile from Lee's apartment. An hour later, as Lee sat in the dark in the nearly empty movie house, he was accosted by police and booked for the murder of the president and that of Dallas police officer J. D. Tippit (which we will examine ahead).

Some assassination authors have suggested that Lee may have been programmed to shoot the president (a "Manchurian Candidate"). This was not the case. It is well known that such programming was unreliable and unpredictable. While there was evidence of MKULTRA activity, it is apparent that Lee was not programmed to be an assassin, but to be a fall guy.

The Warren Commission claimed that three shots were fired, all by one gunman who was firing from a sixth-floor window in the Texas School Book Depository.[795] This theory has since been refuted by additional physical evidence, eyewitness statements, film analysis, and medical testimony produced in later years.

The Warren Commission's view was based on an expedient scenario created by commission counsel Arlen Specter[796] (US Senator from Pennsylvania, 1981–2011). He held that one shot hit President Kennedy in the back of the neck and exited his throat and that the same bullet then hit Governor Connally in the back, broke a rib, exited his chest, continued to travel down, hit his right wrist, passed through it, and then ended up in his left thigh. A second shot hit the president in the right rear portion of the head. And a third shot apparently missed, according to Arlen Specter.[797]

Yet later analysis, including crucial information that the FBI failed to give the Warren Commission, has shown that the lone gunman-magic bullet theory is preposterous.

The best evidence, based on the number of wounds and angles of the shots, indicates that there were three gunmen and four shots fired.[798] The first shot hit the president in the back. When the bullet struck, the president raised his elbows and clenched his fists in front of his face to protect himself.[799] The angle and direction of the shot, based on the wound evidence, indicate that the bullet was apparently shot from the sniper's nest on the sixth floor, southeastern corner window in the Texas School Book Depository. The bullet struck the president's back approximately five inches below the collar and two inches to the right of the spine.[800] It penetrated only about two inches, according to the autopsy doctors' statements.[801] Some researchers believe that this bullet was found on a stretcher at Parkland Hospital.[802]

The second shot was fired a split second after the first shot, too close in time to have been fired from the same bolt-action weapon. While the Warren

Commission claimed the shot that hit Connally first hit President Kennedy, this is refuted by the Zapruder film that shows no sign of this. As Connally himself has stated, "you can see (in the film) the grimace in the president's face. You cannot see it in mine. There is no question about it. I haven't been hit yet."[803] When Connally was hit, he looked as if the wind had been knocked out of him. The shot that hit him struck him in the back, and after that, the bullet apparently traveled the path described above in the Warren Commission Report. However, the report claimed that this was the bullet found on a stretcher at the hospital, despite the fact that it was in pristine condition after having broken two bones and caused numerous wounds.[804] This second shot was fired from a location on the east side of Dealey Plaza, most likely from the roof of the County Records Building or the Dal-Tex building, both on Houston Street. This is based on the fact that the trajectory measured a downward angle of twenty-seven degrees and the left-right angle of twenty degrees.[805]

The third shot struck the president in the back of the head, driving his body forward, as witnessed in the film.[806] This was the second shot fired from the Book Depository.

At almost the same moment, the fourth shot hit, also striking the president in the head, but from the opposite direction. The president was thrust backward and to the left and collapsed into his wife's lap.[807] This shot was fired from behind the stockade fence on the grassy knoll. This source location is based on accounts of witnesses who heard the sound of the shot behind them on the knoll.[808] It is also based on the medical evidence. A host of doctors at Parkland Hospital described a massive exit wound in the back of the head. Neurosurgeon Dr. Kemp Clark described it as "a missile (that) had gone in and out the back of his head."[809] The opening "appeared to be an exit wound in the posterior portion of the skull," said Dr. Ronald Jones.[810] Dr. Robert McClelland stated, "probably a third or so, at least, of the brain tissue, posterior cerebral tissue, and some of the cerebellar tissue had been blasted out."[811] Others doctors present who corroborated this evidence included Dr. Malcolm Perry, Dr. Charles Baxter, and Dr. Gene Akin.[812]

As for the throat wound observed at Parkland Hospital, analysts have determined that it was too small to be either an entrance or an exit wound. Most likely it was caused by bone fragment driven out by the force of the rear head shot.[813] Another fragment hit the curb on Main Street near the underpass, nicking onlooker James Tague in the cheek.[814]

Some sixty-four eyewitnesses would later report their observations of the assassination. Thirty-three said the shots came from the grassy knoll, twenty-five said the Book Depository building, and the remaining gave other responses.[815]

In addition to all of this evidence, modern-day forensic science has produced new findings that also suggest the existence of more than one gunman. In October 2008, nationally known experts, including Dr. Henry C. Lee of Connecticut, convened at an assassination symposium at Duquesne University in Pittsburgh. Dr. Lee told the author that participants discussed the results of neutron activation tests of fragments of bullets recovered from the JFK assassination. Neutron activation is superior to spectrographic analysis because it shows the exact composition in parts per billion. Dr. Lee stated that the tests showed "no match;"[816] that is, the batches of bullets were different. This indicates a high probability of more than one gun having been fired.

Returning to Dealey Plaza, November 22, 1963, and Lee Harvey Oswald, this mind-boggling attack on the president's motorcade must have stunned Lee as much as anyone who was there. He knew that all security agencies of the government would immediately go on full alert. As a loyal covert operative of the CIA, he knew also that he would be responsible for joining in the effort to capture the assassins. He needed to get home to retrieve his revolver and then meet with his control agent for further instructions. It is not unusual for agents to meet in such places as parks and movie theaters. In Lee's case, it was at the Texas Theater on Jefferson Boulevard, located ten blocks south of his rooming house.

Since Lee did not have a car or a driver's license, he left the Texas School Book Depository, walked several blocks east on Elm Street, and jumped on a public transit bus. Three witnesses claimed to have seen Lee on the bus: the driver, Cecil J. McWatters; a teenage passenger, Roy Milton Jones; and a woman who had been Lee's landlady for a brief time, Mary Bledsoe.[817] Bledsoe would later testify that Lee wore a torn shirt with buttons missing and looked like a "maniac." Yet no other witness saw this. McWatters and Jones both reported that Lee had on a jacket, and the landlady's description of his demeanor was contrary to their recollections. What's more, both the driver and the young male passenger said they do not recall Ms. Bledsoe even being on the bus.[818]

The bus was traveling towards Dealey Plaza and after only a couple of blocks, it was caught in a traffic jam as police tried to secure the area amidst the grief-stricken crowds. Lee took a transfer stub from the bus driver, disembarked, and walked to a nearby Greyhound Bus Terminal on Lamar Street. There he hailed a taxi. At the same time, an elderly woman also wanted a cab; Lee offered her his. She declined, and Lee took the ride out to Oak Cliff. Cabbie William Whaley said he drove Oswald to the 700 block of North Beckley Avenue.[819] Lee arrived home at the rooming house at approximately 1 p.m.

and changed his clothes, according to housekeeper Earlene Roberts.[820] There is no doubt Lee's movements were being closely monitored by his handlers. After all, spies spy. Since the plotters' intent was to frame Lee for the assassination, in order to ensure that Lee's side of the story was never told, they needed to have him killed prior to a trial. They had to make certain that the public and the media would believe the fiction that Lee was a "lone nut assassin." Again, for their conspiracy to succeed, the plotters knew they had to arrange for the police to detain Lee and then make sure that he was silenced as soon as possible while "escaping" from police custody. They could not afford for Lee to be allowed to talk. But, as we shall see, things did not go as smoothly as planned.

Meanwhile, at Parkland Hospital, President Kennedy's wife Jacqueline waited in a state of shock outside the trauma room where doctors huddled over the president's lifeless body. The First Lady was brought into the room when the priest arrived. Father Oscar Huber administered the last rites of the Catholic Church while Jacqueline held her husband's hand and pressed it to her cheek. Filled with emotion, Dr. Charles Crenshaw and others on the surgical team stood by as she placed her wedding ring on the president's little finger and then kissed him. Father Huber traced the sign of the cross with holy oils on the president's forehead, and then Jacqueline and the doctors exited the room.[821]

At Parkland Hospital, a shaken Vice President Lyndon Johnson confided his anxiety to White House assistant press secretary Malcolm Kilduff. Johnson said, "We don't know whether this is a worldwide conspiracy, whether they are after me as well as they were after President Kennedy." Johnson then asked Kilduff not to announce the president's death until after he was back at the airport and on Air Force One.[822]

Soon after, President Kennedy's body was flown back to Washington, and that evening an autopsy was performed at the Naval Medical Center in Bethesda, Maryland, led by senior pathologist Commander James J. Humes.[823]

The official announcement of the president's death had been released at Parkland Hospital in Dallas by press aide Kilduff at about 1:30 p.m. Oddly, among those present at the hospital for the announcement was Carousel Club owner and local mobster, Jack Ruby, according to a reporter and another witness. The reporter, Seth Kantor, previously with the *Dallas Times Herald*, later testified that he exchanged "hellos" with Ruby. The second witness corroborating Kantor's story was Wilma Tice who reported her sighting to the FBI. Ruby denied that he was present at Parkland Hospital at the announcement of the president's death, and the Warren Commission dismissed the two witnesses' accounts.[824] The question remains as to what Ruby's purpose was for going to the hospital.

The Warren Commission's fiction continued in its depiction of the next sequence of events in the life of Lee Harvey Oswald. Lee had arrived home at his rooming house in the Oak Cliff section at about 1 p.m., and according to the housekeeper, Mrs. Earlene Roberts, he only spent three or four minutes in his room.[825] He then took his pistol, a Smith and Wesson .38 caliber Special Model revolver,[826] and left. According to the official Warren Commission Report, Lee walked several blocks to the southeast and at approximately 1:15 p.m. at 10th Street between Patton Avenue and Denver Street, he encountered a police cruiser driven by officer Jefferson Davis (J. D.) Tippit. The rest of the Warren Commission version is as follows: "Tippit was driving slowly in an easterly direction on East 10th Street in Oak Cliff. About one hundred feet past the intersection of 10th Street and Patton Avenue, Tippit pulled up alongside a man [allegedly Lee Harvey Oswald] walking in the same direction. The man met the general description of the suspect wanted in connection with the assassination. He walked over to Tippit's car, rested his arms on the door on the right-hand side of the car, and apparently exchanged words with Tippit through the window. Tippit opened the door on the left side and started to walk around the front of his car. As he reached the front wheel on the driver's side, the man on the sidewalk drew a revolver and fired several shots in rapid succession, hitting Tippit four times and killing him instantly."[827]

The Warren Commission claims as evidence—much of it incomplete or fabricated—the following: that two eyewitnesses saw the shooting and that seven saw the gunman fleeing and identified him as Lee Harvey Oswald; recovered shot shells matched Lee's gun; and a jacket found on the route taken by the fleeing gunman belonged to Lee.[828] The facts, however, tell a vastly different story.

First of all, the murder scene, at 404 10th Street, was located nine tenths of a mile from Lee's rooming house, at 1026 North Beckley Avenue, just about a mile away. No one saw Lee walking, or running, that mile.[829] Also, the official version states that the murder occurred at 1:15 p.m., yet according to witnesses, it took place before 1:10 p.m. Lee left his place at 1:04 p.m. It was physically impossible for Lee to have made it on foot to Tippit's location in that time frame.

One witness, T. F. Bowley, thirty-five, who was driving along 10th Street, stated that he saw the police cruiser parked at the curb and spotted an officer lying in the street next to it. He pulled over, and, checking his watch, noted it was 1:10 p.m. He tried to help Tippit, but knew it was too late. He used the squad car radio to call in the shooting to the police dispatcher.[830] (The Warren Commission Report mistakenly credited another witness for having made the call, Domingo Benavides, who was driving by as the shooting took place. Benavides told police that he could not identify the gunman.)[831]

As for the two eyewitnesses whom the Warren Commission says saw the shooting, one was William Scoggins, a taxi driver, and the other was Helen Markham, a waitress. Scoggins was parked at Patton and 10th and claimed that he saw Tippit fall to the ground and that he then saw a gunman run across a yard, into bushes, and south on Patton. However, he admitted to the Warren Commission that when the authorities later showed him pictures of suspects, he was told that he "picked the wrong picture."[832] Scoggins and cabbie William Whaley had attended the same line-up in which Lee appeared with several others. Whaley said anyone would have picked Lee simply because he was "bawling out the policemen." Whaley said Lee was angry because he felt that he was put in line with several teenagers, and that "they were trying to railroad him and he wanted his lawyer . . ."[833]

The other eyewitness, Mrs. Helen Markham, was even more interesting. She stated that she was standing at the northwest corner of 10th Street and Patton when she saw a police car slowly drive up and stop next to a man who was walking down the block. She said the man spoke to the policeman at the right front window. The policeman then got out and walked to the front of the car when he was shot several times. He fell next to the left front wheel of the car. As the gunman ran down Patton, she screamed and ran to the officer's side.[834]

The Warren Commission neglected to point out numerous discrepancies in Markham's story. For example, she said the killer talked with Tippit through the front right window. Yet, crime scene photos show that the window on the passenger side of the cruiser was closed. In addition, Markham claimed to have spoken for a while with the fallen officer until the ambulance arrived. Yet the medical evidence showed Tippit died instantly.[835] What's more, two witnesses claimed that Markham was not even present in the minutes immediately following the shooting.[836] Other problems with her testimony include a description she gave one investigator in which she identified the gunman as short, heavy, and bushy-haired (Lee was thin).[837] Finally, in an unusual exchange with counsel, Markham repeatedly told the Warren Commission that she was unable to identify the suspect in the line-up. But when prompted (or rather, led) by counsel, "was there a number two man in there?" she responded, "number two is the one I picked."[838]

Despite descriptions of Helen Markham's questionable state of mind, the Warren Commission depended upon her to build the case against Lee. Clearly, the commission wanted to be able to state that Lee Harvey Oswald killed Officer J. D. Tippit, and therefore he must have killed the president.

The police report on Helen Louise Markham's condition when she was brought in to identify Lee in a line-up indicated that she was "hysterical." Joseph Ball, senior counsel for the Commission, would later characterize Markham as "an utter screwball,"[839] and he disparaged her testimony as "utterly unreliable" and "full of mistakes."[840] Another Commission attorney, Wesley Liebeler, who interviewed Markham, told Norman Redlich, special assistant to the Commission's General Counsel J. Lee Rankin, that Markham's statements were "contradictory" and "worthless."[841] Nevertheless, the Commission went along with her. After all, she suited its purposes. However, there may have been a valid reason for Markham's odd testimony, an explanation that has not been considered previously. She may well have been conditioned or hypno-programmed, as we shall see ahead.

Turning to the physical evidence in the Tippit murder, Dallas police produced four bullets that were recovered from the body of the fallen officer; three were Winchester-Westerns and one was of a Remington-Peters manufacture. Four cartridge cases were found in the vicinity of the crime scene; two were Winchester-Westerns and two were Remington-Peters. Based on an examination of this evidence, the Warren Commission concluded that five shots may have been fired. One bullet of Remington-Peters manufacture is missing, along one Winchester-Western shot shell.[842] This evidence actually leans in the direction of there having been two gunmen rather than one because of the two types of ammunition and the total number of shots fired.

It was not possible to obtain a ballistics analysis because the recovered bullets were too mangled to be compared with test bullets fired from Lee's revolver.[843] As for the cartridge cases, while the Warren Report claims that experts found they were fired from Lee's gun,[844] independent experts agree that the shot shells found at the Tippit murder scene could not have been fired from a .38 Special, the revolver Lee apparently owned. This is because spent shells from a .38 Special have a bulge in the middle caused by the lengthened cylinder due to the re-chambering.[845] This characteristic does not appear in the recovered shells. Clearly, the evidence shows that Lee did not shoot Officer J. D. Tippit.

Officer Tippit's fate, however, appears to have been closely tied to that of Lee Harvey Oswald. Tippit was an eleven-year member of the police force, married, and the father of three children, although his marriage was on the rocks.[846] He worked part-time at a restaurant, Austin's Barbecue Drive-In.[847] The establishment was owned by a close friend of Jack Ruby's.[848] While Ruby would later tell Warren Commission investigators that he was unsure if he knew J. D. Tippit, witnesses at the Carousel have stated that Ruby knew him "quite well," and that Tippit was a frequent patron of the club.[849] And, as noted earlier, Lee was a patron as well. So, it is not inconceivable that the two knew each other.

Tracing Officer Tippit's movements from the time of the assassination, we find him heading towards the Oak Cliff section of Dallas, which was Jack Ruby's neighborhood. Fifteen minutes after President Kennedy was shot, at 12:45 p.m., police reportedly radioed a description of the alleged suspect: "white, slender, weighing about 165 pounds, about five feet ten inches tall, and in his early thirties" (Lee was twenty-four).[850] The description was based on an eyewitness account by Howard L. Brennan, who was standing across the street from the Texas School Book Depository, according to the Warren Commission. Yet, in a later reconstruction of the scene, Brennan could barely find the sixth-floor stand-in, let alone describe his features. He also stated the suspect was standing while firing, yet the window was open only at the bottom. The assassin had to have been crouching.[851] Two days after the assassination in a TV interview, Dallas Police Chief Jesse Curry was asked if the police had a witness who saw the actual shooting. Curry responded, "no, sir. We do not."[852] Obviously, the police radio description broadcast at 12:45 p.m. on November 22, 1963 was provided by a source other than the Dallas police.

Virtually the entire patrol force was ordered to Dealey Plaza. Yet J. D. Tippit was sent to Oak Cliff to be "at large for any emergency."[853] Lee also lived in Oak Cliff, about a mile from Ruby's apartment. But the only address he had given out to his boss, Roy Truly, was the Irving home where Marina lived with Ruth Paine and the children, at 2115 West 5th Street. In fact, Dallas Police Captain Will Fritz stated he was preparing to go there. But his rationale is vague, since many employees of the Texas School Book Depository, not just Lee, had left the building and had not returned.[854] In fact, it is estimated that of the approximately seventy-five people who were working in the building that day, some forty-eight were outside watching the motorcade and an unknown number dispersed soon after the shots were fired.[855] Clearly, it appears that Captain Fritz's aim to find Lee must have been initiated by those directing the plot.

Meanwhile, Officer Tippit arrived in Oak Cliff and pulled over at a record shop on Jefferson Boulevard, one block from the Texas Theater, where he used the shop phone. Witnesses said he was only there a minute.[856] It was 12:59

p.m. According to the Dallas Police dispatch record, Tippit did not respond to a radio call to his cruiser at 1 p.m.[857]

Recall that Lee had arrived home at this time, according to his housekeeper, Mrs. Earlene Roberts. Lee's rooming house was located straight north, several blocks from Jefferson Boulevard on North Beckley. Mrs. Roberts said that shortly after Lee's return home, she noticed that a police cruiser had stopped in front of the house. She told the Warren Commission that the driver beeped a few times and then drove off. (She said it appeared there were two occupants, however, investigators have noted patrols were routinely solo, and that the driver may have had a shirt hanging in the window.) Mrs. Roberts had glanced at the car and gave investigators several possible cruiser numbers, 106, 107, or 207, none of which matched a car that could have been in the vicinity, according to the Warren Commission.[858] Tippit drove alone in car number 10.[859] If Mrs. Roberts saw a police car, Tippit's was the most likely candidate.

Tippit seems to have been an unwitting pawn in a chess game played with brutal precision by professionals in their field, men who knew that Lee had to be silenced as quickly as possible. Tippit was simply a means to that end.

According to Mrs. Roberts, when she last saw Lee, he had departed and was standing at the bus stop in front of the house.[860] To determine what happened next, it is necessary to logically fit together the many pieces of the puzzle based on the most reliable witness accounts and an accurate examination of the physical evidence. The result is the most plausible scenario, which is as follows: Officer Tippit arrived at Lee's house, honked, and then drove around the block and picked up Lee a few minutes later (knowing Lee could not drive). Tippit was no doubt just following orders to deliver Lee to a certain address, and given Lee's known clandestine connections in the Ageny and his probable relationships formed at the Dallas police force's favorite club, Jack Ruby's Carousel, such an errand would not have been unthinkable. Meanwhile, Lee's handlers, apparently unbeknownst to Tippit, selected a location for Lee's demise, a quiet residential neighborhood at 10th Street and Patton Avenue in Oak Cliff.

The plotters wanted few witnesses. The chosen spot was almost a mile from Lee's rooming house and five blocks from the Texas Theater, a movie house where apparently Lee was assigned to go in order to meet his contact.[861] The 10th Street location was also where waitress Helen Markham could be found, an ideal witness. (Interestingly, the location was also only a few blocks from Jack Ruby's apartment on Ewing Avenue, the same Jack Ruby whom the plotters would soon call on to shoot Lee two days later in the parking garage of the Dallas Police Department Headquarters.)

Lee probably did not know who had killed the president, nor who was behind it. Nor did he realize that he was being set up to be framed for it.

Lee heard the police cruiser honk and saw it was one of his bar associates. He left immediately to go with him. Lee needed to get to his handler as soon as possible to receive his assignment in the wake of the presidential assassination. As this national crisis unfolded, Lee no doubt believed that Tippit was on emergency orders to bring him to the covert command post for a dragnet briefing. Certainly all operatives, overt and covert, were called upon to handle this crisis, told where to meet, and given the roles they would play in the massive manhunt to find JFK's killer or killers. Many must have felt that a coup d'etat was underway. While Lee had worked under the guise of a leftist radical, he was a good, loyal, and patriotic CIA operative. As such, he may well have suspected anti-Castro Cubans were behind the assassination. He knew many of them, and he knew of their intense disapproval of President Kennedy's actions, particularly during the Bay of Pigs crisis.

After Tippit beeped and drove around the block, Lee waited momentarily at the bus stop in front of his rooming house. When Tippit returned, Lee jumped in, and the two sped away. It seems Tippit's orders were to meet two other men about five blocks before the Texas Theater on Jefferson, about a mile south of Lee's rooming house, at 10th Street, between Patton Avenue and Denver Street. The two men may have been Lee's handlers or hitmen hired by them. We do know that Tippit pulled over to the curb and parked at 404 10th Street, near Patton, and got out of his cruiser. Witnesses reported individuals sitting in a gray car, possibly a 1951 Plymouth, which was parked at this point across the street and facing Tippit's police car.[862]

The most likely scenario, based on accounts of eyewitnesses named below, is that two men approached Tippit, probably exiting from the gray car. They talked with Tippit and then motioned for Lee to get out of the cruiser. Lee must have spotted their guns, or perhaps knew the men and sensed trouble. He bolted from the police car, dove into the nearby bushes, and fled for his life. The gunmen fired at Lee and missed. They knew their mission's cover was blown and that the conspiracy was immediately apparent to Tippit. They had to silence him. J. D. Tippit was shot four times by the two gunmen. He fell to the ground dead, as the assailants jumped into their car, the gray vehicle across the street, and sped away.

This description of the Tippit murder is based on several eyewitnesses' statements. Acquilla Clemons was standing one block west of Tippit's cruiser. She stated that she saw two men approach Officer Tippit. One was short and heavy, and the other was tall and thin and was wearing a white shirt with khaki pants.[863] Neither was Lee Harvey Oswald, she said. Apparently, the men talked with Tippit and then, she said, the heavy man started shooting and the two then ran off. The Warren Commission ignored Mrs. Clemons's statements.[864] Frank Wright, a neighbor who lived a half-block east of the murder scene, said he heard the shots and went outside to investigate. He said that he saw a gunman wearing a long coat standing next to the fallen Officer Tippit,[865] and that the man ran to a gray car parked across the street and fled, driving west on 10th Street.[866] Another witness, Jack Tatum, was driving west on 10th moments before the murder. As he drove his red Ford Galaxy past Tippit's police car, he heard shots and looked back. He stated that he saw the officer lying on the ground and that the killer then walked over and shot Tippit in the head, execution style.[867]

Clearly, Lee was supposed to have been killed at 10th Street and Patton Avenue, and when that plan failed, the conspirators' back-up plan kicked in— to kill Lee at the Texas Theater on West Jefferson Boulevard, five blocks away.

Shortly after Tippit's murder, Lee slipped into the Texas Theater to seek refuge. Meanwhile, a couple of blocks from the Tippit murder scene, according to the Warren Commission Report, police found a light gray jacket in a lot on East Jefferson Boulevard. The Warren Commission alleged that the jacket was tossed off by Lee as he fled.[868] Yet Mrs. Roberts, Lee's housekeeper, has stated that when Lee left the house, he was putting on a dark jacket.[869] The jacket that was found had a laundry tag on it. However, Marina Oswald testified that Lee had a gray jacket, but that she always washed Lee's clothes; he never brought them to a commercial laundry.[870] Finally, the Warren Commission reported that the discarded jacket was discovered under a car behind a gas station by Dallas Police Captain W.R. Westbrook. Yet Westbrook has admitted it was not he who found it. The Dallas Police have since been unable to identify the finder of the jacket[871] or who planted it.

While it seems that the Dallas Police have a lot of explaining to do regarding their actions in both the JFK assassination and the Tippit murder cases, much of the evident mischief was no doubt the handiwork of the conspirators who were intent on incriminating Lee to protect themselves. Their intimidation of witnesses was brutal. For example, Mrs. Acquilla Clemons, noted above, who described the two men she saw murder Tippit, was soon victimized herself. Mrs. Clemons later told an independent investigator that shortly after she had divulged her account of the Tippit shooting, a man whom she assumed was a policeman paid her a visit. The man warned her that if she gave her testimony to the Warren Commission, "she might be killed."[872] Tippit witness Domingo Benavides, a truck driver who was at the murder scene, said he felt that he was in danger after the killing.[873] He believed that his brother Eddy was mistakenly murdered instead of him three months later. Eddy Benavides was shot in the back of the head in February 1964.[874] Witness Harold Russell, who worked at a car dealership on Jefferson Boulevard, told investigators that moments after the Tippit shooting, he saw the gunman, whom he could not identify, run down Patton Avenue to Jefferson Boulevard. Russell reportedly later believed that he was going to be killed. At a party three years after the Tippit murder, he broke into a violent frenzy. He was arrested and reportedly died in jail after being hit by a policeman.[875] Another witness who was standing with Harold Russell at the motor company on Jefferson Boulevard was Warren Reynolds. He, too, saw a gunman and stated that he could not give a positive identification. Two months after the assassination, following his interview with investigators, Reynolds was shot in the head while entering his basement office. He did not see his assailant, and robbery was reportedly not considered a motive. When Reynolds recovered from his head wound, fearing for his wife and daughter,[876] he changed his story to say that the gunman was Lee.[877] Meanwhile, a suspect in Reynolds's case had apparently talked about the shooting of Reynolds while in a drunken state. The suspect, Darrell Garner, was picked up and arrested. But a short time later, Garner was released based on an alibi provided by a woman who said she had been with Garner at the time Reynolds was shot. The woman, a former stripper at Jack Ruby's Carousel Club, was Betty Mooney MacDonald (a.k.a Nancy Jane, Marilyn Magyar). Ms. MacDonald herself was arrested a week later after a fight with her roommate. Hours later, she was found dead in her cell; she was hanging by her slacks.[878]

How much of a role MKULTRA played in these scenarios and in the overall assassination cover-up is unknown. But there are several instances that stand out. One example is the Warren Commission's prime witness to the Tippit murder, Helen Markham. It is interesting to note that she was connected to Jack Ruby. She worked as a waitress at the Eatwell Restaurant in downtown Dallas, which was an establishment frequented by Jack Ruby.[879] But the question of whether she was a true witness or a "fabricated" witness needs to be examined. We do know that Ms. Markham's dubious testimony was oddly "out of touch" with reality. For example, she believed she spoke *alone* with Officer Tippit as he lay dying for some *twenty* minutes. Yet, in fact, Tippit died instantly, and a crowd gathered immediately after the shooting.[880] Finally, when Ms. Markham referred to a police identification line-up of suspects that included

Lee, she said, "I looked at him. When I saw this man (Oswald) I wasn't sure, but I had cold chills just run all over me."[881] Granted, the expression "cold chills" is not uncommon. But, interestingly, shivering and complaining of the cold are symptoms that have been reported and recognized as aftereffects of hypno-programming and conditioning. Sirhan Sirhan began to "shiver violently" when examined by doctors shortly after the Robert Kennedy assassination. He also exhibited the same symptoms in his cell following hypnosis sessions by doctors before his trial.[882] While this particular physical response—having chills—does appear in Ms. Markham's testimony, whether or not MKULTRA was applied in her case remains uncertain. However, if it were, it would certainly explain her responses. In such a scenario, Ms. Markham would simply have been told under hypnosis what to say by Agency conspirators who had infiltrated the investigation. Indeed, MKULTRA could easily have made her believe she had witnessed something that she had not.

Returning to Lee Harvey Oswald's predicament, he fled the Tippit murder at 10th Street near Patton Avenue, and, according to the Warren Commission Report, endeavored to avoid being seen by police cruisers racing to the crime scene. Several blocks away, on Jefferson Boulevard, Lee ducked into a shoe store lobby. Johnny Brewer, the store manager, heard sirens and looked up. He saw Lee leave his entranceway and then watched him as he entered the nearby Jefferson Theater without buying a ticket. His suspicions aroused, Brewer walked over and reported this to the box office cashier, Julia Postal, who had apparently stepped away from her window when Lee slipped in. She called the police.[883]

Inside the theater, Lee sat down near the middle aisle towards the rear. There were only a dozen or so spectators in the audience. Minutes later, some fifteen policemen entered from both the front and the rear of the main floor. Johnny Brewer appeared on the stage and pointed out Lee's location to Patrolman M. N. McDonald, who then moved slowly towards the back of the theater, stopped in front of Lee, and ordered him to stand up.[884]

Lee knew that if he were taken into custody, he would be framed for the murder of Officer Tippit and probably that of President Kennedy. Lee also knew that if he bolted, he would be shot, unless he could surprise them and in the commotion somehow manage to swiftly vanish. He immediately decided to bolt.

Lee took a swing at Officer McDonald, but he was not quick enough to escape. McDonald grabbed Lee's gun and wrestled him to the floor, at which point four or five more policemen piled on. Lee was beaten and handcuffed in short order. As he was being led out of the front door of the theater at 1:51 p.m., he shouted "police brutality."[885] According to a *New York Times* story, Lee "received a black eye and a cut on his forehead."[886] But he knew that at least he was still alive. He may have also realized that the theater ambush could well have been the conspirators' back-up plan to silence him to protect themselves. Although there was no evidence as to the identity of the president's assassin, one officer reportedly shouted, as Lee was brought down, "Kill the president will you?"[887] Indeed, if Lee had tried to run from the theater, he would have been killed instantly.

Plans to kill Lee at 10th Street and Patton Avenue and in the Texas Theater had failed. The conspirators' options were few, and time was running out. They needed someone who roamed freely in police circles and who took orders from their covert ally, the mob hierarchy. Local mobster Jack Ruby was chosen. With his connections inside the Dallas Police Department, he was in a perfect position to take out Lee Harvey Oswald. Given the mob's power in Dallas, Ruby knew that refusing a Mafia order would have meant his own early demise. At the same time, the conspirators planned to ensure that Ruby's actions would not be characterized by the media as a mob hit, but rather as a crime of passion. If the public bought this story, Ruby may well have felt that through his killing of the alleged assassin of President John F. Kennedy, public opinion would consider him a patriot, thus earning him a lighter sentence. At any rate, Ruby set out to stalk Lee Harvey Oswald at police headquarters.

As noted earlier, the strip club owned by Jack Ruby was a police hangout. In fact, there are reports that in return for acting as a police informant, Ruby received police protection for his low-level narcotics trafficking, in addition to his gun-running, gambling, and prostitution rackets. The Dallas drug operations were run by the Joe Civello family, which was linked to mob bosses Carlos Marcello in New Orleans and Santo Trafficante in Florida.[888] It is also known that in September 1963, at about the same time Ruby was meeting with Johnny Rosselli in Miami, Richard Helms's lieutenant David Phillips was meeting with Rosselli associate David Morales at the CIA station in Miami. Rosselli, years later, admitted to journalist Jack Anderson that Ruby was "one of our boys."[889]

Several hours after Lee was brought to police headquarters at Harwood and Commerce Street in downtown Dallas, Ruby was following him. Witnesses reported that Ruby was seen on the third floor of the police building at 6 p.m. and again an hour or so later outside the room in which Lee was being questioned by Captain Will Fritz. Ruby reportedly knocked and asked if he could come in. A policeman guarding the door replied, "You can't go in there,

Jack." Ruby then left. He called back at 10:30 p.m., asked if he could bring in sandwiches to the officers on duty, and was told,"No, thank you." Finally, when a press conference was called for midnight to present Lee to the media, Lee's stalker, Jack Ruby, showed up in the crowded room.[890]

The press conference was conducted by Dallas District Attorney Henry Wade. It is interesting to note that, at one point, when Wade was describing Lee's background, the attorney mistakenly stated that Lee was involved with the "Free Cuba Committee" (a right-wing group). Jack Ruby immediately spoke up, correcting the D.A., "Henry, that's the Fair Play for Cuba Committee" (a left-wing group). Obviously, Ruby was closely attuned to his quarry.[891]

Lee had been arraigned for the murder of Officer J. D. Tippit at about 8 p.m. At the midnight press conference, the media asked Lee if he had killed President Kennedy. He replied, "No, I have not been charged with that. In fact, nobody has said that to me yet. The first thing I heard about it was when the newspaper reporters in the hall asked me that question."[892]

An hour or so after the twenty-minute press conference, at 1:30 a.m. on November 23, 1963, Lee was charged with the assassination of the president.[893] During his ordeal, Lee was questioned for approximately twelve hours from November 22 (Friday) through November 24 (Sunday). His prime interrogator was Dallas Police Captain Will Fritz of the homicide bureau, along with FBI and Secret Service agents. No notes or tapes were kept.[894] But even more importantly, Lee had no representation during his questioning.[895]

As for Lee's true identity as an undercover intelligence operative, a telling incident in this regard occurred a couple of hours after Lee was brought in to police headquarters. As questioning began in Captain Fritz's office, a deputy sheriff, Roger Craig, stopped in to meet the detainee. Craig said that he had seen a young man jump into a car on Elm Street at the grassy knoll near the Texas School Book Depository just moments following the assassination of the president. Craig reported that the car was a light-green, Rambler station wagon being driven by a Latin-looking man. Before he could reach the car to question them, the vehicle sped out of Dealey Plaza, heading west. When Craig saw Lee in Captain Fritz's office, he claimed that Lee was the man he had seen. Fritz then asked Lee, "What about the car?" (You will recall that Lee and Marina's friend, Ruth Paine, drove a Rambler wagon.) Lee responded to Fritz, "That station wagon belongs to Mrs. Paine. Don't try to drag her into this." He added, grousing, "Everybody will know who I am now."[896] Cleary, Lee felt that if Ruth Paine were checked out by investigative reporters in the media, and it was found out that she had intelligence connections (besides her father, William Avery

Hyde, as noted earlier), then perhaps his own cover would be blown. After all, his wife and two daughters lived with Ruth Paine. If, indeed, Lee thought that Ruth Paine's car had been used to pick up someone at the Texas School Book Depository, he must have thought it was just another ploy to try to implicate him in the assassination. And since he liked and respected Ruth Paine, his statements above show that he sincerely wanted to shield her from any hassles with the authorities. As it turned out, nothing resulted from Deputy Sheriff Roger Craig's story. Immediately following Lee's remarks, Captain Fritz was called to a meeting in another building and the questioning was curtailed.

Another intriguing aspect of the interrogation of Lee Harvey Oswald was his reported sense of control over the situation in which he found himself. Dallas Police Chief Jesse Curry stated later that he was impressed by Lee's answers. He said he seemed to have been trained in "resisting interrogation techniques." And Assistant District Attorney William Alexander remarked that "it was almost as if (Lee) had been rehearsed, or programmed, to meet the situation that he found himself in."[897] These statements by Chief Curry and Assistant D.A. Alexander indicate that Lee's demeanor and his responses were unusual compared to those of other suspects. Of course, Lee's knowledge that he was innocent obviously helped him to withstand the grilling. But beyond that, we must remember that Lee's handlers had a huge stake in Lee's interrogation. The conspirators' paramount objective was to keep Lee from identifying the names of his colleagues: David Ferrie, Guy Banister, and George de Mohrenschildt, as well as Agency superiors such as E. Howard Hunt and David Phillips. One way for them to have accomplished this goal would have been through MKULTRA hypno-programming (you'll recall that David Ferrie was a master hypnotist).[898] Lee would simply have been conditioned beforehand so that when questioned, he would avoid divulging any information about his covert intelligence activities. Whatever the modus operandi, it apparently worked.

Lee was forceful in his brief media appearances during several scheduled and impromptu press conferences. For example, at one point before he was formally charged, when asked if he had shot the president, he replied, "I didn't shoot anybody, no sir." As he was led through the corridor to his jail cell, he spoke to the TV cameras, asking if someone watching would "come forward to give me legal assistance."[899] Later on in the evening of November 22, after a reporter told him he had been charged with the assassination, Lee looked stunned and replied, "Then I'm the patsy."[900] Following his arraignment for the murder of the president, he stated that the charges were "ridiculous," and stuck to his story.[901]

Lee's brother Robert came in to see him at the visitors' cubicle in the jail. Having read about the alleged evidence against his brother—essentially the rifle lying on the sixth floor of the Texas School Book Depository—a bewildered Robert sat down in front of Lee and asked, "Lee, what in the Sam Hill is goin' on?" In a tense voice, Lee responded, "I just don't know what they're talking about. Don't believe all this so-called evidence." Robert has written that at this point he then stared into Lee's eyes hoping to find an answer. Lee quietly told him, "Brother, you won't find anything there."[902]

Dallas Police Chief Jesse Curry summed up his thoughts regarding Lee Harvey Oswald in an interview sometime later. Chief Curry stated, "We don't have any proof that Oswald fired the rifle, and never did. Nobody's yet been able to put him in that building (the Texas School Book Depository) with a gun in his hand."[903]

Indeed, Lee had no motive.[904] Moreover, Lee was known to have liked President Kennedy. The Russian-speaking community in Dallas voiced this belief about Lee, as did Lee's relatives in New Orleans, Lillian and Marilyn Murret. Lee's friends Michael Paine, Paul Gregory, and George de Mohrenschildt all stated that Lee was an admirer of Kennedy and his family.[905]

With Lee incarcerated at this point, his wife Marina and his mother Marguerite escaped the onslaught of reporters by hiding out in a motel in Irving, a few miles outside of Dallas.[906]

Less than forty-eight hours after the assassination, on Sunday morning, November 24, 1963, Lee was brought from his cell via elevator down to the basement parking garage of the Police Headquarters and City Jail building. The plan was to transfer him to the county jail at Dealey Plaza.[907]

Meanwhile, at Jack Ruby's apartment on Ewing Avenue in Oak Cliff, about four miles west of downtown, the phone rang. It was 9:30 a.m. Sunday morning. Ruby's roommate, George Senator, who also worked at the Carousel, later stated that the call was for Ruby. He added that after Ruby hung up, "He began to pace nervously from room to room."[908] It appears that Ruby must have been told what time Lee Harvey Oswald would be in public view and where. He knew he had no choice; disobeying a mob order would have resulted in his own death.[909] He also must have been aware of the fact that his silencing Lee would eliminate the need for a trial, a trial that could possibly expose the assassination plot. It is doubtful that he would have also known that, at this point, key mob figures were pawns of the Helms-Angleton faction of the CIA—the architects of both the assassination and the cover-up.

Ruby dressed in his business suit and prepared for his assignment by packing his piece. It was not unusual for him to wear a handgun. In the previous fourteen years, he had been arrested eight times by Dallas police, and two of those arrests were for carrying a concealed weapon. He was not charged either time. Indeed, Ruby had friends in the Dallas Police Department.[910]

According to the Warren Commission Report, no one saw Ruby arriving at the parking garage in the Police Headquarters where Lee was to be transferred to a vehicle and driven to the county jail. However, the Commission stated that Ruby "probably" entered the basement by walking alone down a ramp on the Main Street side of the building, three minutes before the shooting.[911] But this account is disputed by two witnesses who were stationed at that ramp. Terrance McGarry of the United Press International, and Harry Tasker, a taxi driver, both said that no one entered the building via the ramp during that time period.[912] The policeman on guard duty, Officer Ray Vaughn, also testified that Ruby never passed by him. And another Dallas policeman, Red Davis, has stated that Jack Ruby was actually brought down to the basement garage by Assistant Chief of Police Charles Batchelor.[913]

The press had been notified of Lee's planned transfer and had set up their TV cameras, microphones, and lighting, preparing for a live telecast from the basement. In living rooms across the nation, viewers were closely watching the broadcast (the author included). According to the Warren Commission, some forty to fifty newsmen were gathered in the garage, along with between seventy and seventy-five police officers.[914] As Lee got off the elevator and walked toward the cameras and the waiting vehicle, he was escorted by Captain Will Fritz in front, Detective James Leavelle on his right, Detective L. C. Graves on his left, and Detective L. D. Montgomery following the group. It was 11:21 a.m.[915] CBS newsman Ike Pappas, standing a few feet from Lee, asked, "You have anything to say in your defense?"[916] Suddenly, Jack Ruby pushed forward, drew his .38 caliber revolver, and fired one shot hitting Lee in the abdomen.[917] "There's a shot! Oswald has been shot! Oswald has been shot!" Pappas yelled into his microphone.[918] Lee collapsed to the ground, and Ruby was tackled by several officers. Viewers who had been intently watching the presidential assassination coverage were stunned. A grieving nation was shocked once again.

Lee was rushed to Parkland Hospital and operated on by Dr. Charles A. Crenshaw and his team. Lee suffered hemorrhagic shock followed by cardiac arrest. He died in surgery at 1:07 p.m.[919] Lee Harvey Oswald was twenty-four.

Lee was buried the next day at Rose Hill Cemetery in Fort Worth, Texas. His immediate family gathered to bid him farewell, while news reporters, who were covering the interment, served as pallbearers.[920] Years later, Marguerite Oswald would be buried next to her son following her death from cancer in a Fort Worth hospital in 1981.[921]

On November 25, 1963, the same day Lee was buried, President John F. Kennedy was laid to rest in Arlington Cemetery. At least one historian has termed it "the greatest funeral in America in the twentieth century."[922] All eyes focused on the veiled Jacqueline Kennedy with her children Caroline, six, and John, three.

Robert Kennedy soldiered his extended family through the public mourning, the Mass, and the graveside service. But the sudden loss of his brother had traumatized him. Kennedy aide Pierre Salinger described Bobby as "the most shattered man I had ever seen in my life. He was virtually non-functioning. He would walk for hours by himself."[923] Nine months later, in August 1964, Bobby eulogized President Kennedy at the Democratic National Convention in Atlantic City, New Jersey. When he rose to speak, pandemonium broke out on the floor. The ovation lasted twenty-two minutes. Bobby then addressed the convention, speaking softly, and concluding with five lines of poetry:

When he shall die
Take him and cut him out in little stars
And he will make the face of heaven so fine
That all the world will be in love with night,
And pay no worship to the garish sun.[924]

After Jack Ruby gunned down Lee Harvey Oswald, many reporters wrote that Ruby had committed a crime of passion when he shot Oswald. The morning of the murder, Ruby had heard that Lee was to be transferred to the county jail, so while running errands downtown, he sneaked into the police headquarters basement and shot Oswald as he walked by. Other reporters have suggested that Ruby would have killed Oswald for money, if the payoff were large enough. Ruby was reportedly deeply in debt, and he knew that if he were convicted of a crime of passion, he could perhaps receive only a five-year sentence.[925]

As it turned out, Ruby defended his crime by testifying that he killed Lee "out of love for our beloved president" and "to spare Mrs. Kennedy" from having to attend Oswald's trial. However, a document discovered three years later, after Ruby had died, revealed that Ruby's lines—using the First Lady as an excuse—were apparently given to him by his attorney, Tom Howard.[926]

But despite Ruby's ploy, a number of journalists felt that if they knew Ruby's true role, they would have the key to understanding the president's assassination. On Sunday night, November 24, 1963, after Ruby had shot Oswald, two journalists appeared at Ruby's apartment on Ewing Avenue in Oak Cliff. They met with attorney Tom Howard, Ruby's roommate George Senator, and another Ruby lawyer, Jim Martin. The reporters were James Koethe of the *Dallas Times Herald* and Bill Hunter of the *Long Beach Independent Press Telegram*. It is not known what they discussed. But less than a year and a half later, the two journalists and one of the lawyers were dead. Hunter was shot in a police station in California in April 1964; Koethe was murdered in his apartment in Dallas in September 1964; and Howard suffered a fatal heart attack in Dallas in March of 1965.[927]

Jack Ruby feared for his own life as well. While in jail, Ruby was interviewed by Earl Warren, Rep. Gerald Ford (the future president), and other Commission members. In one session, Ruby asked if he could be taken out of Dallas. He said, "I would like to request that I go to Washington. . . ." He added, "Gentlemen, my life is in danger here." He also said, "I want to tell the truth, and I can't tell it here." And finally, he stated, "Well, you won't ever see me again. I tell you that. A whole new form of government is going to take over the country, and I know I won't live to see you another time."[928]

The Warren Commission claimed that it found no evidence that Ruby was part of a plot to assassinate the president. Of course, the commission also did not want to uncover a conspiracy.[929] Ruby was tried and convicted for the murder of Lee Harvey Oswald. On March 14, 1964, the jury returned a guilty verdict, and Judge Joseph B. Brown handed down the death penalty. Ruby appealed.[930] Eventually, the Texas Appeals Court reversed this decision based on Judge Brown's refusal to change the location of the trial and other technicalities.[931] A new trial was ordered on December 7, 1966, this one in Wichita Falls, Texas, rather than Dallas. Many observers felt that the outcome would be much different—finding murder without malice, thus giving Ruby a much lighter sentence. On December 9, 1966, Ruby fell ill and was admitted to Parkland Hospital for tests. Doctors found that he was suffering from inoperable lung cancer. Less than one month later, on January 3, 1967, Ruby died.[932] He had been correct when he told Earl Warren that he would never see them again.

Lee's murder at the hands of Jack Ruby had prompted Marina Oswald to take her two children and move from Ruth Paine's house to a place of her own. As soon as the Oswalds left, Michael Paine moved back in with his wife,

Ruth. According to one Warren Commission record, the FBI had placed a wiretap on Ruth's phone immediately after the assassination. A conversation was recorded between Ruth and Michael Paine in which Michael stated that he felt Lee had shot the president. But he said that he did not think Lee was responsible. He added, "We both know who is responsible."[933] Again, Agency ties seem very much implied here.

As noted earlier, Richard Helms and James Angleton were the true source of power in the Agency at this time. It is also known that they felt nothing but contempt for both John and Robert Kennedy.[934] The day after the assassination, Helms sent a personal letter of condolence to Bobby Kennedy. He wrote, "There is nothing for me to say that has not been said better by many others. When you sent me to see the president Tuesday afternoon, he never looked better, seemed more confident, or appeared more in control of the crushing forces around him. Friday struck me personally. Mrs. Helms and I extend our deepest sympathy and heartfelt condolences to you and the family. We pray that you will continue to give us your leadership. Respectfully and sadly, Dick Helms." Bobby's cool reply was simply, "My thanks to you."[935]

About ten years before Helms died in 2002, he appeared on a national talk show, the *Phil Donahue Show*. He was asked why so many people who know the truth concerning the assassination do not come forward with evidence or information. Helms responded, "It is very difficult in real time to get people to talk, particularly when there may be sanctions against them—and the young lady who is twenty-five, who wants to take on one of these powerful figures sometime by saying something she knows about them, does so at her own peril. Ahhh, I don't want to emphasize that anything is going to be done to her, but by the time the newspapers, or somebody, gets through with her, she'll wish she hadn't done it."[936]

# 7

# *Sirhan Bishara Sirhan, an Involuntary Pawn*

O N AUGUST 28, 2002, one of the world's preeminent authorities on the Robert F. Kennedy assassination, Judge Robert J. Joling of Green Valley, Arizona (formerly of Kenosha, Wisconsin), spoke at the University of New Haven. He had traveled to Connecticut to donate his extensive collection of RFK documents to the university's Dr. Henry C. Lee Institute of Forensic Science. A gathering of one hundred, including students, faculty, law enforcement officers, and reporters, came to listen to Judge Joling's findings. The facts of the thirty-four-year-old murder case would surprise many in the room. The forensic evidence showed that the convicted assassin, Sirhan Bishara Sirhan, a twenty-four-year-old Palestinian immigrant who was apprehended with gun in hand, was *not* in fact, the killer.[937]

As we shall see ahead, other respected historians have concurred with Judge Joling's assessment. In addition, nationally recognized investigators have also concluded—based on eyewitness accounts—that there were two other gunmen, both wearing suits, as well as a uniformed security guard, all with guns drawn.

Sen. Robert Kennedy, forty-two, was ambushed in the kitchen pantry of Los Angeles's Ambassador Hotel shortly after midnight on June 5, 1968. He had just delivered a rousing victory speech, having won the California Democratic presidential primary earlier that night. Amidst thunderous applause in the hotel ballroom, he and his wife Ethel and entourage exited the dais and took a shortcut through the pantry on their way to a press conference in another room on that floor. A hotel employee guided Kennedy through the swinging doors of the pantry. Bobby greeted hotel workers as he walked through. Some seventy people—supporters, staff, friends, reporters, photographers, and others—crowded into the kitchen. Witnesses reported that the gunfire sounded like someone had set off a string of firecrackers. Five bystanders were wounded. They survived. Kennedy was hit at point-blank range in the back of the head and the back. He collapsed to the floor with arms outstretched, mortally wounded. The next day, June 6, 1968, at Good Samaritan Hospital, Bobby died.

Sen. Robert Kennedy would have most likely been the next president of the United States. He had won the final primary, defeating Minnesota senator Gene McCarthy, another popular antiwar candidate. Kennedy was expected to win the Democratic Party's presidential nomination at the Chicago national convention in August 1968. From there, most pundits felt that Kennedy would have gone on to beat Republican Richard Nixon for the White House in November. As it turned out, following Bobby's death, the Democrats at the Chicago convention chose Vice President Hubert Humphrey as their party's nominee. He lost in the general election to Richard Nixon. During Nixon's tenure, the United States endured five more years of war in Vietnam.

Bobby's assassination shocked the world. At the crime scene in the Ambassador Hotel kitchen, the apparent assailant, Sirhan Sirhan, had been pummeled and then quickly taken into custody. Sirhan later stated in his jail cell that he had no memory of murder and even when questioned later under hypnosis he had no recall of the shooting. As for the forensic evidence, the bullets test-fired from Sirhan's .22 caliber handgun could not be conclusively matched to any of the victims' bullets.[938] The state also produced a forty-eight-page diary to show evidence of premeditation; Sirhan has no memory of writing it. A prison psychiatrist, Dr. Eduard Simson-Kallas, a PhD from Heidelberg and Stanford, spent a number of sessions analyzing Sirhan at San Quentin Prison shortly after his sentencing.[939] His work indicated that Sirhan was mentally normal, but that he had been hypno-programmed by someone. Since then, no further work has been done to try to unlock Sirhan's mind.[940]

Sirhan is serving a life sentence. At this writing, he is sixty-nine years old and resides at Coalinga, California's Pleasant Valley State Prison. He has been imprisoned for forty-five years.[941]

Following President John F. Kennedy's assassination in 1963, the media reported that Robert Kennedy publicly backed the Warren Commission's views. However, the media did not know that Bobby was also quietly seeking answers to the questions surrounding his brother's murder. Unbeknownst to the general public, he soon became one of the strongest believers in a conspiracy involving his brother's death.[942]

At the time of this writing, Bobby's son, Robert F. Kennedy Jr., a New York attorney and environmentalist, has come out in support of his father's views. According to an *Associated Press* story written by Jamie Stengle, published on January 12, 2013, RFK Jr. has stated that he, too, is convinced that there was more than one gunman involved in President Kennedy's assassination. He made the comments during an appearance with his sister Rory in an interview with journalist Charlie Rose in Dallas.

Early on in the aftermath of the assassination, Bobby Kennedy confided in Walter Sheridan, a close Kennedy family friend, formerly with the Justice Department, asking him to see what he could find out. Both men came to realize that JFK's assassination was the result of a "powerful conspiracy."[943] It is not known if they knew for certain who was behind it, but Sheridan's widow Nancy has revealed that they intended to crack the case when Bobby was elected president. Until then, both men kept their investigation secret in order to protect their families from any danger.[944] Ironically, during the 1967 investigation by New Orleans District Attorney Jim Garrison, both Kennedy and Sheridan opposed Garrison's probe. Bobby felt that the CIA plots to kill Castro would be disclosed and blamed on the Kennedys.[945] Recall that when the Kennedy administration had found out about the attempts on Castro's life, such schemes were ordered halted. Neither Bobby nor Walt Sheridan trusted the CIA.[946] They knew their best course of action was to wait for Bobby to be elected president, and then reopen the John F. Kennedy assassination case when they would have the power to get to the bottom of it. Both men also knew that the CIA was monitoring Robert Kennedy's movements very closely. For example, in South Africa in June 1966, Bobby had received an overwhelming reception from the impoverished masses there when he toured the countryside speaking out vigorously against apartheid. Throughout his travels, Richard Helms's CIA was continuously spying on Kennedy and his advisors.[947] Indeed, Helms, James Angleton, and others in the CIA and in the Johnson administration viewed Bobby Kennedy as a threat, particularly because of his views on the war in Vietnam.[948]

Three and a half years after the assassination of President Kennedy, the Vietnam War was raging. Bobby's outward ambivalence toward running for the presidency masked an inner drive that would not be deterred. Richard Helms, no doubt, foresaw Bobby and his allies working in tandem with the growing antiwar movement and sensed a formidable campaign team emerging. The young senator appeared unstoppable.

Meanwhile, under Helms's watch, Agency drug and hypnosis experiments continued unabated,[949] with the ultimate goal of producing a sophisticated, fail-safe, executive action plan (i.e., assassination program). D-day would come on June 5, 1968, the night on which the nightmare of November 22, 1963 would repeat itself.

Sirhan Bishara Sirhan was born on March 19, 1944 in Jerusalem[950] and although he was a Palestinian, he was not a Muslim. The Sirhans were Orthodox Christians.[951] Indeed, after their arrival in the United States, Sirhan's mother, Mary, worked at a local Presbyterian Church nursery.[952]

Life was not easy for the Sirhan family in the Holy City. According to author Robert Kaiser, Mary Sirhan told him about several horrific occurrences that beset the family while living in Jerusalem. At the age of four, Sirhan saw one of his older brothers run over by a truck and killed during a skirmish between Zionists and Palestinian Arabs.[953] When part of their home was dynamited, the Sirhans fled to another section of the city.[954] There, the seven-member family set up home in a fifteen-by-thirty-foot room with only a camping stove for cooking meals.[955] On another occasion, Sirhan fetched a bucket full of water and brought it into the apartment without noticing what was in the water. He screamed at the sight of a hand floating on the surface.[956]

Sirhan's father, Bishara, brought the family from Jerusalem to California in January 1957 when Sirhan was twelve.[957] The family had obtained immigration visas through the assistance of the Church World Service and sponsorship from the Rev. Haldor Lillenas of the Church of the Nazarene.[958] But soon after their arrival, Bishara Sirhan became unhappy with life in the United States. Bishara left and returned to Jerusalem six months later, abandoning his family.[959]

The Sirhans eventually settled at 696 East Howard Street in Pasadena, California.[960] The family consisted of Sirhan, who was called "Sol" by his friends, his mother, and two brothers, Adel, who was five years older than he, and Munir, who was three years younger.[961] Tragically, a sister, Aida, died of leukemia at age twenty-nine when Sirhan was twenty-one.[962] Finally, there were two brothers, Sharif and Saidallah, who lived away from home.

Sirhan's first educational experience in the United States was the sixth grade at Longfellow Grammar School in Pasadena, where school records show thirteen-year-old Sirhan was "cooperative, well-mannered, and well-liked." He also made "many new friends." He graduated elementary school with a C-plus average, an accomplishment considering his having had to master English as well.[963]

Sirhan earned above average grades at John Muir High School and went on to Pasadena City College. However, he did not do as well there and left at age twenty-one in 1965.[964]

Sirhan's school years were not unlike those of most teenagers. He apparently had no serious romantic involvements, but did have infatuations. For example, he was interested in a young woman named Gwen Gumm, whom he had met at Pasadena City College.[965] He had asked her out for a date several times, but they had never actually gone. They had also seen each other at Santa Anita Racetrack (more regarding Ms. Gumm ahead).[966]

Although a number of historians have tried to portray Sirhan as a loner, he was far from that. At school, and at his several workplaces, he had a variety of friends. One pal was a classmate, a "short pudgy fellow" by the name of Walter Crowe.[967]

Walter Crowe and Sirhan first met in the sixth grade when they had adjoining paper routes.[968] They attended John Muir High School together and both went on to Pasadena City College for two years. At that point, in 1965, Sirhan went to work with horses as an exercise boy, and Walter transferred to UCLA to major in History.[969]

Walter Crowe's political beliefs at the time were Marxist, as were those of many college students in the late 1960s. At Pasadena City College, Crowe attempted to organize a chapter of the Students for a Democratic Society (SDS), a left-wing organization. He also tried to recruit his buddy Sol, but Sirhan was not interested, and in fact, the chapter never materialized. According to Crowe, Sirhan was apolitical.[970]

It was at this time that Walter Crowe was under surveillance by intelligence units for his extracurricular activities, according to the late author Philip Melanson, who had been a professor at the University of Massachusetts in North Dartmouth, Massachusetts.[971] As noted earlier, the intelligence community was working closely with key municipal police departments during this era to quell civil unrest, race riots, and antiwar demonstrations. So, the long arm of the intelligence community found itself in the heart of Sirhan's world. Since Sirhan was a companion of Walter Crowe, Sirhan was certainly observed by covert operatives when the two young men were together at school, even though Sirhan's interests were purely social, not political. At the same time, a number of operatives were very busy seeking individuals for agency hypnosis and drug experiments. As noted earlier, thousands of persons were selected unwittingly for MKULTRA research programs.

The evidence that US intelligence was interested in Sirhan comes from a Military Intelligence report on Sirhan from San Francisco that surfaced in the LAPD's files at the time of Sen. Robert Kennedy's death.[972] Intelligence officer, Timothy Richdale, who was at the LAPD command center immediately following the assassination, reported the existence of an intelligence background check or surveillance report on Sirhan that was written prior to the assassination. The report, which had been filed by Army intelligence officer Terry Fall in San Francisco, listed the schools Sirhan had attended: Pasadena City College, John Muir High School, George Washington Junior High, and Longfellow Grammar School.[973]

Of course, in order for an individual to have been unwittingly selected as a potential subject for any kind of MK program, an intelligence file would have been a prerequisite. The fact that this file was shared with local law enforcement personnel is indicative of the strong ties at that time between the intelligence community and large city police departments. According to author Philip Melanson, former CIA officer Victor Marchetti discovered during 1967 that Los Angeles police were indeed being trained at CIA headquarters. Marchetti has reported he was informed that the training, which lasted for several days, was for "sensitive" activities approved by Richard Helms and conducted by the CIA's Clandestine Services Division.[974]

After leaving Pasadena City College, Sirhan sought work to support himself and to help out his mother, as did his brothers. Adel made his living as a musician playing an oud (a guitar-like instrument) at a bar called the Fez on North Vermont Street in Los Angeles.[975] The youngest brother, Munir, worked as a retail clerk at a Nash Department Store.[976] As for Sirhan, his goal in life was to be accorded the title of jockey. The aspirations of five-foot-four-inch, 120-pound Sirhan motivated him to concentrate on the most humble aspects of the vocation. He was soon hired at Santa Anita Racetrack as an exercise boy and groom. He also briefly worked in the same capacity at Del Mar Racetrack. Both were frequented by mobsters, and Sirhan became friendly with a few of the low-level mob types.[977]

It is important to note that subjects unwittingly ensnared in Richard Helms and James Angleton's MKULTRA experiments were many times found at locations where agency and Mafia paths crossed. These included racetracks where high-level intelligence and mob figures were known to meet. Even J. Edgar Hoover, FBI director, along with his friend and assistant Clyde Tolson, patronized mob meeting places at the Santa Anita and Del Mar racetracks. Under Hoover, the Mafia had enjoyed a comfortable existence. According to Arthur Schlesinger, in 1959, just prior to John Kennedy's election, at the FBI's New York office, there were some four hundred agents investigating the "Communist threat." At the same office, there were four agents working on organized crime. It is even reported that a couple of years later, when Robert Kennedy was attorney general, he called the New York office for an update on the mob. He was told by the agent in charge that he wouldn't be able to provide the latest information because there was a newspaper strike in progress![978] By all appearances, Hoover's forces had a high-level, nonaggression pact in place with the mob, one that would—from a public relations viewpoint—benefit both parties, at least in Hoover's mind.[979]

As in the CIA, FBI and mob heads took careful note as Robert Kennedy's star began to rise again in 1966. All of these organizations recalled how Robert Kennedy's Justice Department had rode herd over mob families in America's largest cities in 1962 and 1963. In those years, a total of 404 wiseguys had been convicted. And the Patriarca family of Rhode Island and the DeCavalcante family of New Jersey had been effectively shut down.[980] Mafia heads in other key cities were outraged. Prior to Bobby's murder, Hoover knew of threats to Kennedy's life, but he chose to leave his nemesis unprotected and even told his staff that this was the way it would be.[981]

Given Hoover's relationship with the mob and his loathing of Robert Kennedy, it is easy to deduce what his mission would be after the assassination: to keep the investigation within the limits of the lone gunman scenario. This strategy would protect both the FBI and the mob from being framed by the CIA. At the same time, the CIA-mob association would essentially provide Richard Helms and James Angleton's lieutenants at the Agency the perfect cover.

At age twenty-one, after leaving college, Sirhan worked from October 1965 to the spring of 1966 as a groom at Santa Anita Racetrack. According to author John Davis, racetrack gambling was controlled at that time by racketeer Mickey Cohen.[982] Cohen would appear virtually every day at either Santa Anita or at Del Mar racetrack. The mob, which had supported Richard Nixon since 1946, had a vested interest in helping whoever was plotting against Robert Kennedy. (At this time, Cohen was stealing millions from the San Diego track. His activities would finally land him in prison by 1971.[983])

Besides the racetrack, other mob meeting places included strip joints, some of which also have a reputation for mob involvement. Sirhan was known to patronize several topless bars including the Cat Patch, located about eight miles from the Santa Anita track.[984] He probably also visited the Briar Patch as well, another topless bar that was less than a mile from the track. Clubs were typical of the venues utilized by Helms's Agency MKULTRA operations. Such places were ideal for picking up unwitting individuals for drug and hypnosis experimentation.

At Santa Anita Racktrack, one individual with whom Sirhan became acquainted was a horse trainer by the name of Henry Ramistella of New Jersey, who was also known as Frank Donneroummas.[985] Donneroummas had an arrest record in Miami and New York for a variety of crimes including theft, narcotics possession, and perjury. He had also been banned from the tracks on the East Coast.[986] Donneroummas befriended Sirhan, and when Sirhan decided to leave Santa Anita to seek a more prestigious position in the racing business, it was Donneroummas who helped him land a new job. With Frank's introduction, Sirhan was hired in the spring of 1966 at a breeding farm called the Granja Vista del Rio Ranch located in Norco, near Corona. It was managed by Bert C. Altfillisch and owned by a group that included staunch anti-Castro Cuban Desi Arnaz, actress Lucille Ball's husband. Along with Arnaz, other horse owners who got to know Sirhan well were actor Buddy Ebsen and TV personality Dale Robertson.[987]

Sirhan was enthusiastic about his good fortune. He next sought a place to stay, hoping to avoid a long daily commute from Pasadena. Taking out his 1956 pink and white DeSoto Fireflight,[988] he drove the back roads in the Granja Vista area until he found a quiet motel along the way. After briefly speaking with the motel manager, Edward Van Antwerp, who lived there with his wife, Sirhan was able to secure a bed for himself. He ended up living there for five months.[989]

In Sirhan's work as a groom and exercise boy at Granja Vista, he developed successful relationships with the staff and the clients. Again, this differs sharply with popular belief that he was a loner. One particular horse owner who enjoyed Sirhan was Robert Prestwood. His wife also liked Sirhan. According to author Robert Kaiser, the couple wanted Sirhan to eventually become the jockey for their colt, Jet Spec.[990]

As an exercise boy at the ranch, Sirhan tried to help his fellow employees to gain better working conditions, and they applauded his efforts, even though he was unsuccessful. For example, Sirhan is known to have taken the lead in representing his coworkers in issues with the ranch manager, Bert Altfillisch. According to several employees, Altfillisch and Sirhan had differences of opinion regarding workplace policies, yet they still respected each other. While Altfillisch maintained firm control over the staff, he allowed Sirhan to air his views, and there was reportedly never any animosity between them.[991]

One of Sirhan's coworkers, Terry Welch, described Sirhan as someone who "indicated a strong liking for the United States and never exhibited any particular loyalty or feeling toward the country of his birth (Jordan)." He added that Sirhan's political beliefs were strongly opposed to Communism.[992] And having been brought up as a Christian, Sirhan also had little interest in Muslim fundamentalism. In fact, he once told author Robert Kaiser while awaiting trial, "I don't identify with the Arabs politically or any other way except for the fact that their blood flows in my veins. Their food I don't go for. Their clothing I don't dig. Their robes and all that bullshit. Their politics I can't understand and don't want to understand . . . Hell, I'm an American."[993] While not even remotely an Arab freedom fighter, he would eventually come to be seen as one.

As for Sirhan's emotional life, it appears that he was interested in a young female coworker at the ranch named Peggy Osterkamp. An attractive young woman, she was the daughter of a Corona dairyman. However, according to Peggy, they never dated.[994]

Sirhan worked at Granja Vista throughout 1966, and during that time, he had several bad falls from a horse. The worst was on September 25, 1966, when Sirhan was racing two fellow trainers on an exercise track. Fog rolled in and Sirhan, riding a chestnut mare at full gallop, crashed into the outer rail. He was in a semicoma when the ambulance arrived to take him to Corona Community Hospital. Several stitches later, his prognosis was good, but he would still spend many weeks pursuing medical specialists in order to find relief for the pain in his left eye.[995]

The horse fall also exacted an emotional toll on the aspiring jockey and gave rise to an element of fear within his psyche. As ranch manager, Bert Altfillisch, commented, "The kid had a lot of ambition, but he never could have become a jockey. He sort of lost his nerve."[996] Sirhan began to see his dream slip away.

Heartbroken, Sirhan soon found a new source of inspiration in the literature of the occult, now known as New Age books. This avocation was introduced to him by a coworker at the breeding farm, forty-year-old Walter Thomas Rathke. Rathke's appearance in Sirhan's life at this time, and his role as Sirhan's mentor and close companion, had numerous, and curious, overtones, as we shall see ahead. Rathke, a bearded man who was known as "Tom," was seventeen years older than Sirhan. He had been married, yet apparently lived alone. He was college educated and had worked for the phone company. However, at this point in his life, he was working in the stables with Sirhan at Granja Vista.[997] He exhibited a deep knowledge of the occult, while at the same time he was known to have maintained beliefs that were far to the right. Indeed, in many ways, his action profile closely resembled that of Lee Harvey

Oswald's friend George de Mohrenschildt. In intelligence circles, such a person is labeled a control agent or a handler.

When he was not at the racetrack with Rathke, Sirhan followed Rathke's lead pursuing his quest for knowledge and power in local bookstores, primarily in the New Age section. One store he particularly favored was Broughton's Bookstore on Lake Street in Pasadena.[998] He would many times just read in the stacks—the books were expensive—and then, based on recall, he would try the mental experiments at home. Some of the topics he and Rathke discussed included astral projection, auras, clairvoyance, and reincarnation. Rathke introduced Sirhan to such books as *The Laws of Mental Domination; Thought Power: Its Control and Culture; and Meditation on the Occult Life: The Hidden Power.*[999]

Sirhan was not known to have indulged in recreational drugs; he smoked L&M cigarettes and drank Tom Collins.[1000] His "highs" appear to have come from winning at the track and from his psychic experimentation. Physically, Sirhan's recovery from his September 1966 horse fall was slow, and as a result, he pursued a workmen's compensation claim to recover lost wages and at least some return for what he had gone through.

On December 6, 1966, Sirhan drove to the Granja Vista ranch and collected his last paycheck. He had had his fill of the breeding farm, and although he knew he would miss some of his friends there, he saw little future in the ranch for himself. Sirhan was twenty-two at this point. He hoped to have a more prosperous new year in 1967, and until a better position came along, planned to continue betting on the horses, and along with his friend Tom Rathke, delving into the world of mysticism.[1001]

At the same time, a fascination with all things Eastern had become fashionable in the summer of 1967. Clothing, philosophy, and the music of India captured the imagination of America's youth. In Monterey, California, the musical hit at the famous pop festival that year was Ravi Shankar.

Indeed, Sirhan enjoyed his New Age studies and would continually search for practical uses, such as relief for his eye pain, which doctors had been unable to completely resolve. Sirhan soon found a master hypnotist not far from his home and visited his library several times. The man, Manly Palmer Hall, was an author and the founder of the Philosophical Research Society, which was housed in a temple near Griffith Park off Los Feliz Boulevard in Los Angeles.[1002] Hall practiced his craft with his German-born wife, and Sirhan reportedly met with both of them and read in their library. It is interesting to note that one of Hall's longtime clients was LA Mayor Sam Yorty, the same official who, following Sirhan's arrest, exclaimed that Sirhan was involved with a "Communist organization" because of his membership in a New Age society.[1003] When police searched Sirhan's car after his being taken into custody, they found a copy of Manly Palmer Hall's book *Healing: The Divine Art*. Oddly, the book was not listed in the grand jury exhibits.[1004]

At home in Pasadena, Sirhan and his brothers Adel and Munir lived a harmonious existence and would share ideas on the news of the day. Although Sirhan was apolitical, he was curious about many subjects, including news from his homeland. Ominous reports from the Middle East that spring made the headlines with Israel's discovery that Arabs were mobilizing their troops in Egypt, Jordan, Syria, and Iraq. War erupted when Israel swiftly attacked its enemies on June 5, 1967. Known as the Six Day War, it was a stunning victory for the Jewish nation. Israel had wiped out the Egyptian air force on the ground, taken over the Gaza Strip, and brought its tanks to the Suez Canal. When it was over, Israel had quadrupled its size, occupying Gaza, Golan, Sinai, the West Bank, and the Old City of Jerusalem. The Israelis had suffered one-tenth the number of Arab casualties and succeeded in creating an added safety zone around their country. US politicians, including Robert Kennedy, supported these efforts. American politicians saw a strong Israel as a counterforce to the Soviets, who had begun to make inroads in the region, enlarging their presence in Egypt and Syria. Indeed, the United States was unwavering in its backing of Israel, both economically and politically. As we shall see ahead, Sirhan was erroneously perceived by many as having had a motive for the RFK assassination that stemmed from the Six Day War. This viewpoint holds that the killing of Robert Kennedy was an act of vengeance due to his support for Israel. The fact of the matter is that none of the candidates for president favored Palestinian or Arab military dominance in the Middle East, which makes this motive moot.

The embarrassing Arab defeat prompted national columnists to applaud Israel's armed forces. In one article, *Time* magazine called upon Jordan's King Hussein to "find sources of pride and confirmation of manhood in causes other than holy war."[1005] Indeed, military historians have concluded the army of Egypt's President Gamal Abdel Nasser clearly was not prepared for this ordeal. Meanwhile, Sirhan Sirhan, at this point, was known to have had only a passing interest in Middle East politics. But soon, this noncommittal stance would abruptly warp into an intermittent, uncharacteristic hostility.

By 1967, Robert Kennedy had begun his third year as senator from New York. He had made great strides in overcoming his grief and deep depression caused by the murder of his brother a little over three years earlier. Happily married with ten children, he and his wife Ethel spent as much time together as his job would allow. He found great satisfaction in directing his energies toward the plight of the poor of New York and drawing public attention to the issues of those living in the worst slums of America. His speeches reflected this compassion and sense of purpose:

"Today in America, we are two worlds. . . . But if we try to look through the eyes of the young slum-dweller—the Negro, and the Puerto Rican, and the Mexican-American—the world is a dark and hopeless place."[1006]

Kennedy wanted to change that. And he knew the power lay in the presidency. But at this point, he was still uncertain about a run for the Oval Office in 1968. President Lyndon B. Johnson, who had been elected in 1964, had an iron grip on the Democratic party, and most observers felt he would run again in 1968. He had promised to win both the war in Southeast Asia and the war at home. Most voters did not know that President John F. Kennedy, just days before he was assassinated, had drawn up departure plans for Vietnam. After he was assassinated, the Pentagon canceled the plans and in late 1963 began to increase military aid to South Vietnam.[1007] At this point, it became "Johnson's War." The year 1967 saw American troop strength in Vietnam climb to nearly a half million. While Johnson continued to bomb North Vietnam, the number of US troops killed in the war was escalating daily. In 1966 and 1967, more than fifteen thousand Americans died in Southeast Asia.[1008] Despite the rising numbers of US troops being sent to Vietnam, the Communists refused to talk unless the bombing was halted. This brought out Johnson's greatest fear: if he acquiesced, he would be considered a coward and an appeaser, just as the British had appeased the Nazis at Munich prior to World War II. President Johnson summed up his philosophy in a crude way: "If you let a bully come into your front yard one day, the next day he'll be up on your porch, and the day after that he'll rape your wife in your own bed."[1009] As B-52 bombers dropped napalm and cluster bombs on North Vietnamese Army camps along the coast near the South Vietnamese border, President Johnson continued to reiterate that the best course of action was to escalate the bombing of North Vietnam's key cities.

Robert Kennedy's response was that this would only bring about the destruction of Vietnam and its people, not peace. Sen. Eugene McCarthy of Minnesota and George McGovern of South Dakota supported Kennedy's view. Richard Nixon's answer was that Kennedy was in effect prolonging the war by encouraging the enemy.

Back in Virginia, Bobby Kennedy enjoyed the late summer weather, tossing a football and playing with his many children. His wife Ethel, his biggest cheerleader, was always up for a good time, whether it was taking the family sailing, horseback riding, or skiing. She could often be found hosting parties at their Hickory Hill home in McLean, Virginia. The large house and grounds had been the headquarters of General George B. McClellan during the Civil War. In 1957, Robert Kennedy bought the manor from his brother Jack.[1010] Ten years later, it had become a headquarters of sorts where family and a broad spectrum of friends would meet for both diversion and serious discussion on the topics of the day. All the while, in the back of Bobby's mind, he was continually weighing his options for the future, and specifically whether or not to run for the presidency. It would be the most important decision of his life.

Sirhan at this time had discovered that betting at the track was not bringing in the income he had hoped it would. Fortunately for him, his mother took the initiative and found him a job. She called on a friend from their church, John Weidner, a Dutch immigrant who owned a health food store at 1380 North Lake Avenue.[1011] Weidner was happy to be able to help Mary Sirhan. Her son's new job entailed working in the stockroom and making deliveries by car, driving to Monterey Park, Downey, and other area locations.[1012]

With the arrival of fall, tempers in the cities nationally cooled somewhat following the summer's brutal race riots. October 1967 also marked a turning point in America's struggle at home against the war in Vietnam. From this point on, it seemed that there was light at the end of the tunnel—for the doves, not the hawks. There was a wave of hope among the protesters that they were making their point heard and that the power of the people, or at least of the youth, would bring the soldiers home and leave Vietnam at peace.

The war protesters believed that after twenty-five years of warfare in Vietnam, first with the Japanese, then the French, and now with the United States, peace could finally come to Indochina. This, without dishonor to the United States, if only America would admit its mistake and pull out. Such was the feeling that pervaded the antiwar groups who were preparing at that point to join the first counterculture march on Washington, DC.

A majority of the country was suddenly seeking a change at the top. Public opinion polls, which had shown President Johnson leading over Robert Kennedy in July 1967 by 45 percent to 39 percent, had flipped. The autumn polls gave Kennedy 51 percent compared to Johnson's 39 percent.[1013]

From San Francisco, the "flower power" movement had spread rapidly to the East Coast. By the fall of 1967, the nation's capital had been chosen as the host city for a nationwide antiwar and antidraft protest. The mass demonstration, sponsored by the National Mobilization Committee to End the War, was set for October 21, 1967. Protesters planned to march to the Pentagon and confront the authorities there. On the day of the event, more than one hundred thousand people showed up, including Abbie Hoffman and Jerry Rubin, who headed up the Youth International Party (Yippies). The marchers, mostly long-haired students in blue jeans, thronged the roadways as they walked. Some waved flags, handed out flowers, or smoked pot along the way. They represented a broad range of backgrounds and experiences, and although most were young students, there were those who had served in Vietnam, enrolled in college, and had turned against the war. Some were outraged by the endless fighting and wanted it to end, but were secure in the knowledge that they had high draft numbers and hence could not be reached by the long arm of the federal government. And there were those who knew they were about to be drafted and were debating whether or not to take refuge in Canada. There were parents, grandparents, and young children, arriving by the busload from the cities and from the countryside, from every part of the United States. Signs read, LBJ, PULL OUT NOW, LIKE YOUR FATHER SHOULD HAVE DONE. END THE DRAFT, PEACE NOW; HELL NO, WE WON'T GO. Among the speakers at the event were nationally known figures, including authors Norman Mailer and Dr. Benjamin Spock.

Many of the demonstrators were well-versed in civil disobedience and knew what their actions could result in. But that was their goal: to create a huge event, bring worldwide attention to it, make their message known, and then pay the price, if needed, by going to jail. In their minds, the government was fighting an illegal war—and those in charge of it were the individuals who should have been arrested, not the war protesters.

As the marchers approached the Pentagon, headquarters of the Department of Defense, they were met by twenty-five hundred armed soldiers. Then, suddenly, the police arrived and chaos ensued. Those who refused to disperse were arrested for disorderly conduct and hauled into paddy wagons. According to the *Washington Post*, there were 681 arrests, including those of Mailer and Hoffman.[1014] The yippies' goal of getting their message out to millions nationwide had been accomplished.

For Sirhan, the war and its ensuing political and social unrest at home was merely a TV spectacle, as it still was for many Americans. But even though Sirhan had never attended a protest rally or joined a peace group, there is evidence that US intelligence, then monitoring antiwar leaders, was interested in him. As noted earlier, a military intelligence report from San Francisco regarding Sirhan surfaced in the LAPD's files following the Robert Kennedy assassination.[1015]

Meanwhile, in the eyes of the public, the wheels of American democracy ground forward, as Democratic senator Gene McCarthy of Minnesota, age fifty-one, with his wife Abigail by his side, began to capture the hearts and minds of legions of college students in state after state. Older Democrats viewed McCarthy's campaign as a threat to their party's incumbency. At a time when party unity was needed, McCarthy was creating a major division that many feared would doom the Democrats' chances of reelection. Those who supported him felt that his candidacy was desperately needed because he was entering the primaries primarily to oppose the Vietnam War policies of Lyndon Johnson. Senator McCarthy was quoted before announcing he would run, "The only way to get Johnson to change course is for someone to run against him."[1016]

Gene McCarthy had the support of many prominent intellectuals and liberals, and he saw himself as destined for the White House eventually. He was an eccentric of sorts and before entering politics in 1949 had taught at a Benedictine college and was known to read an "enormous missal" while on airplane flights.[1017] He had served with distinction in the House prior to winning his Senate seat. In 1960, the year John Kennedy won the presidency, McCarthy was quoted as saying during the campaign, "I should be the candidate for president. I'm twice as liberal as Humphrey, twice as smart as Symington, and twice as Catholic as Kennedy."[1018] He had ended up supporting Adlai Stevenson that year. In the next presidential election in 1964, McCarthy was considered by President Johnson for vice president, but Johnson instead chose the senior senator from Minnesota, Hubert Humphrey. Now, three years later, McCarthy saw it as his turn, despite reportedly slim financing for a national campaign.

According to Kennedy speechwriter and advisor Arthur Schlesinger, Bobby Kennedy was surprised when Gene McCarthy announced his run for the Democratic presidential nomination. At the same time, he apparently looked at it in a positive light. His brother, Ted, however, was quoted at the time as urging Bobby not to run himself. Ted's feeling was that Bobby should wait another four years. He was sure President Johnson would win reelection in 1968, and he thought that running that year would hurt Bobby's chances for 1972.[1019]

Indeed, Bobby's resurgence and his campaign for the Democratic presidential primary nomination were the nascent hopes of many, but still a major question mark. By 1967, with the horrendous casualty figures coming out of Vietnam, Robert Kennedy's feelings against the war began to solidify. Arthur

Schlesinger has written that American troop strength in Vietnam had grown from twenty-three thousand in 1964 to 525,000 at the end of 1967.[1020] In that year, 7,482 American troops were killed. Kennedy saw this tragic loss of life as unwarranted, and he viewed the war as a senseless power struggle with no end in sight. He began to openly sympathize with antiwar protesters and viewed their transgressions not as acts bordering on treason, but as voices crying out in the wilderness. Speaking in the defense of the peace demonstrations, in one speech Senator Kennedy stated, "When we talk about the violence and the people walking out (protesting) and the lawlessness, there is no other way for people to express their point of view, and I think that is most unfortunate."[1021]

Kennedy was fully aware of the key role the war would play in the upcoming presidential race. Yet, it seemed as if he were debating within himself exactly which road to take. By opposing President Johnson, he was dividing the Democratic Party, and this, he knew, could lead to its defeat. On a more visceral level, he also no doubt felt that what had happened to his brother Jack could easily happen to him. Behind the scenes, Kennedy watched and listened and prayed. And as a father of ten, he was torn between his loyalty to his family and to his country.

Timing was another crucial factor for Kennedy to take into consideration. The New Hampshire primary, which was set for March 1968, was fast approaching, and the deadline loomed for him to make a decision. (As it turned out, he would miss this traditional kick-off of the presidential campaign season.)

The former professor, Sen. Eugene McCarthy, officially announced on November 30, 1967 that he was running against President Johnson.[1022] Students from across the country promptly answered his call to end the war. Dubbing McCarthy "Clean Gene," they joined his grassroots campaign in droves. President Johnson reportedly saw McCarthy's challenge as an onerous sign that Robert Kennedy also would step into the fray.

Kennedy, who did not find Senator McCarthy terribly exciting or visionary, kept to the sidelines, intently watching the race unfold. Just four days prior to McCarthy's announcement, Kennedy appeared as a guest on CBS's *Face the Nation*. The question came up as to whether or not he planned to run against Johnson for the presidency. Without disclosing his intentions, Kennedy proclaimed his opposition to the war with the passion of a moral crusader. He stated: "We're killing innocent people because we don't want a war fought on American soil, or because [the Viet Cong are] twelve thousand miles away and they might get eleven thousand miles away. . . . Do we have the right . . . [to] make millions of people refugees, killing women and children, as we have?"[1023]

Tortured inside over the continuing war, Robert Kennedy nevertheless remained undecided on a presidential run, even as several of his colleagues joined the McCarthy campaign. Three of his best friends, Richard Goodwin, Allard Lowenstein, and John Kenneth Galbraith soon left to help McCarthy prepare for the New Hampshire primary, the important, first battle of the 1968 Presidential race.[1024]

Robert Kennedy knew that if he did run as a peace candidate, he would face the same issue that his brother had. President Kennedy had been murdered shortly after he had begun to phase out troops from Vietnam. Would he, too, face the same fate?

The forces opposed to Robert Kennedy saw candidate Gene McCarthy as a wild card. But with the elimination of Bobby, they assumed that at the convention cooler heads would prevail and the more conservative Vice President Hubert Humphrey would win the Democrats' nod, which he did. Republican Richard Nixon was also considered a safe choice, given his record as an unrepentant cold warrior during and after his years as vice president under two-term president Dwight D. Eisenhower.

Clearly, those responsible for President Kennedy's assassination had determined that this time around—if Bobby ran for president and his nomination were assured—they would end his campaign before the general election in November 1968. Secret Service protection had not yet been extended to candidates in the primaries;[1025] it would be instituted following the assassination of Robert Kennedy.

Meanwhile, in Pasadena, Sirhan was busy testing his New Age knowledge with his friend Tom Rathke at Hollywood Park. There, he attempted to impact the performance of horses by concentrating his "powers" of mental telepathy on them. An example of his zeal was later recounted by John and Patricia Strathman, who were friends of Sirhan. John had been in Sirhan's high school class, and he and his wife had stayed in touch, getting together with Sirhan several times in 1966 and 1967 to eat and chat. Patricia shared Sirhan's interest and encouraged his stories. One night, while visiting the Strathmans, Sirhan regaled Patricia with his newly acquired knowledge. He spoke of how he hoped to develop the ability to see mystical bodies and his guardian angel.[1026] John Strathman, a heavyset bearded man and confirmed skeptic, remarked a year or so later that he felt Sirhan was being led down an ill-starred path by Tom Rathke.

Strathman stated that it seemed to him that Rathke held Sirhan "transfixed" on the occult.[1027] Indeed, Rathke's dominant presence in Sirhan's life had raised some suspicions in their minds.[1028] The mysterious Tom Rathke may have captivated Sirhan, but he did not leave a warm impression with the Strathmans. According to author Robert Kaiser, John Strathman stated that he "got a sinister picture" of Rathke's relationship with Sirhan.[1029]

In December 1967, Sirhan invited Rathke over to the family bungalow for dinner. This was Rathke's last visit to Sirhan's home before moving to Northern California.[1030] Shortly thereafter, Rathke reportedly moved to Livermore, in the vicinity of the Lawrence Radiation Lab, east of Oakland, where he took a job as a groom at the Pleasanton Race Stables.[1031] Rathke did not return again until March, three months later, according to a friend of Mary Sirhan's, Lynne Massey Mangan. These visits coincide with the beginning and the ending of the gap in Sirhan's timeline, the period in which information on Sirhan's whereabouts for three months is missing from the LAPD's records. A source from the LAPD, who wished to remain anonymous, confided this fact to authors William Turner, a former FBI agent, and Jonn Christian, a former broadcast journalist.[1032] In addition, a review of the records in LAPD's possession shows that there are details on people with whom Sirhan came in contact while working at the Health Food Store, except for the time period from December 1967 through March 1968; there are no details during the weeks that he was unaccounted for.[1033]

The whereabouts of Sirhan during his weeks away from home are uncertain. Again, his amnesia has blocked any attempt to recall this missing time span. We do know, as would be expected, Mary Sirhan was very worried. According to a neighbor's statement to the FBI, Mary was extremely upset because her son was gone for "quite some time."[1034] This was unlike Sirhan.

Sirhan's brothers presumed he had gone north to visit Tom Rathke, which was logical given the bond between the two. It is interesting to note, regarding their relationship, while Rathke was extremely conservative politically, Sirhan was apolitical for the most part. However, despite his neutral stance, Sirhan is known to have stated that he admired the Kennedys. Asked during his trial about his feelings about President Kennedy, Sirhan said, "I loved him." He then went on to describe Kennedy's efforts to find a solution to the Palestinian refuge problem. He said he recalled that Kennedy had consulted with Arab leaders and promised to work with Israel to help repatriate the refugees.[1035] Sirhan later on told a court appointed psychiatrist, Dr. George Y. Abe, that, in fact, he would have voted for Bobby Kennedy "because Kennedy was for the underdog."[1036]

Leading up to Sirhan's disappearance, the three-month-time-gap, it is known that he had sought a remedy for the pain in his left eye from the injury he had sustained in the bad fall he had taken while working at the racetrack. His search had brought him to at least seven medical specialists. According to Professor Philip Melanson, it is important to note that at this time, one of the most common covers for CIA hypnosis testing was the pretense of giving medical treatment.[1037] It is possible that through these various contacts in the medical community, Sirhan eventually encountered Dr. William J. Bryan Jr.[1038] Dr. Bryan, fifty-four, was the nation's leading expert in the field of hypnosis and had worked for the CIA as a hypnosis expert. While Sirhan has stated that he has no memory of Dr. Bryan, Bryan is known to have confided to several colleagues that he had hypnotized Sirhan.[1039]

Dr. Bryan's office was located on Sunset Strip in Los Angeles, where he conducted sex and hypnosis workshops at his American Institute of Hypnosis. He billed himself as an expert in "the successful treatment of sexual disorders."[1040] A large man—he weighed in at 386 pounds—Bryan also had a large appetite for women. In 1969, the California Board of Medical Examiners cited Bryan for unprofessional conduct. He had been sexually molesting four female patients while they were under hypnosis. The board placed Bryan on probation for five years, with the condition that he have a woman present when treating female patients.[1041]

According to Professor Philip Melanson, who interviewed several CIA consultants and professional colleagues of Dr. Bryan's, they all stated that Bryan was with the CIA. One, whom Melanson gives the pseudonym Gilbert Marston, told Melanson that Bryan had mentioned to him that he not only worked as a CIA consultant, but that he had been asked to hypnotize Sirhan Sirhan.[1042] Marston did not say if the hypnotizing was conducted before or after the assassination (during the trial). But the evidence indicates that it was both (that is, preassassination programming and later postassassination conditioning to influence his statements on the witness stand).

Dr. William Bryan was skilled in tricking subjects under hypnosis to do things they ordinarily would not do. He also had mastered the art of concealing his work by establishing amnesia—or a mental block—in subjects to prevent them from remembering him or what had happened, or what they had done while they were hypnotized.

Bryan denied in a 1974 interview with writer Betsy Langman that he had hypnotized Sirhan Sirhan.[1043] Yet regular female companions[1044] and close colleagues of Bryan's have confided that he told them he did hypnosis work for the CIA and had performed hypnosis work on Sirhan.[1045] Two intrepid investigators who reported this link between Bryan and Sirhan were authors William

Turner and Jonn Christian. They obtained the information from two women who disclosed this news without really knowing its importance. The two young ladies were Beverly Hills call girls who were intimately involved with Bryan.[1046] Working as a duo, they had been regularly taking care of their corpulent customer despite his enormous girth.

During Bryan's chats with his two mistresses, according to the women, the name Sirhan Sirhan came up several times. Over the four-year period they were involved with Bryan, they said he had frequently repeated his stories. Both were certain that he had said Sirhan had been one of his subjects, and they also said he bragged about working for the LAPD and for the CIA on "top secret projects."[1047] This breaking of the code of silence would not have been an issue for a man like William J. Bryan. He was an egomaniac. At the time he was with these women in the early 1970s, he was also known to have become addicted to drugs.[1048] As a result, his ramblings may have been more frequent and repetitious.

As for Dr. Bryan's early years, he claimed that during the Korean War in the 1950s he was—in his words—"chief of all medical survival training for the US Air Force, which meant the brainwashing section."[1049] Bryan's work ostensibly involved preparing soldiers for the mental challenges they could face in the event they were captured by the enemy.[1050]

Dr. William Bryan's consulting work also included Hollywood. He served as technical advisor for the 1962 Frank Sinatra movie *The Manchurian Candidate*, mentioned earlier.[1051]

While sex was a favorite preoccupation of Bryan's, in addition to his CIA work, he also was involved in consulting on legal cases. Attorney F. Lee Bailey once referred to Dr. Bryan as "the most knowledgeable man I knew on the subject of hypnosis."[1052] Bailey utilized Bryan's services for several famous murder trials, one involving the Boston Strangler case of Albert DiSalvo.[1053] According to Bailey, in 1965, Bryan flew to Boston and drove with him to a Bridgewater, Massachusetts, mental hospital. After consulting with officials there, Bryan put DiSalvo into a trance and then regressed him to the murder of the last strangling victim. Questioning him under hypnosis, he concluded that DiSalvo's psychopathic behavior stemmed from his disabled daughter's taking away his wife's affection for him. The session climaxed with DiSalvo lunging at Bryan's throat. Bryan responded by grabbing his subject's shoulders and ordering him to sleep. The command was successful. DiSalvo fell to the floor without a clue as to what had happened.[1054]

Dr. William Bryan, like master hypnotist Manly Palmer Hall, had also authored several books on the occult and had great interest in mystical orders and hypnosis. He had carried out extensive research into the practices of the ancient Egyptians, which also play a key role in Rosicrucian (AMORC— Ancient Mystical Order of Rosicrucian) beliefs. AMORC's San Jose headquarters features an Egyptian museum and the organization claims its roots go back to the Egyptian schools of 1500 BC.[1055] Ahead, we shall see that Sirhan joined and attended one meeting of this group.

Both Hall and Dr. William Bryan were top hypnotists, but whether they were affiliated is not known. Both knew Sirhan and as a result, some investigators have suggested that Hall could have been the one who introduced Sirhan to Bryan. Although Sirhan has no recollection of Bryan at all, Bryan could have met him while he (Sirhan) was in a hypnotized state. Given Hall's and Bryan's skills at hypnosis, combined with the Agency's knowledge of drugs, erasing memories could easily have been accomplished.

Bryan was a CIA consultant at a time when hypnosis and drugs, including LSD, were central elements of programs such as MKULTRA. A profoundly secret arena of the CIA, the work encompassed the mind control and behavior modification research of that era. Much of the records of this work have been destroyed, but again, it is estimated that perhaps thousands of unwitting subjects were used in the Agency's various drug and hypnosis experiments.[1056]

Indeed, intelligence operatives with mob connections at the track also could have very easily linked an unwitting exercise boy, Sirhan, to Dr. William J. Bryan as a brainwashing candidate. Neither the mob nor an Agency "recruiter" would have needed to know the ultimate objective of the conditioning operation—creating a fall guy for an assassination.

According to CIA-contract hypno-programmers, after a research subject was temporarily "appropriated" (sometimes through an early version of today's date-rape drugs slipped into a drink at a club), the individual would be taken to a secure place for the conditioning to be conducted. Experiments were carried out in such places as prisons, safe houses, and hospitals or other clinic-type settings. Besides studying individual responses, the research also involved testing various drugs, hypnosis, and the administering of electroshock treatments.[1057] One of the objectives of the research was to determine the best equation for achieving temporary control over a subject without his or her knowing it, and at the same time obliterating any memory of the experience.

After the programmer induced hypnosis, the subject would be "bombarded" with audio messages and given electric shocks for reinforcement. Audiotape players "looped" (i.e., repeated) the messages, which were fed through speakers placed under the subject's pillow in a "sleep room." This process would last from fifteen to thirty days.[1058] The content of the audio messages would depend on the desired response and the type of operation planned for the subject. According to hypnosis expert Milton Kline, successful hypno-programming can take up to three months.[1059]

New York psychiatrist Dr. Herbert Spiegel, a professor at Columbia University, has stated that Sirhan had a natural capacity to be easily hypnotized. Based on Dr. Spiegel's evaluation of the psychiatric reports, Sirhan placed in the top 5 to 10 percentile in this regard.[1060] This unusual susceptibility to hypnosis no doubt played a key role in the selection of Sirhan as a fall guy.

During Sirhan's three-month time gap, it is apparent that he underwent some sort of conditioning and that notebook writing was an integral part of this hypno-programming process. Two green spiral notebooks—which Sirhan has no memory of using—turned up at the Sirhan home at 696 E. Howard Street in Pasadena the day of the assassination. As Police Sgt. Will Brandt searched Sirhan's home, he found the notebooks in Sirhan's bedroom. One was on a table and the other on the floor near his bed.[1061] Again, Sirhan has no recollection of writing the notebooks, and as a matter of fact, he asked the psychiatrists studying him prior to his trial if they would hypnotize him to try to bring forth the memory. He stated, "whatever I say (about the notebooks) I will face when I'm done." He still drew a blank. Prosecution psychiatrist Dr. Seymour Pollack responded, "That bothers me."[1062]

The notebooks—so-called diaries—consist of a total of forty-eight pages of writing. Many of the words are broken, and phrases and sentences are written in a disjointed, repetitive fashion. Two of the pages relate to assassinating Robert Kennedy. Taken at face value, the lines in these two pages are certainly indicative of premeditation. But in light of the facts surrounding Sirhan's situation and context of the writings taken as a whole, it is clear that the notebooks were a key part of the frame-up; they were designed to incriminate an unwitting person.

The content of the majority of the pages relates to the names of friends, the names of horses, anticapitalist rhetoric, New-Age jargon, and an unsent message to his mother. A handwriting analyst has verified that the notebooks were written by Sirhan.[1063] And thorough investigations of these strange writings have indicated that they are the work of an individual immersed in a drug-induced state. Given that the notebook pages are Sirhan's and that they were written while he was in some sort of stupor, based on what is known of Sirhan's home life, it is apparent that he did not write them at home. If he were ever in a stupor at home, it would have been observed and later revealed.

Richard Helms, CIA director, right, and Senator Frank Church, 1975, Washington, D.C. (© Bettmann/CORBIS)

James Angleton, CIA chief of counterintelligence, 1975, Washington, D.C. (© Harvey Georges/AP/AP/CORBIS)

**David Phillips, CIA western hemisphere division chief, right, 1976, Washington, D.C. (© Bettmann/CORBIS)**

**Lee Harvey Oswald, 1963, New Orleans. (© Mary Ferrell Foundation)**

**George de Mohrenschildt, 1964. (© Bettmann/CORBIS)**

**Jack Ruby, 1963, Dallas. (© Mary Ferrell Foundation)**

Dealey Plaza—the grassy knoll, left, the Texas School Book Depository, center, and the Dal-Tex Building, right, Dallas.

President John F. Kennedy and First Lady Jacqueline Kennedy. (© Abbie Rowe, White House Photographer, John F. Kennedy Presidential Library and Museum, Boston)

**Robert Kennedy, 1964, New York.**

**Sirhan Sirhan, 1968, Los Angeles. (© California State Archives)**

President John F. Kennedy and Robert F. Kennedy, standing behind, to the right of the president, 1961, Washington, D.C. (© JFK Library)

Kitchen pantry of the Ambassador Hotel, 1968, Los Angeles. (© California State Archives)

Sirhan Sirhan, 2011, California. (© Ben Margot/AP/AP/CORBIS)

Senator Robert F. Kennedy and his wife Ethel, left, minutes before the shooting, June 5, 1968, Los Angeles. (© Bettmann/CORBIS)

Dr. Henry C. Lee, forensic scientist, Connecticut.

Researchers involved in the study of brainwashing use the term "automatic writing" to describe the notebook phenomenon. During automatic writing, the subject, while in a drug-induced state, answers questions posed by his handlers or simply transcribes either live voices or audiotapes. As noted above, CIA experiments in brainwashing techniques typically entailed the use of tape recordings, especially for mind control and behavior modification.[1064]

While most of the pages consist of jumbled stream-of-consciousness messages and responses to questions, mixed in with doodling, some passages read like dictation, that is, cleanly written diatribes taken down by Sirhan, but coming from the mind of a skilled behavior-modification and mind-control programmer. Indeed, one of the fragmented lines in the Sirhan notebooks refers to one of Dr. William J. Bryan's favorite stories, Albert DiSalvo and the Boston Strangler. The notebook line reads: "God help me, please help me. Salvo Di De Salve Die S Salvo."[1065] When the name DiSalvo appeared in Sirhan's notebook, many investigators agreed that it was not unlikely that Dr. Bryan had left behind his calling card. As noted earlier, Dr. Bryan was a talkative man, especially when he was boasting of his exploits.

The name of Sirhan's friend, horse trainer Henry Ramistella, a.k.a Frank Donneroummas, appears in one of the notebooks, written by an exceedingly drugged subject: "happiness hppiness Dona Donaruma Donaruma Frank Donaruma pl please ple please pay to 5 please pay to the order of Sirhan Sirhan the amount of 5 . . . "[1066]

Several other strange sentences seem to relate to Sirhan's best friend Tom Rathke. It is not known if Sirhan had contact with Rathke during his three-month absence. However, in the notebooks, Sirhan apparently was made to appear to be trying to contact him: "Hello Tom How will I contact you after I arrive at the airport—I am—coming up sometime Tuesday afternoon. Sirhan Sirhan Sirhan afternoon—Did you really."[1067] Another page reads: "perhaps you could use the enclosed $ Sol Sol perhaps you could use the enclosed $ Sol Sol $ $ $ $ Sol $ perhaps you could use the Hello Tom - perhaps you could use the enclosed $ $ $."[1068]

The strange writing in the notebooks is typically repetitive, but one page is inordinately so. On this page, the word "feed" is written fifteen times.[1069] It is not known how Sirhan lived in terms of food and lodging during the three-month time gap. He was not independently wealthy, and in fact, he did not even have a bank account.[1070] His insurance settlement money for his horse injury would not arrive until April 1968, at which point he had already returned home. Certainly, expenses for three months would have put a dent in Mary Sirhan's savings. According to author John Marks, Richard Helms's Agency behavior-modification experiments many times included such components as sensory or food deprivation. While repetitively writing the word "feed" fifteen times, Sirhan may well have been crying out for a meal.

In addition to these fragments and the numerous nonsensical phrases in the Sirhan notebooks, the words "drugs" and "electric shock" appear four times.[1071] On another page, written upside down, is "Electronic equipment this seems to be the right amount of preponderance."[1072] Again, Sirhan has no memory of this or the reason these words were written.

For the perpetrators, the crucial test for programming a patsy would be knowing for certain that the amnesia would hold up during subsequent police interrogations. The subject's memory of the posthypnotic suggestion, the pro-grammed act itself, and the identity of the hypnotist all had to be irretrievable.

Following the assassination and after days of being questioned in his jail cell by author Robert Kaiser, Sirhan spoke to this issue. Asked what he felt about his amnesia, Sirhan suggested to Kaiser that perhaps someone had been "playing with" his mind. Relying on his knowledge of the occult, he added, "I always try to guard against that."[1073] Sirhan then asked Kaiser to help him find out more about this. Two years later, Kaiser told the *Chicago Tribune* that it was his personal opinion that Sirhan had been programmed by someone.[1074]

To test Sirhan's credibility, according to authors William Turner and Jonn Christian, a former army intelligence officer named Charles McQuiston ana-lyzed audio interview tapes of Sirhan. McQuiston concluded that Sirhan had told the truth. Using a PSE (Psychological Stress Evaluation) instrument, which is similar to a lie detector test, McQuiston evaluated stress that can be caused by attempted deception. He concluded that Sirhan's stress level was low, and that therefore Sirhan's answers were truthful and genuinely sincere. The test also appeared to indicate, based on the phrases that Sirhan used, that he had been hypno-programmed. These results were corroborated by Dr. John W. Heisse Jr., president of the International Society of Stress Analysis, who also reviewed the results.[1075]

One facet of Sirhan's conditioning involved creating within his personality beliefs that previously did not exist. For example, Sirhan believed that he had been taught hypnosis and self-programming by the AMORC.[1076] Yet, the Rosi-crucians do not delve into these subjects. No doubt Sirhan was told this while under hypnosis during his programming. Those who told him this knew that his believing that AMORC had been "playing" with his mind would serve as a perfect cover for their own tinkering.

Sirhan's notebooks also show that his conditioning included references to some of the major figures in the world of New Age literature. This was precisely the kind of knowledge with which Dr. William Bryan was intimately familiar, having written volumes on the subject.

For example, in Sirhan's notebooks, the name of the Tibetan mystic Master Koot Hoomi appeared. However, Sirhan spelled the great master's name as if he had heard it, not read it. Master Koot Hoomi was misspelled "Master Kuthumi."[1077] Clearly, Sirhan was writing it phonetically, in response to a verbal delivery. This is another sign of automatic writing.

Koot Hoomi was believed to have guided the writings of the founder of the Theosophical Society, Madame Helena Blavatsky. Madame Blavatsky was born in Russia and moved to New York City in 1875. She later lived in India and England, where she died in 1891. During her life, she wrote extensively. Her most famous work, *The Secret Doctrine*, was a six-volume set that examined mysteries of the unexplained and studied man's hidden powers.[1078] While in England, Madame Blavatsky named her group of theosophists "the Illuminati."[1079] Interestingly, the same name would be used one hundred years later in the United States to label the "one-world conspiracy" movement. In the 1970s, the right wing blamed the so-called "Illuminati" for the assassinations of John and Robert Kennedy.[1080] This canard would hide the truth and helped to steer the public away from legitimate conspiracy theories. After Bobby's assassination, when Sirhan was asked in jail concerning the term "Illuminati" appearing in his notebooks, he replied that he knew nothing about it, unless it was connected in some way to Manly Palmer Hall's organization.[1081]

In reading a random page of Sirhan's writings, the tone is suspiciously akin to a brainwashing scene from a Hollywood movie. Sirhan was simply a young, aspiring jockey. He had no strong ideological convictions nor any interest in the Communist party. So, for him to suddenly write passionate political statements in a notebook is dubious at best.[1082] "I advocate the overthrow of the current president of the fucken United States of America. I have no absolute plans yet, but soon will compose some . . . . I firmly support the Communist cause and its people—whether Russian, Chinese, Albanian, Hungarian, whoever—Workers of the world unite. You have nothing to lose but your chains and a world to win."[1083] This last sentence is repeated three times.

Clearly, the perpetrators knew that when the authorities were looking for evidence of premeditation, such pages would help build their case. Anyone who read these passages after the assassination could draw but one conclusion: this person could be dangerous. These lines were written at the height of the

Cold War; in the spring of 1968, Communist Russia had invaded upstart Czechoslovakia. To many American observers, it certainly appeared that "workers of the world" were advancing on all fronts. And since a motive for the assassination was severely lacking, the authorities would snatch up pages such as this to establish one. Again, Sirhan was far from being a Socialist. He was a typical, young immigrant who dreamed of wealth and the pleasures it could bring.

As noted earlier, Sirhan was an Orthodox Christian brought up in the Christian sector of Jerusalem; he was not a Muslim.[1084] Given Sirhan's background, the perpetrators were hard-pressed to create a personality that would pass as the profile of an assassin. Consequently, they attempted to use Sirhan's unwitting automatic writing sessions to produce notebook pages that would portray him as an Arab militant. Out of the forty-eight pages of writings, there are three pages referring to charismatic, Socialist, Egyptian President Gamal Abdel Nasser (1956-1970).[1085] Two of these pages naming Nasser are in English, and one is written in Arabic. The former consists of jumbled words and letters on the pages, and the latter is mostly nonsense phrases.[1086] The English reads: "Lo Long live Nasser long live live Long live long Nasser Long live Nasser Long live Nasser Long live Communism Long live Communism Long live Communism Long live Nasser Nasser Nasser Nasser Nasser Nasser." And the second English page reads, "Long live Nasser Nasser Lo Long Live Nasser N N N Nasser is the greatest man that ever lived in this world, Nasser is the greatest man that ever lived in this world Nasser is the greatest man that ever lived lived lived N N N N Nasser is the greatest man that ev eve ev ever lived."[1087] Of course, Sirhan was known, at this point, to have had only a passing interest in Middle East politics.

Indeed, Sirhan's brothers and his friends saw him as a peaceful and spiritual person. As Sirhan told author Robert Kaiser before his trial, "Hatred was very foreign to me; I can't understand it."[1088]

Sirhan's acquaintances Peggy Osterkamp and Gwen Gumm, noted earlier, are also named in the notebooks. Peggy's name is repeated many times, as is her home address, which is written: "Miss Peggy Osterkamp, 13290 Archibald Ave, Corona, Calif 80113." The house number and zip code vary each time the address is repeated.[1089] One page contains the words, "I love you," and "Sol and Peggy."[1090] Gwen is also frequently named in the notebooks, along with her address.[1091]

While both of these young women are known to have had no serious involvement with Sirhan, their names appear prominently. Again, during automatic writing, since the subject is in a trancelike state, what is written is typically whatever has been commanded. If Sirhan were asked about past infatuations, perhaps these names came to mind. If this were the case, then it appears that the programmer was playing with Sirhan's "heartstrings" to achieve his objective.

There also exists the possibility that someone who knew both women and Sirhan—perhaps someone from the track—was present during the automatic writing session and brought up the girls' names. One person who apparently knew all three persons was Tom Rathke.

Another reason the girls' names may have appeared in the notebooks is equally sinister. It is known that while under hypnosis, a person can be told that a stranger who is present is actually someone the subject knows and loves. The subject will then not only accept this as true, but will act accordingly, as if he sees his lover instead of the individual present.[1092] For example, if a woman unknown to Sirhan was with Sirhan during the hypno-programming process, and Sirhan was told under hypnosis that she was one of his recent infatuations, he would have believed this was the case. Such an occurrence would have been highly motivating for Sirhan, since it would have brought into play his deepest emotions. This, in turn, would have enhanced an already potent dose of hypnotic suggestions, routinely laced with mind-altering drugs. The net result was that by adding Sirhan's emotional cravings to the equation, the programmer may have made him more willing, or ready, under hypnosis, to carry out whatever commands he was given.

As it turns out, there does appear to have been a young woman in Sirhan's life at this time, although Sirhan only recalls a brief moment with her. Numerous witnesses at the Ambassador Hotel the night of the assassination saw Sirhan with a mysterious woman in the Embassy Room and in the kitchen pantry area. Her presence, and his lack of memory regarding much of that night, have led some investigators to believe that she was his controller or handler—and his cue. Sirhan does not remember accompanying anyone in particular that evening, except for his being with a woman at one point late in the evening when he became very tired and sought a cup of coffee. Sirhan told NBC reporter Jack Perkins in an interview a year later that he remembers following a girl into the pantry. They found a large coffee urn.[1093] He poured a cup for the girl and one for himself. He does not remember her name. After that point, all he can recall is being beaten by the crowd. Immediately after the shooting, the girl was seen by many witnesses fleeing the pantry while everyone else was trying to get in.[1094] As we shall see ahead, the young woman who was with him during the assassination may have played an integral part in his programming. If she was Sirhan's control, then no doubt during the conditioning process she would have had to have learned as much about his unwitting part in the plot as about her own. This is especially true if her cues were to be the "on" button for Sirhan's prehypnotically, programmed actions. She may have also played the role of Sirhan's fantasy lover, keeping him occupied during his conditioning. There would have been the numerous routine tasks involved in keeping Sirhan in the programming mode, properly medicated, and adequately fed for the three months he was away from home.

While a Tom Collins laced with a knockout drug probably precipitated Sirhan's entry into a three-month state of amnesia, a cup of coffee in the Ambassador Hotel pantry may have been his final cue. The girl with Sirhan that night, whom witnesses all reported as being attractive and having a "good figure," may have been his "control" from the time of his initial induction at the end of 1967. This individual would keep Sirhan mesmerized through various cues and drug-enriched drinks while carrying out the instructions of superiors as to where Sirhan should be and when. And perhaps she even kept him alive.

During Sirhan's time away from home, the three-month time gap, his mother received no communication from her son. As if to account for, or remove suspicion over this obviously uncharacteristic behavior of Sirhan's, an unsent letter to Mrs. Sirhan was written in one of the notebooks. It is one of the few pages written mainly in the Arabic language, Sirhan's native tongue. Author Robert Kaiser's book contains a translation: "My reverend mother, God keep her and bless her. . . . Everything with me is at its best and I am in the best of health. I wish and hope that the same will be with you. Enclosed find ten dollars for the purpose of buying stamps to be placed on all letters you may send to me from Pasadena and especially envelopes and publications from Rosicrushay (sic) from Shener and other mail. I am also waiting for a check from the American Treasury Department which you are also to send P P Peggy. This envelope contains also papers with my address written on them which you are to use only for sending the letters to me here. I especially beg of you in a special way to discuss the matter of my location with no one at all at all. Many thanks in advance Sirhan Sirhan Sirhan Sirhan Sirhan Sirhan your son your son your son Sirhan Sirhan Sirhan Sirhan. . . ."[1095]

Again, Sirhan has no memory of writing this. Asked after the assassination by his attorneys about this page, Sirhan noted that the girl mentioned in the letter could have been Peggy Osterkamp, someone he had not even thought about since 1966, two years earlier.[1096] Obviously, the perpetrators intended for the eventual readers of these notebooks to be led to believe Sirhan was operating of his own free will and attempting to calm his mother's fears—to make it appear that he was trying to assuage his guilt over leaving home without telling his family where he was going or when he would return. He appears to be telling them where he can be reached, but this is another ploy—the line reads, "This envelope contains also papers with my address written on them . . ." But, of course, there is no envelope or papers with his address. It is not a letter that was sent; it is another automatic writing episode, designed by Sirhan's handlers to cover up his conditioning by making it later appear to investigators that he knew where he was, when, in fact, he did not.

In Sirhan's forty-eight pages of notebook writings, there were only two pages that referred to Robert Kennedy. One page read, "My determination to eliminate RFK is becoming more and more of an unshakable obsession. RFK must die. RFK must be killed. Robert F. Kennedy must be assassinated . . ." This sentence was repeated twelve times. At the end of the page, it read, "Robert F. Kennedy must be assassinated before June 5 1968."[1097] Again, Sirhan has no memory of writing these lines. Moreover, he is unaware of having had an "unshakable obsession" regarding Robert Kennedy, nor anyone else, for that matter.

The second page that contained a Kennedy reference stated, "Kennedy must fall." It was repeated eight times.[1098]

Conventional wisdom holds that "under hypnosis you won't do anything you normally wouldn't do." However, experts have discovered that there is also another principle at work in hypnosis: that of the moral imperative (also described in an earlier chapter). Under this rule, a subject will do what he thinks is right by his own set of standards. If someone is convinced through hypnosis that a threat exists to his loved ones, he will react on their behalf to defend them, even striking out at the perceived enemy. According to the principle of moral imperative, for subjects under hypnosis, a need to take action in a way that is morally right (in their own minds) takes over, or becomes imperative. Thusly, forensic scientists familiar with the history of hypnosis have concluded that a person's reluctance to commit a crime can be overridden if the person is conditioned to believe the act they are committing has a high moral purpose.[1099]

For example, if the average hypnotized subject believes that innocent, defenseless people are in some way threatened by imminent danger, he or she will want to take some action to try to protect them. Under this principle, a subject can be given information and commands, but will respond in accordance with the subject's own morals, even taking actions that override inhibitions to achieve that which the subject believes is right for him. By the same token, a hypnotist can trick a subject into doing something against his or her will by triggering the moral imperative. In such a case, the hypnotized subject is given erroneous information and commanded to carry out an action. The subject then obeys the command, believing that his or her action is morally right, and therefore, imperative.[1100] In Sirhan's case, during the pre-trial phase, court psychiatrists using hypnosis discovered something very interesting about their subject. While questioning him about the assassination, Sirhan, under hypnosis, uttered the word "bombers." The doctors then attempted to detect the meaning and context of this response by testing Sirhan's reactions under hypnosis. The psychiatrists told him that Israeli bombs were killing and maiming innocent children in the villages of Gaza. A hypnotized Sirhan began to weep uncontrollably.[1101] It is known that the effectiveness of hypnotism as a programming tool depends in large measure upon the individual being hypnotized. The subject must have passions that can be exploited. Indeed, hypnoprogramming is most successful when based on strong emotions.

In Sirhan's case, probably the most significant emotional factor motivating him, given his childhood experiences during the first Arab-Israeli War, was self-preservation. He was driven to protect himself and his family. Clearly, Sirhan's hypno-programming instilled in him exaggerated anti-Israeli feelings. Feelings that the Jews were directly responsible for the deaths of his family members and the destruction of his homeland had begun to overwhelm him. Added suggestions that Robert Kennedy was advocating military support of Israel focused Sirhan's deepest fears on Bobby. With such posthypnotic suggestions embedded in Sirhan's subconscious mind, a skilled mind control practitioner simply needed to supply the appropriate stimulus to effect the desired behavioral response. This, in turn, triggered Sirhan's self-preservation mechanism, which, while he was under hypnosis and drugs, moved him to strike out at this perceived threat to his family in the person of Bobby Kennedy. In a drug-induced, hypno-programmed state, the so-called moral imperative superseded Sirhan's docile nature.

Returning to the notebooks and viewing them as a product of Sirhan's three-months of conditioning, we can see that they actually build a case for hypno-programming, not premeditation. For example, some of the pages in the notebooks are dated, as if written to look like a diary with journal entries. But the dates make little sense and are out of order. In addition, given that they were created before Sirhan returned home in March of 1968, some dates were obviously postdated. For instance, the statement about Sirhan's "unshakable obsession" has "May 18 9.45 AM - 68" written at the top of the page.[1102] This was no doubt designed to appear as if Sirhan made this entry two and a half weeks before the California primary on June 4. By using a date closer to the assassination, the case for premeditation became more immediate and more incriminating.

The commonly held concept regarding hypnosis, that one cannot be hypnotized without consent, also has been found to be flawed. Resistance to hypnosis can be easily bypassed through the use of drugs and brainwashing techniques, such as sensory deprivation.[1103] Indeed, Sirhan's overpowering emotional response marked a stark contrast to his normal self. When in a nonhypnotized state, Sirhan's actual personality was quite the opposite. For example, during the trial when Sirhan spoke of his feelings toward Robert Kennedy, he stated, "I was hoping he would continue what his brother (had) started . . . I was for him, very much so."[1104]

As for the efficacy of conditioning or programming a subject, psychiatrist Dr. Herbert Spiegel has stated that it is "definitely attainable."[1105] Additionally, a subject can be programmed to not recall who the programmer was. The hypnotist can do this by giving himself another identity in the subconscious mind of the subject.

Dr. Bryan was a master at infusing posthypnotic suggestions into subjects. He was also seen as one of the cleverest practitioners in the art of being able to use the tricks of the trade for the greatest possible impact. This is evident in the case of Sirhan Sirhan. For example, as we shall see ahead, based on evaluations of Sirhan completed in his jail cell, he appears to have been programmed to believe that he could hypnotize himself using a mirror (which is impossible). By having him believe that he could put himself in a trance, he would, after the assassination, believe that he was a person who could shoot another person and not remember it later. Thus, the conditioning would disguise in Sirhan's mind the fact that he had actually been hypno-programmed. And this would provide a firewall between the assassination and the actual operatives and hypno-programmers.

Sirhan's whereabouts during his three-month time gap remain a mystery. CIA conditioning experiments typically took place, as previously described, at certain medical facilities in Canada and in the United States and in agency safe houses. In Sirhan's case, he may have been programmed in a location within Dr. Bryan's geographical area.

We do know that it was not unusual for skilled Agency operatives to disguise covert operations by using doubles. Such ruses would enable the Agency to manufacture evidence by creating the illusion that someone was involved in an activity when in fact they were not even there. We saw the use of a double at the embassy in Mexico, two months prior to the JFK assassination, where security photos revealed that the alleged visit by Lee Harvey Oswald was actually staged by an imposter. The use of a Sirhan double during his three-month disappearance is also a strong possibility. A Sirhan look-alike would have created the cover that Sirhan was away from home visiting friends for three months, while he was actually being held in an Agency conditioning facility. As we shall see, such a ploy would later lead investigators into that place James Angleton liked to call "a wilderness of mirrors."

There are witnesses who have stated that during Sirhan's three-month time gap—in early 1968—they frequently saw a young person they later identified as looking like Sirhan riding horses along the Santa Ana riverbed in Santa Ana, about thirty miles southeast of Pasadena.[1106] The witnesses were area rancher Bill Powers, who owned Wild Bill's Stables, and his employee John Beckley.[1107] They reportedly witnessed Sirhan riding with a neighbor, Oliver Brindley Owen, fifty-five. There is no indication that Sirhan spoke with Powers and Beckley.[1108] Given that Sirhan has no recall of this period, if the person were he, he was probably in a trancelike state during these rides. Or, as noted above, the "Sirhan" witnessed by Powers and Beckley was actually a double.

Rancher Bill Powers had known Owen for four years, and his business was located near Owen's in Santa Ana.[1109] Owen, who went by the name Jerry Owen, was a horse trader and an old-time preacher.[1110] He billed himself as the "Walking Bible" because of his phenomenal recall of chapter and verse. Indeed, several years after the assassination, he became the host of his own television program of the same name.[1111] Besides preaching the Bible part-time and trading horses, Owen was a former prizefighter. He stood over six feet tall and weighed nearly 250 lb. He was known also for his extreme mood swings.[1112] According to writers Turner and Christian, from the time Owen was twenty-six years old until age fifty, he had problems with regard to arson.[1113] His record shows he had been involved in insurance claims resulting from six church fires and collected settlements from some of them. The blazes occurred in locations stretching across the continent from Castro Valley, California, to Oregon, Texas, Kentucky, Maryland, and ending in Tuscon, Arizona.[1114] Jerry Owen could easily have been characterized as a con man.

In Sirhan's so-called diary, the same name appears, written as "J Jee Jeerry" in the notebook pages.[1115] Following Bobby Kennedy's assassination, Sirhan's fingerprints were found on a pickup truck that Owen used. The truck had been found abandoned in Barstow and was turned over to the FBI.[1116]

Despite these links between Sirhan and Owen, the LAPD's final report on the assassination makes no mention of eyewitnesses who saw Owen and Sirhan together.[1117] Numerous investigators, and even Sirhan's mother Mary, have asked Sirhan about Jerry Owen. Yet he cannot recall him. His amnesia block prevails.[1118]

Jerry Owen was very familiar with many of those involved in area horse-racing circles. He frequented Santa Anita and Hollywood Park in 1965 and 1966, just as Sirhan did.[1119] In early 1968, Owen had been boarding two horses at Powers' Wild Bill's Stables in Santa Ana.[1120] According to Powers, Owen had early on mentioned to him that he knew of an exercise boy at the track who could handle his horses better than Powers's employee, Johnny Beckley, could. Owen, who was very serious about the care given his horses, told Powers that a young man named Sirhan would make a good replacement if Beckley didn't work out.[1121]

But Powers was also wary of Owen's eccentric behavior. He later told investigators that Owen seemed like the type who could "have you bumped off. He wouldn't just think about it—he'd do it. And then he'd say a little prayer."[1122]

After the assassination, when Bill Powers was interviewed by two police officers, Powers says that they warned him not to tell anyone that he had seen Owen with Sirhan.[1123] According to LAPD's Sgt. Dudley Varney, Johnny Beckley, Powers's assistant who was at Powers's stables breaking in horses owned by Owen, ended up denying he saw Sirhan. But later on, after Beckley heard he would be called in for further questioning, he vanished.[1124] He reportedly fled to Missouri. According to authors Turner and Christian, he said he "feared for his life."[1125]

Before Beckley left, he told a young, fellow stable hand, John Chris Weatherly, that if any of them disclosed that Owen knew Sirhan, they'd be in deep trouble because, as he put it, "the preacher had enough money to get us all knocked off."[1126] Although Owen was known by some as the voice of scripture, he was deeply feared by others. When Weatherly told the police that his co-workers had seen Owen with Sirhan, Sergeants Varney and Manuel Gutierrez told him that he "shouldn't speak to anyone," that it "would be against the law." [1127] Weatherly was shot at one night in August 1971 while sitting in his truck in front of his house. The bullet narrowly missed him as it tore through his vehicle.[1128] Indeed, Weatherly, Powers, and Beckley all paid a price for releasing this information.

As we shall see ahead, Owen was chosen to unwittingly play the role of a decoy. His presence not only served as a distraction, it also may have been designed ironically to quell some suspicions about Sirhan's critical three-month gap. Having Sirhan ride horses with a "man of God" for three months would be viewed as a perfectly harmless activity. It was also the perfect cover for what was actually happening to Sirhan behind closed doors. Neither Owen nor anyone else without a need to know would have been privy to Sirhan's programming and his handlers' ultimate objective. In covert operations, it is routine to compartmentalize information or knowledge of the plan. Each participant only knows a segment. But none of the segmented bits contains enough information to give away or compromise the operation. This was most likely the case with Jerry Owen.

As for the exact location at which Sirhan's conditioning was conducted, it may have been in Owen's locale where witnesses saw the young man who looked like Sirhan. Or Sirhan was taken there for horse rides at times during the three-month conditioning period. Indeed, Sirhan may even have undergone conditioning at an institution, perhaps covertly flown to Montreal where evidence of Agency-funded mind-control experiments is well documented.[1129] In such a place, he would have been hypno-programmed without detection and without interference of any kind.

Meanwhile, at home in Pasadena, Mary Sirhan prayed, read her Bible, and sought consolation from her son Adel who was living at home with her. Their anguish and sense of loss during Sirhan's absence mirrored in many ways the torment American families across the nation endured during the war in Southeast Asia.

On January 30, 1968, most US soldiers stationed in Vietnam anticipated a quiet night. It was the Vietnamese lunar New Year holiday, known as Tet, a time of joy and celebration. At American outposts in the Vietnamese countryside, troops tried to get some sleep, while those on night watch stared out over sandbags that surrounded their bunkers. Suddenly, without warning, in scores of locations throughout Vietnam, enemy troops emerged from the jungles and attacked. At most bases, perimeter trip wires went off, detonating land mines across no-man's land, decimating the invaders. Waves of Communist replacements continued to rush forward, overrunning the outposts in many areas. US air bases were pounded by mortar shells, blowing apart planes and damaging barracks, hangars, and runways. At the US embassy in Saigon, a rocket attack was followed by a direct assault on the main gate of the compound. Several embassy personnel were killed before the Marines were able to stop the insurgents and secure the area. The attackers in the northern part of the country consisted of North Vietnamese regulars who poured across the

Demilitarized Zone, while in the south, raids were led by the Vietcong. The enemy's Tet Offensive took the nation and Washington by surprise.

Combined forces of North Vietnamese and Vietcong troops totaling some seventy thousand soldiers had launched an assault against US forces all across Vietnam. More than one hundred towns and cities were hit in the incredibly coordinated surprise attack.[1130] In the following month, more than two thousand American troops died before the offensive was stopped. Pentagon sources reported a high number of US troops were killed in Hue and other provincial capitals. Hue was actually captured by the Vietcong, and it would take the United States a month to free the city.

The Communist attack on the US embassy was part of a strategy to foment an uprising against the Saigon regime and against the Americans, according to military historian Stanley Karnow.[1131] He has written that the Tet offensive, as planned by Ho Chi Minh's officers, was heavily promoted in North Vietnam. Their government media declared the massive offensive as their people's best chance to free South Vietnam from the American "aggressors" and to put an end to the corrupt Saigon regime.[1132] The Communist attempt failed. However, it did succeed in gaining the attention of Americans at home. President Johnson had been hurt politically, with his credibility rating in the polls falling from 40 percent to 26 percent. Clearly, trust in Johnson was nearly gone. His response to the Tet Offensive was to call it "a complete failure" on the part of the Communists.[1133]

A week after Tet, on February 8, 1968, Sen. Robert Kennedy appeared before a large audience in Chicago.[1134] The reaction of many listeners would be one of surprise as Kennedy laid all his cards on table. He asserted that his brother's administration had been wrong in its decision to go to war in Vietnam, and he insisted that the present course was not the path to peace. "For twenty years, first the French and then the United States have been predicting victory in Vietnam. In 1961 and 1962, as well as 1966 and 1967, we have been told that the tide is turning, that there is light at the end of the tunnel, that we can soon bring our troops home, that victory is near, the enemy is tiring. Once, in 1962, I participated in such predictions myself. But for twenty years, we have been wrong," Kennedy said.

As Kennedy spoke, there were a half million American troops in Vietnam. Allied Vietnamese forces totaled seven hundred thousand. The enemy forces consisting of North Vietnamese and Vietcong troops were estimated at six hundred thousand.[1135]

Kennedy's Chicago speech was his strongest antiwar message and anti-Johnson diatribe to date: "The history of conflict among nations does not record such a lengthy and consistent chronicle of error as we have shown in Vietnam. It is time to discard so proven a fallacy and face the reality that a military victory is not in sight, and that it will probably never come. Unable to defeat our enemy, or to break his will, at least without a huge, long, and even more costly effort, we must actively seek a peaceful settlement."[1136]

The settlement to which Kennedy referred was a proposal that would have given the Vietcong an opportunity to participate in South Vietnamese politics.[1137] This, of course, was traitorous to those prosecuting the war from the highest echelon of the military and the CIA. Many in Kennedy's audience that day in Chicago also remained unconvinced.

The first announcement of Bobby's regarding his running for the presidency was over dinner with relatives on January 19, 1968. He told his sisters Jean Smith and Pat Lawford and his brother-in-law Steve Smith that "he thought he would run" and joked that he'd be looking to them for funding.[1138] However, despite private family talks, Kennedy continued to deny his intentions in the press. He said he had no plans at that point to take on President Johnson. Slowly, he worked on his message as he waited in the background for the right moment to declare. He knew there would be no turning back once he made his break from the party establishment and had become, in effect, a renegade. He also knew preparation was essential.

By February 1968, hopes had vanished for a swift end to the war in Vietnam. The conflict raged on as US troops vigorously fought to recover from the Tet Offensive. Secretary of Defense Robert McNamara four months earlier had tried to level off the amount of bombing over North Vietnam and had planned a halt in two months if the enemy would come to the negotiating table. He also had refused to increase troop levels, putting the war into a "holding action," despite deep opposition from the Pentagon. His reasoning was that the Communists would not negotiate until after the November elections.[1139] US military and CIA officials, incensed at these restrictions, had quietly approached right-wing politicians in Congress. Sen. John Stennis of Mississippi, a veteran of the armed services committee, and other senators interceded on their behalf with President Johnson.[1140] They were convinced that slowing the air war would be disaster.[1141]

McNamara responded by arguing that North Vietnam could not be forced into negotiations by more bombing. He also insisted the South Vietnamese government take on more responsibility for their own security. The right wing strongly criticized this change in course and protested that it would show our enemies that we had lost our will.[1142] In early February 1968, President Johnson finally removed McNamara from office and gave him the presidency of the World Bank. Johnson's friend and vociferous McNamara critic Clark Clifford was appointed to the post of Secretary of Defense.[1143]

According to author Stanley Karnow, McNamara's friendship with Robert Kennedy was a major reason for his ouster. President Johnson reportedly stated, "Every day Bobby would call up McNamara, telling him that the war was terrible and immoral, and that he had to leave (Vietnam)."[1144]

Apparently Johnson's neuroses regarding the Kennedys compelled him to take action. Historian Doris Kearns Goodwin recalled Johnson saying that he felt Secretary of Defense McNamara was having a mental breakdown, and that given the pressure of the job, it would be "unfair" to keep him on.[1145] At his farewell party, McNamara reportedly did break down emotionally, overtaken with grief and regret over the futility of the air campaign.[1146]

With Clark Clifford in place, the admirals and generals were in charge; the air war and ground war would both accelerate. Their orders: Communist expansion would be stopped and even driven back where feasible. The war would be won, one way or another. This was the game plan of the military and the intelligence establishment.

At the same time, rogues in the CIA were considering even more extreme measures at home.

At the end of Sirhan's three-month absence, before he was brought home or returned to his old DeSoto (perhaps in the parking lot of a bar from which he had been unwittingly escorted following a surreptitious roofie-laced drink), his memory of his whereabouts had been wiped clean. As noted previously, John Marks's book, *The Search for the "Manchurian Candidate,"* describes how CIA contract hypnotists merely had to create a mental block in the mind of the hypnotized subject. Despite numerous examples of CIA hypno-programming experiments, the Agency was able to keep these activities secret for decades. To ensure that the amnesia would last, programmers could also embed a threat in the minds of subjects that harm would befall them if they disclosed information regarding the programming. For example, the subject could be told while under hypnosis that if he crossed a "memory boundary" delineated by the hypnotist as off limits, he would then die. If Sirhan believed he was at death's door every time he was probed regarding his trances or his automatic writing, this could certainly have made him very uncomfortable.

The conditioning of Sirhan instilled in him particular responses to various cues, but more importantly, it was no doubt also designed to deeply impact his emotions. This is because emotions are among the fundamental keys to controlling behavior; involvement of the emotions is critical to motivating a subject. It appears that Sirhan was led to believe on a visceral level that his people faced grave danger from a potential Kennedy presidency. The feelings of fear, horror, and dread, buried in his psyche from living through the first Arab-Israeli War of 1948, made Sirhan a perfect "candidate" for an assassination conspiracy. These emotions—when tied to distorted visions of an RFK presidency—provided potent motivation for the tasks required. For the plan to work, i.e. making Sirhan a patsy, the hypno-programming had to build in Sirhan a sense that Robert Kennedy was not only pro-Israel, but also anti-Arab. Fear was kindled in Sirhan—through hypnosis—that Israel was going to destroy the Palestinians. These new fears and thoughts were expressed by Sirhan upon his return home. His conditioning had instilled in him a feeling of anger toward Israel that family and friends indicated was not there previously.

Sirhan's return after three months was a great relief to his mother. His brothers Munir and Adel seemed to take it in stride, although they, too, had no information as to where their brother had been. Sirhan must have been embarrassed that he was not aware of any missing time, and he probably quickly changed the subject whenever it popped up. At the same time, he was no doubt very annoyed at not knowing what was happening to him—not recalling recent events that had happened in his life and the lives of others, having strange feelings and desires, and exhibiting new behaviors.

He had returned home irritable, withdrawn, and suffering from amnesia with regard to his disappearance. It is hardly a coincidence that these symptoms are similar to those of individuals known to have participated in CIA behavior-modification programs of that time. Investigators and witnesses, who may be unaware of such programs, have tried to attribute Sirhan's personality change to his spill from a horse. But the facts do not support this conclusion: the accident had occurred a year and half earlier, in September 1966, and, according to doctors, it was not a serious head injury.[1147] From the perspective of his having been conditioned, his irritability is perfectly understandable; the subject was grappling with new feelings, mysterious urges, and thought patterns and had no idea what was happening to him.

It was Sirhan's family that first recalled a change in his behavior, with several members noting that he had become withdrawn and "touchy." One of Sirhan's older brothers, Sharif, who lived in his own apartment, has stated that in the months prior to the RFK assassination, Sirhan had gone from being a polite and kind kid brother to being irritable all the time.[1148] His family and his friends recalled that where he had once been "gentlemanly," he had become, according to his brother Sharif, "abnormal."[1149]

Robert Kaiser has described how one morning Sirhan punched his younger brother Munir over a cup of tea.[1150] Some have described this change in Sirhan as a sign that he was experiencing a mental breakdown, but there is no evidence of this. Dr. Eduard Simson-Kallas, noted earlier, examined Sirhan in prison and determined that he was sane. Sirhan exhibited no symptoms of being paranoid schizophrenic or psychotic.[1151] This diagnosis was corroborated by San Quentin's chief psychiatrist, Dr. D. G. Schmidt.[1152] The doctors found him to be a normally functioning person. However, in retrospect, it is clear that the fact that he was uncharacteristically depressed and irritable was a telling sign of a malady directly related to his uniquely enigmatic situation.

Upon his return home, Sirhan resumed his job as a delivery man at the Pasadena organic health food store, but only for a short time. Interestingly, in LAPD Chief of Detectives Robert Houghton's book, *Special Unit Senator*, Houghton writes that Sirhan worked at the health food store from September 1967 to March 7, 1968.[1153] He has neglected to report Sirhan's documented three-month disappearance.[1154]

According to store owner John Weidner, when Sirhan had originally started, he was "very happy" working there. However, Weidner also noted that later on Sirhan became "touchy" and that they had had several arguments.[1155]

Weidner stated that Sirhan made comments about the state of Israel, such as, "They have stolen my country." Regarding the United States, Sirhan complained, "there is no freedom in America."[1156] Weidner said Sirhan became nervous and arrogant during this time.[1157] Sirhan's disagreements with his boss—over such things as the sequence in which he made his deliveries—became major disputes. Suddenly, Sirhan quit.[1158] It was early March 1968, shortly after the three-month time gap. Sirhan's uncharacteristic behavior clearly coincides with a type of conditioning designed to make him angry—angry enough to fire unwittingly and on cue.

About this same time, Sirhan's companion, Tom Rathke, reappeared, at the Sirhan home for dinner, according to family friend Lynne Massey Mangan.[1159] Author Robert Kaiser probed the nature of Sirhan's relationship with Rathke during a conversation with Sirhan in his jail cell prior to the trial. At one point, Sirhan reported that he had received "mental protection" from Rathke, although he never explained what this meant.[1160] It is assumed that, at least in Sirhan's mind, protection involved some kind of thought waves.

It is uncertain whether Rathke played a part in Sirhan's predicament, for example, as a liaison between an unwitting Sirhan and the hypno-programmer. Following the assassination, when Rathke was interviewed by investigators, he gave one of the most detailed descriptions of the personality change in Sirhan. While Rathke was very close to Sirhan, he ironically painted a picture of a very *unlikable* companion. For example, Rathke stated that Sirhan had gone from being a "boy . . . (with whom) you'd talk and laugh and have fun . . ." to someone who was "rigid" and "like a paranoid."[1161] If Rathke were aware of the actual circumstances of Sirhan's missing three months, then he may have been attempting to disguise Sirhan's true condition.

With Tom Rathke's encouragement, as soon as Sirhan returned from his three-month absence, he joined two New Age organizations. First, he mailed in his dues to the San Jose-based Ancient Mystical Order of the Rosae Crucis (Rosicrucians). He only attended one meeting, which was held at the group's Pasadena Lodge on May 28, 1968, and left early.[1162] As for the other organization, Sirhan attended a meeting of the Pasadena chapter of the Theosophical Society, according to investigators Turner and Christian.[1163] Clearly, those conditioning Sirhan wanted to establish Sirhan as a fringe-type individual, a person who was seeking some kind of out-of-the-ordinary power. By linking him to these occult organizations, however briefly, they were able to later portray him as one who could have immersed himself deeply into some kind of trancelike state. It would even make him appear, to some, as an individual who was mentally unstable enough to kill a presidential candidate in a crowded room. While reasonable minds know that these characterizations of the behavior of occult enthusiasts are unfair, they are the perceptions that influenced many who were unfamiliar with New Age literature and philosophy. The occultist image would later paint the murder suspect in such a way that the discovery of his hypnotic, drug-induced, trancelike state would be conveniently disguised as Sirhan's own handiwork, in the mind of the general public.

While speaking with author Robert Kaiser before the trial, Sirhan discussed the possibility of his having been conditioned, perhaps by someone close to him, such as Tom Rathke. Sirhan stated that he could not accept the theory that his friend would have done this.[1164] Indeed, there is no indication that Rathke possessed the professional experience needed to have carried out such a sensitive programming operation himself. Some of the challenging variables—the notebooks, the amnesia, the girl, the cues—all required precise coordination, along with expert brainwashing techniques, in order to succeed without a hitch. The process of conditioning an individual is essentially the programming of their psyche with a series of posthypnotic suggestions. Amnesia also was a key part of the equation, in part drug-induced, in conjunction with cues leading to rapid immersion into a trancelike state.

As we shall see ahead, in the days after Sirhan returned home and leading up to Bobby Kennedy's assassination, Sirhan was witnessed in a trancelike state at various locations. Such states are not self-induced. They had to have been produced by his handlers who would have had to have been closely monitoring him during this period. In addition to close surveillance, it would have been necessary for Sirhan's handlers to test his conditioning. These occurrences in which Sirhan was "zoned out" were no doubt induced by his handlers to allow them to check out the posthypnotic suggestions and cues that they had given to Sirhan. These occasions also allowed them to reinforce Sirhan's conditioning, to embed new suggestions, and to further establish premeditation.

Prior to his conditioning, Sirhan was not a "gun person." He did not own a gun. His only brief experience with one had been in the Muir High School ROTC.[1165] Yet, soon after he returned home, he suddenly and uncharacteristically had the urge to purchase a weapon. Again, a hypnotic suggestion to this effect—to buy a gun—could have been made in such a way that the subject would have felt that he had to comply, whatever the cost.

According to Sirhan's brother Munir, shortly after Sirhan's return, he asked Munir if he could find him a used handgun. This took Munir by surprise. He feared that his brother was contemplating suicide. When Sirhan dismissed this notion, Munir pressed the issue and replied, "'You swear on sis?'"[1166] Munir was referring to their sister, Aida, who died of leukemia at age twenty-nine in 1965.[1167] Sirhan agreed and swore.

Munir said it was a mystery to him why Sirhan "would want anything to do with guns."[1168] He and his brother both knew that as aliens, it was unlawful for them to own firearms. According to Munir, Sirhan explained that the gun would be used just to practice at the firing range. He also promised to keep it in the car, out of their mother's sight.[1169]

Munir may have thought that his brother wanted a gun for protection, especially given the fact that Sirhan had just come home from a mysterious three-month absence. Munir himself had recently spent nine months in jail for possession of marijuana. So he, no doubt, understood the vagaries of life.[1170]

Munir spoke with a coworker at F. C. Nash Department Store in Pasadena who had a .22 caliber revolver for sale.[1171] The colleague, George Erhard, was a gun collector, and had purchased the 8-shot Iver-Johnson revolver from a neighbor. He agreed to sell it for twenty-five dollars. According to Munir,

Erhard drove to the Sirhan house, where he listened to some records for a while and then closed the sale.[1172]

If a successful posthypnotic suggestion prompted Sirhan to obtain a handgun, an equally effective suggestion caused amnesia to shroud any memory of his carrying and using it. Following the assassination, when Sirhan's defense psychiatrists queried him under hypnosis regarding the gun, he had no memory of it.[1173] Of course, if Sirhan had not come into ownership of a handgun at home, his handlers would have had an alternative plan to acquire one, since a gun was an essential component of the operation.

At this point in time, Robert Kennedy was still publicly undecided regarding his candidacy for president. On March 11, 1968, Bobby accepted an invitation from California farmworker organizer Cesar Chavez, forty-one, who was on a hunger strike. Chavez, the founder of the National FarmWorkers Association (predecessor of the United FarmWorkers of America), had been fasting for three weeks with the goal of drawing attention to the exploitation of farmworkers and to protest violence in the vineyards between the workers, the Teamsters, and the growers. He had asked Bobby to be with him when he ended his fast and to break bread at a celebration of the Mass.[1174] Following in the footsteps of India's Mahatma Gandhi, Chavez had previously walked some three hundred miles to Sacramento for his fellow workers.[1175] At this point, Chavez had lost thirty pounds and was down to 120.[1176] As author Richard D. Mahoney has colorfully described the story, Bobby flew to Delano, California, where more than six thousand farmworkers greeted him with shouts of "Viva Kennedy."[1177] After the Mass, and the sharing of a piece of Mexican bread, Kennedy congratulated Chavez and the other laborers in their struggle for justice for all farmworkers and for Hispanics in general.[1178] Kennedy also urged them to uphold Chavez's principle of nonviolent protest. The crowd responded in Spanish with shouts of "Run! Run!" Those few hours with a desperate Cesar Chavez and his fellow farmworkers had convinced Bobby more than ever that he was needed. The public could see Bobby's power, he could see it, and his enemies also could see it. After boarding the plane for his return trip home, Bobby called his wife Ethel and told her it was time for him to announce his candidacy.[1179]

Meanwhile, on the East Coast, the state that traditionally kicked off the nation's presidential primary season had become a mecca for college students who turned out from across the land to campaign for Gene McCarthy. In New Hampshire's towns and villages, young people stood outside in the cold and snow, smiling and handing out campaign buttons, pamphlets, and bumper stickers. The newly politicized students urged residents to vote on March 12, 1968. Their mantra exhorted residents to dump Johnson, support Clean Gene, and get America out of Vietnam.

McCarthy was the only Democrat to challenge the incumbent, President Lyndon Johnson, at this point. What McCarthy's campaign lacked in funding, it made up for in enthusiasm and in numbers of young supporters. This grassroots campaign was responsible, in part, for the New Hampshire presidential primary's robust turn out. Some fifty thousand Democratic voters went to the polls. Of course, many of these voters did not necessarily support the peace plank; they were simply dissatisfied with the current administration and wanted change.[1180]

When the ballots of the first primary of the presidential race were tallied, the results stunned the nation. Senator McCarthy, the peace candidate, had lost to President Johnson by only three hundred votes.[1181] This incredible near-victory over a sitting president was totally unexpected. The immense turnout for McCarthy in conservative New Hampshire sent a signal of strong discontent with the war in Vietnam. Indeed, President Johnson's career was at stake. Many pundits gave credit to the more than five thousand students who had flocked to the Granite State to campaign for the Minnesota senator.

Four days after the New Hampshire primary, on March 16, 1968, Robert Kennedy publicly announced his intention to run for presidency of the United States. He delivered his statement in the same room in which his brother had announced his candidacy in 1960, the Caucus Room of the Old Senate Office Building in Washington, DC. At Bobby's side were his wife and nine of their ten children.[1182]

Kennedy's speech was broadcast live to millions of homes across America: "I am announcing today my candidacy for the presidency of the United States. I do not run for the presidency merely to oppose any man, but to propose new policies. . . . My decision reflects no personal animosity or disrespect toward President Johnson. The issue is not personal, it is our profound differences over where we are heading and what we want to accomplish. . . . I seek new policies—policies to end the bloodshed in Vietnam and in our cities, policies to close the gap that now exists between black and white, between rich and poor, between young and old in this country and around the rest of the world." [1183]

Although some historians feel that Robert Kennedy had waited in the wings to see how President Johnson would fare in New Hampshire before jumping into the race, one of Bobby's closest friends, author Arthur Schlesinger Jr., has written that this was not the case. Kennedy had already decided a week earlier to run for president. According to Schlesinger, "only a change in Vietnam policy would have canceled it."[1184]

The Democratic party, meanwhile, was still President Johnson's. The party bosses, union leaders, and many in the press favored the president. At the same time, Gene McCarthy had his huge following from the college campuses. Hence, Bobby's desperate need to go to the people directly. But this approach was also very much in keeping with his progressively radical bent. He chose to reach out to the poor, the downtrodden, the minorities, the voiceless, and the disenfranchised. They were his reason for wanting to lead America: to work to help improve the lives of those most in need. He felt that this would thereby improve the quality of life for everyone, while setting an example for the rest of the world. The starting point for Kennedy was to try to find a way to end the carnage in Vietnam and bring America's troops home. In this regard, Kennedy's campaign was scandalous to Cold War warriors throughout the Johnson administration, the military, and the intelligence community. These factions suddenly began to sense that their grip on power was in jeopardy once again, much as it had been just prior to November 22, 1963.

Robert Kennedy embarked on the campaign trail with gusto, quickly making up for lost time. While decrying the nation's war in Southeast Asia, the campaign was also seen as a celebration of America. Young supporters who joined the crusade associated the Kennedy theme with Woody Guthrie's "This Land Is Your Land." Throngs turned out to greet the young candidate at every key stop on the campaign trail. In West Virginia, where eight years earlier John Kennedy had won a very close primary fight, Bobby retraced his brother's footsteps. He rode standing up in an open convertible, as well-wishers pressed against his car and reached out to shake his hand. During a campaign stop at Courthouse Square in Beckley, West Virginia, one young housewife emerged from the crowd and handed Kennedy a mug of beer. He sipped it and smiled to the applause of the crowd.[1185]

In Welch, West Virginia, on the courthouse steps, Bobby leaned into a microphone and spoke to the townsfolk about an editorial that had appeared in their local newspaper. "A local editor wrote this about me in an article in today's paper," said Kennedy. "He said I am un-invited, unwanted, undesirable, unethical, un-American, unfit, unprepared, unshorn, unpopular, unloved, and overrated. But I wanted him to make sure he knew I had my hair cut, though." Laughter and applause filled the air and a man in the crowd responded, "We love you, Senator Kennedy."[1186]

214

Indeed, an incredible presidential campaign was unfolding before voters' eyes. Captivated TV audiences across the country watched with growing excitement as the Kennedy troops took to the campaign trail covering fifteen states in two weeks' time. Journalists called Bobby's marathon a blitzkrieg, while historians have defined it as a unique experience in American politics, given the amount of territory visited and its impact on people. According to author Richard Mahoney, in Arizona and Alabama Kennedy's reception was "merely positive," but in every other state the crowds were ecstatic.[1187]

On March 17, 1968, fifteen thousand students turned out to hear Bobby Kennedy deliver the Alfred M. Landon Lecture at Kansas State University. The audience in the packed field house was considered to be primarily conservative, coat-and-tie-wearing students. Kennedy anticipated a generally cool response due to his antiwar mantra. Nevertheless, he pressed ahead with his message, his voice filled with emotion: "Can we ordain to ourselves the awful majesty of God—to decide what cities and villages are to be destroyed, who will live and who will die, and who will join the refugees wandering in a desert of our own creation? In these next eight months, we are going to decide what this country will stand for—and what kind of men we are."[1188] When he had finished, as one writer would report, the applause sounded like the roar of Niagra Falls.[1189]

When Bobby Kennedy's campaign blitz arrived in Nashville, Tennessee, the candidate continued to raise the ante. He spoke in support of the antiwar movement as he assailed the policies of the Johnson administration: "When we are told to forego all dissent and division, we must ask: who is truly dividing the country? It is not those who call for change, it is those who make present policy." Instead of the "public commitment of a few years ago . . . (the young have chosen) lives of disengagement and despair, turning on with drugs and turning off America."[1190]

Kennedy found his most enthusiastic reception in California, where shrieking thousands complemented the intensity of his remarks: "'Our brave young men are dying in the swamps of Southeast Asia. Which of them might have written a poem? Which of them might have cured cancer? Which of them might have played in a World Series or given us the gift of laughter from the stage or helped build a bridge or a university? Which of them would have taught a child to read? It is our responsibility to let these men live. . . . It is indecent if they die because of the empty vanity of their country.'"[1191]

Bobby wrapped up this initial two-week, whirlwind campaign drive on March 29 in Arizona. At the Navaho town of Window Rock, he appealed to the plight of the Native Americans. He criticized the Bureau of Indian Affairs (BIA) and called their policies a form of colonialism. Then he stressed the importance of the Indian cause and stated, "You have your culture. You have your history. You have your language."[1192] According to author Richard Mahoney, whose father, William P. Mahoney, headed up the Arizona Kennedy campaign, Kennedy connected with the local populace as no one had done so before. After listening to Bobby speak, one Navaho reportedly told Mahoney, "I have waited all my life for a white man to say that."[1193]

Two days later, on the evening of March 31, 1968, President Lyndon Johnson sat at his desk in the Oval Office and stared intently into a TV camera. He spoke slowly in his soft southern drawl, as he addressed the nation. "Good evening, my fellow Americans. Tonight I want to speak to you of peace in Vietnam and Southeast Asia . . ." His speech appeared to be a routine update on the administration's latest war plans, or possibly some movement towards starting up peace talks with North Vietnam. But when he came to the end, he took the nation by surprise with the announcement that he was dropping out of the 1968 presidential race: "I have concluded that I should not permit the presidency to become involved in the partisan divisions that are developing in this political year. Accordingly, I shall not seek, and I will not accept, the nomination of my party for another term as your president."[1194]

The frustrations of the war had broken Johnson's spirit. He was unable to find a way to win both abroad and at home, and he also understood the political realities of that election season. His policies were under continual attack from Richard Nixon, Gene McCarthy, and Robert Kennedy. His ability to carry out the duties of the office had become seriously impaired as a result, and the prognosis for his administration was not good. As Arthur Schlesinger has pointed out, pollsters in Wisconsin had predicted an embarrassing two-to-one loss for LBJ in that state's upcoming primary.[1195]

The day President Johnson announced his withdrawal from the primary race, Bobby Kennedy had just arrived at LaGuardia Airport in New York, concluding his two-week campaign blitz.[1196] Kennedy took a short break before continuing his crusade back to the heartland of Indiana.

Meanwhile, those in the Pentagon and the CIA who were prosecuting the war knew that without President Johnson, a like-minded president was needed to fill the vacuum if victory in Vietnam was to be achieved. Their success depended on ensuring the election of a commander in chief who would continue to support US forces in Southeast Asia. They found such a candidate in Richard Nixon. In his quest to be the Republican Party's standard-bearer, he

216

was opposed primarily by New York's Nelson Rockefeller. Although Nixon had been out of politics since his loss to John Kennedy in 1960, he still had strong backing from key Republican Party loyalists. He had gained their support during his two terms as vice president under Dwight Eisenhower from 1952 to 1960. It was during these years that he had established a reputation as a close ally of the generals, the admirals, and the intelligence community. In 1954, he was one of the few advisors who had suggested sending US troops to Vietnam in the event France was defeated in its colonial war with the independence-minded Indo-Chinese colonies. Nixon even went so far as to advocate using atomic weapons in Southeast Asia.[1197] French forces were overrun in 1954 at Biendienphu. However, President Eisenhower decided it was not the time to rush into a land war in Asia.

By March 31, 1968, there were 550,000 American troops involved in the war effort in Vietnam.[1198] Again, the military and the CIA were confident that victory could be achieved, but not if Bobby Kennedy were elected president.

Besides Robert Kennedy, Dr. Martin Luther King Jr. was probably the most serious threat to the war effort. America's foremost civil rights champion and Nobel Peace Prize winner, King had joined the antiwar movement in the spring of 1967.

In early 1968, King's immediate priority was to fulfill a promise he had made to intercede in a strike by sanitation workers in Memphis, Tennessee. The city's garbagemen had walked off the job on February 12, 1968, after the city refused their demands for improved wages and working conditions.[1199] Most of Memphis's thirteen hundred black sanitation workers had joined the walk-out. Carrying signs that read I AM A MAN, they demanded the right to form a union. An earlier demonstration had been broken up by police wielding nightsticks and spraying mace. With the strike entering its sixth week, Dr. King arrived in Memphis. He was confident their march would be nonviolent.

That night, April 3, 1968, despite heavy rains, more than two thousansd people turned out at Mason Temple to meet him. Many listeners later said that they felt King's words were prescient: "I don't know what will happen now. We've got some difficult days ahead. But it really doesn't matter with me now. Because I've been to the mountaintop. Like anybody, I would like to live a long life. Longevity has its place. But I'm not concerned about that now. I just want to do God's will. And he's allowed me to go up to the mountain. And I've looked over. And I've seen the Promised Land." As the large audience erupted in applause and cries of "Yes, sir," and "Go ahead, doctor," King continued. "But I want you to know tonight that we as a people will get to the Promised

Land. So, I'm happy tonight. I'm not worried about anything. I'm not fearing any man. Mine eyes have seen the glory of the coming of the Lord. I have had a dream this afternoon that the brotherhood of man will become a reality. With this faith, I will go out and carve a tunnel of hope from a mountain of despair. . . . With this faith, we will be able to achieve this new day, when all of God's children—black men and white men, Jews and Gentiles, Protestants and Catholics—will be able to join hands and sing with the Negroes in the spiritual of old, 'Free at last! Free at last! Thank God almighty, we are free at last.'" [1200] It was Martin Luther King Jr.'s last sermon.

The next day, April 4, 1968, Robert Kennedy had begun campaigning in Indiana. He spoke in Muncie that afternoon, and that evening he planned to stop in Indianapolis, where he was scheduled to speak in the ghetto. [1201]

Meanwhile, in Memphis, Martin Luther King Jr. and his closest friend, the Rev. Ralph Abernathy, were staying in room 306 at the modest two-story Lorraine Motel. [1202] It was cool that evening. At approximately 6 p.m., King opened the door of his room and stepped out onto the balcony. Accompanied by the Rev. Samuel Kyles, they prepared to go to Kyles's house for dinner. King's chauffeur, Solomon Jones, waited by the limousine in a parking lot below the balcony. Others in the entourage included James Bevel, Ben Branch, Jesse Jackson, Bernard Lee, James Orange, Hosea Williams, and Andy Young. [1203]

Jones called out to King, reminding him to bring a topcoat. King then asked Abernathy to bring it out with him. Turning to his friends in the parking lot, King commented to musician Ben Branch, "Ben, make sure to play 'Precious Lord, Take My Hand' at the meeting tonight. Sing it real pretty." Branch replied, "Okay, Doc, I will." King kidded with Jesse Jackson, twenty-six, as Kyles started to walk down the stairs to the limousine, leaving King alone on the balcony. [1204]

On the other side of the parking lot, an embankment covered with trees and brush rose up to the back yard of a row of old brick buildings. King was leaning against the iron railing on the motel balcony when suddenly the crack of a high-powered rifle shot exploded across the parking lot. King was thrown to the floor of the balcony, the right side of his jaw and neck torn away. [1205]

Abernathy rushed from the room to his friend's side and held his head as a pool of blood spread across the floor. The others in the group raced up the stairs to help their fallen leader. King was rushed by ambulance to St. Joseph's Hospital, where he was pronounced dead at 7:05 p.m. [1206]

It is now known that the civil rights leader was under constant surveillance by Richard Helms's CIA, as well as the FBI and the military. [1207] These groups worked closely with the local Memphis Police Department. And, in fact, Memphis's public safety director, Frank Holloman, had served in the FBI for twenty-five years and had managed the Memphis FBI office.[1208]

Andrew Young, an aide of Martin Luther King Jr.'s, said he believed that King's assassination was directly related to "the fear that officialdom had of his bringing large numbers of poor people to the nation's capital (the planned Poor People's March)."[1209] According to King's closest supporters, Bobby Kennedy's staff had been hard at work assisting King in organizing the march on Washington. Shortly before his death on April 4, 1968, "Brother Martin" was planning to endorse Robert Kennedy for president. King was quoted as saying, "We've got to get behind Bobby."[1210]

Robert Kennedy had received word that Martin Luther King Jr. was dead while he was en route by plane to his next campaign stop in Indianapolis. Bobby wanted to speak in a ghetto there, although the mayor and the police had advised him not to.[1211] He went anyway. It was a cold night, yet a large crowd had assembled in a parking lot to hear him speak. Kennedy knew that the audience had not yet received word that Martin Luther King Jr. had been killed.[1212] Arriving at the site, Kennedy stepped from his car, walked over to a flat bed truck, and climbed up to the microphone. Softly he spoke, "I have bad news for you, for all of our fellow citizens, and people who love peace all over the world, and that is that Martin Luther King Jr. was shot and killed tonight." The crowd gasped.[1213]

Historians agree Kennedy's speech not only defined his campaign, but defined the man. It was simple and from the heart. "Martin Luther King Jr. dedicated his life to love and to justice for his fellow human beings, and he died because of that effort. . . . For those of you who are black and are tempted to be filled with hatred and distrust at the injustice of such an act, against all white people, I can only say that I feel in my own heart the same kind of feeling. I had a member of my family killed, but he was killed by a white man. . . . My favorite poet was Aeschylus. He wrote: 'In our sleep, pain which cannot forget falls drop by drop upon the heart until, in our own despair, against our will, comes wisdom through the awful grace of God.' What we need in the United States is not division; what we need in the United States is not hatred; what we need in the United States is not violence or lawlessness, but love and wisdom, and compassion toward one another and a feeling of justice towards those who still suffer within our country, whether they be white or they be black. . . . We've had difficult times in the past. We will have difficult times in the future. It is not the end of violence; it is not the end of lawlessness; it is not the end of disorder. But the vast majority of white people and the vast majority of black people in this country want to live together, want to improve the quality of our life, and want justice for all human beings who abide in our land. Let us dedicate ourselves to what the Greeks wrote so many years ago; to tame the savageness of man and to make gentle the life of this world. Let us dedicate ourselves to that, and say a prayer for our country and for our people."[1214]

That night there were riots in 110 US cities, thirty-nine people were killed and twenty-five hundred injured. Over seventy-five thousand National Guard troops were called out. But after Kennedy's speech, Indianapolis remained calm. It was one of the few cities that did.[1215]

After an international manhunt, James Earl Ray, an escaped convict with little experience shooting a rifle,[1216] was arrested in England two months later. Ray believed that he was framed. Nevertheless, he ended up pleading guilty because he was told by his attorney that if he did not, he would receive the death penalty. Ray was sentenced to a ninety-nine-year prison term after a two-hour-and-seven-minute "trial." The truth was never adjudicated.[1217] Within days, Ray retracted his plea, and despite his many attempts to prove his innocence, he never received a full trial. He died in prison in 1998 at age seventy. (A number of historians believe that Ray, too, was an innocent patsy, and that he was conditioned through an MKULTRA program to be an unwitting fall guy.)

Meanwhile, in Pasadena, on April 5, 1968, Sirhan received a check in the mail from the Argonaut Insurance Company. It was the workman's compensation for his horse accident, money for which he had waited many months. The amount totaled $1,705, the balance of his $2,000 claim after medical and legal fees were taken out.[1218] In the days when cigarettes cost forty cents a pack and a gallon of gas was about the same price, possessing $1,705 bestowed upon Sirhan a feeling of affluence. He immediately cashed the check. He asked his mother to be his "banker," depositing with her $1,000 which he would draw on as needed. Sirhan also gave some of the money to his brother Adel, according to Mary Sirhan.[1219] As for saving or investing his money, Sirhan's plan for financial growth consisted of betting at Hollywood Park. But instead of increasing his earnings, he lost hundreds.[1220]

At the same time, Sirhan's unusual personality change, particularly his depression, became evident to his mother. In mid-April 1968, she decided to do something about it. She mentioned to a colleague of hers, the mother of Sirhan's former classmate, Walter Crowe, that it had been a long time since Walter had been over to see Sirhan. Mrs. Crowe agreed and asked Walter to give Sirhan a call. It had been three years since the two friends had been out together. They arranged to meet on May 2, 1968 at Bob's Big Boy Restaurant located across the street from Pasadena City College.[1221] The night of their reunion at Bob's Big Boy, Walter was celebrating his having started a new job that day at the Los Angeles County Department of Welfare.[1222] Their conversation revolved around Walter's work and Mideast politics, something they always enjoyed discussing. For example, on the topic of the Six-Day War, fought less than one year earlier, Sirhan lamented the fact that the Arab people had lost so much land. He said he was confident they would wait and fight again another day. Walter viewed the situation as a proxy war and discussed Russia's role as an arms supplier in support of the Arab cause.[1223] The topic of Robert Kennedy reportedly did not come up. As for Sirhan's attitude, or any noticeable personality change, Walter later noted that Sirhan had seemed very quiet. He also said that he seemed to have lost some of his earlier idealism.[1224]

For their night on the town, Sirhan had called another old friend from the college to join them, Ivan Garcia, a native of Guatemala. Garcia arrived at Bob's Big Boy Restaurant with one of his friends, Joseph Marcovecchio, a Colombian student.[1225] In an interview with authorities after the assassination, Garcia described his friend Sirhan as a law-abiding citizen. "I never knew Sirhan to violate any laws of any kind," Garcia stated.[1226]

While Sirhan may have appeared as straight as usual, he seemed to have lost some of his spontaneity. The four friends exited Bob's Big Boy and proceeded to two topless bars and a Mexican restaurant. They first drank pitchers of beer at the Hi-Life at 1958 East Colorado, and again at the Cat Patch at 2211 East Foothill Road, Pasadena.[1227] Sirhan continued to exhibit his subdued disposition, as even his penchant for erotic dancers began to diminish. According to Crowe, at one point in the evening, Sirhan apparently asked the others why the strippers were "demeaning themselves."[1228] His friends told him to lighten up. Although Sirhan was still buying beer for everyone, this remark was yet another out-of-character sign, clearly stemming from the unusual circumstances related to his state of mind. The four young men ended up the night at Ernie's Taco House on Colorado and Fair Oaks. The next day, Walter reported to his mother that Sirhan had seemed "withdrawn."[1229]

Meanwhile, on the campaign trail, Robert Kennedy had hit a rough stretch in Indiana where anti-Kennedy signs had begun to appear. Demonstrators standing on the fringes of the crowds waved placards that read: GO BACK TO MASS. MOPHEAD and HOW MANY DID YOU BETRAY AT THE BAY OF PIGS? Some even complained of the way in which Kennedy pronounced the name of the state, "Indian-er" versus "Indianuh."[1230]

Indeed, the young Democrat's reception in Indiana initially ranged from cool to hostile. Many voters in the rural areas of Southern Indiana did not identify with Kennedy's stand against the war and his call for social justice.

While speaking to medical students at Indiana University Medical Center, Bobby was booed. According to author Richard Mahoney, when Kennedy was asked by one medical student where he planned to find the money to finance new social legislation, Bobby responded, "From you." He continued, "I look around this room and I don't see many black faces who will become doctors. Part of civilized society is to let people go to medical school who come from ghettos. I don't see many people coming here from slums, or off of Indian reservations. You are the privileged ones here. It's easy for you to sit back and say it's the fault of the Federal Government. But it's our responsibility, too. It's our society, too. . . . It's the poor who carry the major burden of the struggle in Vietnam. You sit here as white medical students, while black people carry the burden of the fighting in Vietnam."[1231]

Kennedy's honesty inspired the several dozen reporters following him, which in turn resulted in more positive press. Gradually, voters began to see Kennedy's genuine concern. As Marshall McLuhan stated, Bobby began to come across on TV as a "reluctant hero," giving him a persuasive edge.[1232]

Turning to the northern part of the state of Indiana, the political environment took a major turn for the better. Urban minorities and factory workers in South Bend, Gary, and smaller communities, flocked to every stop to see Kennedy, and to try to touch him. On Indiana's primary day, May 7, 1968, Kennedy won decisively over McCarthy, 42 percent to 27 percent.[1233] The campaign trail next headed west for key primaries in Nebraska on May 14, Oregon on May 28, and the crucial California contest on June 4, 1968.

"I like rural people . . . they listen to me," said Robert Kennedy in Nebraska.[1234] The farmers there were apparently more open to Bobby's message, which by this point he had hardened and refined. He petitioned the common man to take up his cause. Speaking from a flat bed truck to a large group of farmers in a cornfield, he stated, "I come to Nebraska in my campaign because I need your help. We're taking on the Establishment. And we are taking on the political figures of this country." This was a turning point in the campaign and in Bobby Kennedy's life. He had signaled the Establishment by name that he intended to defeat them and their candidates and go on to change American society. He had given his opponents fair notice.

The small cabal who did not want any part of a new Kennedy administration had already determined how they would stop this "one man revolution." If they could not win at the polls, there was no other alternative but "executive action." This brutal course stemmed from the mentality of this era: the United States was at war overseas and at home. And both sides in the fight were certain they were right.

Nebraskans turned out in droves for the primary. At the end of the day, Kennedy had crushed McCarthy 51 percent to 31 percent.[1235] Hubert Humphrey had not announced his candidacy until April 27, 1968, and was therefore too late to enter the primaries in Indiana and Nebraska. Immediately following Johnson's announcement of his withdrawal from the race, Humphrey had signed on two hawks on Vietnam to head up his campaign, Sen. Walter Mondale and Fred Harris.[1236] Both were friends of Robert Kennedy's, but disagreed with him over the war. Humphrey's support of the war effort readily gave him Johnson's votes. Since he also maintained a strong base of support from big labor and southern politicians, Humphrey's position in the spectrum made him an increasingly decisive factor in the contest for the Democratic party nomination. If Kennedy could defeat McCarthy prior to the convention in Chicago and then pick up Johnson's supporters who were still "on the fence" with respect to Humphrey, he could win the nomination.

Robert Kennedy had taken the Midwest by storm. The question on everyone's mind was whether this momentum would last. There remained only three weeks until the most important primary—California on June 4. But before that, there stood one more challenge that was expected to be an extremely tight race—Oregon.

At this time in Sirhan's life, from May 20, 1968 forward, Sirhan was seen by various witnesses at a number of locations, places that were not part of his usual routine. In most of these sightings, witnesses said they observed him with a young woman. Her description stayed essentially the same from witness to witness: a Caucasian in her mid-twenties, approximately five feet six inches, medium-blond, shoulder-length hair, and having a good-looking figure.[1237]

The sightings painted a picture of Sirhan and a female companion pursuing Robert Kennedy. Yet, it was known that Sirhan was not closely watching the Kennedy campaign. He had little knowledge—if any—of the campaign schedule, times, locations, driving directions, audience size, sponsors, and so forth. Indeed, if he had been hunting Kennedy, he would have had to have been accompanying someone who possessed this logistical information. Sirhan has no memory of these so-called "stalkings." Nor does he recall the woman, except for the few moments when he poured coffee for her in the kitchen pantry of the Ambassador Hotel minutes before the assassination.

Witnesses who recalled seeing Sirhan during these few weeks prior to the assassination reported behaviors that were uncharacteristic of him. Their descriptions indicate that something was influencing Sirhan's mental state. He was alternating between frenzied responses and being immersed in a trance-like state, both symptoms of hypno-programming.

The young woman seen with Sirhan at most of the nine or so sightings was usually accompanied by a man who also remains unidentified. The man's role seemed to be to oversee the woman while she evidently served as Sirhan's cueing mechanism. The man would also have been needed to drive Sirhan's DeSoto while the woman drove their vehicle and watched over a "zoned-out," hypno-programmed Sirhan.

Some investigators have suggested that the sighting of Sirhan and the woman at a Kennedy function on May 20, 1968 was a "dry run," planned and carried out under the direction of those who conditioned Sirhan as a test to prepare an unwitting Sirhan and the woman for their roles in the actual shooting, in the event that Kennedy won the California primary on June 4. In fact, most of Sirhan's two-week "sightings" phase was a practice exercise to test their cues. By having Sirhan suspiciously appear in nine locations over a fifteen-day period, the plotters also made it appear that Sirhan was stalking the candidate, thus establishing a pattern of premeditation. Creating the impression of a premeditated act meant that the murder could be viewed as a capital offense. This could result in the death penalty and hence the planned elimination of the patsy.

The first sighting occurred on May 20, 1968 at Robbie's Restaurant in Pomona, where Bobby Kennedy was scheduled to speak at a campaign luncheon for approximately four hundred guests.[1238] A full house awaited Kennedy for the reception. Witnesses later reported they saw Sirhan accompanied by the woman who carried a purse with her. Sirhan carried a jacket over his right arm, despite the fact that it was a hot day.[1239] Together, they walked through a side dining room and approached the kitchen door, the woman leading the way. Police Officer William Schneid stopped them at that point and informed them that that entrance was closed. The woman then asked which way Senator Kennedy would enter the luncheon, and Schneid responded that most likely he would go upstairs to the next floor, whereupon she and Sirhan abruptly turned and headed for the front staircase.[1240]

Officer Schneid later reported that he saw the woman at the luncheon upstairs. He gave this account to the FBI, yet he was never interviewed by

LAPD.[1241] As it turned out, LAPD's practice of ignoring witnesses whose testimony pointed to the existence of a conspiracy became commonplace throughout the investigation of the assassination. Indeed, investigator Philip Melanson has uncovered numerous incidences in which LAPD tried to discredit witnesses who saw the woman "whose presence coincides with (Sirhan's) loss of memory."[1242]

Dozens of Kennedy supporters, tickets in hand, filled the lobby of Robbie's Restaurant eagerly working their way to the staircase, hoping for a good seat for Bobby's speech. When Sirhan and the woman finally reached the stairs to the main reception area on the upper level, they were blocked by the night manager, Albert LeBeau, thirty-five, who had been called in to work that day to collect tickets. When LeBeau spotted the couple climbing over a side railing to get onto the stairs behind him, he grabbed the woman's arm and asked for their tickets. The woman said they were with the senator's party, but LeBeau insisted that they needed tickets for admission. The couple then left him.[1243] However, they eventually made it to the upper-level dining room, where once again LeBeau bumped into Sirhan. This time Sirhan and the woman were listening to Kennedy's speech while standing in the midst of the overflowing crowd lining the back wall of the reception hall.[1244] According to author Robert Kaiser, LeBeau asked the couple how they got in, and Sirhan, apparently startled, replied, "What the hell is it to you?"[1245] LeBeau kept walking.

Once again, the rage intrinsic to Sirhan's conditioning surfaced in an emotional outburst. His conditioning triggered his self-preservation mechanism, and this moved him to lash out at this perceived threat. The so-called moral imperative superseded Sirhan's docile nature.

As for LeBeau, he later recognized Sirhan's photo from a group of twenty-five pictures provided by the police. Yet, in their final summary, LAPD reported that he "admitted he lied" regarding recognizing Sirhan. This false account of LeBeau's testimony showed the lengths to which the police would go in order to nip in the bud any possible conspiracy leads.[1246]

A week later in Pasadena, early in the evening on May 28, 1968, Sirhan appeared at his first and only meeting of the Ancient Mystical Order of Rosicrucians (AMORC). A sign on the door of the lodge at 2030 East Villa Street displayed the organization's logo: a triangle, a rose, an all-seeing eye, and the letters AMORC.[1247] Sirhan signed the register and entered the hall. The organization is nonpolitical and nonsectarian. This is the same group Los Angeles Mayor Sam Yorty had exclaimed was a Communist organization when he later referred to Sirhan's membership. Bemused reporters corrected him.[1248]

Sirhan sat quietly and read AMORC literature while surrounded by a dowdy assortment of middle-aged lodge members. An example of the benign nature of the Rosicrucians' beliefs is seen in the presentation that Sirhan participated in during his brief meeting with them. The lodge master, Ted Stevens,[1249] spoke about the mentalist technique of perceiving objects by sensation only, without seeing them. This is apparently a prerequisite to learning how to develop one's "inner powers," such as extrasensory perception. Sirhan participated in the lesson by identifying various objects while blindfolded.[1250] He reportedly then left the meeting early. This brief "sighting" of Sirhan attending a Rosicrucian meeting and then leaving early seems trivial in hindsight, if it were not for the unusual, singular importance Sirhan later gave it, as we shall see ahead.

At the same time Sirhan was attending the AMORC meeting, the polls were closing for the presidential primary in the state of Oregon. A win there was crucial to both Kennedy and McCarthy, since the victor would gain added momentum going into the all-important California primary one week later. A win by McCarthy would derail Kennedy's campaign, perhaps irreparably. At the same time, a Kennedy victory would send a signal to undecided Democrats at the convention that a sizable number of party people wanted a regime change at the top of the party. Such an eventuality would have given Kennedy a lock on the nomination over Humphrey, according to many observers.

Still, Humphrey had picked up enough Johnson votes during May to come within reach of the nomination himself. One media survey had shown by this point that there were some 1,280 delegates favoring Humphrey. The number needed to win was 1,312.[1251]

The Oregon battle saw Gene McCarthy step up his offensive. Although his stand on the war was the same as Kennedy's, he found many issues on which to attack Bobby. They ranged from sarcastic comments related to Kennedy's youth, to Bobby and his brother being responsible for American involvement in Vietnam. On another touchy issue, McCarthy argued against Kennedy's stand in favor of gun control legislation.[1252]

Bobby, on the other hand, found that he had little in common with Oregon voters. For the most part, their gun rights were not to be infringed upon; Robert Kennedy had supported some type of gun control since the assassination of President Kennedy.

Another problem for his campaign was the fact that the state's population of minorities was only two percent.[1253] Yet Kennedy's strongest supporters had always been the poor and the minorities. In addition, factory workers, who had backed the Kennedys in the northeast, seemed to have little interest in Bobby's speeches.

Their view of the world was far different from his. A perfect example of this discordance was demonstrated in author Richard Mahoney's description of Bobby's style on the campaign trail. While on the plane to Portland to kick off the Oregon primary race, Kennedy and his entourage never tired of singing one of the peace movement's hallmark folk songs, "Where Have All the Flowers Gone?"[1254]

Sen. Kennedy lost the Oregon primary. The vote, 44.7 percent for McCarthy to 38.8 percent for Kennedy, was Kennedy's first defeat, and it came at a critical time.[1255] Now, everything depended on the California primary one week later on June 4, 1968.

Ironically, the defeat in Oregon added to Kennedy's appeal for California voters. His public image became "less ruthless, almost an underdog," according to Arthur Schlesinger.[1256] Jackie Kennedy's mother, Janet Auchincloss, wrote to Bobby, "The first defeat makes you a more sympathetic figure."[1257] It also showed that he was human. As Bobby himself concluded, "Let's face it, I appeal best to people who have problems."[1258]

Two days later, on May 30, 1968, five days before the assassination, the next sighting of Sirhan occurred.[1259] According to witness descriptions, Sirhan and the young woman, accompanied by another man, made a brief visit to the Kennedy campaign office in Azusa, California. With the primary election imminent, enthusiastic Kennedy volunteers were filled with anticipation. Two of the campaign workers, Laverne Botting, forty-one, and Ethel Creehan, forty-five, noticed Sirhan and the two others as they entered the office. According to witnesses, Sirhan was the only one who spoke. He reportedly told Ms. Botting that he was from the Pasadena campaign office, and he then asked if Robert Kennedy would be coming to Azusa. She replied that he would not. Ms. Creehan overheard the brief conversation and corroborated it. Apparently, Sirhan then turned, joined the young woman and the other man who stood some distance away, and departed with them.[1260]

As soon as the photo of Sirhan was published in the newspapers following the assassination, Ms. Botting and Ms. Creehan called the FBI and told them what they knew. Later, they both picked out Sirhan's picture from a line-up of police photos. Yet, neither of them was allowed to see Sirhan in person. They also gave descriptions of the woman that were consistent with other witnesses' sightings: a female in her early twenties, five feet seven inches, excellent figure, with brownish-blond hair. Ethel Creehan added that the girl had a "prominent" nose, a distinctive feature that also was noticed by a number of other witnesses at various sightings. Neither woman gave a description of the other man who was with Sirhan and the woman.[1261]

The police dismissed both of these witnesses' accounts and discredited Ms. Botting because she had said Sirhan had a "broad nose and shoulders." Yet, everything else in her description was accurate. (And Sirhan does have a broad nose.) The police concluded, "She must be mistaken."[1262] As for Ms. Creehan, her account matched Sirhan except for his height; she said he was five feet eight inches instead of five feet four inches. The police reported, "It is doubtful if the person she observed was Sirhan."[1263] Apparently, if a sighting involved the woman, then LAPD did all that it could to deny it.

Officer C. B. Thompson, who wrote the interview summaries for these two witnesses, also reported another mysterious incident in connection with Ms. Botting. She had received a threatening phone call after she gave her eyewitness account. According to Ms. Botting, the caller had said, "'I hear you think you saw Sirhan. You had better be sure of what you are saying.'"[1264] This menacing, anonymous call fits a pattern of intimidation. As we shall see, the investigation eventually came to resemble more of a grand cover-up than a search for the truth. Again, the Azusa visit is one of the events leading up to the assassination that Sirhan does not recall. The woman and the man who were with Sirhan would never be identified. But the fact that they existed is evident, based on the number of witnesses and their matching testimony. These volunteers are people who had no reason to lie, or to make up stories. They were actually putting themselves at some risk in trying to help the police, given that they knew that conspirators were still on the loose. Again, it seems clear that the perpetrators arranged the sightings to test their control systems, i.e., to determine whether Sirhan was responding appropriately to the cues given to trigger posthypnotic suggestions. At the same time, they intended for the accomplices to remain in the background in order to create a lone-gun scenario. Those conditioning Sirhan would not have wanted witnesses later testifying to having seen the girl and the other man.

The next sighting of Sirhan occurred on June 1, 1968, this time at a gun shop called the Lock, Stock, and Barrel in San Gabriel, California.[1265] According to the store clerk, Larry Arnot, a retired Pasadena fireman, Sirhan entered the shop that Saturday afternoon accompanied by two men. They bought four boxes of bullets consisting of two hundred rounds—two boxes of .22 caliber and two boxes of Super-X Westerns. After the assassination, the receipt for $3.99 from the Lock, Stock, and Barrel was found in Sirhan's car.

Police interviewed Arnot, and later on he testified at the trial. But in court, Arnot's testimony took a bizarre turn. The prosecution noted that Arnot, who had undergone a polygraph test conducted by LAPD detective Hank

Hernandez, had stated that he remembered the sales transaction but did not recall Sirhan after all. However, the gun shop's coowner Donna Herrick corroborated her employee's original claim and said that she, too, had seen Sirhan at their store.[1266]

Obviously, purchasing ammunition is not a crime. But it is interesting that the story of a sighting with apparent accomplices made it to the trial. At the same time, not unexpectedly, both the prosecution and the defense refused to broach the matter of who was accompanying Sirhan. Rather than allow possible implications of a conspiracy to arise, they quickly concluded their inquiries with "'no further questions.'"[1267] All the while, both sides were aware that for an alleged "lone gunman," Sirhan was accompanied by others quite often.

Meanwhile, in San Francisco that evening, June 1, 1968, Sen. Robert Kennedy and Sen. Eugene McCarthy faced off for their eagerly awaited, nationally televised debate. The candidates were seated in a TV studio with moderator Frank Reynolds of ABC News stationed between them. An estimated twelve million viewers tuned in that night.[1268] For many, the Kennedy-McCarthy debate was comparable to the John Kennedy-Richard Nixon debates eight years earlier. Robert Kennedy framed his positions clearly and simply, without the rhetoric of his opponent, who was a former college professor. Kennedy stated, "I do think we have some commitments around the globe. I think we have a commitment to Israel, for instance, that has to be kept. But what I don't think is that we can be policemen of the world, and go all over the rest of the globe and settle every internal dispute with American soldiers or American arms."[1269]

At this point, a *Los Angeles Times* telephone poll showed that the move toward McCarthy was reversing. Kennedy was picking up on-the-fence voters and even a number of McCarthy supporters. All the while, McCarthy maintained a positive and upbeat tone, but his message seemed to lack a sense of reality. "I think that I sense what the young people of this country needed," said McCarthy. "As young students were dropping out and were saying the establishment was no good, we've had a genuine reconciliation of old and young in this country, and the significance of that is I think that throughout the whole country now there's a new confidence in the future of America."[1270]

Following the debate, pollsters named Kennedy the winner by 2.5 to 1.[1271] Bobby's success rippled across the electorate, and crowds turning out to see him grew larger and more enthusiastic across the widely diverse and pivotal state of California.

By this point, many observers felt that if Kennedy were to win the California primary June 4, there would be little chance of his being defeated at the Chicago convention. Winning the Golden State would garner him the immense momentum of a nationally televised convention. Consequently, many prognosticators believed that in Chicago, Kennedy would handily win the party's nomination. At the same time, Kennedy was opposed by powerful people in the intelligence community and the military, some southern leaders, and organized crime bosses. Even Democratic President Johnson was known to have wanted a Republican candidate to win, rather than a Democrat who would oppose his war policies.[1272]

If Robert Kennedy lost the California primary, then the issue of his becoming the new moral leader of the burgeoning peace movement would be moot. Of course, if he had lived, he may well have attempted a run again in 1972. But at this moment, Bobby Kennedy was at his most influential and his most vulnerable point. Kennedy's antiwar stand was considered by some as anti-American. The rogue element that flourished in the upper echelon of the CIA saw Communism as an evil force in the world, and to some, Kennedy's antiwar stand was seen as siding with evil. In the minds of a few, taking extreme measures to destroy Kennedy was justifiable. They carefully planned their covert operation to eliminate him, all the while knowing full well the tactical problems they would face.

For example, once Sirhan was put into a trance, would he shoot on cue? What would the police do if witnesses reported they saw the guns of the actual gunmen? What if Sirhan shot the other gunmen? What if the police counted more than eight .22 caliber bullets at the murder scene; how would they contend with a second gun? From numerous witness accounts, many of which were not available until more than twenty years after the assassination, the extent of the planning has become apparent.

The reliability of Sirhan's being able to shoot on cue—given his trancelike state—had to be tested and confirmed beforehand. A sighting of Sirhan, in which Sirhan—accompanied by a young woman and a man—was seen rapid-firing his gun in a practice session, occurred on June 1 in the Santa Ana Mountains.[1273] This was the same day that Sirhan allegedly purchased ammunition from Larry Arnot at the Lock, Stock, and Barrel. The sighting occurred in a remote area south of Corona, California, according to Dean Pack, an insurance man, who had been hiking in the area with his son.[1274] Pack called police following the assassination and told them he had recognized Sirhan from news accounts. He said he had seen Sirhan, along with a girl in her early twenties with brunette hair, and another man, in the mountains practicing shooting with a pistol, firing at tin cans. The man was described as being six feet tall with light brown hair. Apparently, he did all the talking. Pack reported that they were "unfriendly" and that Sirhan had "glared" at him.[1275] He added that he and his teenage son then quickly left the area.

Once again, LAPD dismissed the sighting by saying that Pack did not make a positive ID. Yet, Pack has claimed the police did not even show him a photo—the interview having been done via phone. Pack had expected to show the site of the encounter to the FBI and was surprised when they, too, were not interested.[1276]

The description given by Pack of Sirhan's face—the angry glaring—occurred at many of the sightings. Again, Sirhan has no recollection of these activities. Given Sirhan's trancelike state the night of the assassination, it is probable he was also in a trance or similar condition while pistol-shooting in the Santa Ana Mountains. It was a practice session set up to guarantee that Sirhan, while in a trance, would fire on cue, based on a posthypnotic suggestion.

Two days before the California presidential primary election, Sunday, June 2, 1968, Sirhan rose early to drive his mother to church; he also picked her up afterwards. That afternoon, at about 2 p.m. Sirhan was sighted at the RFK campaign office on Wilshire Boulevard in downtown Los Angeles, according to two volunteers, Ellenor Severson, a housewife, and Larry Strick, eighteen, a high school student.[1277] Larry Strick asked Sirhan if he needed help with anything, and Sirhan reportedly replied, "I'm with him," as he pointed to another volunteer in the room named Khaiber Khan.[1278] Ellenor Severson later corroborated Strick's account.[1279]

The campaign worker to whom Sirhan had motioned, forty-four-year-old Khaiber Khan, was a wealthy Iranian exile who had been a former spymaster for the Shah of Iran. Khan and Shah Mohammad Reza Pahlavi had since had a complete falling out,[1280] although Khan reportedly still had ties within the Shah's intelligence organization, SAVAK.[1281] SAVAK was a secret police agency closely allied with the CIA.

Khan's background in Iranian intelligence dated back to his work with British intelligence during World War II. When he was twenty-nine, in 1953, he assisted the CIA in the overthrow of the leftist government of Mohammad Mossadegh in Iran, the regime change that installed the Shah.[1282] In the 1950s, when Khan and the Shah of Iran were building SAVAK, two of their most ardent supporters were James Angleton, head of the CIA's Israeli desk, and

Richard Helms. CIA chief Helms had maintained a cordial relationship with the Shah for many years (recall that although six years apart in age, he and the Shah were both alums of the same prep school in Switzerland). As noted earlier, when Helms left the CIA in 1973, he was appointed ambassador to Iran by Richard Nixon.[1283]

In the early 1960s, Khan broke off his relationship with the Shah and charged the Shah's administration with the theft of US foreign aid.[1284] Khan fled with his wealth to London, while at the same time keeping in touch with his intelligence network. He also claimed to have American contacts, one of whom was Walter Sheridan, a former FBI agent whom Robert Kennedy had hired in 1958 as an investigator for the Senate Labor Rackets Committee.[1285] Walter Sheridan, you'll recall, was helping Bobby to find out who killed his brother, President John F. Kennedy.

In 1965, Khaiber Khan was reportedly nearly nabbed by the Shah's operatives in Switzerland before he sought safe haven in the United States.[1286] He lived in New York, and in 1968 moved to Los Angeles where he was also known as Goodarzian, or "Goody."

On June 1, 1968, Khan joined the Robert Kennedy campaign as a volunteer at the LA headquarters office on Wilshire Boulevard. He only worked there for four days, from June 1 to 4, 1968, during which time he was involved in recruiting Arab volunteers. He apparently signed up twenty or so.[1287] According to author Professor Philip Melanson, Khan's covolunteers did not easily warm up to him. They described him as "a playboy," "strange," "a phony," and "overbearing."[1288]

Campaign workers Ellenor Severson and Larry Strick came forward immediately after the assassination and gave statements to the FBI relating the fact that they had seen Sirhan with Khaiber Khan at the Wilshire campaign office two days before the election. Khan claimed in a FBI interview that he was not at the headquarters office until later that day.[1289] He added, however, that he, too, had witnessed Sirhan with a young woman dressed in a polka dot dress at the campaign office two days later, on primary day, June 4, at about 5 p.m. He also reported to the FBI that he had seen the woman with another man sitting in a car outside the headquarters the day before, Monday, June 3, 1968.[1290] A similarly described woman in the company of Sirhan would be observed by many witnesses at the Ambassador Hotel on the night of the assassination.

If Helms's ally, the SAVAK, had been chosen to participate in the assassination, then knowledge of this covert operation—killing Kennedy—which was planned for June 4 following Sen. Robert Kennedy's victory speech, may have been secretly reverberating within the spy community. Clearly, Khaiber Khan wanted to see Kennedy win. Khan knew that Kennedy could help Iran initiate a change in its repressive government. He also knew that a win would be politically advantageous for him. He could perhaps regain some of the power he once wielded in his glory days. But, most importantly, Khan may well have chosen to volunteer at the Wilshire Boulevard campaign headquarters because he suspected that someone was plotting an attempt on Kennedy's life, and he intended to find out who.

The questions surrounding Ellenor Severson and Larry Strick's statements regarding Khan, and Sirhan's alleged comment, "I'm with him," remain unanswered. But, given Sirhan's conditioning and its influence on him during these "sightings," it is not difficult to picture Sirhan following a command that implicated him with Khaiber Khan. Such a scenario would have constituted a plot within a plot. While the handlers of Sirhan had targeted Robert Kennedy, they may also have seen Khan as an equally significant adversary due to his anti-Shah activities. Linking Khan to the assassination plot could terminate his intelligence career, and at the same time provide additional cover for the actual perpetrators. In addition, by sowing a posthypnotic suggestion whereby Sirhan felt that he was one of Khan's recruits, Sirhan's programmers would advance their efforts to further mislead investigators.

Khan has claimed he did not attend Kennedy's victory speech at the Ambassador Hotel following the primary election.[1291] Neither the FBI nor LAPD questioned him as to where he was the night of the assassination.[1292]

While the FBI accepted the statements of witnesses Severson, Strick, and Khan, the LAPD, on the other hand, would accept none of them. LAPD rejected Khan's claims of sighting Sirhan based on the fact that he seemed "unsure."[1293] According to the LAPD, witness Larry Strick retracted his statements after being unable to identify a photo of Sirhan. This was strange, since Strick had identified the FBI's photos of Sirhan, and he had called his colleague Ellenor Severson after identifying Sirhan in a TV news report.[1294] As for Severson's testimony, LAPD ignored it as if she did not even exist.[1295] The authorities also elected not to pursue further detail on the background of Khaiber Khan.[1296]

The same day that Sirhan was seen at the RFK headquarters, Sunday, June 2, 1968, Robert Kennedy was spending some much-earned time off with his family at a strawberry festival in Garden Grove. Afterwards, the family decided to drop in at Disneyland, not far from there, where the children wanted to ride through "The Pirates of the Caribbean."[1297]

Returning to downtown Los Angeles that evening, Kennedy was late for a scheduled speech at a brief rally at the Coconut Grove, a night club in the Ambassador Hotel. As it turned out, several witnesses had seen Sirhan awaiting his arrival, according to LAPD Chief of Detectives Robert Houghton. Susan Redding and her husband reported that they saw Sirhan, standing "sullen and silent," along with a young woman. Another witness, Bert Blume, a Kennedy For Youth member who knew Sirhan from the health food store, recognized Sirhan in the lobby.[1298] Sirhan and the woman apparently left before Kennedy's arrival.

California voters at this point—just two days away from the decisive presidential primary election—were inundated with news coverage of the race. On many substantive issues, the leading candidates found common ground. However, the way they approached the voters and their campaign styles differed greatly, as their public appearances would attest. Gene McCarthy carried out his campaign primarily through radio and TV interviews. This format was most efficacious for displaying his professorial qualities. Sitting at a large microphone in a quiet studio he expounded on his political philosophy in a serious and thoughtful manner. Bobby Kennedy, on the other hand, campaigned outside where he greeted crowds of supporters face-to-face.

Kennedy crisscrossed California by plane, carrying out a relentless schedule of rallies, speeches, and handshaking. Whites, blacks, Latinos, Asians, the young, and the old turned out by the thousand to touch him—in San Francisco, Long Beach, Watts, San Diego, and Los Angeles.[1299] At nearly every key stop, Mexican-Americans, with hope in their faces, waved signs that read VIVA KENNEDY. A bond existed between Kennedy and minorities and the poor, and from it sprang an amazing outpouring of affection.[1300]

At a rally across San Francisco Bay in West Oakland, Kennedy's car was stopped in traffic while leaving the event. According to the Rev. Hector Lopez and other witnesses, a fascinating thing happened after the rally. Many of those who had been "raising all the hell," including Black Panthers, suddenly acted as guards clearing people from the car, so Kennedy could get through, parting the masses and allowing the candidate to move on.[1301]

On Monday, June 3, 1968, the last day of the California campaign, Bobby collapsed while speaking at a convention center in San Diego.[1302] Exhaustion had set in. He was quickly revived and brought back to LA to rest while awaiting the outcome of the following day's vote.

Campaign strategists for both Kennedy and McCarthy knew heading into California that the race would be too close to call. The strategists planning Bobby Kennedy's assassination knew this, as well.

# 8

# June 5, 1968,
# the Assassination of
# Sen. Robert F. Kennedy

TUESDAY MORNING, JUNE 4, 1968—the day of the California presidential primary election—the polls had already been open for a couple of hours when Sirhan started up his DeSoto parked out in front of the house. His mother had been urging him to start looking for a job in the help wanted ads. She had reluctantly given her son the last of the insurance settlement money, $400, and at the same time begged him to quit gambling away his money at the track. But Sirhan was insistent that the money was his and that he needed it right away. That night, following the assassination, police found $409 in his pockets.[1303] Interestingly, Sirhan's brother Adel later stated that Sirhan had spoken about investing in a horse. Also, the horse-trading preacher Jerry Owen, referred to earlier, would later report in a rambling statement to police that he had offered to sell one of his horses that day to a hitchhiker, and he claimed the man he had picked up was Sirhan Sirhan, as we shall see ahead. It should be noted here that while this link between Sirhan and Owen has intrigued investigators, it was clearly a red herring, another diversion designed to throw off investigators. As we have seen, such operations were routinely used by agency rogues—Hunt, Phillips, Angleton, and Helms—to manufacture misleading evidence.

Throughout the state of California, this particular primary day was generating more excitement than usual as voters across the state waited in line for their turn to vote. This was especially true in urban neighborhoods, where polling stations were reporting a turnout that surprised many observers. As for Sirhan Sirhan, he was witnessed late that morning in Duarte, California, at the San Gabriel Valley Gun Club. During this sighting, some fifteen people reported having seen him.[1304] From their reports, it also known that Sirhan was accompanied by the young woman previously seen with him, and the taller man. Sirhan signed the range's guest book, something few patrons bothered with. He wrote in the registry: "Sirhan B. Sirhan, 696 East Howard St., Pasadena, Cal." He was then observed rapid firing—which is against range rules—for several hours.[1305] As with earlier sightings, Sirhan says that he does not understand why he went to the firing range. This fact came out later during the jury selection phase of his trial, when at one point he whispered to defense counsel investigator Michael McCowan, "Find out if they were racing on Election Day. I told Pollack (Dr. Seymour Pollack, the prosecution's psychiatrist) that I looked at the entries and didn't like them. That's why I went to the (pistol) range."[1306] Sirhan was telling McCowan that he made up his reason for going to the gun club. He knew he would have gone to the track under normal circumstances, and he needed to explain why he ended up at the gun club, even though he had no memory of why he went there. Rather than sounding like someone who has trouble telling the truth, this exchange indicates that Sirhan had no idea why he had gone to the firing range and did not know why he did not know. Indeed, this exchange accurately portrays a man who had been operating under the influence of a posthypnotic suggestion sown in his psyche.

According to witness descriptions, the young woman at the gun club that day matched the girl seen in earlier sightings. Range employees, Harry Hicks and Russell Weaver, said they were busy painting when the young woman walked by them. They described her as "quite shapely."[1307] She was seen sometime before noon with a man (not Sirhan).[1308] The man carried a rifle, and the woman brought a pistol. Sirhan appeared at approximately the same time, they said. The man headed to the south end of the range, toward the area reserved for rifle shooting.[1309]

Sirhan exhibited a number of unusual behaviors during his time at the gun club. For example, college students Henry Carreon and David Montellano later told LAPD that the man they identified as Sirhan had difficulty communicating. They said his speech was "hesitant," and when he did speak, "he talked so fast they could hardly understand him."[1310] They also found it very odd that he did not know if his weapon was single-or double-action, and they wondered why he was firing so rapidly.[1311]

At about 11 a.m., two witnesses observed Sirhan firing a rifle. Richard and Roberta Grijalva, nineteen-year-old twins, gave very detailed descriptions.

They stated that Sirhan shot the rifle for about a half hour.[1312] The Grijalvas also saw him rapid firing a .22 at the pistol range. The LAPD later dismissed the twins' account by claiming the person they identified was merely someone who happened to look like Sirhan. Yet, Sirhan was the only person there that day who looked like him, according to all of the patrons interviewed.[1313]

Another witness who came forward, Michael Soccoman, also a college student, stated that he had swapped guns with Sirhan to try out his. Later, concerned that his fingerprints were on Sirhan's gun following the assassination, he called the police. Soccoman claimed that Sirhan told him he "had been practicing for four months up north."[1314] This is interesting, because Sirhan had spoken at home about his best friend Tom Rathke's having moved "up north." Indeed, pistol practice seems to have been part of his conditioning, since he ordinarily would have had no interest in such things.

The range master, Everett Buckner, also spotted Sirhan and noticed the young woman who was with him. According to Buckner, at one point Sirhan offered to help her, and she responded, "Get away from me, goddamn it, someone will recognize us."[1315] Interestingly, Buckner saw Sirhan as oblivious to the woman's disapprobation.[1316]

There is little doubt that the handlers of Sirhan wanted him to appear to be alone to avoid the complications arising from a conspiracy case. Thus, it was crucial that they disconnect any linkage between Sirhan and the two witnessed handlers.

As it turned out, after the assassination, when news leaked out that Sirhan had been witnessed at the San Gabriel Valley Gun Club in the company of a young woman, conspiracy theories became a hot topic. Soon, LAPD produced a witness whom they claimed had come forward saying she was the woman in question, that Sirhan was a stranger to her, and that she had practiced with his gun that day. Interestingly, she was a barmaid who worked at a topless club, the Briar Patch, which is located near the Santa Anita Racetrack where Sirhan had worked. It is also a few miles from another topless bar that Sirhan was known to visit.[1317] The Briar Patch was frequented by law enforcement personnel, and the woman stated she knew "quite a few sheriffs" who "come in practically every day" to drink at the bar.[1318] In her strange story, she said that she and her husband had left their two children with a babysitter and had decided to squeeze in some shooting practice. However, she claimed that they did not know how to get to the San Gabriel Club, so they traveled miles out of their way to the Briar Patch bar to get directions and then allegedly drove back, arriving at the firing range at 4 p.m.[1319] Her story that she had swapped guns with Sirhan late in the day was inconsistent with every other witness. Range master Buckner, who had first told the FBI about the young woman with Sirhan following the assassination, had said that he was certain that he had seen her in the morning just after he arrived for work. Moreover, two other witnesses, Ben Trower and Jim Langlois, stated there were no women there at that time (4 p.m.), the time the barmaid said she had been there.[1320] In addition, other witnesses reported Sirhan and the couple had left by 3 p.m. Eventually, Buckner was questioned by LAPD's Sgt. Hank Hernandez. Oddly, despite the evidence to the contrary, Buckner stated that the barmaid very closely resembled the woman he had seen.[1321] Clearly, LAPD needed a witness to resolve the dilemma of Sirhan having accomplices, if the department wished to avoid having to announce that there was a conspiracy. And apparently the department's insistence that there was no conspiracy made a significant impression on Everett Buckner.

At the firing range that day, Sirhan was in a state of high anxiety. Again, witnesses reported that he spoke quickly and was firing his handgun rapidly for hours.[1322] This behavior, the fast pace of his speech, and reported mumbling, was very similar to his condition at the time of his arrest.[1323] It is also considered a sign of having been in a deep hypnotic trance. Within an hour after the assassination, according to police reports, Sirhan was calm, his speech was normal, and he had stopped mumbling. His behavior had changed significantly. While the police noticed this change and knew that it was very different from the behavior of alcohol abusers, they did not understand the implications of it.

If we look at Sirhan's behavior when he was in the presence of the young woman and the other man and compare it to the times he was driving his mother to work, we see a radical difference. His altered consciousness when with the couple seems to have been triggered by an outside stimulus. It could have been a visual sign, such as the sight of the young woman, hearing particular words, or surreptitiously induced through a drug. When Sirhan was accompanied by the other two, he was in fact put into a hypno-programmed state in which he functioned within a continuous "streaming" posthypnotic suggestion. The cue for this strange behavior would have had to have been planted in his subconscious during his conditioning. His hyperactivity, trance-like states, and such inexplicable personality changes parallel the effects of drugs and posthypnotic suggestions. Taking this into account, it is logical to question whether he was even able to drive to the range that day. Or did, in fact, someone else drive, i.e., the girl or the other man? When Sirhan's final hours of freedom are analyzed, it becomes evident that his normal consciousness was suspended intermittently for lengthy stretches of time.

After departing the San Gabriel Valley Gun Club firing range, Sirhan next appeared at Bob's Big Boy restaurant near Pasadena City College at about 6 p.m. In a conversation with writer Robert Kaiser in jail later on, Sirhan spoke about the hours before the assassination. He was perplexed and he wondered aloud why he had not gone to the races that day, as he had routinely done. He asked himself why he had gone to Bob's Big Boy and then concluded, abashedly, "It was like some inner force."[1324]

In order to complete their mission, those controlling Sirhan had to carefully watch and guide all of his movements up until the shooting in the Ambassador Hotel kitchen pantry. To do this effectively, a third-party "synchronizer" was an essential element, as we shall see. Sirhan was rarely witnessed alone at the various sightings, and although he appeared to be by himself at Bob's Big Boy restaurant, this may not have been unintended. The perception the perpetrators wanted to create was for Sirhan to appear as a loner stalking his prey.

According to LAPD Chief of Detectives Robert Houghton, Sirhan met an acquaintance at the restaurant counter, a student from India named Gaymoard Mistri.[1325] Sirhan appeared to be still in his hyper mode. Over a hamburger and coffee they discussed horses, a mutual interest of theirs, and the Middle East troubles. After they finished eating, they took a short walk over to the college to look at course offerings posted for the upcoming semester. There they briefly conversed with three Arab students who were about to head off for their 7 p.m. classes: Marouf Badran from Jerusalem, Anwar Sayegh, whom Sihan had known from the college's Arab student organization, and a new student, named Abdo Jabra Malki, from Jordan.[1326]

Shortly after meeting with them, the students left for class, and Sirhan and Mistri returned to their cars. During Sirhan's trial, prosecutors stated that they agreed with the defense that there was obviously nothing conspiratorial regarding Sirhan's meeting with three Arab students hours before the assassination. What happened next, however, was unusual. After arriving back at their cars, Sirhan asked Mistri if he felt like shooting some pool. The Indian student replied that he already had plans for the evening at another friend's house.[1327] What was odd was that Sirhan's invitation sounds suspiciously like the conversation of a young man simply looking for something fun to do for the evening. After Mistri replied he was busy, they went their separate ways.

To understand Sirhan's state of mind at this point, given his behavior a few hours earlier and in the hours to come, it appears that while he was with Mistri at the restaurant and during the visit to the college, he was coping. Sirhan's recall of the evening is vague. As the hours progressed from 7 p.m.

to midnight, the night became hazier and then reached a point where it was blank. It is not known precisely at what places and times his programming took over, or, as he stated, the "inner force" kicked in. Nor does Sirhan know what motivated him to go to the Ambassador Hotel.

The fact of the matter is, given the trancelike state that eventually enveloped Sirhan, he may *not* have driven himself to the Ambassador Hotel at all, as noted earlier. It is known that Sirhan's DeSoto Fireflite, number JWS-093, was found by police the next day. It was parked illegally on New Hampshire Street, one-half block south of Wilshire Boulevard, three blocks from the Ambassador Hotel.[1328] But it is not known for certain that Sirhan had actually driven it, or if he had been a passenger, either in his car or in his handler's vehicle. In retelling the story later, he may well have filled in gaps in his memory by making up logical connections, imagining himself driving to the hotel rather than having been driven.

As for Sirhan's reason for going to the Ambassador Hotel, he claimed later at his trial that he simply wanted to go out and have a good time. He has stated that he remembers thinking that he was going to a parade, but he is not sure why. He has added, "If the horses had been running that night I would have been down at the track."[1329] Once again, he appears to be trying to make sense of bits and pieces of the evening, some of which he can recall, and some of which are merely stories that he has heard from others since that night.

Sirhan stated that after supper at Bob's Big Boy he drove downtown because he had seen a newspaper ad for the "Miracle March for Israel" being held on Wilshire Boulevard.[1330] He wanted to see what was happening.[1331] A Jewish rally had been planned to celebrate the first anniversary of the Six-Day War commemorating Israel's victory over the Arabs. Sirhan claimed that when he arrived, he found out that he had the wrong date; the event was scheduled for the following night.[1332] However, he noticed that there was a storefront party in progress at that location for US Sen. Thomas Kuchel. Sirhan said he then heard there were more parties at the Ambassador Hotel nearby, so he decided to drop in.[1333]

Three candidates' celebrations were scheduled at the Ambassador that night: Kuchel's opponent US Senate Republican candidate Max Rafferty's in the Venetian Room, Democratic US Senate candidate Alan Cranston's in the Palm Court, and the largest, the Kennedy reception, in the Embassy Room.

As citizens throughout the state were busy voting, California's Primary Day found Sen. Robert Kennedy with his family at a friend's home in Malibu. Film director John Frankenheimer, thirty-eight, had given Bobby his Malibu beach house to use while in Los Angeles, providing Bobby a respite and a chance to be with Ethel and six of their children.[1334] At the time, Frankenheimer was in the midst of making a documentary about Robert Kennedy's campaign. He had been shooting film across the country for more than two months. The footage was going to be used in the anticipated contest against Richard Nixon in the fall. Ironically, Frankenheimer also had directed the movie *The Manchurian Candidate.*

Early in the evening, Tuesday, June 4, 1968, Frankenheimer drove his Rolls-Royce out of his driveway and headed off with his friend, Robert Kennedy, to the Ambassador Hotel to await the California primary returns. They had just left a dinner party he had arranged for Bobby, Ethel, and some of his Hollywood friends.[1335] At this point, Frankenheimer was anxious to get Kennedy to the hotel so that the candidate could relax for a few hours before the hoped-for victory celebration. According to author Robert Kaiser, Frankenheimer missed the exit for the hotel at Vermont Avenue and ended up in a traffic jam. Listening to him curse his predicament, Bobby counseled him: "Take it easy, John. Life is too short."[1336]

On the radio, news coming out of Vietnam was much like any other day during these months and years. Reports of body counts no longer surprised most listeners; they had become inured. "In fighting near Khesahn, eighty-three enemy were killed yesterday as they attacked a marine position east of the outpost in the early morning darkness. Marines put their own losses at fourteen dead, ninety-seven wounded. Meanwhile, thunderstorms raging near the North Vietnamese border limited American pilots to only ninety-five bombing missions yesterday."[1337]

At the same time, grief over the loss of so many young Americans was increasingly taking its toll, and divisions within American society were approaching the breaking point.

As the polls closed in California, Kennedy campaign workers, volunteers, and supporters streamed into 3400 Wilshire Boulevard in Los Angeles, the posh Ambassador Hotel. In a fifth-floor suite, the Kennedy camp was glued to the television, anxiously following the networks' election coverage.

Bobby's main Democratic rival, Sen. Gene McCarthy and his camp had gathered in the Beverly Hilton, where supporters watched optimistically as the returns from the suburbs began coming in.[1338] By 9 p.m., their candidate was leading in the raw vote. But in the large cities—where Kennedy would find his greatest support—the votes were still not counted. Indeed, the black and Mexican vote were sizable. In the Kennedy suite, novelist Budd Schulberg confidently told Bobby, "You're the only white man in this country they trust." Kennedy grinned.[1339] The networks were expected to announce their predictions shortly.[1340]

Besides Kennedy's advisors, also at Bobby's side were his wife Ethel—three months pregnant with their eleventh child—and four of their children, David, Michael, Courtney, and Kerry. Other Kennedy family members on hand were his sister Pat Lawford and sister Jean with her husband Steve Smith.[1341] Kennedy friends and supporters came from all walks of life: politics, government, the media, the unions, and the sports world. Men who had worked for John Kennedy were in the suite, including Pierre Salinger, Ted Sorenson, and Larry O'Brien; writers Theodore White and George Plimpton; and union leaders Cesar Chavez, Dolores Huerta, and the United Auto Workers' Paul Schrade.[1342] World-famous athletes included Los Angeles Rams tackle Roosevelt Grier and Olympic champion from UCLA, Rafer Johnson. And rounding out the group, America's first astronaut who had orbited the earth six years earlier, was John Glenn.[1343]

Meanwhile, at about 9 p.m. downstairs on the main floor, Sirhan's odyssey at the Ambassador Hotel began. From his arrival at the hotel until the assassination at 12:15 a.m., Sirhan says he can recall very little of the entire three-hour period, nor can he understand what was propelling him.[1344] Based on various witness interviews, we can follow his movements.

At first Sirhan was in a loquacious, arrogant mood. An hour later, he had suddenly descended into a trancelike state, mesmerized in front of a teletype machine in the Colonial Room of the hotel.[1345] Having just eaten at Bob's Big Boy in Pasadena, a few mixed drinks should not have had the impact that Sirhan experienced—not without some assistance, either internally or externally applied. Sirhan was exhibiting traits that were not considered part of his normal personality. His disposition was initially irritable and touchy, accompanied by arrogance and aggressiveness, characteristics not uncommon in those who have undergone conditioning processes.

Sirhan was first witnessed at the hotel's Venetian Room where a party was being held for Senate Republican primary candidate Max Rafferty, who was running against Sen. Thomas Kuchel. Sirhan had gone to high school with Rafferty's daughter Kathleen.[1346] It was here that more obvious signs of Sirhan's trancelike state began to emerge. A Venetian Room waiter apparently refused to serve Sirhan a drink because he was not appropriately dressed for the occasion. According to authors Christian and Turner, Sirhan angrily tossed a crumpled bill at the man and stomped out.[1347]

A few minutes later, Sirhan was seen, drink in hand, outside the same room. Rafferty's party was getting underway, and although Sirhan did not meet Rafferty's daughter, Kathleen,[1348] he did mix with two other revelers, Enrique Rabago, a car mechanic, and Rabago's friend Humphrey Cordero.[1349] Rabago, a Kennedy supporter, asked Sirhan, "Are we going to win?"[1350] He replied affirmatively. But when Rabago added that Gene McCarthy was in the lead at that point, as if on cue, Sirhan retorted, "Don't worry if Senator Kennedy doesn't win. That son of a bitch is a millionaire. Even if he wins, he won't do anything for you or me or the poor people." Rabago and Cordero took this as a sign that Sirhan was "disgusted" with the clientele at Rafferty's party. They later testified that they did not feel Sirhan was intoxicated.[1351]

Shortly after this, Sirhan came upon a man working in a sound booth nearby, an electrician named Hans Bidstrup.[1352] They chatted briefly about Bidstrup's job, the primary election returns, and where the candidate was staying at the hotel. According to Bidstrup, Sirhan seemed "half drunk and very tired," and he said that Sirhan left abruptly.[1353]

Another hotel worker, Gonzalo Carillo Cetina, a waiter, bumped into Sirhan in front of the men's room outside the hotel's Palm Court bar. Apparently, Sirhan was tired and wanted to sit down. Cetina reported that Sirhan asked him to hold his glass while he fetched a chair from a stack to sit on.[1354]

According to the FBI, about 10 p.m., a witness named Lonny L. Worthey and his wife had tried to get into the Embassy Room where the Kennedy reception was underway, but found that it was already packed, so they decided to go to the nearest bar in the hotel. While getting his wife a Coke, Worthey leaned over and accidentally bumped into a young man he later recognized as Sirhan. Worthey excused himself, but Sirhan said nothing. Sirhan was standing with a young woman at the end of the crowded bar. According to Worthey, the two seemed to be together.[1355] Sirhan was observed sipping a Tom Collins with the woman. Later in jail, when Sirhan was questioned while under hypnosis by psychiatrists Pollack and Diamond, he stated that he had had four Tom Collinses that evening.[1356]

The description of the woman who appeared at Sirhan's side matched the earlier sightings, including her distinctive facial looks. She had been identified consistently as having an unusual nose, which was described by various witnesses as "prominent," "funny," "upturned," and "pudgy."[1357] This particular evening, she was wearing a polka dot dress. As the night progressed, numerous witnesses placed Sirhan in the company of the young woman in a polka dot dress and another man. The other man wore a white shirt with a yellow or gold sweater and dark pants, witness Sandra Serrano, a twenty-year-old Youth for Kennedy volunteer, later told the FBI.[1358]

The sighting at the bar was the first point at which Sirhan was seen motionless, as if in a stupor. It was also the first sighting that night of Sirhan with the young woman by his side. Sirhan's sudden mood swing and the presence of the woman occurred together. Again, for a hypno-programmed individual, a trance can be induced by any number of external stimuli, including hearing particular words or seeing a particular face. Sirhan's behavior had rapidly undergone a major transformation. He had ceased being arrogant and talkative, and was entering a deep, trancelike state, as we shall see ahead.

Upstairs in Room 511, Bobby Kennedy poured himself a cold drink, sat down, and lit up a small cigar. For a few minutes, he felt relaxed; there was an air of confidence in the Kennedy suite.[1359] The number crunchers had expected Vice President Hubert Humphrey to pick up Lyndon Johnson's delegates across the country. But it now appeared that a Kennedy win in California could give Bobby enough delegates to put him over the top, defeating McCarthy and Humphrey at the convention. Kennedy aide Richard Goodwin began placing phone calls to key McCarthy supporters Allard Lowenstein and Kenneth Galbraith.[1360]

According to Arthur Schlesinger, Galbraith felt he would join Bobby as soon as he had a chance to meet with Gene McCarthy first, and Lowenstein promised that if Galbraith switched sides, he would, too.[1361] The time had come to join forces if they expected to stop Humphrey at the Chicago convention.

Kennedy advisors and friends conversed quietly, keeping an eye fixed on the TV for the latest election returns. Meanwhile, across the hall in room 516, journalists mingled with campaign aides, enthusiastically sharing a moment filled with anticipation.[1362] Writers Jimmy Breslin, Pete Hamill, and Jack Newfield were on this floor along with other close associates of Bobby's: Fred Dutton, Adam Walinsky, Ted Sorensen, Charles Evers, John Lewis, and California Democratic chieftain, Jesse Unruh.[1363] As some began to contemplate the convention strategy, others optimistically wondered what new plans Bobby would initiate once settled in the White House.

*The New York Times* had reported that day that candidate Richard Nixon's newly appointed chief of staff H. R. Haldeman said he was confident Nixon would win the Republican nomination. At the same time, in New York, Nixon rival Governor Nelson Rockefeller called Nixon a chronic loser. Rockefeller added that the tide was actually turning in his own direction.[1364]

Finally, at 10 p.m. the networks announced their projections. While Senator McCarthy had taken the early lead, the urban areas were now beginning to report. The tide had turned. CBS and NBC—without yet having received the figures for Los Angeles—predicted a win for Sen. Robert Kennedy.[1365] On the fifth floor, euphoria reigned.

Meanwhile, downstairs the newspaper organizations had set up a temporary news headquarters in their assigned space in the Colonial Room. Kennedy had agreed to meet the press there following his victory speech in the Embassy Room.[1366] The route between the two rooms would take Kennedy through the kitchen pantry.

The news media's space in the Colonial Room was cooler compared to the hot, overflowing Embassy Room. At approximately 10:30 p.m., in one area of the media room, a Western Union teletype operator, Mary Grohs, looked up from her work and noticed a young man "staring fixedly" at her teletype machine. It was Sirhan Sirhan.[1367] Grohs asked him if he needed help, but she received no response. Assuming he wanted election results, she then directed him to a different teletype machine, but he remained where he was, as if mesmerized. She then noticed that he had a vacant look in his eyes. Later, she would state to author Robert Kaiser, "I will never forget his eyes."[1368]

Curiously, Grohs also informed Kaiser that the police had told her not to talk about the incident.[1369] One police officer who checked out Sirhan after the assassination reported that the pupils of his eyes were dilated. The police also found that during his initial interrogations, he had appeared "detached," but they did not pursue the matter.[1370]

Leaving Ms. Grohs, Sirhan turned slowly and walked out of the Colonial room and into a passageway leading to the Embassy Room. A Kennedy press aide, Judy Royer, saw Sirhan at that point coming towards her.[1371] Royer, who was the secretary to California Governor Pat Brown, was stationed near the press room for the election night coverage. She had been told that only the media were to be allowed in that area near the Colonial Room and behind the stage area in back of the Embassy Room. Realizing Sirhan obviously was not a reporter, she asked him to leave. Sirhan then walked through a nearby doorway and into the Embassy ballroom.[1372]

Clearly, Sirhan's dazed demeanor had become more pronounced. Although he had apparently been alone for a few minutes, he would link up with the young woman again shortly.

In less than one hour, Robert Kennedy would deliver his victory speech on the Embassy Room stage. Due to the overflowing crowd, the doors of the large ballroom had been closed, and only those with passes were allowed to enter. Well over one thousand revelers, many festooned with Kennedy hats, banners, buttons, and balloons, sang and intermingled as they eagerly awaited the arrival of their candidate.

Meanwhile, in the middle of the crowd in the Embassy Room, the young woman in the polka dot dress searched the sea of joyous faces. She had apparently become separated from Sirhan. A young Kennedy campaign volunteer, Susanne Locke, who had noticed the woman's "out-of-place" look, has stated that her face appeared "expressionless."[1373] She described the woman as in her early twenties, having long brown hair, being well proportioned, and wearing a white polka dot dress with blue dots. Locke also noted that the girl was not wearing a yellow admission badge. Finding this odd, she brought it to the attention of the head volunteer coordinator, Carol Breshears, who informed one of the guards. There is no record of the police following up this matter.[1374] The woman in the polka dot dress quickly disappeared into the boisterous crowd.

Then came the announcement from the stage. The networks were projecting a victory for Senator Kennedy. The ballroom erupted in wild cheering, and immediately the chanting began: "We want Bobby! We want Bobby! We want Bobby!"

The vote count had been delayed for hours due to a snafu in Los Angeles County. This was the first time computers were being utilized to tabulate the vote, and unfortunately, in their debut, the new IBM scanners were having trouble with the punch cards.[1375] History would repeat itself even more vividly thirty-two years later when glitches in Florida's punch card count postponed the results of the 2000 presidential election. A court ruling finally settled the matter in favor of George W. Bush over Al Gore.

In 1968, the count was just as critical. More than 40 percent of the California vote came from Los Angeles County, yet by 10 p.m., because of the glitch, these votes were still not in. The city's voter turnout, particularly in the minority communities, was high, and that was Kennedy turf. The final results showed Kennedy with 46.3 percent to McCarthy's 41.8 percent.[1376]

Jesse Unruh, leader of the California delegation, commandeered the microphone on the Embassy Room stage and informed the exuberant crowd. Bobby would be coming down to give his victory speech within the hour.

At this point, approximately 11 p.m., Sirhan has stated that he recalls feeling very sleepy, and he vaguely remembers returning to his car parked on New Hampshire Street, three blocks from the hotel. His memory of actually getting in the car apparently does not exist. Sirhan has stated that he felt that he must have been too tired to drive and consequently decided to return to the hotel to look for coffee.[1377]

While preparing for Sirhan's trial, psychiatrist Dr. Seymour Pollack analyzed Sirhan under hypnosis to try to unlock any memory of his returning to his car. Dr. Pollack was unsuccessful. He was also unable to find out how Sirhan's gun was brought into the Ambassador Hotel.[1378] It appears that Sirhan had reached a point of total immersion in a trancelike state by that time.

At approximately 11:30 p.m., Sandra Serrano, noted earlier, the cochair of the Pasadena-Altadena Youth for Kennedy Committee, had decided to escape the heat of the hotel's Embassy Room and cool off for a few minutes outside.[1379] She sat down on the metal steps of an emergency exit staircase and was sipping a vodka and orange juice when she witnessed a group of three climbing the stairs—a young woman in a polka dot dress, a taller man, and a person she later recognized as having been Sirhan. They brushed past her as they entered the hotel.[1380]

Serrano's descriptions match those of other witnesses who also saw them in the hotel's kitchen pantry, either just prior to the shooting or while running out afterwards. These witnesses included Darnell Johnson, a campaign field worker; Robin Casden, a teenage Kennedy supporter;[1381] Thomas Vincent DiPierro, a waiter and college student; George Green, a campaign worker; Evan Freed, a press photographer;[1382] and Booker Griffin, a black organizer.[1383]

Based on Serrano's account, the woman, her male companion, and Sirhan quickly ascended the staircase and disappeared down a hallway. The three then entered the pantry located between the Embassy Room and the Colonial Room. There they were observed by Griffin, and waiter Thomas DiPierro, who described the woman as "attractive" and wearing a "white dress with black or dark purple polka dots."[1384] DiPierro stated that he felt that the woman was with Sirhan because "it looked like she was almost holding him."[1385] The woman had been witnessed carrying an "all white sweater,"[1386] an unnecessary item for a warm evening, but ideal for concealing a small Iver-Johnson Cadet revolver with its two-and-one-half-inch barrel.

Sirhan has recalled glimpses of being in the pantry "having coffee with a pretty girl."[1387] But he can remember nothing immediately preceding this and nothing following, until the point where he was being pummeled immediately after the assassination.[1388] As he would state numerous times, "I have no mental images of shooting Robert Kennedy."[1389] During the trial, Sirhan would tell his attorney, Grant Cooper, that he vaguely remembered a large shiny coffee urn, but was not sure exactly where it was in the hotel.[1390] Witnesses have stated it was in a short hallway off the pantry. According to Professor Melanson, Sirhan recalled being with the girl in a dark place in the hotel. They were tired and she wanted coffee. Sirhan stated that he poured for her, and they sat down. He also said that "she appeared to be Armenian or perhaps Spanish."[1391]

In prison, Sirhan told authors Turner and Christian that he recalls an image of meeting a girl whose name he does not remember. "I met the girl and had coffee with her. She wanted heavy on the cream and sugar."[1392] As Sirhan told NBC's Jack Perkins in 1969, the only thing he can recall after the coffee is "choking and the commotion."[1393] Again, Sirhan is not sure why he was there and has no memory of the assassination.[1394] As for the woman in the polka dot dress, she was seen by many witnesses fleeing the pantry (after the shooting) while everyone else was trying to get in.[1395] Sirhan was asked about the woman later by Dr. Diamond for the defense. Under hypnosis, Sirhan wrote out his answers. The page read, "She did not tell me her name . . . . she wanted she wanted coffeeeeeee No No No No."[1396]

Interestingly, tests later performed by Doctors Diamond and Pollack on Sirhan, while he was under hypnosis, have provided some insight into his state of mind at that moment in the kitchen pantry. Sirhan was asked who was with him when Kennedy was shot. He replied by writing the answer, "Girl the girl the girl." When asked her name, Sirhan only groaned.[1397] Asked if she saw his gun, Sirhan wrote, "she wanted she wanted coffeeeeeee."[1398]

The young woman and Sirhan were next seen standing by a tray stand in the pantry. Waiter DiPierro, who was the son of one of the hotel maitre d's, said he noticed that she and Sirhan smiled at each other and added that Sirhan was wearing a "sick-looking" smile.[1399] At this point, witnesses said that the woman was joined in the kitchen pantry by her male companion in the white shirt and gold sweater with whom she had come in and two suited men, one dressed in a dark and one in a light suit. They planted themselves next to her and Sirhan.[1400] This group was spotted by campaign workers Darnell Johnson and Robin Casden.[1401] Their descriptions matched those of other witnesses who minutes later saw the two suited men shooting Robert Kennedy,[1402] and saw them escaping afterwards.[1403] Much of the witness information regarding accomplices was obtained by the FBI. But in the LAPD's final report, stories differing from the lone-gun version were termed "unreliable" without any explanation.[1404] LAPD also wrote that some of these witnesses had retracted their statements, when in fact they had not.[1405]

Based on the accounts of five witnesses, there were two gunmen besides Sirhan. One was on the side of Robert Kennedy and one directly behind him.

Sirhan was in front of Kennedy. One gunman wore a dark suit, and the other a lighter color. The five witnesses were Evan Freed, Dr. Marcus McBroom,[1406] Lisa Urso, Don Schulman, and Martha Raines (a pseudonym supplied by author Philip Melanson).[1407]

The assassination planners no doubt picked the pantry as the location for the murder for a number of reasons. The ambush had to take place away from the media so that no record of the assailants would exist on newsreel film or in photographs. The "death zone" would also have to allow escape routes for the gunmen and at the same time be small enough to limit the number of witnesses. The plotters knew that Senator Kennedy would deliver his victory speech in the Ambassador Hotel's Embassy Room and then walk from the back of the stage towards the Colonial Room where he was to take questions from the media. This route would pass through the kitchen pantry, a location where the press following Kennedy most likely would not be filming due to the dim lighting and narrow, restrictive space. There was, in fact,  no live TV, film, or video shot of the assassination of Robert Kennedy.[1408] (However, there were sound recordings, described ahead.) The film crews had turned off their equipment as they headed for the Colonial Room. As for still photos, there was at least one photographer, a high school student named Jamie Scott Enyart,[1409] whom we shall discuss later.

For the Kennedy campaign, the route through the pantry offered a convenient shortcut for Bobby to meet the press. Instead, he would meet a hail of gunfire.

Wild applause erupted in the Embassy Room as a smiling Robert Kennedy stepped up to the microphone, eager to thank the voters and his hundreds of devoted followers. His wife Ethel, looking radiant in a light summer dress, stood close by him on the stage. They were surrounded by staff members Frank Mankiewicz, Fred Dutton, Dick Tuck, Bill Barry,[1410] and other aides and supporters. The cheering gradually subsided as Kennedy addressed his audience: "I would hope now that the California primary is over, that we can now concentrate on having dialogue on what direction we want to go in the United States . . . what we are going to do in the rural areas of this country; what we are going to do for those who still suffer in the United States from hunger; what we are going to do around the rest of the globe; and whether we are going to continue the policies that have been so unsuccessful in Vietnam . . . I think we should move in a different direction."[1411]

As he spoke, Senator Kennedy was calm and confident, humorous and grateful. He made a special point of thanking his family and friends. "I'd like to express my appreciation to Steve Smith, who was ruthless but effective, and I want to say how much—how grateful I am to him, to his wife, my sister Jean, to my sister Pat, and to my mother, and all those other Kennedys. I want to thank an old friend, Rafer Johnson. My thanks to Rosey Grier, who said he would take care of anybody who didn't vote for me. I want to express my gratitude to my dog Freckles, who has been much maligned in this campaign. And I don't care what they say—as Franklin Roosevelt said—I don't care what they say about me, but when they start to attack my dog. . . . I'm not doing this in any order of importance, but I also want to thank my wife Ethel. Her patience during this whole effort was fantastic."[1412]

At this point, Kennedy was approaching the end of his remarks. He stuck to his message, reaching out to the entire country:

Here is California, the most urban state of any of the states of our Union; South Dakota, the most rural of any of the states of our Union. We were able to win them both. I think we can end the divisions within the United States.[1413]

What I think is quite clear is that we can work together in the last analysis, and that what has been going on within the United States over a period of the last three years—the division, the violence, the disenchantment with our society, the division between black and white, between the poor and the more affluent, or between age groups or over the war in Vietnam—is that we can start to work together. We are a great country, an unselfish country, and a compassionate country. I intend to make that my basis for running.[1414]

Robert Kennedy finished his last campaign speech with the following words: "What I think all of the primaries have indicated, whether they occurred in Colorado, or Idaho, or Iowa, wherever they occurred, is that the people in the Democratic Party and the people in the United States want change. The country wants to move in a different direction. We want to deal with our own problems in our own country and we want peace in Vietnam.[1415] Mayor Yorty has just sent me a message that we've been here too long already. So, my thanks to all of you. And now it's on to Chicago and let's win there."[1416] It was shortly after midnight, June 5, 1968.

Amidst enthusiastic cheers, Bobby exited with his wife at the back of the stage enroute to the Colonial Room via the kitchen pantry. Someone in the group by the stage said, "This way, Senator."[1417] Maitre d' Karl Uecker took hold of Kennedy's right hand to lead him toward the pantry. At the same time, the ACE guard service's Thane Eugene Cesar held his right arm.[1418] They were ahead of the rest of the Kennedy entourage, which included Ethel, ex-FBI agent Bill Barry, spokesman Frank Mankiewicz, Speaker of the California Assembly Jesse Unruh, attorney Frank Burns, Pierre Salinger, and others.

Upon entering the kitchen pantry, Robert Kennedy met three hotel employees and shook hands with each of them: busboy Juan Romero, waiter Martin Patrusky, and porter Jesus Perez.[1419]

The pantry was overflowing with people as Kennedy continued walking, past Evan Freed and towards Lisa Urso, and the group with Sirhan. One witness reported he heard a voice yell out, "Kennedy, you son of a bitch."[1420] According to witness Evan Freed, who was standing four feet from Kennedy, the first shot came from the man in the dark suit who had stepped behind Kennedy, opposite Sirhan. He fired upwards at point-blank range. The angle and muzzle distance—less than one inch away—corresponds with Dr. Thomas Noguchi's autopsy findings.[1421] Another witness, interviewed by author Philip Melanson, Martha Raines (pseudonym) also saw the dark-haired man in a suit firing a weapon.[1422] Kennedy's head jerked forward, from the impact of being shot from behind. He then fell backwards and collapsed onto the floor, stated witness Lisa Urso.[1423] At the same time, Urso saw the blond man in the light suit, who was standing "by Kennedy," placing a handgun back into a holster.[1424] Based on the ballistics and powder burn evidence, it is clear that one of the gunmen had jammed his pistol into Kennedy's back and shot at point-blank range.[1425] His accomplice had hid his gun under a newspaper, according to witness Dr. Marcus McBroom,[1426] and apparently shot into the ceiling, resulting in bullets ricocheting back down into the floor and into the crowd. LAPD criminalist DeWayne Wolfer was later quoted as saying, "It's unbelievable how many holes there are in the kitchen ceiling."[1427] (Five or six ceiling panels were removed by the police but were destroyed while the case was still being appealed.[1428])

Sirhan, firing his eight-shot revolver, was slammed against a steam table by maitre d' Karl Uecker. After the second shot, Uecker held the gun down away from Kennedy.[1429] The barrage of gun shots (from all of the weapons firing) sounded like a string of firecrackers popping, according to photographer Boris Yaro and Kennedy advisor Frank Burns.[1430] While the two suited gunmen hastily concealed their guns, Sirhan's pistol was clearly visible. Bill Barry along with Rafer Johnson tackled Sirhan. Struggling to rip the gun from Sirhan's hand, Jack Gallivan and George Plimpton dove into the fray. Finally, Roosevelt Grier twisted the gun away while others joined in to hold the suspect down. Radio reporter Andy West repeatedly shouted, "Hold him! Hold him! We don't want another Oswald!"[1431]

As others screamed for a doctor, West flipped on his tape recorder and reported, "Senator Kennedy has been shot! Senator Kennedy has been shot; is that possible? Is that possible? Is it possible, ladies and gentlemen . . . it is possible, he has. Not only Senator Kennedy. Oh my God, Senator Kennedy has been shot and another man, a Kennedy campaign manager, and possibly shot in the head. I am right here."[1432]

When the smoke cleared, Robert Kennedy lay on his back, blood spreading across the floor. In the midst of the pandemonium, Ethel fought her way to his side. She grasped his hand, in which someone had placed rosary beads, and held on to him.[1433] According to author Richard Mahoney, before Bobby slipped into unconsciousness, a friend heard him whisper, "Jack. Jack."[1434]

Kennedy was shot three times, and a fourth bullet went through the right shoulder pad of his coat. All of the shots were fired as close as one inch away as indicated by the powder burns.[1435] Two of the bullets hit him in his back below his right shoulder. The fatal bullet entered behind his right ear and lodged in his brain.[1436]

Karl Uecker and other witnesses all reported that the Sirhan gun had never come within several feet of Robert Kennedy. LAPD's five best witnesses concurred, and some witnesses stated it was six feet away. The shots were fired into Kennedy's back and behind the right ear, yet witnesses placed Sirhan in front of Kennedy. Also, the paths of the bullets that struck Kennedy were at a steep upward angle, while Sirhan's gun was shooting straight on.[1437] Author Dan Moldea, writing about the discrepancy in the distances, has theorized that perhaps Robert Kennedy was accidentally pushed into Sirhan's gun. However, this scenario conflicts with all of the eyewitness accounts. Moreover, according to both Sirhan and his brother Adel—following Moldea's prison interview with Sirhan at which Adel was present—Moldea fabricated an admission by Sirhan of knowingly firing at Kennedy.[1438] Again, Moldea has attempted to bend reality to fit the official version of events, regardless of the cost.

Five other people who had crowded into the pantry were also hit by gunfire along with Robert Kennedy. Irwin Stroll, seventeen, was hit in the knee. Ira Goldstein, nineteen, in the left hip. William Weisel, thirty, in the stomach. Elizabeth Evans, forty-three, in the forehead. And Paul Schrade, forty-three, who also suffered a head wound. All five survived.[1439]

While one gunman had concentrated on hitting Kennedy, the other had aimed away from the first gunman and fired ricochets off the ceiling into the crowd (which accounts for the five injured having suffered less severe wounds than Kennedy). This scenario left Sirhan, still in a trancelike state, pointing his gun at both of the other gunmen. The perpetrators, however, had taken the necessary precautions to avoid being shot. Based on the evidence later discovered, they protected themselves, the young woman in the polka dot dress, and the taller man from being hit by having loaded Sirhan's revolver with blanks beforehand. After the assassination, an inspection of Sirhan's weapon indicated that there was lead in the barrel. Yet, the bullets found in the victims were copper-jacketed. These bullets would have cleaned out the lead. The ammunition Sirhan was firing at the range earlier that day—wad cutter target bullets—leaves a lead coating.[1440] With this coating still there, Sirhan had to have been firing blanks that night in the kitchen pantry. While the sound of firing blanks is the same as the sound of shooting live rounds, there is a major observable difference between them in the length of the flame shooting out. As it turned out, witness Lisa Lynn Urso saw "flames" shooting out of Sirhan's gun.[1441] Other witnesses, who saw the first shot, said the flame was six to twelve inches in length. Normal gunfire has only a one-inch flame. The longer flame is consistent with that of a gun firing blanks.[1442]

The plotters used blanks instead of live rounds in Sirhan's gun in order to ensure that the actual assassins did not get hit. One of the gunmen fired four shots at Bobby and the other fired ricochets off the ceiling and into the crowd, hitting and wounding five bystanders.

Sirhan has stated that he does not recall firing a handgun or Kennedy even being in the kitchen.[1443] Symptoms of his stupor were observed by witnesses. During the shooting, Sirhan was beaten by a half-dozen men, yet he clung to his gun. Writer George Plimpton, who helped bring him down, stated, "He was very strong for a small man." He added that Sirhan's eyes seemed "enormously peaceful."[1444] Both of these images fit the description of one who is in a hypnotic trance.

Forensic analyses of the recovered bullets also indicate that more than one gun was fired. An independent criminalist with thirty years of experience, William W. Harper of Pasadena, examined the bullet evidence two years after the assassination. Using his Balliscan camera, he studied the victim bullets and those test-fired with Sirhan's gun. Contrary to the LAPD's version, Harper's results showed major discrepancies.[1445] For example, Harper discovered that a bullet recovered from one of the victims, ABC's William Weisel, had no characteristics in common with one taken from Senator Kennedy's body.[1446] In August 1971, the day before Harper was to testify before a grand jury looking into the RFK firearms evidence, Harper was shot at while driving his car in Pasadena. He was shaken but unharmed.[1447]

In yet another test performed several years later, a seven-member panel of firearms experts made the same comparison. The report, issued by Los Angeles Judge Robert A. Wenke on October 6, 1975, disclosed that experts found significant differences in the striations (markings) found on the bullets test-fired from Sirhan's gun when compared to the victim bullets.[1448]

There are also additional eyewitness accounts that reported seeing other gunmen firing at the scene of the assassination. Donald Schulman, a runner for KNXT-TV of Los Angeles who has steadfastly maintained his story over many years, was standing behind Kennedy when the gunfire erupted. He has stated that he was "absolutely positive" that he saw plainclothes men with guns drawn in the pantry.[1449] He also saw the security guard, Thane Eugene Cesar, with his gun in hand, and he mistakenly assumed the guard also was responsible for the gunfire. From his viewing position, Schulman could not see Sirhan shooting.[1450] Cesar was at Kennedy's right side. It was at this same moment that other witnesses saw the gunman in the dark suit move directly behind Kennedy, plunge his gun into Kennedy's back, and fire.

In an interview with Jeff Brent of Continental News Service radio at the murder scene, Schulman, who was quite shaken, said, "The security guard fired three times." He adds, "The security guard then fired back hitting him (Sirhan) and he is in apprehension (was apprehended)."[1451] Schulman's language is confusing. Obviously, Sirhan was not shot, and no one witnessed Cesar fire his gun. Given the trauma of the moment, Schulman's statements are unclear, but they do indicate more than one gun was being fired. In a follow-up statement, Schulman was one of the few who accurately stated that Kennedy was hit three times. In a 1975 interview with LA Special Counsel Tom Kranz, Schulman— who was not a publicity seeker—testified, "I had thought I saw three guns. I saw other guns pulled and possibly fired."[1452] The LAPD dismissed this line of inquiry in their final report by concluding that Schulman was "unable to furnish information that materially affected the investigation."[1453] His name was not even listed in LAPD's list of those in the pantry at the time of the murder.[1454]

It was customary for the Ambassador Hotel to hire rent-a-cops from Ace Guard Service for crowd control. The night of the assassination, part-time Ace Guard Thane Eugene Cesar, twenty-six, was assigned to the kitchen pantry area.[1455] He was at Kennedy's right side as Kennedy entered the kitchen pantry. At the moment of the assassination, Cesar has stated that he was knocked down, but he regained his footing. He then drew his pistol, but did not fire.[1456]

In an interview with reporter John Marshall of KFWB radio immediately following the shooting, Marshall asked Cesar, "Officer, can you confirm that the senator has been shot?" Cesar replied, "Yes, I was there holding his arm when they shot him."[1457] Cesar was able to correctly identify Kennedy's three wounds before the doctors did some twenty minutes later.[1458] In the famous photograph taken just after the shooting, the snap-on black neck tie lying on the floor next to Kennedy is Cesar's.[1459]

Cesar has claimed that he was carrying a .38 caliber pistol the night of the assassination. He also owned a .22 caliber pistol, but told police he had sold it prior to the assassination.[1460] However, it was later discovered that he had sold it after the murder.[1461]

According to William Gardner, chief of security at the Ambassador Hotel, Kennedy aides had told him that Bobby did not want uniformed officers or armed individuals around him.[1462] One reason reportedly given by campaign staffers was that it would be bad for his image. Another view suggested that the candidate feared an attack from an individual posing as a policeman. Presumably, Cesar's assignment was simply to control the crowd as Kennedy entered the pantry.

Because Cesar was carrying a gun and was positioned inches from Kennedy, some case experts have concluded that he may have been one of the gunmen. However, the facts indicate that if Thane Eugene Cesar played any part at all in the assassination conspiracy, it was an unwitting role to take out *not* Bobby Kennedy, but Sirhan Sirhan, as we shall see ahead. Investigators have suggested that Cesar may have been working for the CIA. As authors Turner and Christian have pointed out, his day job was with Lockheed working in a restricted area related to the CIA's U-2 spy plane facility.[1463] Author Philip Melanson has shown that Cesar was hired by Ace Guard Service for part-time work only a few days before the assassination, according to company records.[1464] Cesar had told the FBI that he was assigned to watch the hotel's kitchen pantry area that night at 10:50 p.m.[1465] Yet, he claimed he did not see Sirhan and the others waiting there, while other witnesses did see them.[1466] Cesar has also reportedly stated that he had no love for the Kennedys.[1467]

Another writer has suggested that Cesar may have been working in league with the California mob, which feared a Bobby Kennedy presidency.[1468] Author John Davis has suggested that Cesar may have had ties to gambling czar of San Diego, John Alessio, and has also noted that the Ambassador Hotel had been partly owned by investors who had mob connections.

While some investigators have portrayed Cesar as an agency operative or a mob hitman, an assassination of this magnitude would not have been conducted through the use of a rent-a-cop. It would have been professionally carried out to ensure the mission was accomplished. If, indeed, Cesar was involved, it is more likely that his role was to shoot Sirhan. Cesar was assigned to the kitchen pantry for crowd control and to guard Senator Kennedy. At the commencement of shooting, Cesar would have been expected to use his weapon to stop Sirhan, who was standing in front of him holding an exposed gun. (The two other gunmen attempted to keep their weapons hidden while firing.) By silencing Sirhan, a messy trial would have been avoided (as occurred when Jack Ruby killed Lee Harvey Oswald), the case would have been put to rest, and possible exposure of Sirhan's hypno-programming would have been limited. As it turned out, the kitchen pantry area was packed with people, some seventy in all. When the shooting started, Cesar witnessed Kennedy being hit in the back and the head. Cesar then fell and Sirhan was buried under Kennedy supporters. Shooting Sirhan was out of the question; Cesar could not find Sirhan in his line of sight.

Again, given the sophistication of the operation, it is unlikely that Cesar, known to work full-time at a CIA-related facility, would have been used to kill a presidential candidate. With such obvious ties to the Agency, it clearly would not have been advisable. By having Cesar kill Sirhan, on the other hand, the Agency would have been seen as an employer of an alert and responsible citizen who tried unsuccessfully to protect the candidate and in an exchange of gunfire fatally shot the assailant.

Because of Cesar's circumstances—the fact that he had been walking next to Kennedy and was carrying a gun—he ended up as a suspect, although he was never arrested. Experts involved in the case, who knew that there was evidence of a second gun, found in Cesar a simple solution to the puzzle. But when the assassination is viewed as a covert operation, it becomes clear that the true perpetrators stood to gain more by having both Sirhan and Kennedy eliminated. Indeed, by using a uniformed guard to shoot the patsy, the plotters were layering in more protection for themselves, and also for those who were intent on controlling the outcome of the 1968 presidential race.

To return to the Ambassador Hotel's kitchen pantry and the scene of the assassination, as soon as the fusillade of gunfire had ended, the woman in the polka dot dress fled the scene. She was seen running out of the rear door of the pantry along with the gunmen. There were seven witnesses who reported seeing her with either one, or both of the assailants, moments after Robert Kennedy was shot: Evan P. Freed, a press photographer who years later became an attorney for the City of Los Angeles; Marcus McBroom, a doctor; George Green, thirty-three, a real estate salesman; Jack Merrit, a guard; Richard Houston, twenty-one; Darnell Johnson, a campaign worker; and Booker Griffin, twenty-nine, a black organizer from Watts. None of these witnesses had any reason to invent a story. Yet their statements were either ignored by the LAPD or misstated in its final report.[1469]

Witness Dr. Marcus McBroom had been standing just outside the kitchen when the gunfire started.[1470] He said he did not immediately comprehend what was happening until suddenly the young woman in the polka dot dress ran out of the kitchen followed by a man wearing a suit.[1471] Over his arm the man had a newspaper with a gun protruding from it. When McBroom and an ABC cameraman noticed the weapon, they stepped back. According to McBroom's account, as the girl ran out, she shouted, "We got him" or "We shot him."[1472] McBroom also provided a description of the gunman's face. He said it was sweat-covered, and that the man appeared to be an "Arab looking person."[1473] Recall that at that time, the Iranian intelligence organization, SAVAK, was closely allied with Richard Helms's CIA.

Booker Griffin, the head of the Negro Industrial and Economic Union, reported that when he saw the girl with a taller man running out, he shouted, "They're getting away!" He has stated that he ran after her and searched outside in the parking lot to no avail.[1474]

The polka dot dress woman and her male companion had exited the building, descended the metal staircase, passed Sandra Serrano still sitting on the steps,[1475] and disappeared into the night. The two suited gunmen had vanished as well.

In the pandemonium of the Embassy Room, over the cries of the shocked, grief-stricken, angry crowd, announcers called repeatedly for a doctor. Dr. Stanley Abo, a radiologist, was the first to arrive at Kennedy's side. He placed ice on the back of his head.[1476] Minutes later, Bobby was taken out on a stretcher and rushed by ambulance to Good Samaritan Hospital in Los Angeles.

Officers Arthur Placencia and Travis White and three other policemen arrived at the hotel at 12:22 a.m. They found Sirhan being held down in the kitchen pantry. Quickly they seized him, fought their way through the crowd to a squad car, and drove off to Rampart Station.[1477] At the same time, Sgt. Paul Schraga set up a command post in the parking lot. The forty-year-old veteran police officer, known for his excellent record, had received a radio report of the shooting and drove his patrol car to the Ambassador Hotel lot. As soon as he arrived, a couple in their fifties named Bernstein rushed up to him. They reported they had seen a young woman in a polka dot dress and a man run by them. The woman had shouted, "We shot him!" The Bernsteins asked, "Who?" "Senator Kennedy," was the reply. Sergeant Schraga called in the report. Minutes after the assassination, LAPD issued an all-points bulletin that read: "Prior to shooting, suspect observed with a female cauc. Twenty-three to twenty- seven [years old], five feet six inches, wearing a white voile dress, three-fourth inch sleeves, with small black polka dots . . ."[1478] At 1:41 a.m., a senior LAPD officer canceled the bulletin. Later on, according to Sergeant Schraga, his report of the incident ended up "missing." When he eventually refused to go along with the official version of the assassination, Schraga said, his service ratings began to fall. As a result, a year later he chose to leave the department.[1479]

In addition to those mentioned above, others who came forward to report seeing the woman in the polka dot dress in the Embassy Room, most of the time with Sirhan, were Lonny Worthy, Margaret Hahn, Judith Groves, John Ludlow, Eve Hansen, Nina Ballantyne, Susan Locke, and Jeanette Prudhomme. The LAPD dismissed all of these accounts.[1480] Soon, however, word spread that a woman in a polka dot dress may have been involved in the assassination. The LAPD tried to stem the publicity by producing a Santa Barbara college student who had been at the Ambassador Hotel that night and had worn polka dots. Her name was Valerie Schulte. She had been some fifteen feet behind Senator Kennedy—not next to Sirhan as the polka dot dress woman had been. Also, her dress was green with yellow dots, and she had, in fact, been on crutches that night with a cast on one leg, barely able to walk, let alone run.[1481]

When Sirhan was thrust into the waiting patrol car after the shooting, he was still in a trancelike state. It gradually phased out after he was taken into custody. At the police station, he became hyper and aggressive once again, just as he had before entering the trance. And finally, after several hours in jail, he returned to his normal, polite, and rational self. When looked at analytically, Sirhan's symptoms formed a bell-shaped curve. These are the kinds of changes that are known to be caused by hypno-programming.

Interestingly, following Sirhan's arrest, the LAPD did not administer an alcohol or drug test, even though this is considered a routine practice in any serious crime. Officer Arthur Placencia, who rode with Sirhan in the police cruiser on the way to Rampart Station, has stated that he checked Sirhan's eyes by shining a flashlight in his face. In an interview with a defense investigator, Placencia stated that Sirhan's pupils were dilated.[1482] This is typically evidence of alcohol or drugs in the person's system. Officer Travis White stated that he, too, had checked Sirhan's eyes, but found them to be normal. No one reportedly tested Sirhan with a breathalyzer.[1483]

In California law, premeditation is defined as the capacity to maturely and meaningfully reflect on the gravity of a contemplated act.[1484] Consequently, if it were shown that Sirhan had been intoxicated or drugged, he would therefore have probably not been in a position to "meaningfully reflect," and hence, he would have been eligible for a more lenient sentence than capital punishment.

At the police station, initially Sirhan was hyperventilating and his voice was nearly inaudible. As police tapes have indicated, his speech was rapid and his behavior was aggressive. An hour later, in a second interview, according to Sgt. William Jordan, Sirhan was "relaxed, polite, and composed."[1485] Clearly, more than alcohol was influencing the suspect's state of mind.

Another odd reaction of Sirhan's was noted by the doctor who examined him shortly after his incarceration: Sirhan was shivering "violently," yet the room was warm.[1486]

In addition to these behavioral changes, it is interesting to note that the content of Sirhan's speech also was bizarre. Sirhan has insisted that he did not know what had happened or where he was and consequently had refused to identify himself when brought to the police station. The police saw this as simple stubbornness and expected him to say something about the assassination that had just taken place. Oddly, Sirhan instead struck up a conversation about another case that had occurred at the time. It involved a deputy district attorney, Jack Kirschke, who had killed his wife and her lover. As authors Turner and Christian have pointed out, it was very curious that this subject was on Sirhan's mind at this point in time. In that particular case, Jack Kirschke's lawyer had taken the unusual step of asking the court if *hypnosis* could be used to obtain information in the case. It was denied.[1487]

As Sirhan chatted, no one mentioned the assassination. In fact, Sirhan claims he did not know Robert Kennedy had been shot until an attorney, A. L. Wirin of the ACLU, arrived at the jail to meet with him in his cell.[1488]

When Sirhan was searched in the station, the police found that he was not carrying a wallet. However, his jeans pockets were stuffed with a number of other items: four one hundred dollar bills, along with a five dollar bill, four ones and change; a newspaper ad for a June 2 Kennedy rally at the Ambassador Hotel, an RFK song sheet, two .22 bullets, a slug, a comb, his car keys,[1489] and a newspaper article from the May 26, 1968 issue of the *Pasadena Independent Star News*. The column, written by David Lawrence and headlined "Paradoxical

Bob," criticized Kennedy for supporting military aid to Israel while opposing the war in Vietnam. The article stated, "Presidential candidates are out to get the votes, and some of them do not realize their own inconsistencies."[1490]

Sirhan was not a regular newspaper reader, preferring to get his news via TV or radio. Nor was he a news article collector. If he had clipped a column and was carrying it, he most likely would have been planning on sharing it with someone. But it is doubtful the opinion piece "Paradoxical Bob" rose to this level of interest, neither on his part nor that of his friends.

The clipping is meaningful, however, when one considers Sirhan's condition. He has no memory of the assassination or of preparing for it in any way. Yet, when he was searched in an interrogation room following the assassination, he was found to be carrying an item that could show premeditation—a story about Kennedy, the peace candidate, planning to aid Israel in its struggle with the Arabs. For those who orchestrated Sirhan's actions, having him taken into custody with this article in his possession was one more way for them to create the appearance of a motive.

The other items also gave the impression of a man with a motive. For example, some investigators would assume that the bills were getaway money; the newspaper ad was for a rally that Sirhan had actually attended; the song sheet would presume additional stalking; and his lack of a wallet or ID led authorities to suspect that he wanted to slow investigators down to allow any accomplices time to disappear. Yet the same pocket evidence would not be unexpected if found on an unwitting fall guy, one who was "brainwashed" to believe that Robert Kennedy's support for aid to Israel would destroy his homeland and his family.

Meanwhile, that morning in Pasadena when Sirhan's brother, Munir, saw the morning news, he was stunned. He and Adel immediately went to the police station to inform the authorities that the suspect was their brother.[1491]

LAPD Sgt. William Brandt led the squad that searched the Sirhan home at 696 East Howard Street, Pasadena. As mentioned earlier, in Sirhan's bedroom, one spiral notebook was found on the floor and another on his desk.[1492] Sgt. Brandt also found a large envelope from the IRS, US Treasury Department. On it was written, "RFK must be disposed of like his brother was." At the bottom it said, "Reactionary."[1493] In the trash in the backyard another envelope was discovered the next day by Pasadena officer Thomas Young.[1494] This one was from the Argonaut Insurance Company. It read: "RFK must be be be disposed of d d d disposed disposed d of disposed disposed of properly Robert Fitzgerald (sic) Kennedy must soon die die die die die die die die die."[1495]

At Sirhan's trial, handwriting expert Laurence W. Sloan testified that these words were indeed written in Sirhan's handwriting.[1496] Sirhan does not recall writing on the envelopes nor the notebooks, as explained earlier.[1497] But they are clearly additional samples of automatic writing.

Placing these items in Sirhan's bedroom and in the trash can outside would have required a simple black-bag job. Such operations are not uncommon in intelligence work, and local police forces are also known to participate in these activities. Such jobs may be required, for example, to plant bugs or listening devices for mob surveillance, as well as for homeland security to counter would-be terrorists. Rogue operatives familiar with such routines needed to simply choose a time during which the Sirhans were not at home or the family was asleep, pick a door lock or enter a window, and drop off the notebooks and envelopes. One of the most notable black-bag jobs of this era was the Watergate break-in in which operatives, all with CIA connections, broke into the Democratic National Headquarters in Washington in June 1972. The burglars were caught in the act. The fallout from the Watergate break-in, and the subsequent revelations of abuses of power, became Nixon's undoing. Although Nixon handily won a second term in November 1972, within two years he was forced to resign.

On the evening following the shooting in the Ambassador Hotel, President Lyndon Johnson addressed the nation. In a televised speech, he said, "It would be wrong, it would be self-deceptive, to ignore the connection between lawlessness, hatred, and this act of violence. It would be just as wrong, just as self-deceptive to conclude from this act that our country is sick, that it has lost its sense of balance, its sense of direction, and common decency. Two hundred million Americans did not strike Robert Kennedy last night no more than they struck John F. Kennedy in 1963 or Martin Luther King Jr. in April of this year. But those awful events give us ample warning that in a climate of extremism, of disrespect for law, of contempt for the rights of others, violence may bring down the very best among us. A nation that tolerates violence in any form cannot expect to be able to confine it to just minor outbursts."[1498] The president also announced the formation of a commission to study the causes of violence in the United States.

At Good Samaritan Hospital in Los Angeles, Senator Kennedy's condition was deteriorating. Dr. Henry Cuneo and Dr. James Poppen had done all they could to try to save his life.[1499] Outside the front entrance of the hospital, a crowd held a vigil for Bob Kennedy. On a nearby hill, young people wore orange signs that read PRAY FOR BOBBY.[1500] By evening, the doctors reported that cortical activity had ceased; the brain was dead, but his heart continued to beat through the evening, then gradually slowed and stopped.[1501]

Sen. Robert F. Kennedy died at 1:44 a.m. on June 6, 1968. He was forty-two.[1502]

At his funeral in St. Patrick's Cathedral in New York City, Sen. Edward (Ted) Kennedy delivered a moving eulogy:

> My brother need not be idealized, or enlarged in death beyond what he was in life, but be remembered simply as a good and decent man, who saw wrong and tried to right it, saw suffering and tried to heal it, saw war and tried to stop it.
>
> Those of us who loved him and who take him to his rest today, pray that what he was to us and what he wished for others will some day come to pass for all the world. As he said many times, in many parts of this nation, to those he touched and who sought to touch him:
>
> 'Some men see things as they are and say why. I dream things that never were and say why not.'[1503]

Following the funeral, Robert Kennedy's flag-draped coffin was brought by train from New York to Washington, DC. All along the route, people stood by the tracks in the hot sun to bid him farewell. Many waved or placed their hands over their hearts, and many cried. Bobby was buried next to his brother John in Arlington Cemetery.[1504]

The investigation into the assassination of Robert Kennedy was carried out by a LAPD team called SUS, or Special Unit Senator. The Chief of Police at the time of the assassination was Thomas Reddin.[1505] His Chief of Detectives Robert A. Houghton appointed Hugh Brown, chief of homicide detectives, to head up the special unit.[1506] The SUS team was set up to function as a separate operating unit from the normal LAPD organizational structure. According to the FBI's senior officer on the case, Roger J. LaJeunesse, SUS ran everything themselves.[1507]

Hugh Brown assigned Lt. Manuel Pena, forty-nine, to manage the details of the investigation. Sgt. Hank Hernandez, thirty-seven, who was under Pena, was tasked with looking into the possibility of a conspiracy. (Hernandez was promoted to lieutenant shortly after his appointment to SUS.) Both Pena and Hernandez were known to be also working with the CIA[1508] and had participated in operations in South America.[1509] According to documents released by the Agency, during the 1960s the CIA had conducted training sessions for LAPD personnel and police from other key cities.[1510] According to the FBI's LaJeunesse, Pena had carried out special assignments for the CIA for ten years.[1511] Pena's covert role was revealed also by his brother, a teacher, who had praised his CIA work in a conversation with TV reporter Stan Bohrman.[1512] Hank Hernandez's CIA links involved an assignment in Venezuela. Hernandez was also honored for his work involving a Latin American CIA training program.[1513] Both Pena and Hernandez worked diligently to keep the investigation focused on Sirhan as a lone gunman.

One of the first witnesses to come forward immediately following the assassination of Robert Kennedy was Jerry Owen, the preacher and horse trader mentioned previously. Owen was the man witnesses had seen with a young man, whom Owen believed was Sirhan, riding in the Santa Ana riverbed several months earlier, during the period in which Sirhan was missing. Clearly, Owen feared he would be implicated in the shooting. Shortly after the assassination, he walked into an LAPD substation and gave a long-winded story, telling the police that he had never met Sirhan but had picked him up hitchhiking the day before the murder, had briefly met some of Sirhan's associates, and that he had struck a horse deal with Sirhan[1514] which fell through.[1515]

Owen gave varying versions of his story with each telling, which was ironic since he was known as the "Walking Bible" because of his amazing memory.[1516] Essentially, Owen told police that he had picked up Sirhan hitchhiking at 7th and Grand Avenue in LA on June 3, 1968, the day before the Democratic presidential primary in California. He claimed that he had also picked up another young man at the same time, and that he stopped the truck when that man spotted four people he knew at a street corner: a suited man with a "dirty blond" girl[1517] and two other young men.[1518] The young man with Sirhan jumped out at that point, according to Owen. Owen also claimed that during the ride, he made a deal with Sirhan to sell him a palomino for three hundred dollars.[1519] He said he dropped off Sirhan in Hollywood, and they arranged to meet there later to close the horse sale. Owen said that that night Sirhan, accompanied by the young woman, and the suited man whom he had seen earlier, got together. Sirhan was unable to pay the full amount, so they agreed to meet again the next day. The next day, Owen claimed, the couple told him that Sirhan could not get the money until that night, and that they wanted him to meet them at 11 p.m. at the rear of the Ambassador Hotel.[1520] At that point, Owen informed them he had obligations in Oxnard that evening but promised to return the next day, June 5, 1968.[1521] Indeed, the hitchhiker story leaves the impression that Owen knew all about the accomplices, but made it appear that their meeting was happenstance.

At the police station, Owen claimed that he could not recognize the mug shots of Sirhan that he was first asked to identify.[1522] Again, as noted earlier, the "Sirhan" Owen is describing in his report may well have been a double. As for the horse deal, this part of the story happens to match Sirhan's brother Adel's information. According to Adel, Sirhan drew down three hundred dollars from his "account" with his mother—a day or two prior to the assassination—for the purpose of purchasing a horse.[1523] However, Adel has also stated that Sirhan never hitchhiked.[1524]

Another witness who shone some light on the nature of Jerry Owen's role was his long-time friend, Rev. Jonathan Perkins. An elderly preacher, Perkins stated in an interview with writer Jonn Christian that Owen had dropped in on him shortly after Kennedy's murder.[1525] Perkins said Owen was in great fear that he was "about to get mixed up in that thing (the assassination)."[1526] He noted that Owen had mentioned being at the Ambassador Hotel where he was supposed to meet a stable boy who wanted to buy a horse. Owen said that he had been driving a truck with a horse trailer, and that the trailer would have been a good place for a fugitive to hide. Perkins said Owen added, "They was gonna use me as a getaway, as a scapegoat. They could have gone four or five miles and shot me in a vacant lot."[1527]

After the assassination, Bill Powers, Owen's neighbor at Wild Bill's Stables in Santa Ana, met Owen in a local store and the topic of Sirhan came up. Powers has stated that Owen confided to him that he "kinda got mixed up in the deal," and he exhorted Powers to not disclose anything if asked by the police.[1528] Powers has stated that he was visited several times by men who claimed to be FBI, and that they told him he should not speak to anyone about what he knew, and that he had better "cooperate."[1529] According to Powers, Owen implied that the entire arrangement with Sirhan must have been part of a larger plot. Powers said that Owen felt he had been unwittingly set up to "take Sirhan out of the country in that little truck with the horse in back."[1530]

After several interviews, LAPD decided that Owen's story had holes in it and that it had changed each time Owen told it. The police decided that the hitchhiker tale had been a case of mistaken identity and that there was no connection between Owen and Sirhan.[1531] SUS's Hank Hernandez considered Owen a publicity seeker and stated that his analysis indicated that Owen had made up the entire story.[1532]

Jerry Owen has argued that he had nearly been set up by Sirhan. However, based on the evidence of his past involvement with Sirhan or a Sirhan-double, Owen knew that he had, in fact, been set up by the handlers of Sirhan. In the end, Owen's perceived involvement benefited the actual perpetrators by drawing public attention towards Owen and away from them.

Given the circumstances of the assassination, it is entirely possible that Owen and his horse trailer may have been "assigned" as an escape route, but not for Sirhan. Four other individuals would have wanted that vehicle waiting outside the hotel, just in case anything went wrong with the assassination plan. They were: the young woman in the polka dot dress, the taller man who accompanied her, and the two suited men packing weapons. Whether or not Owen was aware of the fact beforehand—that he may have been an escape option for an assassination team—is not known. Nor is it known if, in fact, he did provide this service. As noted earlier, the truck was later found abandoned in Barstow and turned over to the FBI. Sirhan's fingerprints were found on it.[1533]

Finally, it is also interesting to note that Jerry Owen was a friend of the mayor of Los Angeles at the time, Sam Yorty.[1534] This relationship may well have been one reason the conspirators chose Owen as the perceived Sirhan "caretaker" during his missing time gap, his conditioning period. Owen's link to Yorty gave the authorities an added incentive to pursue the "lone gunman" scenario, which was certainly a safer, and less messy course of action than attempting to establish a connection between an associate of the mayor—Jerry Owen—and the alleged assasin, Sirhan Sirhan.

In the final analysis, the entire Jerry Owen episode should be seen as a diversionary tactic designed as a part of the assassination plan to provide an explanation concerning Sirhan's whereabouts, to involve other innocent people, to confuse investigators, and to set off a wild goose chase into the "wilderness of mirrors." This is particularly true if, indeed, the young person whom Owen knew as Sirhan was instead an unwitting double.

The SUS team was particularly adept at handling reports of accomplices and other conspiracy theories by preventing corroborating accounts from surfacing.[1535] For example, witnesses who saw the young woman in the polka dot dress in the pantry were either ignored or pressured into revising their stories. One key witness who strayed from the lone assassin theory was Sandra Serrano. As noted earlier, she had seen the young woman and her male companion rushing down the Ambassador Hotel's outside staircase, the same route they had used earlier with Sirhan when entering the kitchen.

Serrano was still sitting on the steps sipping a vodka and orange juice,[1536] when, as she has stated, the fleeing woman shouted "We shot him!" "We shot him!" Serrano asked who, and she replied, "We've shot Senator Kennedy."[1537] Another witness, Albert Ellis, later told the FBI that he, too, had heard the same cry.[1538]

Soon after the assassination, NBC's Sander Vanocur interviewed Serrano for nationwide television.[1539] She gave the same account she later gave the police. In fact, her descriptions of the young woman and the male companion and Sirhan match those of other witnesses who also saw them in the pantry, either just prior to the shooting, or while running out afterwards.[1540] The LAPD tried numerous times to persuade Serrano to change her story with regard to the woman announcing, "We shot him." She steadfastly refused. Two weeks after the assassination, on June 20, 1968, at 9 p.m., Serrano submitted to a polygraph test administered by Sgt. Hank Hernandez.

Professor Philip Melanson has chronicled the methods employed against Serrano based on a surviving audiotape of the test.[1541] Hernandez insisted to Serrano that she did not hear the young woman say, "We shot him." And rather than asking "yes" or "no" questions, Hernandez's approach involved using harassment and intimidation to persuade her to change her story. His stream of rhetoric resulted in continual arguing with the witness. Excerpts of his statements demonstrated the lengths to which SUS would go to suppress evidence of a plot. The following is a quote of Hernandez's voice on tape: "You owe it to Senator Kennedy. . . . Be a woman about this. . . . Don't shame his death by keeping this up. . . . What you saw is not true. Tell me why you made up this story. . . . If you loved the man, the least you owe him is letting him rest in peace, and he can't. . . . This is going to make an old woman out of you before your time. . . . There's people out there waiting for you if you don't tell me the truth." On the verge of tears, the twenty-year-old caved in. She agreed to recant her statements. Twenty years later, in 1988, when the California State Archives released the LAPD's files on the case, Serrano was asked to speak on a local radio program. She summed up her Hank Hernandez polygraph test by saying, "I became unglued. . . . I said what they wanted me to say."[1542]

While the young woman in the polka dot dress appeared to have been a triggering mechanism relative to the actions of Sirhan, at the same time she may have been conditioned to some extent as well. In this context, her words served to help deflect suspicion away from the masterminds of the murder and the professional hitmen in their employ. Such legerdemain is in keeping with the modus operandi of a covert action operation.

Another witness interrogated by Hank Hernandez regarding the young woman with Sirhan in the kitchen pantry was waiter Thomas Vincent DiPierro, the son of one of the hotel's maitre d's, also noted earlier.[1543] Two days following the assassination, on June 7, 1968, DiPierro testified before the grand jury that indicted Sirhan. His account was similar to Sandra Serrano's original testimony: that there were accomplices. LAPD could not afford to let this stand; not if they intended to maintain their "lone nut" theory. On the heels of Sandra Serrano's withering polygraph test, Sgt. Hank Hernandez knew how to approach DiPierro.[1544] The college student and part-time waiter was brought in for a similar session and told in no uncertain terms that he should state that there was no young woman with Sirhan. DiPierro recanted his story.[1545]

DiPierro was not comfortable with this situation, and one year later he decided to write to a radio reporter, Art Kevin of KHJ, who was airing a series of reports on the RFK case and the existence of the polka dot dress woman. According to authors Turner and Christian, Art Kevin had been urged by LAPD to avoid the issue, but he refused.[1546] In his letter, DiPierro praised Kevin for "the first real true report" on the matter and added, "I was deeply interested in hearing the facts straight for a change."[1547]

The facts regarding the physical evidence found in the kitchen pantry were the key to proving whether there was more than one gunman. If more than eight shots were fired, then there had to have been a second gunman. LAPD's lead criminalist, DeWayne Wolfer, reported to SUS team leaders Manny Pena and Hank Hernandez that seven bullets were recovered and one was lost in the ceiling space.[1548] According to LAPD's official ballistics report, two bullets were recovered from Senator Kennedy's body, five bullets were taken from the five surviving victims, and one bullet was lost in the "ceiling interspace," for a total of eight bullets.[1549] But FBI documents, released under the Freedom of Information Act, reveal evidence of five additional bullets. In its examination of the murder scene, the FBI reported finding two bullet holes in the doorjamb of the pantry's swinging doors, two in the center divider post, and one in the stage door jamb. These five added to the LAPD list produce a total of thirteen bullets fired.[1550]

FBI agent William Bailey, who inspected the crime scene shortly after the assassination, discovered the evidence of two unaccounted for bullets lodged in the center divider between the swinging doors in the kitchen pantry.[1551] Two additional bullets that SUS neglected to report became public information when FBI photos of the hotel kitchen pantry evidence were released in 1975.[1552] Since both the LAPD and the FBI knew of these in 1968, it is clear that both were working together to ensure that evidence of a conspiracy remained secret, at least initially. Another hole with a bullet in it was discovered by two LAPD officers, Robert Rozzi and Charles Wright. The two policemen were photographed by the AP at the crime scene pointing to the bullet hole, which was located in a doorjamb a foot above the floor in a hallway leading into the pantry.[1553] The door frames were quickly removed by the police and destroyed by them a year later.[1554]

In the decade following the assassination, a battle raged over the exact bullet count due to the serious consequences of having more than eight, the alleged murder weapon having been an 8-shot Iver-Johnson. One witness, Nina Rhodes, whose account mentioned hearing more than eight shots, found out in 1992 that her statement to the FBI, given in 1968, had been rewritten. The summary released in 1992 indicated that while at the hotel kitchen entrance on the night of the murder she had heard "eight distinct shots." Upon reading the report, she was amazed. She immediately wrote back to inform the Los Angeles grand jury, "I would like to stress . . . I heard twelve to fourteen shots, some originating in the vicinity of the senator not from where I saw Sirhan . . ."[1555]

LAPD has maintained its position that no additional bullets were found at the scene of the assassination. In addition, when asked to produce the spectrographic report, which would determine if all of the recovered bullets had the same metallic makeup and hence were likely from the same "batch," the department responded that the scientific evidence was "either lost or destroyed."[1556]

An acoustic analysis of ABC's broadcast tape from the Embassy Room was conducted in 1982 at the Stanford Research Institute in Menlo Park, California, according to writers Klaber and Melanson. The results ascertained that no fewer than ten gunshots had been fired.[1557]

Neither the defense nor the prosecution brought up the matter of the extra bullets at Sirhan's trial. Sirhan's lead attorney, Grant Cooper, wanted to avoid the distinction because a count of over eight bullets meant that there was a second gun and therefore a conspiracy. A conspiracy would indicate premeditation, which would have hurt his client.

Besides the number of bullets fired and the number of gunmen, of equal importance is understanding Sirhan's state of mind during the assassination. Two psychiatrists were brought in by the court to examine Sirhan and try to unlock his memory, Dr. Bernard Diamond for the defense and Dr. Seymour Pollack for the prosecution. According to author William Klaber, Dr. Diamond, hypnotized Sirhan eight times.[1558] He discovered signs that Sirhan had been hypnotized many times before. He was also struck by how reliably Sirhan would perform in a waking state what had been suggested to him under hypnosis, without recalling having been told to perform and without recalling having been hypnotized. [1559]

For example, in one test conducted in the presence of author Robert Kaiser, Dr. Diamond hypnotized Sirhan and then told him that when he took out his handkerchief, he (Sirhan) would climb the bars of his cell. Dr. Diamond then woke up Sirhan and a while later the doctor blew his nose. Sirhan began climbing. Asked why he was doing this, he replied that he was "getting some exercise."[1560] This was a simple example of his being effectively programmed.

According to Dr. Diamond, Sirhan's hypnotic trances came on quickly by using just a coin, and they were unusually deep. Sirhan did not need a monotonous sleepiness patter.[1561] After the psychiatrists had hypnotized Sirhan, at one point they asked him to write down his answers. When they asked Sirhan to write his name, he wrote Sirhan B. Sirhan, and then he kept repeating the line, only stopping when he had filled the page.[1562] Asked additional questions, he continued to repeat writing his answers again and again until told to stop.[1563] This turn of events surprised the doctors. Clearly, Sirhan was exhibiting "automatic writing." When Dr. Diamond asked him why he was writing "crazy," Sirhan wrote "practice, practice, practice, practice, practice . . . mind control mind control mind control."[1564]

Dr. Diamond also determined that in addition to Sirhan's unusual susceptibility to hypnosis, he had been subjected to extensive hypnosis previously. Dr. Diamond asked Sirhan if he had ever studied hypnosis, but Sirhan said he did not know much about it. After being put under hypnosis, Dr. Diamond again asked Sirhan where he had experienced hypnosis. Sirhan replied, "AMORC." Yet AMORC did not teach hypnosis.[1565] When Dr. Diamond asked Sirhan at another point, "Who hypnotized you?" he answered, "Mirror, mirror, my mirror, my mirror. . . ."[1566] Leading experts in hypnosis agree that the notion that one can hypnotize oneself by looking in a mirror is absurd.[1567] Clearly, Sirhan's programmer planted the belief in Sirhan's mind that he (Sirhan) had been self-hypnotizing using a mirror. In this way, he wrote himself out of Sirhan's memory—a fairly simple task for an expert hypnotist. As noted earlier, Dr. William Bryan, CIA consultant and hypnotist extraordinaire, was well-versed in the occult practices of ancient Egypt and modern-day Rosicrucians. He also no doubt anticipated that the authorities would attempt to break through Sirhan's amnesia and identify the true conspirators. By making Sirhan believe AMORC was responsible for his condition, another veil was placed over the identity of those who were actually responsible.[1568] Again, the Rosicrucians do not delve into hypnosis and such subjects. And Sirhan's hypno-programmers knew that his believing that AMORC had been "playing" with his mind would serve as a perfect cover for their own tinkering. Sirhan, in fact, attended only one AMORC meeting in May 1968, two months following his return home. He had spent less than a couple of hours with the group, yet his feelings towards this group were unusually strong, for no apparent reason.[1569] In his conversations with author Robert Kaiser, Sirhan adamantly insisted that no harm come to the Rosicrucians because of the assassination.[1570] Indeed, AMORC very conveniently met Sirhan's programmers' needs. They had to disguise their identities and their handiwork, so they simply embedded a posthypnotic suggestion that AMORC had taught him everything.

In the pre-trial evaluations, defense psychiatrist Dr. Diamond asked Sirhan, while under hypnosis, to write something about Robert Kennedy. Sirhan wrote nine times, "RFK must die, RFK must die. . . ." The doctor then asked him "Who killed Kennedy?" Sirhan wrote "I don't know. I don't know."[1571] For his final questions, the psychiatrist asked Sirhan if he had been thinking that night of shooting Kennedy, and if he had done it. Sirhan wrote, "No" in answer to both questions.[1572]

When Dr. Seymour Pollack, the prosecution's psychiatrist, asked Sirhan—while under hypnosis—why he shot Kennedy, Sirhan did not have an answer. When Dr. Pollack asked him again, Sirhan stated, "the bombers." Dr. Pollack then described a scene of bombs hitting Jerusalem. Sirhan burst into tears.[1573] Upon being awakened, Sirhan did not recall any of the discussion about bombers nor about Kennedy. It appears that Sirhan's mind had been compartmentalized, and the death and suffering of Palestinians had become an emotional trigger embedded in his psyche. At Sirhan's trial several months later, the prosecution would attempt to show that the motive for the Robert Kennedy assassination was Bobby's support for Israel.[1574] In a speech on May 26, 1968, at Temple Neveh Shalom in Portland, Oregon, Kennedy had advocated sending fifty bombers to Israel to help defend that country from an Arab attack. Yet, the facts show that Sirhan did not hear the story about the fifty bombers until after the assassination.[1575] Clearly, the prosecution was trying to fill in empty spaces in the picture that the well-concealed hypno-programming had created.

Prior to the trial, Drs. Pollack and Diamond also considered the possibility that Sirhan had been intoxicated the night of the assassination and if this could account for his actions and his memory block. When questioned under hypnosis, Sirhan told them that he had had four Tom Collinses that evening.[1576] Sirhan's defense team brought in a brain specialist to evaluate their client's reaction to alcohol. The test was designed to determine precisely the effect of four Tom Collinses drinks on Sirhan in a controlled setting in his jail cell.[1577] According to author Robert Kaiser, Dr. Edward H. Davis from Beverly Hills conducted an electroencephalogram (EEG) test before Sirhan began drinking and the results were found to be normal. The doctor then determined the effect on Sirhan's brain waves after alcohol was introduced. To simulate Sirhan's intake on the evening of the assassination, he used the hotel's recipe for Tom Collins and mixed it using six ounces of Gordon's gin, which is the equivalent of four drinks.[1578] Sirhan was relaxed as he started the test. After drinking for several minutes, he began to tremble and became anxious. According to Dr. Eric Marcus, a psychiatrist who was observing the test, Sirhan then became mildly delirious and appeared to be choking.[1579] Dr. Marcus' notes reported that Sirhan began crying, "'I'll get even with the Jews, goddamn it. Twenty years is long enough for those Jews. Got to have justice. Didn't have to help them by sending planes. That bastard just can't, he can't help those bastards.'" Sirhan then motioned to Dr. Marcus, calling him "Adel," and then asked to be taken home. When Sirhan was told that Dr. Marcus was not Adel, Sirhan responded, "'Get out of here. You're one of them.'" Marcus also noted that Sirhan thought that the deputies outside his cell were "the Jews."[1580] The experiment's results were intriguing. Sirhan was reliving a scene of terror, one that was not related to his consciousness, but rather to his unconscious. The Tom Collinses appeared to have set off the programming, and in fact, the test showed this drink may well have been an integral part of Sirhan's conditioning.

When Sirhan was awake and in his normal state, he spoke with Dr. Pollack about his recollections of the presidential primary campaign. He told him with respect to Kennedy, "Hell, I was for him."[1581] Again, Pollack suggested that the plight of the Arabs and Kennedy's support for Israel could have caused Sirhan to fire at Kennedy, to which Sirhan—who again had no memory of the murder—responded, "My conscience doesn't agree with what I did. It's against my upbringing. My childhood, family, church, prayers . . . the Bible, and all this, sir. 'Thou shalt not kill,' Life is the thing, you know. Where would you be if you didn't have life? And here I go and splatter this guy's brains. It's just not me."[1582]

Only hours after Robert Kennedy's assassination, Dr. William J. Bryan, the Agency's hypnotism wizard, happened to be a guest on a KABC radio program hosted by Ray Briem. Sirhan had not been identified by name at this point. While Bryan was discussing an unrelated topic with the show host, the CIA consultant stated in an offhand remark that the Kennedy shooting suspect was probably acting under a posthypnotic suggestion.[1583] Given Bryan's well-known oversized ego, it is not surprising that he would interject this insight into the interview, since, as he later told colleagues in confidence, he was the one who had hypnotized Sirhan.

According to Prof. Philip Melanson, Bryan also told a colleague that he had been called by the authorities at one point to work with Sirhan Sirhan "in a prison cell."[1584]

While there is no evidence Bryan visited Sirhan in jail, Sirhan's behavior suggests he did. One example is Sirhan's twenty-minute lecture on the origin of the State of Israel that he delivered during his trial. Sirhan was not a Middle East scholar, nor was he particularly interested in Arab politics and the Islamic way of life, as he stated several times. In fact, he was not even a Muslim; he was a Christian refugee from Jerusalem. Yet suddenly, on the stand, he delivered a monologue on the entire subject. It was reportedly more cogent than the work of many professional newsmen in the courtroom that day.[1585] Sirhan's performance would bolster the assumption of many jurors that Sirhan, an Orthodox Christian, was an Arab freedom fighter.

As you may recall, when the police searched Sirhan's pockets immediately following the assassination they found a Pasadena, California, newspaper clipping concerning Kennedy's support for military aid to Israel.[1586] Obviously, if Sirhan had been an Arab patriot, he would have responded to the police by acknowledging possession of the editorial and voicing an opinion regarding its content. Yet this was not the case. Sirhan does not even recall the article. He also no doubt knew that every candidate in the presidential race supported Israel. So in this respect, Kennedy was no different from the others.

As the trial proceeded, Sirhan became frustrated with his defense team and did not want his lawyers to use mental illness as a defense. He absolutely rejected the notion that he was psychotic (as did his psychiatrist),[1587] and he told author Robert Kaiser prior to the trial, "I want to plead guilty. I don't want to have those people proving I'm insane."[1588] He told Kaiser, "If it's going to cost me my life, I want to help the Arabs."[1589] Sirhan had decided his only "defense" was to be anti-Israeli.

Given the sophisticated nature of the conspiracy to kill Bobby Kennedy, the perpetrators must have realized that their failure to also eliminate Sirhan had to be remedied. A final posthypnotic suggestion was required. Agency hypno-programmer William Bryan would simply need to give his subject a command to accept complete responsibility for the murder. Although he had no memory of the assassination, during the trial Sirhan told the court, "I will ask to be executed. I killed Robert Kennedy willfully, premeditatedly, with twenty years of forethought. That's why."[1590] (Sirhan was only twenty-four years old.) Clearly, Sirhan had become unhinged.

Sirhan's trial had begun in Los Angeles on January 7, 1969, and was given to the jury by April 14, 1969. Three days later, the jury reached its verdict. Sirhan was found guilty of first degree murder and five counts of assault with a deadly weapon with intent to commit murder.[1591] Sirhan was convicted on April 17, 1969,[1592] and was sentenced to death in the gas chamber. His sentence was reduced to life in prison after California abolished the death penalty in 1972.[1593]

D r. Bernard Diamond, psychiatrist for the defense, considered Sirhan to have been *temporarily* insane at the time of the assassination.[1594] Yet, other experts in the field of psychiatry, who have studied Sirhan's background and evaluated his present state of mind, have concluded that the facts do not add up.

After Sirhan was sentenced, the Chief of San Quentin prison's psychological program, Dr. Eduard Simson-Kallas, as noted earlier, took up the challenge of finding out if Sirhan's amnesia was real. He was able to spend thirty-five hours studying Sirhan.[1595] An Estonian by birth, Dr. Simson had some twenty years of experience and was impartial regarding the Middle East situation.[1596] Dr. Simson's findings showed that Sirhan was essentially not deceptive nor mentally disturbed, at least not to the point where he would have murdered someone and then pretended he could not remember it.[1597] Yet, Sirhan was obviously at the murder scene, gun in hand, firing away.

To try to understand this, Dr. Simson extensively examined Sirhan and determined that he was sane; he exhibited no symptoms of being a paranoid schizophrenic or psychotic.[1598] This diagnosis was corroborated by San Quentin's chief psychiatrist, Dr. D. G. Schmidt.[1599]

Dr. Simson also found enough indications to feel confident that Sirhan in fact does not have any recollection of the assassination nor of writing the note-books. He concluded that Sirhan was "prepared by someone. He was hypno-tized by someone."[1600] To find out who did it and why, the psychiatrist decided to try to deprogram him.

First, Dr. Simson studied Sirhan's responses regarding the assassination. He said Sirhan's statements fit a pattern seen in others who have had various types of hypnosis conditioning—they do not remember nearly as much detail as a normal witness would recall. They are unable also to recall having been unwittingly put into a trance. "I don't really know what happened," said Sirhan, "I know I was there. They tell me I killed Kennedy. I don't remember exactly what I did but I know I wasn't myself."[1601]

The fact that Sirhan could recall so few details of the crime is very unusual, unless of course he had been hypnotized, according to Dr. Simson. Dr. Simson also explored the concept of a triggering mechanism, someone who would have set off, in a preplanned way, the responses exhibited by Sirhan in the hotel pantry. The young woman for whom he poured a cup of coffee was the most likely candidate. Dr. Simson believes that if Sirhan had been programmed to respond to her cue, just meeting her could have put him in a trance.[1602] In Dr.Simson's final analysis, he believes that she was the triggering mechanism.[1603] As for a motive, according to Dr. Simson, Sirhan's conditioned responses were probably derived from the passions surrounding the Arab-Israeli conflict.[1604]

Dr. Simson's next step was the deprogramming process. But before he could begin, his work was suddenly stopped by the associate warden of the prison, James W. L. Park.[1605] The prison administrator's rationale was that Dr. Simson's work did not conform to those services offered to other pris-oners. This prompted the psychiatrist to quit after having served at the prison for six years.[1606] Since then, no further work has been attempted to break past the memory blocks in the recesses of Sirhan's mind.

Another bizarre story in the Bobby Kennedy assassination case occurred during the investigation of the forensic evidence. It was alleged that Los Angeles Coronor Dr. Thomas Noguchi had mishandled the Kennedy autopsy. It was Dr. Noguchi who had discovered and released the powder burn evidence that proved that the bullets that killed Bobby were fired from one inch away while Sirhan had been firing from several feet away. Dr. Noguchi's accuser, a man who went by the name of Dr. Donald Angus Stuart, had been hired as the LA deputy coroner in Noguchi's office just prior to the assassination in early

1968.[1607] Noguchi was eventually exonerated. Stunning news came to light in 1972 when Stuart was arrested and charged with perjury. He was an impostor who had made up all of his medical credentials.[1608] It is not known if his placement in the coroner's office was part of the MKULTRA conspiracy to kill the Kennedys.

As noted earlier, there are no known pictures of the moment of the assassination. Jamie Scott Enyart, the high school student previously mentioned, has stated that he was in the Ambassador Hotel kitchen pantry and had taken photos of Robert Kennedy at the moment he was shot.

During a 1992 interview, Enyart described to authors Klaber and Melanson what had happened to him on the night of June 4, 1968. "As I got into the pantry I was about ten feet behind [Kennedy], continuing to take pictures as he began to shake hands with people. All of a sudden I saw him drop from the frame. He fell. And I continued taking pictures. I backed up, jumped up on a table. Everyone in front of me had been shot and fell, and I jumped up to get out of the way."[1609]

The LAPD quickly confiscated his film, taking three rolls,[1610] knowing that such film evidence could contain valuable clues. Several months later, Enyart received eighteen prints back from the police, none of which were pantry shots, and none of his negatives was returned.[1611]

When the Robert Kennedy assassination files were made public in 1988, Enyart sought his photos, but was told they must have been destroyed. According to a police property report, on August 21, 1968, the LAPD had burned 2,410 photos from the Kennedy case in a local hospital incinerator.[1612] The LAPD stated that the discarded photos were all duplicates, although no record was kept indicating which photos they were.[1613]

Enyart sued in 1989. In 1995, the city claimed to have found the negatives in the state archives, but while they were being delivered to the courthouse, the briefcase containing the pictures was reportedly stolen from a courier's car.[1614] Finally, in August 1996, after three weeks of deliberations, the court ruled in favor of Scott Enyart. The jury awarded him $625,600 for the loss of his photographs.[1615] However, the city appealed, and in 1999, the Second District Court of Appeals in Los Angeles set aside the jury's verdict. The court ruled that during voir dire, three of the jurors had improperly concealed their bias against the city. At the end of the day, it is doubtful Enyart would have had to endure the lengthy and sometimes bitter legal process if, in fact, his photos did not contain anything of substantive value related to a conspiracy.

Because of Bobby Kennedy's assassination, for many voters, the 1968 presidential race lost its idealism and hope. Sen. Eugene McCarthy went on to the Chicago Democratic Convention where he lost to Vice President Hubert Humphrey. On November 5, 1968, Humphrey was defeated by Republican Richard Nixon for the presidency of the United States. Nixon easily won the electoral vote. But in the popular vote, he edged out the Democrat by only one half of one percent.[1616]

When Nixon moved into the White House, there were more than five hundred thousand American troops involved in the war effort in Vietnam.[1617] US negotiators and the North Vietnamese had finally agreed to sit down in Paris to start talking peace some six months earlier, on May 10, 1968. As Commander in chief, Nixon continued a charade of peace talks for five long years. In essence, North Vietnam wanted the Viet Cong represented in the South Vietnamese government, while the United States wanted the North Vietnamese out of South Vietnam. Neither side would compromise. During this five-year time span, more Americans died in Vietnam than had been killed there prior to Nixon's election.[1618]

In President Nixon's campaign for a second term in 1972, he was expected to face strong opposition from another popular candidate, Gov. George Wallace of Alabama. Governor Wallace was campaigning in Laurel, Maryland, on May 15, 1972, when he was shot by a lone gunman. Arthur Bremer, twenty-one, an unemployed busboy, was arrested at the scene. Governor Wallace barely survived. (He would spend the rest of his life in a wheelchair.) The attempted assassination fit a pattern witnessed before in the murders of President Kennedy, Martin Luther King Jr., and Robert Kennedy.

Two years later, an interesting connection to the Wallace shooting surfaced that involved CIA hypnosis consultant Dr. William Bryan. In June 1974, New York writer Betsy Langman interviewed Dr. Bryan at his Los Angeles office.[1619] When she broached the subject of hypno-programming, he stormed out of the room denying that he had hypnotized Sirhan. Later, a very upset Ms. Langman spoke with Bryan's secretary out of the office. From her she learned that shortly after presidential candidate Governor George Wallace was shot in Laurel, Maryland, an urgent call regarding the attempted assassination came in for Bryan. The call was from Laurel, Maryland.[1620]

Author Philip Melanson has reported that later in the 1970s, Dr. William Bryan's name was submitted to the House Select Committee on Assassinations as a key witness, according to congressional sources who disclosed this information to reporter Greg Roberts.[1621] However, before Dr. Bryan could testify, he was found dead at the Riviera Hotel in Las Vegas in the spring of 1977. The cause of death was listed as "natural causes."[1622]

At this writing, Sirhan Sirhan is still incarcerated. His attorney is William F. Pepper, a lawyer known for his work on behalf of James Earl Ray who was accused of shooting Martin Luther King Jr. on April 4, 1968, in Memphis, Tennessee. Ray died in prison in 1998 at age seventy. Sirhan has been imprisoned in California for forty-five years. He is sixty-nine years old.

# 9

# *Conclusion*

---

T HE FACTS UNCOVERED in the John and Robert Kennedy assassination investigations clearly support the contention that an operation involving hypno-programmed fall guys and hidden sharpshooters was indeed activated, and that rogue CIA personnel at the highest levels, headed by Richard Helms and James Angleton, masterminded the program. The conspirators' motives were to stop both Kennedy brothers' plans to end the Cold War by negotiating peace with Cuba, North Vietnam, and the Soviet Union.

Two victims of the Agency's MKULTRA program, Lee Harvey Oswald and Sirhan B. Sirhan, both unwitting patsies, suffered similar experiences at the hands of rogue agents.

Both Lee and Sirhan had been befriended by mysterious characters, significantly older than they, who assumed controlling presences in their lives. Lee's older friend was CIA contract agent George de Mohrenschildt, a Russian émigré in Dallas who was introduced to Lee upon his return from the Soviet Union.[1623] George de Mohrenschildt was expected to appear before the House Committee on Assassinations when he was found dead from a gunshot wound, an apparent suicide.[1624] Sirhan's close friend was Tom Rathke, the college-educated horse groom who introduced Sirhan to the occult. Sirhan later came to believe such practices brought on his extraordinary predicament.[1625]

Both Lee Harvey Oswald and Sirhan Sirhan spent months away from home with little or no financial resources. Lee had no trouble affording travel expenses and accommodations neither when he "defected" to the Soviet Union nor when he returned to the United States with wife and child in mid-1962.[1626] And Sirhan disappeared for three months,[1627] from approximately

December 1967 through February 1968. His whereabouts and his means of support during this time period are unknown.

The CIA's presence in the lives of Lee and Sirhan was substantial. Lee had been immersed in the intelligence community early on, attending the military's Defense Language Institute, where he studied Russian,[1628] after which he was assigned to Atsugi, Japan, a key US "CIA listening post."[1629] Upon leaving the Marines, there is evidence Lee became a fake defector to the Soviet Union. It is known that James Angleton oversaw every detail of the defector program and therefore would have been handling Lee's assignments in the USSR. Lee's associations with CIA assets included, besides George de Mohrenschildt, an American Air Force doctor stationed at the US Embassy in Moscow, Captain Alexi Davison of Atlanta, Georgia.[1630] Dr. Davison, who returned home in 1963, was named by the Soviets as a key CIA operative in one of the most important US spy networks in the Soviet Bloc.[1631] David Ferrie, Lee's friend in New Orleans whose agency work was confirmed by director Richard Helms in early 1969,[1632] was a CIA pilot. In addition, Lee was witnessed meeting with one of Richard Helms's top lieutenants, David Phillips, in Dallas in 1963.[1633] Sirhan's ties to the intelligence community initially came from a US Army Intelligence liaison in Los Angeles who reported shortly after the Robert Kennedy assassination that his office had a file on Sirhan that was created *before* the assassination.[1634] Additionally, a key CIA asset, a nationally recognized hypnosis expert, Dr. William J. Bryan Jr. of Los Angeles, later boasted to friends that he had hypnotized Sirhan,[1635] both prior to the assassination and after in his jail cell before the trial.

In both Lee and Sirhan's cases, we see a profusion of so-called incriminating evidence carefully fabricated to frame them. For example, we have Lee's alleged "diary," covering two years of his life, all of which, according to experts, was written in a day or two,[1636] and a faked photo of him posing with a rifle in his backyard.[1637] In Sirhan's case, a forty-eight-page notebook—produced by the prosecution to show alleged premeditation—was apparently penned by Sirhan, but the writings are obviously a product of those who had a special expertise in the methods of hypnotic trances and producing so-called automatic writing. When defense psychiatrist Dr. Bernard Diamond tried to elicit from Sirhan while under hypnosis when exactly the notebooks were written, Sirhan continually answered that he had no memory of them.[1638]

Both Lee and Sirhan's handlers meticulously crafted for both of them their own paths of circumstantial incrimination. Lee believed his assignment was to gain intelligence on anti-Castro forces and pro-Castro Cubans in the

New Orleans area. But by acting as a pro-Castro leftist radical,[1639] Oswald was unwittingly being set up by his handlers to appear to be a potential assassin in the making. In Sirhan's case, he was witnessed with a young woman and a man just prior to the assassination, during which he exhibited a total personality change and signs of being in a frenzied state,[1640] behavior that was highly uncharacteristic of him. They appeared to be "stalking" RFK. Sirhan was also seen practicing shooting with the couple at a gun club and said later that he does not even recall why he was there.[1641]

Critical evidence linking Oswald and Sirhan to the JFK and RFK assassinations is also lacking. Lee was seen by three witnesses four minutes before the JFK shooting—*not* on the sixth floor of the Texas School Book Depository awaiting the presidential motorcade—but relaxing in the first-floor break room and then in the second-floor lunchroom. Two minutes after the assassination, Lee's supervisor, Roy Truly, and patrolman Marrion Baker again witnessed Lee in the lunchroom calmly sipping a Coke.[1642] While Sirhan was apprehended with gun in hand, the forensic evidence showed Bobby was shot from behind as evidenced by the powder burns on his head and back. Sirhan, however, had been positioned *in front* of Kennedy. LA coroner Dr. Thomas Noguchi has documented that it was impossible for Sirhan to have fired the fatal shots.[1643]

In both political murders, eyewitness testimony has indicated the presence of hidden gunmen, expert shooters concealed on the sidelines, who carried out the assassinations, while unwitting fall guys, Lee and Sirhan, were blamed. President Kennedy was hit in a crossfire involving three gunmen.[1644] Eyewitness statements, film evidence, and the autopsy all indicate that shots were fired from the Texas School Book Depository, from another building on Houston Street, and from behind a fence on the grassy knoll in Dealey Plaza.[1645] Robert Kennedy was shot in the kitchen pantry of the Ambassador Hotel, according to eyewitnesses, by two gunmen in suits who stood directly behind Kennedy and at his left side, firing from inches away before escaping in the chaos.[1646] Judge Robert A. Wenke's 1975 panel reported that Sirhan's gun could not be "positively identified" as the murder weapon because the markings on the victim bullets were significantly different from those bullets from the test-fired Sirhan gun.[1647] In fact, Sirhan's Iver-Johnson .22 was later discovered to be coated with lead in the bore, indicating that the gun had been firing blanks,[1648] a ruse Sirhan's handlers used to protect the actual assassins who were in the line of fire.

Lee and Sirhan both appeared confused upon discovering they were being charged with murder. Lee, a young ex-Marine, immediately replied that he was a patsy.[1649] He did not live long enough to disclose details of whom he thought had set him up. When Sirhan was taken into custody, he was found to be in a stupor. He found out that Robert Kennedy was shot when attorney A. L. Wirin arrived at the county jail to meet with him in his cell.[1650]

The true perpetrators intended to make sure that any hint of a conspiracy would be buried with Lee and Sirhan in their graves by silencing both of them. Lee's death came swiftly. Two days after President Kennedy's assassination, Lee was shot in Dallas Police headquarters by mobster Jack Ruby and died two hours later. Strong Agency-Mob ties would have meant Ruby's death if he had not followed orders to silence Lee.[1651] In the Robert Kennedy assassination, at least ten shots were fired in the Ambassador Hotel's kitchen pantry, according to a report on audio recordings from three open news microphones conducted by the Stanford Research Institute in 1982.[1652] Three bullets hit Bobby, a fourth pierced his jacket shoulder, and five people were wounded in the melee. But after RFK staffers piled onto the diminutive Sirhan, none of the gunmen had a clear shot at Sirhan.

The evidence compiled on the rogue agency MKULTRA assassination program indicates that the operation was masterminded by Richard Helms, who served three decades in the CIA, became its Director (1966–1973) and was MKULTRA's major promoter. James Angleton, long-time CIA counterintelligence chief, was also a key MKULTRA backer. Both are now deceased. Richard Helms passed away at eighty-nine from bone cancer in Washington, DC, on October 22, 2002.[1653] James Angleton succumbed to lung cancer. He died in Washington, DC, at age sixty-nine on May 11, 1987.[1654] Their closest associates, David Phillips, CIA western hemisphere chief, died of lung cancer in Bethesda, Maryland, on July 7, 1988, at sixty-five,[1655] and the last remaining member of the group, E. Howard Hunt, CIA disinformation writer and sabotage expert, died of pneumonia in Miami on January 23, 2007 at age eighty-eight.[1656]

In dissecting the assassinations of the sixties, beneath the surface, they involve similar motives, means, and opportunities. The motive of the rogue intelligence operatives was to control America's destiny in their own twisted way. The means by which they intended to accomplish this end was to use a workable version of the MKULTRA plan involving unwitting fall guys along with professional hitmen. The opportunities were readily available, given the wide range of allies supporting them, from various local law enforcement individuals, to mobsters, to foreign spy agencies.

Everyone knows there is a price to pay for ignoring the lessons of our past. Thomas Jefferson forewarned our nation at its very beginning regarding the consequences of apathy and insufficient vigilance. He left us this poignant, poetic reminder: "If a nation expects to be ignorant and free, it expects what never was and never will be."

Ultimately, it is hoped that the information presented herein will aid the cause of those seeking justice for Sirhan Sirhan and the family of Lee Harvey Oswald. May it also serve as a guidepost as we seek to avoid future tragedies like the Kennedy assassinations.

# NOTES

1. "Robert F. Kennedy's Assassin Transferred," <u>Waterbury Republican-American</u> [Waterbury, CT] 3 Nov. 2009: A4.

2. Richard D. Mahoney, *Sons and Brothers: The Days of Jack and Bobby Kennedy* (New York: Arcade Publishing, 1999), p. 294.

3. Arthur M. Schlesinger Jr., *Robert Kennedy and His Times* (New York: Ballantine Books, a division of Random House, 1978), p. 665.

4. Philip H. Melanson, *Spy Saga: Lee Harvey Oswald and US Intelligence* (New York: Praeger Publishers, 1990), p. 117.

5. Thomas Powers, *The Man Who Kept The Secrets: Richard Helms And The CIA* (New York: Alfred A. Knopf, 1979), p. 293.

6. Victor Marchetti and John D. Marks, *The CIA And The Cult Of Intelligence* (New York: Alfred A. Knopf, 1974), p. 18.

7. Gaeton Fonzi, *The Last Investigation* (New York: Thunder's Mouth Press, 1993), p. 302n.

8. Richard M. Helms with William Hood, *A Look Over My Shoulder: A Life In the Central Intelligence Agency* (New York: Random House, 2003), p. 253.

9. Bernard Fensterwald Jr., with Michael Ewing, the Committee to Investigate Assassinations, *Coincidence or Conspiracy?* (New York: Zebra Books, Kensington Publishing Corp., 1977), p. 191.

10. Fensterwald, p. 199.

11. Fensterwald, p. 200.

12. Helms, pp. 14–15.

13. Helms, pp. 24–25.

14. Helms, pp. 29–30.

15. Powers, p. 24.

16. Powers, p. 30.

17. Helms, p. 153.

18. Helms, p. 103.

19. Edward Jay Epstein, *Legend: The Secret World of Lee Harvey Oswald* (New York: McGraw-Hill Book Company, 1978), p. 29.

20. John Marks, *The Search for the "Manchurian Candidate:" The CIA and Mind Control: The Secret History of the Behavioral Sciences* (New York: W.W. Norton & Company, 1979) pp. 225–227.

21. Powers, p. 24.

22. Associated Press, "CIA Shielding Of War Criminals Described," The Hartford Courant 7 June 2006: A4.

23. Marks, pp. 5–6.

24. Marks, p. 24.

25. Marks, p. 31.

26. Philip H. Melanson, PhD, *The Robert F. Kennedy Assassination: New Revelations on the Conspiracy and Cover-up, 1968—1991* (New York: Shapolsky Publishers, 1991) p. 215.

27. Marks, p. 10.

28. Marks, p. 96.

29. Melanson, (*RFK*), pp. 208–209.

30. Marks, pp. 129–130.

31. Marks, p. 4.

32. Marks, p. 58.

33. Marks, p. 72n.

34. Marks, pp. 83–88.

35. Marks, p. 91n

36. "Six Veterans Sue Over Experiments," The Hartford Courant 8 Jan. 2009, 3B.

37. Marks, pp. 74–76.

38. Marks, pp. 73, 135.

39. Marks, pp. 157–159.

40. Marks, p. 168.

41. Marks, pp. 225–227.

42. Marks, p. 61.

43. Marks, p. 63.

44. Marks, p. 198.

45. Marks, p. 202.

46. Marks, p. 202.

47. Melanson, *The Robert F. Kennedy Assassination,* pp. 173–174.

48. Marks, p. 154.

49. Marks, p. 203.

50. Marks, p. 210.

51. Marks, p. 204*n.*

52. William W. Turner and Jonn G. Christian, *The Assassination of Robert F. Kennedy: A Searching Look at the Conspiracy and Cover-up 1968–1978* (New York: Random House, 1978) p. 206.

53. Marks, pp. 202–204.

54. Melanson (*RFK*), p. 176.

55. Turner and Christian, p. 208.

56. Marks, pp. 139–140.

57. Marks, p. 146.

58. Marks, p. 143.

59. Marks, p. 140.

60. Marks, pp. 141–142.

61. Marks, pp. 146–150.

62. Marks, p. 149.

63. Marks, p. 227.

64. Powers, pp. 96–97.

65. Powers, p. 99.

66. Powers, p. 98.

67. Richard Helms with William Hood, *A Look Over My Shoulder: A Life in the Central Intelligence Agency* (New York: Random House, 2003), p. 163.

68. Helms, p. 165.

69. Powers, p. 100.

70. Powers, pp. 98–99.

71. Schlesinger, p. 482.

72. David E. Scheim, *Contract on America: The Mafia Murder of President John F. Kennedy* (New York: Shapolsky, 1988), p. 208.

73. Helms, p. 196.

74. Michael O'Brien, *John F. Kennedy: A Biography* (New York: St. Martin's Press, 2005), p. 573.

75. Schlesinger, pp. 772–774.

76. Marks, p. 197.

77. Marks, p. 109.

78. Marks, p. 109.

79. Marks, pp. 108–109.

80. Marks, pp. 210–211.

81. Marks, pp. 216–217.

82. Marks, pp. 226–228.

83. Powers, p. 172.

84. Marks, p. 215.

85. Schlesinger, p. 783.

86. Stanley Karnow, *Vietnam: A History* (New York: Viking, 1983), p. 525.

87. Mahoney, p. 343.

88. Robert Blair Kaiser, *"RFK Must Die!"* (New York: Dutton, 1970), pp. 209–210.

89. Schlesinger, pp. 857–858.

90. Stephen B. Oates, *Let the Trumpet Sound: The Life of Martin Luther King, Jr.* (New York: Harper and Row Publishers, Inc., 1982), p. 429.

91. Powers, pp. 246–249.

92. "Domestic Spying—Again?" editorial, <u>Hartford Courant</u> 20 Nov. 2002: A9.

93. Schlesinger, p. 883.

94. Karnow, p. 525.

95. Karnow, p. 617.

96. Marchetti, p. 225.

97. Turner and Christian, pp. 64–67.

98. Melanson, *The Robert F. Kennedy Assassination,* pp. 256–257, 298–299.

99. H.R. Haldeman with Joseph DiMona, *The Ends of Power* (New York: Times Books, 1978), p. 37.

100. Haldeman, p. 37.

101. Marks, p. 219.

102. Marks, pp. 219–221.

103. Helms, p. 412.

104. Marks, p. 222.

105. Marks, p. 222.

106. Marks, p. 223.

107. Marks, p. 222.

108. Powers, p. 10.

109. Nora Boustany, <u>Washington Post</u>. "A Judge Who Defied a Tyrant," <u>Hartford Courant</u> 23 Oct. 2005, city ed.: A6.

110. Powers, p. 305.

111. Powers, p. 290.

112. Powers, p. 287.

113. Powers, p. 292.

114. George Lardner Jr., "No Closer to Cracking the Kennedy Case," <u>The Washington Post</u> 21 Nov. 2005: A13.

115. Fensterwald, p. 200.

116. Helms, p. 171.

117. Powers, p. 82.

118. Powers, p. 124.

119. Helms, p. 185.

120. Helms, p. 134.

121. George Michael Evica, *And We Are All Mortal: New Evidence and Analysis in the John F. Kennedy Assassination* (West Hartford: University of Hartford, 1978), p. 256.

122. David Talbot, *Brothers: The Hidden Story of the Kennedy Years* (New York: Simon & Schuster, Free Press, 2007), p. 103.

123. Talbot, p. 103.

124. Talbot, p. 197.

125. Helms, pp. 275–276.

126. Turner and Christian, p. 153n.

127. Schlesinger, p. 520.

128. Helms, p. 134.

129. Helms, p. 202.

130. Fensterwald, p. 191.

131. Marks, p. 109n.

132. Marks, p. 109.

133. Helms, p. 286.

134. Fensterwald, p. 452.

135. Fonzi, p. 239.

136. Mark Lane, *Plausible Denial: Was the CIA Involved in the Assassination of JFK?* (New York: Thunder's Mouth Press, 1991), p. 222.

137. Helms, pp. 288–289.

138. Fensterwald, p. 454.

139. Helms, p. 314.

140. Powers, p. 120.

141. Fonzi, p. 283.

142. Fonzi, p. 293.

143. Fonzi, p. 434.

144. Fonzi, p. 144.

145. Harrison Edward Livingstone, *Killing Kennedy and the Hoax of the Century* (New York: Carroll & Graf Publishers, 1995), p. 289.

146. Mark Lane and Dick Gregory, *Code Name "Zorro:" the Murder of Martin Luther King Jr.*(Englewood Cliffs, NJ: Prentice-Hall, Inc., 1977), pp. 302–303.

147. Karnow, p. 616.

148. Helms, p. 338.

149. Karnow, p. 616.

150. Helms, pp. 431–432.

151. Helms, p. 253.

152. Helms, p. 411.

153. Powers, p. 16.

154. Helms, p. 411.

155. Powers, p. 18.

156. Powers, p. 295.

157. Powers, p. 305.

158. Powers, p. 304.

159. Robert D. Hare, PhD, *Without Conscience: The Disturbing World of the Psychopaths Among Us* (New York: The Guilford Press, 1993), p. 33.

160. Edward Jay Epstein, *Legend: The Secret World of Lee Harvey Oswald* (New York: McGraw-Hill, 1978) p. 12.

161. David Talbot, *Brothers: The Hidden History of the Kennedy Years* (New York: Free Press, 2007) pp. 291–292.

162. Hare, p. 59.

163. Hare, pp. 3–4.

164. Hare, p. 34.

165. Powers, p. 35.

166. Hare, p. 44.

167. Hare, p. 49.

168. Hare, p. 162.

169. Hare, p. 62.

170. Hare, p. 68.

171. Hare, pp. 76–80.

172. Hare, p. 92.

173. Hare, p. 104.

174. Hare, p. 109.

175. Hare, p. 109.

176. Martha Stout, PhD, *The Sociopath Next Door* (New York: Broadway Books, 2005), p. 91.

177. Stout, p. 90.

178. Stout, p. 92.

179. Lane (*Plausible Denial*), p. 216.

180. Powers, p. 305.

181. Tom Mangold, *Cold Warrior: James Jesus Angleton: the CIA's Master Spy Hunter* (New York: Touchstone, Simon & Schuster, 1991), p. 31.

182. Mangold, p. 358.

183. Michael Holzman, *James Jesus Angleton, the CIA, & the Craft of Counter-intelligence* (Amherst: University of Massachusetts Press, 2008), p. 9.

184. Mangold, p. 34.

185. Holzman, p. 18.

186. Holzman, p. 28.

187. Holzman, p. 30.

188. Mangold, p. 38.

189. Mangold, p. 41.

190. Mangold, p. 37.

191. Mangold, p. 35.

192. Mangold, p. 34.

193. Mangold, p. 35.

194. Mangold, p. 36.

195. Mangold, p. 39.

196. David C. Martin, *Wilderness of Mirrors* (Guilford, CT: The Lyons Press/ The Globe Pequot Press, 1980), p. 13.

197. Martin, p. 13.

198. Martin, p. 17.

199. Martin, p. 18.

200. Martin, p. 57.

201. Martin, p. 206.

202. Mangold, p. 37.

203. Mangold, p. 44.

204. Mangold, p. 238.

205. Mangold, p. 238.

206. Mangold, pp. 237–238.

207. Mangold, p. 239.

208. *Idaho Statesman* 1 Oct. 2011

209. Holzman, p. 334.

210. Holzman, p. 83.

211. Holzman, p. 94.

212. Mangold, p. 31.

213. Mangold, pp. 42–43.

214. Martin, p. 206.

215. Mangold, p. 24.

216. Mangold, p. 48.

217. Holzman, p. 81.

218. Holzman, p. 95.

219. Holzman, p. 131.

220. Holzman, p. 170.

221. Mangold, p. 50.

222. Martin, p. 215.

223. Holzman, p. 133.

224. Mangold, p. 51, 153.

225. Holzman, p. 72.

226. Mangold, p. 51.

227. Mangold, p. 52.

228. Mangold, p. 53.

229. Holzman, p. 91.

230. Mangold, p. 49.

231. Holzman, p. 136.

232. Mangold, p. 47.

233. Mangold, p. 52.

234. Mangold, p. 50.

235. Mangold, 52.

236. Mangold, p. 53.

237. Mangold, p. 97.

238. Mangold, p. 305.

239. Martin, p. 184.

240. Joan Mellen, *A Farewell to Justice* (Washington, DC: Potomac Books, Inc, 2005), p. 251.

241. Mangold, pp. 66–67.

242. Mangold, p. 69.

243. Holzman, p. 285.

244. Mangold, pp. 278–279.

245. Mangold, p. 158.

246. Mangold, p. 157.

247. Martin, p. 207.

248. Mangold, p. 128.

249. Mangold, p. 330.

250. Mellen, p. 176.

251. Martin, p. 115.

252. Fensterwald, p. 219.

253. Holzman, p. 207.

254. Holzman, p. 319.

255. Martin, p. 68.

256. Martin, p. 70.

257. Holzman, p. 176.

258. Martin, p. 211.

259. Mangold, p. 312.

260. Holzman, p. 239.

261. Marks, p. 202.

262. Marks, p. 202.

263. <u>CNN Presents</u>, CNN, 4 Mar. 2012.

264. Mangold, p. 60.

265. Mangold, p. 247.

266. Martin, p. 218.

267. Holzman, p. 188.

268. Martin, p. 219.

269. Martin, pp. 139–140.

270. Martin, pp. 144–146.

271. Martin, p. 145.

272. Mangold, p. 76.

273. Mangold, p. 58.

274. Marc Schulman, *JFK History Maker: A Fifty-Year Retrospective* (New Rochelle, NY: MultiEducator, Inc., 2011), p. 203.

275. Mangold, p. 132.

276. Mangold, p. 313.

277. Peter Janney, *Mary's Mosaic: The CIA Conspiracy to Murder John F. Kennedy, Mary Pinchot Meyer, and Their Vision for World Peace* (New York: Skyhorse Publishing, 2012), p. 384.

278. Fensterwald, pp. 184–186.

279. Holzman, p. 302.

280. Mangold, p. 162.

281. Mangold, p. 174.

282. Martin, pp. 155–156.

283. Martin, p. 156.

284. Mangold, p. 175.

285. Martin, p. 165.

286. Mangold, p. 178.

287. Mangold, p. 183.

288. Mangold, p. 178.

289. Mangold, p. 190.

290. Mangold, pp. 198–199.

291. Mangold, p. 403.

292. Mangold, p. 204.

293. Mangold, p. 399.

294. Martin, p. 176.

295. Mangold, p. 206.

296. Mangold, p. 97.

297. Mangold, p. 203.

298. Mangold, p. 201.

299. Mangold, p. 206.

300. Fensterwald, p. 185.

301. Janney, p. 70.

302. Benjamin C. Bradlee, *Ben Bradlee: A Good Life: Newspapering and Other Adventures* (New York: Simon & Schuster, 1995), pp. 267–271.

303. Janney, p. 312.

304. Holzman, p. 220.

305. Janney, p. 84.

306. Janney, p. 384.

307. Mangold, p. 244.

308. Mangold, p. 248.

309. Janney, p. 384.

310. Holzman, p. 236.

311. Holzman, pp. 232–233.

312. Mangold, p. 309.

313. Holzman, pp. 241–242.

314. Martin, p. 70.

315. Holzman, p. 239.

316. Mangold, p. 309.

317. Martin, p. 216.

318. Mangold, p. 318.

319. Holzman, pp. 292–293.

320. Martin, p. 213.

321. Mangold, p. 313.

322. Mangold, p. 316.

323. Mangold, p. 319.

324. Holzman, pp. 300–301.

325. Mangold, p. 350.

326. Martin, p. 216.

327. Mangold, pp. 353–354.

328. Leonard Mosley, *Dulles: A Biography of Eleanor, Allen, and John Foster Dulles and Their Family Network* (New York: The Dial Press/James Wade, 1978), pp. 325–327.

329. Marchetti and Marks, p. 26.

330. Powers, p. 85.

331. Helms, p. 118.

332. Powers, p. 86.

333. Mosley, p. 347.

334. Helms, p. 119.

335. N.C. Aizenman, "Guatemalan 'Social Cleansing' Unchecked," <u>The Hartford Courant</u> 27 Feb. 2006: A2.

336. Powers, p. 90.

337. Marchetti and Marks, p. 29.

338. Powers, p. 91.

339. Marchetti and Marks, p. 114.

340. Mahoney, p. 66.

341. Mosley, p. 462.

342. Helms, p. 168.

343. Powers, p. 146.

344. Fensterwald, p. 206.

345. Karl Evanzz, *The Judas Factor: The Plot to Kill Malcolm X* (New York: Thunder's Mouth Press, 1992), p. 109.

346. Powers, p. 340.

347. Mahoney, p. 93.

348. Marchetti and Marks, p. 34.

349. Mosley, p. 466.

350. Mahoney, p. 108

351. Peter Dale Scott, *Deep Politics and the Death of JFK* (Berkeley: University of California Press, 1993), p. 173.

352. Mahoney, p. 67.

353. Powers, p. 148.

354. Mahoney, p. 67.

355. Mahoney, p. 47.

356. Schlesinger, p. 487.

357. Talbot, p. 48.

358. Jim Marrs, *Crossfire: The Plot that Killed Kennedy* (New York: Carroll and Graf Publishers, Inc., 1989), p. 141.

359. Schlesinger, p. 530.

360. Mahoney, p. 216.

361. Powers, p. 147.

362. Fonzi, p. 334.

363. Powers, pp. 148–152.

364. Fensterwald, p. 515.

365. Helms, pp. 196–200.

366. Schlesinger, p. 531.

367. Fensterwald, p. 189.

368. Mahoney, p. 265.

369. Schlesinger, p. 529–530.

370. Mahoney, p. 287.

371. Schlesinger, p. 594–5.

372. Schlesinger, p. 599.

373. Talbot, p. 94.

374. Talbot, pp. 275–276.

375. Talbot, p. 88.

376. Powers, p. 146.

377. Schlesinger, p. 528.

378. Fonzi, p. 373.

379. Fensterwald, p. 32.

380. Powers, p. 128.

381. Powers, p. 130.

382. Helms, p. 310.

383. Mahoney, p. 279.

384. Powers, p. 135.

385. Schlesinger, pp. 756–759.

386. Karnow, p. 298.

387. Karnow, p. 378.

388. Schlesinger, p. 758.

389. Powers, p. 183.

390. Powers, p. 163.

391. Schlesinger, p. 778.

392. Schlesinger, p. 765.

393. Scott, p. 24.

394. Schlesinger, p. 767.

395. Schlesinger, p. 771.

396. Karnow, p. 298.

397. Karnow, p. 319.

398. Schlesinger, p. 775.

399. Karnow, p. 307.

400. Karnow, p. 304.

401. Karnow, p. 315.

402. Schlesinger, p. 771.

403. Schlesinger, p. 778.

404. Karnow, p. 310.

405. Karnow, pp. 325–326.

406. Karnow, p. 326.

407. Karnow, p. 311.

408. Fonzi, p. 70.

409. Fensterwald, p. 527.

410. Tim Weiner, "Obituary: E. Howard Hunt, Watergate figure who jolted Nixon presidency," *International Herald Tribune* 24 Jan. 2007 http://www.iht.com

411. James H. Fetzer, PhD (editor), *Murder in Dealey Plaza* (Chicago: Catfeet, 2000), p. 298.

412. Harrison Edward Livingstone and Robert J. Groden, *High Treason: the Assassination of JFK and the Case for Conspiracy* (New York: Carroll & Graf, 1998), pp. 110–126.

413. Jim Marrs, *Crossfire: The Plot that Killed Kennedy* (New York: Carroll & Graf, 1989), p. 11.

414. Josiah Thompson, *Six Seconds in Dallas: A Micro-Study of the Kennedy Assassination* (New York: published by Bernard Geis Associates, distributed by Random House, 1967), p. 24.

415. Edward Jay Epstein, *Inquest: The Warren Commission and the Establishment of Truth* (New York: The Viking Press, 1966), p. 46.

416. David Talbot, *Brothers: The Hidden History of the Kennedy Years* (New York: Free Press, 2007), p. 282.

417. Philip H. Melanson, *Spy Saga: Lee Harvey Oswald and US Intelligence* (New York: Praeger, 1990), p. 144.

418. Sylvia Meagher, *Accessories After the Fact: the Warren Commission, the Authorities, and the Report* (New York: Vintage Books, Random House, 1967), p. 269.

419. Edward Jay Epstein, *Legend: The Secret World of Lee Harvey Oswald* (New York: McGraw-Hill, 1978), p. 190.

420. Melanson, *Spy Saga*, pp. 137–138.

421. Meagher, p. 54.

422. Meagher, p. 232.

423. Michael Benson, *Who's Who in the JFK Assassination* (New York: Citadel Press, Kensington Publishing, 1993), p. 329.

424. Epstein, *Legend*, p. 60.

425. Melanson, *Spy Saga*, pp. 41–43.

426. Bernard Fensterwald Jr., director, The Committee to Investigate Assassinations, *Coincidence or Conspiracy?* (New York: Kensington Publishing, 1977), p. 298.

427. Melanson, *Spy Saga*, pp. 40–41.

428. Melanson, *Spy Saga*, p. 34.

429. Melanson, *Spy Saga*, pp. 39–41.

430. Benson, p. 136.

431. Benson, pp. 132–133.

432. Melanson, *Spy Saga*, p. 51.

433. Benson, p. 137.

434. Epstein, *Legend*, p. 62

435. Meagher, p. 244.

436. Epstein, *Legend*, p. 69.

437. Epstein, *Legend*, p. 73.

438. Fetzer, p. 42.

439. Meagher, pp. 107–109.

440. Epstein, *Legend*, p. 64.

441. Epstein, *Legend*, p. 86.

442. Livingstone and Groden, pp. 163–164.

443. Melanson, *Spy Saga*, p. 12.

444. Livingstone and Groden, pp. 139 and 163.

445. Fetzer, p. 363.

446. Melanson, *Spy Saga*, p. 9.

447. Melanson, *Spy Saga*, p. 25.

448. Epstein, *Legend*, pp. 77–80.

449. Benson, p. 63.

450. Epstein, *Legend*, p. 71.

451. Marrs, p. 105.

452. Epstein, *Legend*, p. 72.

453. Epstein, *Legend*, p. 79.

454. Epstein, *Legend*, p. 84.

455. Melanson, *Spy Saga*, p. 11.

456. Marrs, pp. 110–111.

457. Joan Mellen, *A Farewell to Justice: Jim Garrison, JFK's Assassination, and the Case That Should Have Changed History* (Potomac Books, Inc., 2005), p. 176.

458. Melanson, *Spy Saga*, p. 25.

459. Melanson, *Spy Saga*, p. 12.

460. Melanson, *Spy Saga*, p. 25.

461. Epstein, *Legend*, pp. 89–91.

462. Epstein, *Legend*, p. 92.

463. Melanson, *Spy Saga*, p. 13.

464. Epstein, *Legend*, p. 94.

465. Melanson, *Spy Saga*, p. 133.

466. Melanson, Spy *Saga*, p. 100.

467. F. Peter Model and Robert J. Groden, *JFK: The Case for Conspiracy* (New York: Manor Books, 1976), p. 177.

468. Walt Brown, *Treachery in Dallas* (New York: Carroll & Graf Publishers, 1995), p. 312.

469. Model and Groden, p. 188.

470. Epstein, *Legend*, pp. 94–96.

471. Melanson, *Spy Saga*, p. 14.

472. Epstein, *Legend,* pp. 95–96.

473. Epstein, *Legend,* p. 96.

474. Epstein, *Legend,* p. 96.

475. Epstein, *Legend,* pp. 99–101.

476. Mark Lane, *Plausible Denial: Was the CIA Involved in the Assassination of JFK?* (New York: Thurnder's Mouth Press, 1991), pp. 68–69.

477. Epstein, *Legend,* p. 106.

478. Epstein, *Legend,* p. 295.

479. Melanson, *Spy Saga,* pp. 138–139.

480. Epstein, *Legend,* p. 103.

481. Epstein, *Legend,* p. 103.

482. Epstein, *Legend,* p. 103.

483. Epstein, *Legend,* p. 103.

484. Epstein, *Legend,* pp. 107–108.

485. Melanson, *Spy Saga,* p. 138.

486. Epstein, *Legend,* p. 150.

487. Epstein, *Legend,* p. 109.

488. Epstein, *Legend,* pp. 144–145.

489. Melanson, *Spy Saga,* p. 18.

490. Epstein, *Legend,* p. 108.

491. Epstein, *Legend,* p. 109.

492. Epstein, *Legend,* p. 196.

493. Epstein, *Legend,* p. 112.

494. Marrs, p. 126.

495. Epstein, *Legend,* p. 136.

496. Epstein, *Legend,* p. 149.

497. Fensterwald, p. 220.

498. Fensterwald, pp. 220–221.

499. Meagher, p. 346.

500. Mellen, p. 166.

501. Model and Groden, p. 187.

502. Model and Groden, p. 188.

503. Melanson, *Spy Saga*, p. 22.

504. F. Peter Model and Robert J. Groden, *JFK: The Case for Conspiracy* (Manor Books, 1976), p. 188.

505. Meagher, pp. 336–341.

506. Meagher, p. 343.

507. Epstein, *Legend*, pp. 158, 166.

508. Epstein, *Legend*, p. 165.

509. Melanson, *Spy Saga*, p. 107.

510. Mellen, p. 166.

511. Melanson, *Spy Saga*, p. 55.

512. Melanson, *Spy Saga*, p. 46.

513. Melanson, *Spy Saga*, p. 47.

514. Melanson, *Spy Saga*, p. 60.

515. Melanson, *Spy Saga*, pp. 89–90.

516. Melanson, *Spy Saga*, pp. 80–81.

517. Melanson, *Spy Saga*, p. 78.

518. Gaeton Fonzi, *The Last Investigation* (New York: Thurder's Mouth Press, 1993), p. 191.

519. Melanson, *Spy Saga*, p. 89.

520. Fonzi, p. 31.

521. Melanson, *Spy Saga*, p. 77.

522. Epstein, *Legend*, pp. 180–181.

523. Melanson, *Spy Saga*, pp. 76, 79.

524. Epstein, *Legend*, p. 190.

525. Melanson, *Spy Saga*, p. 79.

526. Fensterwald, p. 213.

527. Epstein, *Legend*, pp. 203–206.

528. Epstein, *Legend*, p. 197.

529. Epstein, *Legend*, p. 205.

530. Melanson, *Spy Saga*, p. 80.

531. Epstein, *Legend*, pp. 189, 316.

532. Melanson, *Spy Saga*, p. 82.

533. Epstein, *Legend*, p. 190.

534. Arthur M. Schlesinger Jr., *A Thousand Days, John F. Kennedy in the White House* (New York: Black Dog & Leventhal Publishers, 2005), p. 293.

535. Epstein, *Legend*, p. 316.

536. Epstein, *Legend*, p. 199.

537. Melanson, *Spy Saga*, p. 81.

538. Epstein, *Legend*, p. 203.

539. Meagher, p. 183.

540. Epstein, *Legend*, pp. 194–195.

541. Melanson, *Spy Saga*, pp. 82–84.

542. Lane, *Rush to Judgment*, p. 311.

543. Philip H. Melanson, *The Robert F. Kennedy Assassination: New Revelations on the Conspiracy and Cover-up* (New York: Shapolsky Publishers, Inc., 1991), pp. 183–184.

544. Melanson, *The Robert F. Kennedy Assassination*, p. 200.

545. Epstein, *Legend*, p. 203.

546. Epstein, *Legend*, p. 214.

547. Epstein, *Legend*, p. 184.

548. Epstein, *Legend*, p. 207.

549. Epstein, *Legend*, p. 203.

550. Melanson, *Spy Saga*, p. 58.

551. George Michael Evica, *And We Are All Mortal: New Evidence and Analysis in the John F. Kennedy Assassination* (West Hartford: University of Hartford, 1978), p. 6.

552. Fensterwald, pp. 414–415.

553. Meagher, p. 199.

554. Meagher, p. 184.

555. Melanson, *Spy Saga*, p. 58.

556. Evica, p. 6.

557. Melanson, *Spy Saga*, pp. 121–122.

558. Melanson, *Spy Saga*, p. 83.

559. Fetzer, p. 369.

560. Melanson, *Spy Saga*, p. 118.

561. Melanson, *Spy Saga*, p. 118.

562. Meagher, p. 208.

563. Meagher, pp. 200–201.

564. Melanson, *Spy Saga*, p. 83.

565. Meagher, pp. 202–204.

566. Meagher, pp. 205–206.

567. Meagher, p. 215.

568. Epstein, *Legend*, p. 209.

569. Melanson, *Spy Saga*, p. 86.

570. Melanson, *Spy Saga*, pp. 86–88.

571. Meagher, p. 283.

572. Meagher, pp. 288–290.

573. Meagher, p. 283.

574. Meagher, p. 290.

575. Meagher, p. 287.

576. Meagher, p. 63.

577. Talbot, p. 71.

578. Talbot, p. 77.

579. Talbot, p. 74.

580. Talbot, p. 153.

581. Talbot, p. 158.

582. Meagher, pp. 128–130.

583. Meagher, pp. 286–287.

584. Meagher, p. 287.

585. Epstein, *Inquest*, p. 136.

586. Meagher, p. 241.

587. Epstein, *Inquest*, p. 136.

588. Meagher, p. 320.

589. Meagher, p. 321.

590. Meagher, p. 291.

591. Melanson, *Spy Saga*, p. 74.

592. Melanson, *Spy Saga*, p. 86.

593. Meagher, p. 93.

594. Meagher, p. 220.

595. Melanson, *Spy Saga*, p. 61.

596. Meagher, p. 221.

597. Melanson, *Spy Saga*, p. 73.

598. Melanson, *Spy Saga*, p. 74.

599. Epstein, *Legend*, p. 214.

600. Melanson, *Spy Saga*, p. 79.

601. Fonzi, p. 192.

602. Melanson, *Spy Saga*, p. 90.

603. Livingstone and Groden, *High Treason*, p. 113.

604. Mahoney, 228.

605. Epstein, *Legend*, pp. 216–217.

606. Melanson, *Spy Saga*, p. 86.

607. Fensterwald, pp. 218–219.

608. Melanson, *Spy Saga*, p. 34.

609. Melanson, *Spy Saga*, p. 37.

610. Mellen, p. 132.

611. Livingstone and Groden, p. 251.

612. Lane, *Plausible Denial*, p. 224.

613. Livingstone and Groden, p. 161.

614. Talbot, p. 334.

615. Melanson, *Spy Saga*, pp. 33–34.

616. Melanson, *Spy Saga*, p. 36.

617. Richard D. Mahoney, *Sons & Brothers: The Days of Jack and Bobby Kennedy* (New York: Arcade Publishing, 1999), p. 229.

618. Melanson, *Spy Saga*, pp. 40–43.

619. Mahoney, p. 270.

620. Melanson, *Spy Saga*, p. 93.

621. Melanson, *Spy Saga*, p. 29.

622. Epstein, *Legend*, p. 218.

623. Melanson, *Spy Saga*, p. 32.

624. Epstein, *Legend*, p. 218.

625. Melanson, *Spy Saga*, p. 51.

626. Melanson, *Spy Saga*, p. 63.

627. Fensterwald, p. 38.

628. Meagher, p. 234.

629. Melanson, *Spy Saga*, p. 62.

630. Epstein, *Legend*, p. 219.

631. Melanson, *Spy Saga*, pp. 63–64.

632. Melanson, *Spy Saga*, p. 63.

633. Epstein, *Legend*, p. 221.

634. Melanson, *Spy Saga*, pp. 86–87.

635. Melanson, *Spy Saga*, p. 87.

636. Melanson, *Spy Saga*, p. 87.

637. Epstein, *Legend*, p. 222.

638. Melanson, *Spy Saga*, p. 64.

639. Epstein, *Legend*, p. 224.

640. Melanson, *Spy Saga*, pp. 65–66.

641. Epstein, *Legend*, p. 226.

642. Epstein, *Legend*, pp. 227–229.

643. Melanson, *Spy Saga*, pp. 44–45.

644. Melanson, *Spy Saga*, p. 49.

645. Melanson, *Spy Saga*, p. 39.

646. Turner and Christian, p. 207.

647. Fonzi, p. 408.

648. Lane, *Plausible Denial*, p. 78.

649. Fonzi, p. 421.

650. Melanson, *Spy Saga*, p. 181.

651. Fonzi, pp. 264–265.

652. Fonzi, p. 409.

653. Talbot, p. 389.

654. Fensterwald, p. 487.

655. Fensterwald, pp. 488–489.

656. Mahoney, p. 273.

657. Meagher, p. 232.

658. Benson, p. 354.

659. James W. Douglass, *JFK and the Unspeakable: Why He Died and Why It Matters* (Maryknoll, NY: Orbis Books, 2008), page 168.

660. Fensterwald, p. 388.

661. Fonzi, p. 111.

662. Meagher, p. 380.

663. Fensterwald, p. 388.

664. Fonzi, p. 110.

665. Fonzi, pp. 110–112.

666. Fonzi, p. 113.

667. Epstein, *Legend*, p. 234.

668. Fensterwald, p. 388.

669. Meagher, p. 379.

670. Epstein, *Legend*, p. 234

671. Fonzi, p. 113.

672. Fensterwald, p. 388.

673. Meagher, p. 377.

674. Fonzi, p. 109.

675. Meagher, p. 377.

676. Fonzi, p. 114.

677. Fonzi, p. 116.

678. Talbot, p. 383.

679. Fonzi, pp. 278–280.

680. Fonzi, p. 295.

681. Fonzi, p. 281.

682. Meagher, p. 381.

683. Fonzi, p. 281.

684. Melanson, *Spy Saga*, pp. 94–96.

685. Fonzi, pp. 281–282.

686. Fonzi, p. 282.

687. Melanson, *Spy Saga*, p. 102.

688. Epstein, *Legend*, pp. 237–238.

689. Fonzi, p. 283.

690. Melanson, *Spy Saga*, p. 97.

691. Fensterwald, p. 395.

692. Fonzi, p. 288.

693. Fonzi, p. 288.

694. Melanson, *Spy Saga*, p. 98.

695. Melanson, *Spy Saga*, pp. 95–96.

696. Fonzi, pp. 283–284.

697. Melanson, *Spy Saga*, pp. 99–100.

698. Meagher, pp. 227–228.

699. Peter Dale Scott, *Deep Politics and the Death of JFK* (Berkeley, California: University of California Press, 1993), pp. 41–42.

700. Evica, p. 141.

701. Melanson, *Spy Saga*, p. 100.

702. Melanson, *Spy Saga*, p. 103.

703. Fonzi, p. 285.

704. Melanson, *Spy Saga*, p. 101.

705. Fonzi, p. 294.

706. Talbot, p. 385.

707. Talbot, p. 387.

708. Scott, p. 173.

709. Mahoney, p. 273.

710. Melanson, *Spy Saga*, p. 124.

711. Melanson, *Spy Saga*, p. 152.

712. Epstein, *Legend*, p. 239.

713. Meagher, pp. 196–197.

714. David E. Scheim, *Contract on America: The Mafia Murder of President John F. Kennedy* (New York: Kensington Publishing Corp., 1988), pp. 52–53.

715. Marrs, p. 40.

716. Marrs, p. 41.

717. Epstein, *Legend*, p. 239

718. Meagher, p. 230.

719. Fensterwald, p. 562.

720. Meagher, p. 243.

721. Fensterwald, p. 563.

722. Melanson, *Spy Saga*, p. 57.

723. Melanson, *Spy Saga*, p. 57.

724. Meagher, pp. 365–366.

725. Fonzi, p. 423.

726. Fensterwald, p. 254.

727. Meagher, pp. 213–216.

728. Benson, p. 198.

729. Fensterwald, p. 18.

730. Fensterwald, p. 411.

731. Fensterwald, p. 254.

732. Epstein, *Legend*, p. 246.

733. Fensterwald, p. 255.

734. Lane, *Plausible Denial*, p. 78.

735. Fensterwald, pp. 392–393.

736. Meagher, pp. 370–371.

737. Talbot, p. 272

738. Talbot, pp. 271–272.

739. Schlesinger, *A Thousand Days*, pp. 354–355.

740. Schlesinger, *A Thousand Days*, p. 354.

741. Schlesinger, *A Thousand Days*, p. 356.

742. Schlesinger, *A Thousand Days*, p. 356.

743. Meagher, p. 269.

744. Livingstone and Groden, *High Treason*, p. 251.

745. Marrs, p. 410.

746. Fensterwald, p. 563.

747. Benson, p. 72.

748. Benson, p. 85.

749. Marrs, p. 406.

750. Marrs, p. 406.

751. Benson, p. 324.

752. Marrs, p. 406.

753. Marrs, p. 404.

754. Marrs, p. 406.

755. Fensterwald, p. 563.

756. Mark Lane, *Rush to Judgment: A Critique of the Warren Commission's Inquiry into the Murders of President John F. Kennedy, Office J.D. Tippit and Lee Harvey Oswald* (New York: Holt, Rinehart & Winston, 1966), pp. 142–144.

757. Lane, *Rush to Judgment*, p. 146.

758. Meagher, p. 46.

759. Meagher, p. 234.

760. Lane, *Plausible Denial*, p. 343.

761. Talbot, p. 389.

762. Meagher, p. 36n.

763. Meagher, p. 37.

764. Meagher, p. 18n

765. Josiah Thompson, *Six Seconds in Dallas: A Micro-Study of the Kennedy Assassination* (New York: published by Bernard Geis Associates, distributed by Random House, 1967), pp. 116–117.

766. Livingstone and Groden, p. 116.

767. Thompson, pp. 236–237.

768. Thompson, p. 180.

769. Meagher, pp. 225–226.

770. Thompson, p. 235.

771. Thompson, p. 136.

772. Thompson, p. 245.

773. Thompson, p. 181.

774. Thompson, p. 135.

775. Epstein, *Inquest*, p. 135.

776. Meagher, p. 68.

777. Meagher, p. 68.

778. Thompson, p. 234.

779. Lane, *Plausible Denial*, p. 342.

780. Benson, p. 491.

781. Marrs, p. 65.

782. Thompson, p. 4.

783. *Report of the Warren Commission on the Assassination of President Kennedy, The New York Times Edition* (New York: McGraw-Hill Book Company, 1964), pp. 58–60.

784. Thompson, p. 192.

785. Benson, p. 184.

786. Meagher, pp. 71–72.

787. Meagher, p. 72.

788. Meagher, p. 26.

789. Meagher, p. 25.

790. Meagher, p. 25.

791. Meagher, p. 26.

792. Meagher, p. 25.

793. Thompson, p. 118.

794. Thompson, p. 233.

795. Epstein, *Inquest,* pp. 117–118.

796. Fensterwald, p. 549.

797. Warren Commission, p. 38.

798. Thompson, p. 137.

799. Thompson, p. 39.

800. Thompson, p. 48.

801. Thompson, p. 43.

802. Thompson, p. 45.

803. Thompson, pp. 70–71.

804. Thompson, p. 147.

805. Thompson, p. 130.

806. Thompson, p. 109.

807. Thompson, p. 94.

808. Thompson, p. 126.

809. Thompson, p. 106.

810. Thompson, p. 107.

811. Thompson, p. 107.

812. Thompson, p. 107.

813. Thompson, p. 52.

814. Thompson, p. 230.

815. Thompson, p. 25.

816. Lee, Henry C. Personal interview, Oct. 27, 2008.

817. Meagher, p. 76.

818. Meagher, p. 81.

819. Meagher, p. 83.

820. Lane, *Rush to Judgment*, p. 168.

821. Crenshaw, pp. 96–97.

822. Talbot, p. 283.

823. Fonzi, p. 17.

824. Lane, *Rush to Judgment*, pp. 264–265.

825. Lane, *Rush to Judgment*, p. 168.

826. Marrs, p. 344.

827. Lane, *Rush to Judgment*, p. 177.

828. *Report of the Warren Commission on the Assassination of President Kennedy, the New York Times Edition*, p. 164.

829. Marrs, pp. 347–348.

830. Lane, *Rush to Judgment*, pp. 171–172.

831. *Report of the Warren Commission on the Assassination of President Kennedy, the New York Times Edition*, p. 156.

832. Lane, *Rush to Judgment*, pp. 192–193.

833. Marrs, p. 341.

834. *Report of the Warren Commission on the Assassination of President Kennedy, the New York Times Edition*, p. 156.

835. Epstein, *Inquest*, p. 134.

836. Lane, *Rush to Judgment*, p. 192.

837. Lane, *Rush to Judgment*, p. 186.

838. Lane, *Rush to Judgment*, p. 180.

839. Fensterwald, p. 560.

840. Epstein, *Inquest*, p. 134.

841. Epstein, *Inquest*, p. 135.

842. *Report of the Warren Commission on the Assassination of President Kennedy, the New York Times Edition*, p. 161.

843. Meagher, p. 258.

844. *Report of the Warren Commission on the Assassination of President Kennedy, the New York Times Edition*, p. 160.

845. Marrs, p. 345.

846. Fetzer, p. 79.

847. Fetzer, p. 79.

848. Lamar Waldron and Thom Hartmann, *Legacy of Secrecy: The Long Shadow of the JFK Assassination* (Berkeley: Counterpoint, 2008), p. 125.

849. Lane, *Rush to Judgment*, p. 251.

850. Lane, *Rush to Judgment*, p. 83.

851. Epstein, *Inquest*, p. 135.

852. Lane, *Rush to Judgment*, p. 99

853. Waldron and Hartmann, *Ultimate Sacrifice*, p. 728.

854. Meagher, pp. 86–87.

855. Model and Groden, p. 276.

856. Waldron and Hartmann, *Ultimate Sacrifice*, p. 729.

857. Fensterwald, p. 429.

858. *Report of the Warren Commission on the Assassination of President Kennedy, the New York Times Edition*, pp. 235–236.

859. *Report of the Warren Commission on the Assassination of President Kennedy, the New York Times Edition*, p. 154.

860. *Report of the Warren Commission on the Assassination of President Kennedy, the New York Times Edition*, p. 236.

861. Douglass, p. 292.

862. Waldron and Hartmann, *Ultimate Sacrifice*, p. 732.

863. Benson, p. 81.

864. Fensterwald, p. 559.

865. Marrs, p. 342.

866. Waldron and Hartmann, *Ultimate Sacrifice*, p. 733.

867. Fetzer, p. 72.

868. Lane, *Rush to Judgment*, p. 200.

869. Lane, *Rush to Judgment*, p. 169.

870. Lane, *Rush to Judgment*, p. 202.

871. Lane, *Rush to Judgment*, p. 203.

872. Lane, *Rush to Judgment*, p. 194.

873. Waldron and Hartmann, *Ultimate Sacrifice*, p. 733.

874. Meagher, p. 299.

875. Benson, p. 402.

876. Lane, *Rush to Judgment*, p. 279.

877. Fensterwald, p. 576.

878. Fensterwald, p. 577.

879. Lane, *Rush to Judgment*, p. 282.

880. Lane, *Rush to Judgment*, p. 188.

881. Crenshaw, p. 102.

882. Melanson, *The Robert F. Kennedy Assassination: New Revelations on the Conspiracy and Cover-up*, p. 190.

883. *Report of the Warren Commission on the Assassination of President Kennedy, the New York Times Edition*, pp. 164–165.

884. *Report of the Warren Commission on the Assassination of President Kennedy, the New York Times Edition*, pp. 165–166.

885. *Report of the Warren Commission on the Assassination of President Kennedy, the New York Times Edition*, p. 167.

886. Lane, *Plausible Denial*, p. 353.

887. Model and Groden, pp. 277–278.

888. Waldron and Hartmann, *Legacy of Secrecy*, p. 104.

889. Waldron and Hartmann, *Legacy of Secrecy*, p. 106.

890. Waldron and Hartmann, *Legacy of Secrecy*, p. 190.

891. Fetzer, p. 116.

892. Lane, *Rush to Judgment*, p. 81

893. John H. Davis, *Mafia Kingfish: Carlos Marcello and the Assassination of John F. Kennedy* (New York: Penguin Books, 1989), p. 210.

894. *Report of the Warren Commission on the Assassination of President Kennedy, the New York Times Edition*, p. 167.

895. Lane, *Plausible Denial*, p. 353.

896. Douglass, pp. 273–274.

897. Melanson, *Spy Saga*, p. 15.

898. Melanson, *Spy Saga*, p. 39.

899. Waldron and Hartmann, *Legacy of Secrecy*, p. 191.

900. Lane, *Plausible Denial*, p. 15.

901. Lane, *Plausible Denial*, p. 352.

902. Fensterwald, pp. 50–51.

903. Benson, p. 96.

904. Meagher, p. 236.

905. Meagher, p. 245.

906. Fetzer, p. 116.

907. *Report of the Warren Commission on the Assassination of President Kennedy, the New York Times Edition*, p. 184.

908. Davis, p. 226.

909. Davis, p. 228.

910. Meagher, p. 422.

911. *Report of the Warren Commission on the Assassination of President Kennedy, the New York Times Edition*, p. 203.

912. Meagher, p. 404.

913. Livingstone and Groden, *High Treason*, p. 202.

914. *Report of the Warren Commission on the Assassination of President Kennedy, the New York Times Edition*, p. 199.

915. *Report of the Warren Commission on the Assassination of President Kennedy, the New York Times Edition*, p. 201.

916. Associated Press, "Ike Pappas dies; reported Oswald shooting live on air," Waterbury Republican-American 3 Sept 2008, 5B.

917. *Report of the Warren Commission on the Assassination of President Kennedy, the New York Times Edition*, p. 201.

918. Associated Press, "Ike Pappas dies; reported Oswald shooting live on air," Waterbury Republican-American 3 Sept 2008, 5B.

919. Crenshaw, pp. 189–190.

920. Epstein, *Legend*, p. 254.

921. Marrs, p. 550.

922. Edward Klein, *The Kennedy Curse: Why America's First Family Has Been Haunted By Tragedy For 150 Years* (New York: St. Martin's Press, 2003), 220.

923. Schlesinger, p. 660.

924. Schlesinger, p. 718.

925. Brown, p. 177.

926. Fensterwald, p. 66.

927. Lane, *Rush to Judgment*, p. 284.

928. Matthew Smith, *Conspiracy: The Plot to Stop the Kennedys* (New York: Kensington Publishing Corp., 2005), pp. 99–100.

929. Smith, p. 98.

930. Marrs, p. 424.

931. Marrs, p. 426.

932. Marrs, pp. 431–432.

933. Melanson, *Spy Saga*, p. 80.

934. Talbot, pp. 273, 275.

935. Talbot, pp. 273–274.

936. Crenshaw, pp. 202–203.

937. Joling, Robert J. Personal interview. 28 August 2002, University of New Haven, West Haven, CT.

938. Turner and Christian, pp. 176–177.

939. Turner and Christian, pp. 199–200.

940. Turner and Christian, p. 200.

941. "Robert F. Kennedy's Assassin Transferred," <u>Waterbury (CT) Republican-American</u> 3 Nov. 2009: 4A.

942. David Talbot, *Brothers: the Hidden History of the Kennedy Years* (New York: Free Press, a division of Simon & Schuster, Inc., 2007), p. 281.

943. Talbot, p. 325.

944. Talbot, p. 325.

945. Talbot, p. 329.

946. Talbot, p. 330.

947. Talbot, p. 338.

948. Talbot, p. 346.

949. John Marks, *The Search for the "Manchurian Candidate:" The CIA and Mind Control: The Secret History of the Behavioral Sciences* (New York: W.W. Norton, 1979), pp. 173, 202–205.

950. William L. O'Neill, volume editor, and Kenneth T. Jackson, series editor in chief, *The Scribner Encyclopedia of American Lives, the 1960s, Vol. 2* (New York: Charles Scribner's Sons, 2003), p. 383.

951. Robert Blair Kaiser, *"R.F.K. Must Die!"* (New York: E.P. Dutton, 1970), p.121.

952. Kaiser, p. 202.

953. Klaber and Melanson, p. 180.

954. Kaiser, p. 203.

955. Kaiser, p. 204.

956. Kaiser, p. 204.

957. Kaiser, p. 103.

958. Robert A. Houghton and Theodore Taylor, *Special Unit Senator: the Investigation of the Assassination of Senator Robert F. Kennedy* (New York: Random House, 1970), p. 163.

959. Kaiser, p.197.

960. Kaiser, p. 97.

961. Kaiser, p. 87.

962. Kaiser, p. 142.

963. Houghton, p. 162.

964. Kaiser, p. 417.

965. Kaiser, pp. 545, 549.

966. Philip H. Melanson, PhD, *The Robert F. Kennedy Assassination: New Revelations on the Conspiracy and Cover-up, 1968–1991* (New York: Shapolsky Publishers, 1991), p. 271.

967. Kaiser, p. 111.

968. Kaiser, p. 227.

969. Kaiser, p. 111.

970. Melanson, *The Robert F. Kennedy Assassination* (*hereafter RFK*), p. 155.

971. Melanson, *RFK,* pp. 292–295.

972. Melanson, *RFK,* p. 291.

973. Melanson, *RFK,* p. 291.

974. Melanson, *RFK,* p. 290.

975. Kaiser, p. 209.

976. Kaiser, p. 202.

977. David E. Scheim, *Contract on America: The Mafia Murder of President John F. Kennedy* (New York: Shapolsky, 1988), pp. 321–323.

978. Schlesinger, pp. 283–286.

979. Mahoney, p. 74.

980. Mahoney, p. 193.

981. Mahoney, pp. 351–352.

982. John H. Davis, *Mafia Kingfish: Carlos Marcello and the Assassination of John F. Kennedy* (New York: McGraw-Hill, 1989), p. 393.

983. Davis, pp. 391–395.

984. Melanson, *RFK,* p. 271.

985. William W. Turner and Jonn G. Christian, *The Assassination of Robert F. Kennedy: A Searching Look at the Conspiracy and Cover-up, 1968–1978* (New York: Random House, 1978), p. 220.

986. Davis, p. 392.

987. Turner and Christian, p. 220.

988. Klaber and Melanson, p. 115.

989. Kaiser, p. 233.

990. Kaiser, pp. 209, 586–587.

991. Kaiser, p. 207.

992. Turner and Christian, p. 221.

993. Kaiser, p. 276.

994. Kaiser, p. 190.

995. Kaiser, pp. 207–208.

996. Kaiser, p. 208

997. Kaiser, p. 191.

998. Kaiser, p. 209.

999. William Klaber and Philip H. Melanson, *Shadow Play, The Murder of Robert F. Kennedy, the Trial of Sirhan Sirhan, and the Failure of American Justice* (New York: St. Martin's Press, 1997), pp. 17, 182.

1000. Kaiser, p. 209.

1001. Kaiser, p. 286.

1002. Turner and Christian, p. 225.

1003. Turner and Christian, p. 224.

1004. Turner and Christian, p. 224.

1005. Kaiser, p. 212.

1006. Arthur M. Schlesinger Jr., *Robert Kennedy and His Times* (New York: Random House, 1978), p. 859.

1007. Schlesinger, p. 783.

1008. Stanley Karnow, *Vietnam, a History* (New York: Viking, 1983), p. 524.

1009. Karnow, pp. 336–337.

1010. Schlesinger, p. 161.

1011. Kaiser, p. 214.

1012. Kaiser, p. 214.

1013. Schlesinger, p. 883.

1014. *Washington Post,* 22 October 1967

1015. Melanson, *RFK,* p. 291.

1016. Schlesinger, p. 887.

1017. Schlesinger, pp. 209, 890.

1018. Schlesinger, p. 209.

1019. Schlesinger, p. 895.

1020. Schlesinger, p. 883.

1021. Schlesinger, p. 883.

1022.   Karnow, p. 526.

1023.   Mahoney, p. 344.

1024.   Mahoney, p. 346.

1025.   Mahoney, p. 351.

1026.   Melanson, *RFK*, p. 179.

1027.   Kaiser, p. 292.

1028.   Kaiser, p. 436.

1029.   Kaiser, p. 292.

1030.   Turner and Christian, p. 217.

1031.   Kaiser, p. 191.

1032.   Turner and Christian, p. 224.

1033.   Melanson, *RFK*, p. 201.

1034.   Turner and Christian, p. 224.

1035.   Klaber and Melanson, pp. 161, 184.

1036.   Kaiser, p. 166.

1037.   Marks, p. 197.

1038.   Melanson, *RFK*, pp. 200–201.

1039.   Melanson, *RFK*, pp. 202, 206.

1040.   Turner and Christian, p. 226.

1041.   Turner and Christian, p. 226.

1042.   Melanson, *RFK*, p. 206.

1043.   Turner and Christian, p. 227.

1044.   Turner and Christian, p. 228.

1045.   Melanson, *RFK*, p. 206.

1046.   Turner and Christian, p. 228.

1047.   Turner and Christian, p. 228.

1048.   Turner and Christian, p. 228.

1049.   Turner and Christian, pp. 225–226.

1050.   Turner and Christian, pp. 225–226.

1051. Turner and Christian, p. 207.

1052. F. Lee Bailey and Harvey Aronson, *The Defense Never Rests* (New York: Stein and Day Publishers, 1971), p. 193.

1053. Melanson, *RFK*, p. 205.

1054. Bailey and Aronson, pp. 200–201.

1055. Melanson, *RFK*, p. 208.

1056. Melanson, *RFK*, p. 215.

1057. Melanson, *RFK*, pp. 208–209.

1058. Marks, pp. 144–145.

1059. Marks, p. 204 footnote.

1060. Turner and Christian, p. 204.

1061. Klaber and Melanson, p. 17.

1062. Melanson, *RFK*, p. 159.

1063. Kaiser, p. 392.

1064. Marks, p. 145.

1065. Melanson, *RFK*, p. 207.

1066. William W. Turner and Jonn G. Christian, *The Assassination of Robert F. Kennedy, a Searching Look at the Conspiracy and Cover-up, 1968–1978* (New York: Random House, 1978) p. 220.

1067. Kaiser, p. 573.

1068. Kaiser, p. 569.

1069. Kaiser, p. 548.

1070. Klaber and Melanson, p. 186.

1071. Melanson, *RFK*, p. 209.

1072. Kaiser, p. 568.

1073. Kaiser, p 286.

1074. Melanson, *RFK*, p. 168.

1075. Turner and Christian, pp. 210–211.

1076. Melanson, *RFK*, p. 194.

1077. Kaiser, p. 570.

1078.  Kaiser, pp. 108–109.

1079.  Kaiser, p. 108.

1080.  Turner and Christian, p. 218.

1081.  Turner and Christian, p. 218.

1082.  Melanson, *RFK*, p. 155.

1083.  Kaiser, p. 589.

1084.  Kaiser, p. 121.

1085.  Kaiser, pp. 558, 559, 574.

1086.  Kaiser, p. 574.

1087.  Kaiser, p. 558.

1088.  Kaiser, p. 288.

1089.  Kaiser, pp. 585–586.

1090.  Kaiser, p. 562.

1091.  Kaiser, pp. 545, 549.

1092.  Melanson, *RFK*, p. 178.

1093.  Melanson, *RFK*, p. 235.

1094.  Kaiser, p. 114.

1095.  Kaiser, p. 565.

1096.  Kaiser, p. 324.

1097.  Kaiser, p. 550.

1098.  Kaiser, p. 578.

1099.  Turner and Christian, p. 208.

1100.  Turner and Christian, p. 207.

1101.  Melanson, *RFK*, p. 149.

1102.  Kaiser, p. 550.

1103.  Turner and Christian, p. 207.

1104.  Kaiser, p. 430.

1105.  Turner and Christian, p. 208.

1106.  Turner and Christian, pp. 128, 132.

1107.   Turner and Christian, pp. 128, 132.

1108.   Turner and Christian, pp. 127–132.

1109.   Turner and Christian, p. 130.

1110.   Kaiser, pp. 98–100.

1111.   Turner and Christian, p. 119.

1112.   Turner and Christian, p. 34.

1113.   Turner and Christian, pp. 368–369.

1114.   Turner and Christian, p. 369.

1115.   Kaiser, p. 548.

1116.   Turner and Christian, p. 132.

1117.   Turner and Christian, pp. 135, 138.

1118.   Turner and Christian, p. 366.

1119.   Turner and Christian, p. 97.

1120.   Turner and Christian, p. 133.

1121.   Turner and Christian, p. 12.

1122.   Turner and Christian, p. 133.

1123.   Turner and Christian, p. 133.

1124.   Turner and Christian, p. 139.

1125.   Turner and Christian, p. 14.

1126.   Turner and Christian, p. 129.

1127.   Turner and Christian, p. 128.

1128.   Turner and Christian, p. 150.

1129.   Marks, p. 141.

1130.   Karnow, p. 536.

1131.   Karnow, p. 549.

1132.   Karnow, p. 548.

1133.   Karnow, p. 559.

1134.   Schlesinger, p. 905.

1135.   Karnow, p. 555.

1136. Stuart Television Productions, Part III, *The Life of Robert F. Kennedy*, presented on the Discovery Channel, June 1998.

1137. Schlesinger, p. 905.

1138. Mahoney, p. 345.

1139. Karnow, p. 520.

1140. Karnow, p. 521.

1141. Karnow, p. 522.

1142. Karnow, p. 524.

1143. Karnow, p. 525.

1144. Karnow, p. 525.

1145. Karnow, p. 525.

1146. Karnow, p. 525.

1147. Kaiser, p. 229.

1148. Melanson, *RFK*, p. 180

1149. Melanson, *RFK*, p. 180.

1150. Kaiser, p. 292.

1151. Tuner and Christian, p. 201.

1152. Turner and Christian, p. 201.

1153. Houghton, p. 195.

1154. Turner and Christian, p. 224.

1155. Houghton, pp. 195–196.

1156. Houghton, p. 196.

1157. Houghton, p. 196.

1158. Kaiser, p. 215.

1159. Turner and Christian, p. 217.

1160. Kaiser, p. 286.

1161. Melanson, *RFK*, p. 180.

1162. Kaiser, p. 205.

1163. Turner and Christian, p. 224.

1164. Kaiser, p. 287.

1165. Houghton, p. 69.

1166. Kaiser, p. 215.

1167. Kaiser, p. 98.

1168. Houghton, p. 69.

1169. Houghton, p. 183.

1170. Kaiser, p. 94.

1171. Houghton, p. 175.

1172. Houghton, p. 175.

1173. Melanson, *RFK*, p. 162.

1174. Mahoney, p. 346.

1175. Mahoney, p. 347.

1176. Mahoney, p. 348.

1177. Mahoney, p. 349.

1178. Mahoney, p. 349.

1179. Mahoney, p. 351.

1180. Karnow, p. 572.

1181. Karnow, p. 572.

1182. Kaiser, p. 216.

1183. Stuart Television Productions, Part III.

1184. Schlesinger, p. 917.

1185. Stuart Television Productions, Part III.

1186. Stuart Television Productions, Part III.

1187. Mahoney, pp. 354–355.

1188. Schlesinger, p. 926.

1189. Schlesinger, p. 926.

1190. Schlesinger, p. 927.

1191. Schlesinger, p. 928.

1192. Mahoney, p. 358.

1193. Mahoney, p. 358.

1194. Karnow, p. 580.

1195. Schlesinger, p. 931.

1196. Mahoney, p. 358.

1197. Karnow, p., 594.

1198. Karnow, p. 580.

1199. Oates, p. 451.

1200. Oates, pp. 467–468.

1201. Schlesinger, p. 939.

1202. Oates, p. 470.

1203. Oates, p. 471.

1204. Oates, pp. 471–472.

1205. Oates, p. 472.

1206. Oates, p. 472.

1207. Philip H. Melanson, PhD, *The Martin Luther King Assassination, New Revelations on the Conspiracy and Cover-up, 1968–1991*(New York: Shapolsky Publishers, Inc., 1991), p. 79.

1208. Melanson, *Martin Luther King Assassination,* p. 74.

1209. Schlesinger, p. 938*n*.

1210. Schlesinger, p. 938.

1211. Mahoney, p. 361

1212. Mahoney, p. 361.

1213. Schlesinger, p. 939.

1214. Schlesinger, pp. 939–940.

1215. Schlesinger, p. 942.

1216. Harold Weisberg, *Martin Luther King, The Assassination* (New York: Carroll & Graf Publishers/Richard Gallen, 1971), p. 174.

1217. Kaiser, p. 440.

1218. Kaiser, p. 216.

1219. Turner and Christian, p. 46.

1220. Kaiser, p. 216.

1221. Kaiser, p. 227.

1222. Kaiser, p. 113.

1223. Kaiser, p. 113.

1224. Kaiser, p. 227.

1225. Kaiser, p. 227.

1226. Kaiser, p. 143.

1227. Kaiser, p. 227.

1228. Kaiser, p. 228.

1229. Houghton, p. 166.

1230. Schlesinger, p. 952.

1231. Mahoney, p. 365.

1232. Schlesinger, p. 950.

1233. Mahoney, p. 367.

1234. Schlesinger, p. 954.

1235. Schlesinger, p. 955.

1236. Schlesinger, pp. 949–950.

1237. Klaber and Melanson, p. 123.

1238. Klaber and Melanson, p. 122.

1239. Klaber and Melanson, p. 123.

1240. Klaber and Melanson, p. 123.

1241. Klaber and Melanson, p. 123.

1242. Melanson, *RFK*, p. 235.

1243. Melanson, *RFK*, pp. 218–219.

1244. Melanson, *RFK*, p. 219.

1245. Kaiser, p. 533.

1246. Melanson, *RFK*, p. 221.

1247. Kaiser, p. 273.

1248. Kaiser, p. 97.

1249. Kaiser, p. 274.

1250. Melanson, *RFK*, p. 193.

1251. Mahoney, p. 368.

1252. Schlesinger, p. 972.

1253. Schlesinger, pp. 972–973.

1254. Mahoney, p. 369.

1255. Schlesinger, p. 974.

1256. Schlesinger, p. 975.

1257. Schlesinger, p. 975.

1258. Schlesinger, p. 973.

1259. Melanson, *RFK*, p. 222.

1260. Klaber and Melanson, p. 125.

1261. Klaber and Melanson, p. 125.

1262. Klaber and Melanson, p. 125.

1263. Klaber and Melanson, p. 125.

1264. Klaber and Melanson. p. 125.

1265. Klaber and Melanson, p. 115.

1266. Klaber and Melanson, pp. 115–118.

1267. Klaber and Melanson, p. 118.

1268. Houghton, p. 262.

1269. Houghton, p. 262.

1270. *New York Times*, 2 June 1968.

1271. Schlesinger, p. 979.

1272. Karnow, p. 594.

1273. Turner and Christian, p. 222.

1274. Turner and Christian, p. 222.

1275. Turner and Christian, p. 222.

1276. Turner and Christian, p. 222.

1277. Melanson, *RFK*, pp. 274–275.

1278.  Melanson, *RFK*, p. 278.

1279.  Melanson, *RFK*, p. 279.

1280.  Melanson, *RFK*, p. 275.

1281.  Melanson, *RFK*, p. 281.

1282.  Melanson, *RFK*, p. 281.

1283.  Marks, p. 219.

1284.  Melanson, *RFK*, p. 281.

1285.  Melanson, *RFK*, p. 283.

1286.  Melanson, *RFK*, p. 281.

1287.  Melanson, *RFK*, p. 283.

1288.  Melanson, *RFK*, p. 278.

1289.  Melanson, *RFK*, p. 280.

1290.  Melanson, *RFK*, p. 273.

1291.  Melanson, *RFK*, p. 284.

1292.  Melanson, *RFK*, p. 284.

1293.  Melanson, *RFK*, p. 278.

1294.  Melanson, *RFK*, p. 279.

1295.  Melanson, *RFK*, p. 279.

1296.  Melanson, *RFK*, pp. 276–278.

1297.  Houghton, p. 263.

1298.  Houghton, p. 262.

1299.  Schlesinger, p. 980.

1300.  Schlesinger, p. 957.

1301.  Schlesinger, p. 976.

1302.  Houghton, p. 273.

1303.  Melanson, *RFK*, p. 196.

1304.  Turner and Christian, p. 104.

1305.  Melanson, *RFK*, p. 261.

1306.  Kaiser, p. 332.

1307.  Melanson, *RFK*, p. 267.

1308.  Melanson, *RFK*, p. 262.

1309.  Kaiser, p. 118.

1310.  Kaiser, p 71.

1311.  Kaiser, p. 71.

1312.  Melanson, *RFK*, p. 264.

1313.  Melanson, *RFK*, p. 265.

1314.  Kaiser, p. 117.

1315.  Kaiser, p. 118.

1316.  Melanson, *RFK*, p. 262.

1317.  Melanson, *RFK*, p. 270.

1318.  Melanson, *RFK*, p. 269.

1319.  Melanson, *RFK*, p. 269.

1320.  Melanson, *RFK*, p. 268.

1321.  Kaiser, p. 156.

1322.  Kaiser, p. 71.

1323.  Melanson, *RFK*, p. 189.

1324.  Kaiser, p. 238.

1325.  Houghton, p. 267.

1326.  Houghton, p. 268.

1327.  Houghton, p. 268.

1328.  Kaiser, p. 86.

1329.  Klaber and Melanson, p. 328.

1330.  Klaber and Melanson, p. 183.

1331.  Kaiser, p. 161.

1332.  Klaber and Melanson, p. 183.

1333.  Klaber and Melanson, p. 183.

1334.  Schlesinger, p. 980.

1335.  Kaiser, p. 15.

1336. Kaiser, p. 15.

1337. *New York Times*, 2 June 1968.

1338. Kaiser, p. 19.

1339. Kaiser, p. 21.

1340. Klaber and Melanson, p. 5.

1341. Kaiser, p. 19.

1342. Kaiser, p. 19.

1343. Kaiser, p. 18–19.

1344. Klaber and Melanson. p. 331.

1345. Turner and Christian, pp. 197–197.

1346. Turner and Christian, p. 196.

1347. Turner and Christian, p. 196.

1348. Turner and Christian, p. 196.

1349. Kaiser, p. 437.

1350. Turner and Christian, p. 197.

1351. Turner and Christian, p. 197.

1352. Kaiser, p. 436.

1353. Kaiser, p. 437.

1354. Melanson, *RFK*, p. 181.

1355. Turner and Christian, p. 68.

1356. Kaiser, p. 367.

1357. Melanson, *RFK*, pp. 223–224.

1358. Turner and Christian, p. 70.

1359. Mahoney, p. 372.

1360. Schlesinger, p. 981.

1361. Schlesinger, p. 981.

1362. Mahoney, p. 372.

1363. Schlesinger, p. 981.

1364. *New York Times*, 4 June 1968.

1365. Kaiser, p. 18.

1366. Melanson, *RFK*, p. 76.

1367. Kaiser, p. 531.

1368. Kaiser, p. 531.

1369. Kaiser, p. 532.

1370. Kaiser, p. 532.

1371. Melanson, *RFK*, p. 76.

1372. Melanson, *RFK*, p. 76.

1373. Turner and Christian, p. 69.

1374. Melanson, *RFK*, p. 225.

1375. Kaiser, p. 16.

1376. Mahoney, p. 372.

1377. Klaber and Melanson, p. 329.

1378. Melanson, *RFK*, p. 163.

1379. Melanson, *RFK*, p. 237.

1380. Turner and Christian, p. 70.

1381. Turner and Christian, pp. 70–72.

1382. Klaber and Melanson, p. 128.

1383. Turner and Christian, pp. 69–71.

1384. Melanson, *RFK*, pp. 228, 244.

1385. Klaber and Melanson, p. 13.

1386. Turner and Christian, p. 71.

1387. Klaber and Melanson, p. 329.

1388. Kaiser, p. 251.

1389. Klaber and Melanson, p. 329.

1390. Kaiser, p. 427.

1391. Melanson, *RFK*, p. 235.

1392. Turner and Christian, p. 193.

1393. Melanson, *RFK*, p. 235.

1394. Klaber and Melanson, p. 329.

1395. Kaiser, p. 114.

1396. Kaiser, p. 596.

1397. Kaiser, p. 366.

1398. Kaiser, p. 596.

1399. Turner and Christian, p. 72.

1400. Turner and Christian, p. 71.

1401. Turner and Christian, p. 71.

1402. Melanson, *RFK*, p. 65.

1403. Klaber and Melanson, p. 128.

1404. Klaber and Melanson, p. 135.

1405. Klaber and Melanson, p. 134.

1406. Klaber and Melanson, p. 130.

1407. Melanson, *RFK*, p. 65.

1408. Melanson, *RFK*, p. 20.

1409. Klaber and Melanson, p. 307.

1410. Houghton, p. 281.

1411. Jules Witcover, *85 Days, the Last Campaign of Robert F. Kennedy* (New York: Ace Publishing Corporation, 1969), p. 264.

1412. Hougton, pp. 283–284.

1413. Schlesinger, p. 982.

1414. Mahoney, p. 373.

1415. Klaber and Melanson, p. 6.

1416. Kaiser, pp. 22–24.

1417. Klaber and Melanson, p. 7.

1418. Kaiser, pp. 24–25.

1419. Kaiser, p. 25.

1420. Kaiser, p. 26.

1421. Klaber and Melanson, p. 129.

1422. Melanson, *RFK*, p. 65.

1423. Melanson, *RFK*, p. 19.

1424. Melanson, *RFK*, p. 65.

1425. Klaber and Melanson, pp. 97–98.

1426. Klaber and Melanson, p. 130.

1427. Melanson, *RFK*, p. 41.

1428. Melanson, *RFK*, p. 332.

1429. Melanson, *RFK*, p. 25.

1430. Turner and Christian, p. 186.

1431. Kaiser, p. 31.

1432. Kaiser, p. 28.

1433. Kaiser, p. 30.

1434. Mahoney, p. 374.

1435. Turner and Christian, p. 376.

1436. Kaiser, p. 110.

1437. Klaber and Melanson, pp. 97–98.

1438. Jim DiEugenio, *The Curious Case of Dan Moldea*, (www.CTKA@webcom.com) Probe May-June 1998

1439. Kaiser, p. 32.

1440. Turner and Christian, p. 173.

1441. Kaiser, p. 26.

1442. Turner and Christian, p. 190.

1443. Klaber and Melanson, p. 329.

1444. Melanson, *RFK*, p. 184.

1445. Turner and Christian, p. 160.

1446. Turner and Christian, p. 381.

1447. Turner and Christian, p. 158.

1448. Turner and Christian, p. 177.

1449. Klaber and Melanson, p. 122.

1450. Klaber and Melason, p. 121.

1451. Melanson, *RFK*, pp. 66–67.

1452. Melanson, *RFK*, p. 68.

1453. Melanson, *RFK*, p. 69.

1454. Klaber and Melanson, pp. 120–121.

1455. Turner and Christian, p. 165.

1456. Turner and Christian, p. 165.

1457. Turner and Christian, p. 167.

1458. Turner and Christian, p. 168.

1459. Turner and Christian, p. 167.

1460. Davis, pp. 390–391.

1461. Turner and Christian, p. 166.

1462. Melanson, *RFK*, p. 74.

1463. Turner and Christian, p. 166.

1464. Melanson, *RFK*, p. 85.

1465. Melanson, *RFK*, p. 76.

1466. Turner and Christian, pp. 165–168.

1467. Klaber and Melanson, p. 120.

1468. Davis, p. 391.

1469. Klaber and Melanson, pp. 128–134.

1470. Klaber and Melanson, p. 130.

1471. Klaber and Melanson, p. 130.

1472. Klaber and Melanson, p. 130.

1473. Klaber and Melanson, pp. 130–131.

1474. Turner and Christian, p. 69.

1475. Turner and Christian, p. 70.

1476. Houghton, p. 30.

1477. Houghton, p. 294.

1478. Kaiser, p. 95.

1479. Melanson, *RFK*, p. 100.

1480. Klaber and Melanson, pp. 132–133.

1481. Kaiser, pp. 25, 386.

1482. Melanson, *RFK*, p. 185.

1483. Melanson, *RFK*, p. 186.

1484. Kaiser, p. 447.

1485. Melanson, *RFK*, pp. 188–189.

1486. Melanson, *RFK*, p. 190.

1487. Turner and Christian, pp. 197–198.

1488. Kaiser, p. 428.

1489. Melanson, *RFK*, p. 196.

1490. Kaiser, p. 42.

1491. Kaiser, pp. 87–88.

1492. Kaiser, p. 88.

1493. Kaiser, pp. 88–89.

1494. Kaiser, p. 392.

1495. Kaiser, p. 392.

1496. Kaiser, p. 392.

1497. Melanson, *RFK*, p. 158.

1498. Kaiser, p. 101.

1499. Kaiser, p. 89.

1500. Kaiser, p. 105.

1501. Kaiser, p. 101.

1502. Kaiser, p. 106.

1503. Edward Kennedy, tribute to Robert Kennedy, Funeral Mass, St. Patrick's Cathedral, New York, 8 June 1968

1504. Schlesinger, p. 1.

1505. Turner and Christian, p. 52.

1506. Turner and Christian, pp. 63–64.

1507. Turner and Christian, p. 62.

1508. Turner and Christian, pp. 66–67.

1509. Melanson, *RFK*, pp. 288–290.

1510. Turner and Christian, p. 275 footnote.

1511. Turner and Christian, p. 65.

1512. Turner and Christian, p. 65.

1513. Turner and Christian, p. 66.

1514. Kaiser, pp. 98–100.

1515. Turner and Christian, p. 355.

1516. Turner and Christian, p. 119.

1517. Turner and Christian, p. 324.

1518. Turner and Christian, pp. 362–363.

1519. Turner and Christian, p. 36.

1520. Turner and Christian, p. 38.

1521. Turner and Christian, p. 363.

1522. Turner and Christian, p. 44.

1523. Turner and Christian, p. 46.

1524. Kaiser, p. 166.

1525. Turner and Christian, p. 97.

1526. Turner and Christian, p. 98.

1527. Turner and Christian, p. 99.

1528. Turner and Christian, p. 133.

1529. Turner and Christian, p. 133.

1530. Turner and Christian, p. 133.

1531. Houghton, p. 151.

1532. Turner and Christian, p. 44.

1533. Turner and Christian, p. 132.

1534. Turner and Christian, p. 119.

1535. Melanson, *RFK*, p. 240.

1536. Turner and Christian, p. 70.

1537. Kaiser, p. 47, 59.

1538. Kaiser, p. 115.

1539. Kaiser, p. 47.

1540. Turner and Christian, pp. 69–71.

1541.  Melanson, *RFK,* pp. 248–256.

1542.  Melanson, *RFK,* p. 256.

1543.  Turner and Christian, p. 72.

1544.  Turner and Christian, pp. 80–81.

1545.  Turner and Christian, p. 81.

1546.  Turner and Christian, p. 82.

1547.  Turner and Christian, p. 82.

1548.  Klaber and Melanson, p. 83.

1549.  Turner and Christian, p. 178.

1550.  Turner and Christian, p. 187.

1551.  Klaber and Melanson, p. 82.

1552.  Klaber and Melanson, p. 90.

1553.  Klaber and Melanson, p. 80.

1554.  Klaber and Melanson, p. 85.

1555.  Klaber and Melanson, p. 127.

1556.  Turner and Christian, p. 179.

1557.  Klaber and Melanson, p. 127 footnote.

1558.  Klaber and Melanson, p. 223.

1559.  Klaber and Melanson, p. 223.

1560.  Klaber and Melanson, p. 219.

1561.  Melanson, *RFK,* p. 178.

1562.  Kaiser, p. 364.

1563.  Kaiser, p. 365.

1564.  Kaiser, p. 366.

1565.  Melanson, *RFK,* pp. 191–193.

1566.  Klaber and Melanson, p. 218.

1567.  Klaber and Melanson, p. 224.

1568.  Melanson, *RFK,* p. 194.

1569.  Kaiser, p. 343.

1570.  Kaiser, p. 273.

1571.  Kaiser, p. 365.

1572.   Kaiser, p. 368.

1573.   Melanson, *RFK*, p. 149.

1574.   Kaiser, p. 430.

1575.   Kaiser, p. 421.

1576.   Kaiser, p. 367.

1577.   Kaiser, p. 229.

1578.   Kaiser, p. 229.

1579.   Kaiser, p. 230.

1580.   Kaiser, p. 230.

1581.   Melanson, *RFK*, p. 151.

1582.   Melanson, *RFK*, p. 153.

1583.   Turner and Christian, p. 226.

1584.   Melanson, *RFK*, p. 206.

1585.   Kaiser, p. 420.

1586.   Kaiser, p. 41.

1587.   Klaber and Melanson, p. 239.

1588.   Melanson, *RFK*, p. 153.

1589.   Kaiser, p. 231.

1590.   Melanson, *RFK*, p. 28.

1591.   Houghton, p. 297n.

1592.   Kaiser, p. 498.

1593.   Klaber and Melanson, pp. 258, 283–284.

1594.   Klaber and Melanson, p. 220.

1595.   Turner and Christian, p. 199.

1596.   Melanson, *RFK*, p. 164.

1597.   Turner and Christian, p. 199.

1598.   Tuner and Christian, p. 201.

1599.   Turner and Christian, p. 201.

1600.   Turner and Christian, p. 199.

1601.   Turner and Christian, p. 200.

1602. Turner and Christian, p. 200.

1603. Turner and Christian, p. 200.

1604. Turner and Christian, p. 199.

1605. Turner and Christian, p. 200.

1606. Turner and Christian, p. 201.

1607. Turner and Christian, p. 163.

1608. Turner and Christian, pp. 163–165.

1609. Klaber and Melanson, p. 307.

1610. Klaber and Melanson, p. 303.

1611. Klaber and Melanson, p. 303.

1612. Klaber and Melanson, p. 303.

1613. Melanson, *RFK,* pp. 93–95.

1614. Klaber and Melanson, p. 305.

1615. Klaber and Melanson, p. 322.

1616. Klaber and Melanson, p. 36.

1617. Karnow, p. 580.

1618. Karnow, pp. 580–581.

1619. Turner and Christian, p. 227.

1620. Turner and Christian, p. 228.

1621. Melanson, *RFK,* p. 203.

1622. Turner, p. 228.

1623. Walt Brown, *Treachery in Dallas* (New York: Carroll & Graf Publishers, Inc., 1995), pp. 66–67.

1624. Scheim, p. 58.

1625. Turner, p. 216.

1626. F. Peter Model and Robert J. Groden, *JFK: The Case for Conspiracy* (New York: Manor Books, Inc, 1976), pp. 177, 188.

1627. Philip H. Melanson, PhD, *The Robert F. Kennedy Assassination, New Revelations on the Conspiracy and Cover-up, 1968—1991* (New York: Shapolsky Publishers, 1991) p. 201.

1628. Fetzer, p. 363.

1629.  Fetzer, p. 363.

1630.  Bernard Fensterwald Jr., director, The Committee to Investigate Assas-
       sinations, *Coincidence or Conspiracy?* (New York: Kensington Publishing
       Corp., 1977), pp. 219–220.

1631.  Bernard Fensterwald Jr., director, The Committee to Investigate Assas-
       sinations, *Coincidence or Conspiracy?* (New York: Kensington Publishing
       Corp., 1977), pp. 219–220.

1632.  Fensterwald, p. 298.

1633.  Fonzi, p. 421.

1634.  Melanson, *RFK*, p. 291.

1635.  Turner and Christian, p. 228.

1636.  Melanson, *Spy Saga*, pp. 137–138.

1637.  Fetzer, p. 369.

1638.  Melanson, *RFK*, pp. 149, 157.

1639.  Brown, pp. 227–229.

1640.  Kaiser, p. 71.

1641.  Klaber and Melanson, p. 328.

1642.  Fetzer, p. 366.

1643.  Turner and Christian, p. 162.

1644.  Fetzer, p. 85.

1645.  Fetzer, pp. 39–41.

1646.  Melanson, *RFK*, p. 65.

1647.  Turner and Christian, pp. 176–177.

1648.  Turner and Christian, p. 173.

1649.  Fetzer, p. 369.

1650.  Kaiser, p. 428.

1651.  Davis, p. 228.

1652.  Klaber and Melanson, p. 127n.

1653.  Talbot, p. 100.

1654.  Fonzi, p. 296n.

1655.  Talbot, p. 389.

1656.  Talbot, p. 402.

# INDEX

# Index

# Index